ASPA Classics

Conceived of and sponsored by the American Society for Public Administration (ASPA), the ASPA Classic Series publishes volumes on topics that have been, and continue to be, central to the contemporary development of the field. The ASPA Classics are intended for classroom use, library adoptions, and general reference. Drawing from the *Public Administration Review (PAR)* and other ASPA-related journals, each volume in the series is edited by a scholar who is charged with presenting a thorough and balanced perspective on an enduring issue.

Each volume is devoted to a topic of continuing and crosscutting concern to the administration of virtually all public sector programs. Public servants carry out their responsibilities in a complex, multidimensional environment, and each collection will address a necessary dimension of their performance. ASPA Classics volumes bring together the dialogue on a particular topic over several decades and in a range of journals.

The volume editors are to be commended for volunteering to take on such substantial projects and for bringing together unique collections of articles that might not otherwise be readily available to scholars and students.

ASPA Classics

Public Administration and Law
Julia Beckett and Heidi O. Koenig, eds.

Local Government Management:
Current Issues and Best Practices
Douglas J. Watson and Wendy L. Hassett, eds.

Public Administration and Law

An ASPA Classics Volume

Edited by
Julia Beckett and Heidi O. Koenig

M.E.Sharpe
Armonk, New York
London, England

To Keith, Jacob, and Andrew
and
to Bob, Tom, and Katie
without whose support none of this would be possible.

Library of Congress Cataloging-in-Publication Data

Public administration and law / edited by Julia Beckett and Heidi O. Koenig.
    p. cm. — (ASPA classics)
Includes bibliographical references and index.
ISBN 0-7656-1542-8 (cloth : alk. paper) — ISBN 0-7656-1543-6 (pbk. : alk. paper)
  1. Administrative law—United States. 2. Public administration—United States. I. Beckett, Julia, 1958–
II. Koenig, Heidi O., 1962–   III. Series.

KF5402.P83 2005
342.73′06—dc22
                                                    2004023625

CONTENTS

BOXES, FIGURES, AND TABLES

INTRODUCTION

The Field of Public Administration and Public Law

Law is extremely important to public administration. Law is a source of democratic principles and it is integral in the activities of governance. Public administration is not merely "carrying out the business of government"; public administration is the execution of law. Efficiency, economy, and effectiveness must be sought within the context of statutory authority, limited budgets, personnel rules, and court decrees. Government must be accountable, open, and procedurally fair; government must provide equal protection and equal opportunity as well as promote justice. These democratic values are not merely ethical norms or aspirations, they are fundamental legal imperatives found in the constitutions, statutes, rules, administrative rulings, and court decisions of the state and federal governments. This book incorporates classic writings from the journal *Public Administration Review* that consider the legal foundations of public administration as well as the constraints and challenges faced by public administrators.

This book addresses important questions about law and public administration: How does law affect administrators? How are legal and constitutional values incorporated into or imposed upon administrative practices and processes? How do administrators differ from judges? These are important concerns for students, practitioners, and scholars of public administration. This book seeks to provide articles that address these themes at federal, state, and local levels of administration. There are several excellent books that summarize national administrative law and constitutional law; what this book contributes are articles that address the public administration focus. The articles included here, first, address the framework and values that link law and administration and, second, discuss practical examples of how administrative practice incorporates and responds to legal issues and constraints. This introduction briefly describes the historic separation between law and administration in the United States and notes some distinctions about American conceptions of law and administration. It then summarizes common public administration criticisms of law and arguments that are more supportive of law. Finally, it provides an overview of the structure of the book.

Almost a century ago American public administration writings began to focus on administration as management and to shy away from law as the basis for administrative actions. This administration law separation has its origins in Woodrow Wilson's famous pronouncement that the problem of administration is not how to found a constitution but to run one. This theme was echoed in early twentieth-century American public administration texts that not only separated administration from politics but also divorced administration from its roots in law. Now most administrators recognize that this separation is both artificial and foolhardy.

In America, the focus of governance discussions often begins with considerations of policy and tasks of administration: the legal foundations and connections are downplayed. In many European nations, law is more important than the roots of public administration: there, administration *is* carrying out public law. In many countries, statutes narrowly define and specifically determine what administrators should do, yet in America, administrators are often given broad grants of statutory authority and discretion to fill in administrative details and legal requirements. This book considers American public administration and law because the context matters. A government's administration is affected by that government's history, laws, and traditions. For example, the complexities of American federalism, with distinct governance and legal authority for state and federal governments, affect local public administration decisions about trash disposal or land use.

It is common in American public administration to discuss budgeting, organizations, personnel, research methods, and leadership. Often public management considers policy. Less common are discussions of "interpreting the law" or "implementing the law"; instead, the focus is on developing policy, implementing policy, or understanding missions. Administrative and management issues often are addressed in American texts without considering legal concerns, or law is often presented as a constraint. Administrative commentators frequently present statutes and regulations as limits to administrative action and impediments to managing the public's business. Court cases and judges are portrayed as impeding administration, imposing excessive procedures, or requiring payments outside the budget process. The animosity about law, lawyers, and judges does not serve or benefit public administrators.

An alternative, beneficial view of courts and law is occasionally presented. In this view, law is an integral part of the democratic fabric, civic values, and foundations of government. Statutes and rules provide principles developed in a democratic, participatory manner. Courts serve the general public and public servants in many ways. They referee disputes and make law. They decide issues based on arguments in a manner that provides administrative feedback and balances governmental powers. Adjudication by administrative agencies and courts is part of the transparency, accountability, and openness in a democratic government. Yet executives, legislatures, and courts have roles distinct from administrators. This book concentrates on the administrative interpretations, implications, and impacts of public law.

The legal profession has its own knowledge base and expertise, yet administrators are expected to understand law, both regarding practical matters and as part of the principles of democratic governance. Public administrators are also expected to be competent in the legal areas—the constitutions, statutes, rules, and common law court decisions—

that affect their responsibilities. However, the concerns of governance and administration are not completely reflected in the language of statutes or the issues in court decisions. The chapters in this book focus on the concerns of public administration as they are related to law.

Public administrators need to understand the types of laws and the legal environment of government, as many articles found in the journals of the American Society for Public Administration attest. This book includes twenty articles chosen to balance understanding law and judicial practice with administrative practice. (A few of the articles have been abridged by the editors, but their essence remains intact.) This book is organized around the five ways public law is often presented:

- As constitutional structure and relationships (Part I)
- As courts and judicial decisions (Part II)
- As administrative law based on the Administrative Procedure Act (Part III)
- As adversarial practice and dispute resolution (Part IV)
- As integral to democratic governance (Part V).

PART I

A GOVERNMENT UNDER LAW

America has a government under law both in practice and in democratic theory. Law plays an important role in American society. It defines relationships between all combinations of individuals, businesses, groups, and governments. Many of these relationships are established from social expectations and enumerated through the common law case-by-case development of legal principles. Many other relationships are now specified in statutes and administrative rules. Law is often broadly defined to include constitutions, statutes and legislative authority, regulations and rules, and court decisions. Such laws provide the foundation for public administrators' authority to act as well as establish limits on governmental authority.

Administrators must understand legal and constitutional obligations. For the general public, the old adage that ignorance of the law is no excuse may be adequate. However, more is expected of public servants. They have the duty to know the law and act in a lawful manner.

One definition of public administration is "the execution of the law." Yet determining "what is the law" is complex. Judges and lawyers often view law in the context of a particular legal challenge and their understanding of law is developed predominantly through analysis of appellate court decisions. In this context, law is often technical and specific. Administrators, in carrying out law and implementing policy, may interpret law differently from lawyers. In this context, the administrative concern is law in action. In contrast, the general public's understanding of law differs from the expert views of lawyers and bureaucrats. There are legal, practical, and theoretical aspects of government under the law that public administrators need to understand, and the chapters in Part I are selected to address themes and debates regarding the interplay between the constitutional foundations, the rule of law, and legal specialization.

Understanding public administration and law begins with considering the constitutional foundations of American public administration. The discussions of the legal foundations of government commonly begin with the U.S. Constitution because it is the founding document and the supreme law of the land. The Constitution establishes the foundation and authority of government and provides the structure and functions of the three primary branches: legislative, executive, and judicial. Yet, questions arise regarding the constitutional source and extent of administrative authority. Many chapters in this book consider relationships of legislative delegation, executive authority, administrative discretion, individual rights, and court review.

Every legal inquiry begins by understanding the constitutional and legislative foundations of the administrative activity and only then assesses the questions of constitutionally

1

protected individual rights and civil rights. Administrators must understand and respect constitutional rights, including the First Amendment rights of free speech and petition for redress, the Fourth Amendment limits on unreasonable search and seizure, and the due process and equal protection rights in the Fifth and Fourteenth Amendments. These important rights are closely linked to democratic values. What these constitutional rights are and what is appropriate governmental action has been determined in a long line of Supreme Court cases. Often two or more constitutional values are at issue in a single case. A challenge for both courts and administrators is balancing competing values and important constitutional rights. One thing is certain: The constitutional guarantees of individual and civil rights place obligations and constraints on government and its public servants.

Perhaps the most important constitutional constraint on administrators is that of due process. Due process is an essential democratic and judicial value that does not have a definitive or rigid definition. The constitutional requirement that government cannot take life, liberty, or property without due process of law in the Fifth Amendment applies to federal actions. The Fourteenth Amendment imposes due process on state and local governments. Due process has been expansively interpreted by the courts, which emphasize the equitable concern of fundamental fairness to the individual as more important than traditional administrative concerns of efficiency or economy. Courts separate due process into categories of substantive due process and procedural due process. The former addresses whether government has narrowly crafted and applied statutes when policies that regulate or otherwise provide public benefits may also impose upon constitutional rights. Although substantive due process review is less common, this issue reflects concerns about democratic values and government actions.

Courts are particularly vigilant about procedural due process challenges to administrative hearings. Many of the due process requirements of a trial apply to administrative hearings. The government must give to the defendant: prior and specific notice of the offense; access to government information on the case; an opportunity to present information and arguments; a detailed explanation of the reasons for the decision by the hearing officer; and an opportunity for appeal. What are appropriate and necessary procedures to satisfy due process in one case depend upon the type of rights and the type of setting, but a central question for courts is whether the government has considered fundamental fairness to the individual. Discussions about constitutional due process rights, government responsibilities, and administrative practices are found in many chapters in this book.

Constitutions grant authority to governments to act in certain areas; this is a structural and functional view of the constitution. The structure applies to the intergovernmental relationships between both the branches and the levels of governments. The United States Constitution created a federal government of limited and enumerated powers. States are general-purpose governments with broader powers to protect the health, safety, and welfare of their citizens. Local governments are subordinate to both levels of government. Although the structures and powers may differ for cities and states, the constitutional theories of government under law apply to them.

All levels of government pass laws and regulations to provide for the public must be consistent with constitutional powers. Legislatures enact laws that specify what government will do, such as how to raise revenue and budget spending, what the government will regulate, and what agencies can and must do. Issues relating to the relationships among various forms of government and governmental power have been raised both by scholars and in court cases. For example, a question of federalism arising in a Supreme Court case might ask whether a responsibility should belong to the federal or state government under their Constitutions. Other issues about government powers arise from interpreting statutes in relations to a constitutional clause. For example, the Commerce Clause, "regulating commerce among the several states," is the foundation of many regulatory powers of the federal administrative state. Supreme Court decisions addressing these issues demonstrate a philosophy of governance and administration, yet the Court may be divided on important fundamental questions. What the Court considers appropriate and acceptable changes both over time and in factual context.

Public administrators are ruled by every branch of government. According to long-standing doctrine, the executive is responsible for developing programs, administering policy, and implementing laws. Others contend that political theory means the legislature, elected by and representing the people, is the predominant branch for developing laws and policies. The role of the judiciary is to interpret cases that challenge the legality of statutes and administrative actions. The ultimate government authority interpreting the U.S. Constitution is the Supreme Court. The involvement of three branches of government that dictate administrative action often raises questions in practice regarding roles, interaction, overlap, and cooperation in governance. These themes are considered in all of the chapters in this section.

The source and structure of authority for public administrators is an essential concern in bureaucratic theory. The concepts of hierarchy, chain of command, and unity of command do not fit neatly into the constitutional structure. In addition, there is little direct constitutional language about public administration. This has led to a number of questions: To whom are administrators responsible? How do the differing values and issues for the executive, legislative, and judicial branches affect public administrators? The first chapter, by David Rosenbloom, from 1983, presents a systematic comparison of the three branches and administrative responsibilities.

Interpretation of constitutional authority evolves through many court decisions, but scholarship also plays a key role in understanding the Constitution. A long-standing debate about administrative legitimacy concerns the issue that public administrators are not given a separate article or description in the federal Constitution. Public administration scholars have considered constitutional design and the founders' intent regarding administration. This debate centers on whether the lack of constitutional language about administration affects the importance and legitimacy of public administration practice. A beginning point for discussing public administrative authority is in the constitutional role of the executive, and in Chapter 2 John A. Rohr traces the executive from the history of the constitutional convention, statutory actions, and key Supreme Court decisions.

Rohr asserts there is constitutional confusion about the two types of executive roles—as clerk and as leader—that continues to affect public administrators.

Another aspect of "government under law" is American governments must enact laws before exercising authority. Many legal scholars distinguish public and private legality by specifying that governments have only the power to do those things that are specifically granted and that individuals can do anything unless it is specifically prohibited by law. The clarity, specificity, and purpose of legislation are not always obvious and this raises challenges for public administrators. Broad legislative authority allows policy directives to change with the results of elections or social problems; it allows for administrative interpretation and discretion. Sometimes administrators are tasked to fill in gaps in laws by developing rules and regulations. These two aspects of discretionary authority are part of administrative practice and are areas of concern to scholars.

The nuances of appointing public officials, defining their duties, and determining who can fire officials are examples of why this legislative authority and interpretation matters. Rohr's chapter from 1989 also discusses the role of the executive and how legislative enactment of a new role—the independent counsel—affects executive power. In Chapter 3, in an article that was published as a companion piece to Rohr, Rosemary O'Leary presents five reasons why public administrators must understand law and argues that law should be included in public administration education.

Concerns about specialization of knowledge and duties are familiar in public administration. This is part of bureaucratic and personnel theory. Within governments there are many administrators with professional training and subject matter expertise, such as accountants, engineers, social workers, doctors, and lawyers. Some of the issues that scholars discuss relating the role of professional expertise in governance include: Are there different concerns and appropriate roles for public administrators and government lawyers? Are there distinct domains of public administration and law? Is giving legal advice more narrow and advisory than making choices about public management decisions? The fourth chapter, by Doyle W. Buckwalter and J. Ivan Legler, evaluates these concerns as they relate to city managers and city attorneys. This chapter also provides insight on how legal issues can affect local government management.

In the twentieth century, America developed a wide scope of governmental activities, which Rosenbloom calls "the administrative state." Along with this expansion of the administrative state, administrative law developed through both legislation and court cases. The federal Administrative Procedure Act (APA) enacted in 1946 established practices for developing rules, required procedures for enforcing statutes and rules through hearings, provided for court review of administrative actions, and developed policies for public access to government information. Many states have administrative procedure acts modeled on the APA. Since much of government activity is accomplished through administrators developing and enforcing rules and regulations, consideration of government under law also means understanding how administrative law and the APA affect public administration.

The active regulatory and distributive roles governments take in the modern administrative state often involve combining and practical considerations. The concluding chapter in this section, by David Rosenbloom, written in 2000, addresses a century of progress on how administrators are affected by administrative law, congressional action, and the Supreme Court's constitutional doctrine. As Rosenbloom shows, the interaction between congressional supervision, court review, and administrative practices has developed over time and has many important implications for public administration. Chapters in later parts of this book return to these themes of the interrelationship among procedures, practices, and powers of the executive, legislature, courts, and public administrators.

CHAPTER 1

PUBLIC ADMINISTRATION THEORY AND SEPARATION OF POWERS

DAVID H. ROSENBLOOM

It has been recognized for some time that the discipline of public administration is plagued by a weak or absent theoretical core. This has led some to conclude, along with Robert Parker,[1] that "there is really no such subject as 'public administration.' No science or art can be identified by this title, least of all any single skill or coherent intellectual discipline." Others, including Frederick C. Mosher,[2] have considered it a "resource," that public administration "is more an area of interest than a discipline," since this enables the field to draw upon a variety of disciplines. Still others, such as Herbert Kaufman[3] and James Q. Wilson,[4] have argued that public administration faces a serious and seemingly irresolvable problem in continually seeking to maximize the attainment of mutually incompatible values. The contention of this essay is that the central problem of contemporary public administrative theory is that it is derived from three disparate approaches to the basic question of what public administration is. Each of these approaches has a respected intellectual tradition, emphasizes different values, promotes different types of organizational structure, and views individuals in markedly distinct terms. These approaches are conveniently labeled "managerial," "political," and "legal." They have influenced one another over the years, and at some points they overlap. Yet, their primary influence on public administration has been to pull it in three separate directions. Furthermore, these directions tend to follow the pattern of the separation of powers established by the Constitution. Consequently, it is unlikely that the three approaches can be synthesized without violating values deeply ingrained in the United States political culture.[5]

The Managerial Approach to Public Administration

Origin and Values

In the United States the managerial approach to public administration grew largely out of the civil service reform movement of the late nineteenth century. In the reformers' words, "What civil service reform demand[ed], [was] that the business part of the

From *Public Administration Review* 43, no. 3 (May/June 1983): 219–227. Copyright © 1983 by American Society for Public Administration. Reprinted with permission.

government shall be carried on in a sound businesslike manner."[6] The idea of "business-like" public administration was most self-consciously and influentially discussed by Woodrow Wilson in his essay on "The Study of Administration."[7] There, Wilson considered public administration to be "a field of business" and consequently largely a managerial endeavor. He also set forth the three core values of the managerial approach to public administration: "It is the object of administrative study to discover, first, what government can properly and successfully do, and, secondly, how it can do these proper things with the utmost possible efficiency and at the least possible cost either of money or of energy."[8] Thus, public administration was to be geared toward the maximization of effectiveness, efficiency, and economy.

The managerial approach was strengthened by Frederick Taylor and the scientific management movement.[9] Taylorism sought to enshrine the values of efficiency and economy in a world view that promised to achieve harmony and affluence among mankind. Later, Leonard White's influential *Introduction to the Study of Public Administration*[10] asserted that "the study of administration should start from the base of management rather than the foundation of law, and is, therefore, more absorbed in the affairs of the American Management Association than in the decisions of the courts." When the managerial approach to public administration was at the pinnacle of its influence in the 1930s, it was widely held, along with Luther Gulick, that "efficiency" was "axiom number one in the value scale of administration" and that politics could not enter "the structure of administration without producing inefficiency."[11]

The essence of the managerial approach's values was captured by Simmons and Dvorin in the following terms: "The 'goodness' or 'badness' of a particular organizational pattern was a mathematical relationship of 'inputs' to 'outputs.' Where the latter was maximized and the former minimized, a moral 'good' resulted. Virtue or 'goodness' was therefore equated with the relationship of these two factors, that is, 'efficiency,' or 'inefficiency.' Mathematics was transformed into ethics."[12]

Organizational Structure

The managerial approach to public administration promotes organization essentially along the lines of Max Weber's ideal-type bureaucracy.[13] It stresses the importance of functional specialization for efficiency. Hierarchy is then relied upon for effective coordination.[14] Programs and functions are to be clearly assigned to organizational units. Overlaps are to be minimized. Positions are to be classified into a rational scheme and pay scales are to be systematically derived in the interests of economy and motivating employees to be efficient. Selection of public administrators is to be made strictly on the basis of merit. They are to be politically neutral in their competence. Relationships among public administrators and public agencies are to be formalized in writing and, in all events, the public's business is to be administered in a smooth, orderly fashion.[15]

View of the Individual

The managerial approach to public administration promotes an impersonal view of individuals. This is true whether the individuals in question are the employees, clients, or the "victims"[16] of public administrative agencies. One need not go so far as Max Weber in considering "dehumanization" to be the "special virtue" of bureaucracy or to view the bureaucrat as a "cog" in an organizational machine over which he/she has virtually no control.[17] Yet there can be no doubt that a strong tendency of scientific management was to turn the individual worker into an appendage to a mechanized means of production. By 1920, this view of the employee was clearly embodied in the principles of position classification in the public sector: "The individual characteristics of an employee occupying a position should have no bearing on the classification of the position."[18] Indeed, the strong "position-orientation" of the managerial approach to public administration continues to diminish the importance of the individual employee to the overall organization.

Clients, too, have been "depersonalized" and turned into "cases" in an effort to promote the managerial values of efficiency, economy, and effectiveness. Ralph Hummel explains:

> At the intake level of the bureaucracy, individual personalities are converted into cases. Only if a person can qualify as a case, is he or she allowed treatment by the bureaucracy. More accurately, a bureaucracy is never set up to treat or deal with persons: it "processes" only "cases."[19]

"Victims" may be depersonalized to such an extent that they are considered subhuman, especially where physical force or coercion is employed as in mental health facilities and police functions.[20] The human relations approach to organization theory and some contemporary views argue that reliance on impersonality tends to be counterproductive because it generates "bureaupathologies."[21] Nevertheless, the managerial approach's impersonal view of individuals is deeply ingrained and considered essential to the maximization of efficiency, economy, and effectiveness.

The Political Approach to Public Administration

Origins and Values

The political approach to public administration was perhaps most forcefully and succinctly stated by Wallace Sayre:

> Public administration is ultimately a problem in political theory: the fundamental problem in a democracy is responsibility to popular control; the responsibility and responsiveness of the administrative agencies and the bureaucracies to the elected officials (the chief executives, the legislators) is of central importance in a government based increasingly on the exercise of discretionary power by the agencies of administration.[22]

This approach grew out of the observation of some, such as Paul Appleby, that public administration during the New Deal and World War II was anything but devoid of politics.[23]

Thus, unlike the origin of the managerial approach, which stressed what public administration ought to be, the political approach developed from an analysis of apparent empirical reality.

Once public administration is considered a political endeavor, emphasis is inevitably placed on a different set of values than those promoted by the managerial approach. "Efficiency," in particular, becomes highly suspect, as Justice Brandeis pointed out in dissent in *Myers v. United States* (1926):

> The doctrine of the separation of powers was adopted by the Convention of 1787, not to promote efficiency but to preclude the exercise of arbitrary power. The purpose was, not to avoid friction, but, by means of the inevitable friction incident to the distribution of governmental powers among three departments, to save the people from autocracy.[24]

Rather, the political approach to public administration stresses the values of representativeness, political responsiveness, and accountability through elected officials to the citizenry. These are viewed as crucial to the maintenance of constitutional democracy, especially in view of the rise of the contemporary administrative state, which may be likened unto "bureaucratic government."[25]

One can find many examples of governmental reforms aimed at maximizing the political values of representativeness, responsiveness, and accountability within public administration. For instance, the wide ranging academic controversy concerning the concept of "representative bureaucracy"[26] notwithstanding, the Federal Civil Service Reform Act of 1978 made it "the policy of the United States . . . to provide a Federal workforce reflective of the Nation's diversity" by endeavoring "to achieve a work force from all segments of society."[27] The Federal Advisory Committee Act of 1971 sought to enhance responsiveness through the use of "representative" advisory committees.[28] Earlier, the poverty and model cities programs of the 1960s sought to use "citizen participation" as a means of promoting political responsiveness in administrative operations. The quest for responsiveness has also blended into attempts to promote the accountability of public administrators to political officials through a variety of measures including greater use of the General Accounting Office,[29] the creation of the federal Senior Executive Service, and structural changes such as the establishment of the Office of Management and Budget, the Office of Personnel Management, and the Congressional Budget Office. "Sunshine" provisions such as the Freedom of Information Act and "sunset" requirements are also examples of the attempt to promote political accountability. There is also a growing academic literature on the need to promote representativeness, responsiveness, and accountability in the modern administrative state.[30]

It is important to note that the values sought by the political approach to public administration are frequently in tension with those of the managerial approach. For instance, efficiency in the managerial sense is not necessarily served through sunshine regulations that can dissuade public administrators from taking some courses of action, though they may be the most efficient, and can divert time and resources from program implementation to the deliverance of information to outsiders. Consultation with advisory committees and "citizen participants" can be time consuming and costly. A socially representative public service may not be the most efficient one.[31] Nor is the intended shuffling of Senior Executive Servants from agency to agency likely to enhance efficiency in the managerial sense. Rather it is thought that by providing this cadre of top public administrators a wider variety of experience, they may come to define the public interest in more comprehensive terms and therefore become more responsive to the nation's overall political interests. Moreover, while various budgeting strategies and sunset provisions can promote economy in one sense, the amount of paperwork they generate and the extent to which they may require agencies to justify and argue on behalf of their programs and expenditures can become quite costly. Indeed, a quarter century ago, Marver Bernstein reported that "many officials complain that they must spend so much time preparing for appearing at Congressional hearings and in presenting their programs before the Bureau of the Budget and other bodies that it often leaves little time for directing the operations of their agencies."[32] Managerial effectiveness is difficult to gauge, of course, but federal managers have long complained that their effectiveness is hampered by the large congressional role in public administration and the need to consult continually with a variety of parties having a legitimate concern with their agencies' operations.[33]

Organizational Structure

Public administration organized around the political values of representativeness, responsiveness, and accountability also tends to be at odds with the managerial approach to organization. Rather than emphasizing clear lines of functional specialization, hierarchy, unity, and recruitment based on politically neutral administrative competence, the political approach stresses the extent and advantages of political pluralism within public administration. Thus, Harold Seidman argues that, "Executive branch structure is in fact a microcosm of our society. Inevitably it reflects the values, conflicts, and competing forces to be found in a pluralistic society. The ideal of a neatly symmetrical, frictionless organization structure is a dangerous illusion."[34] Norton Long makes a similar point: "Agencies and bureaus more or less perforce are in the business of building, maintaining, and increasing their political support. They lead and in large part are led by the diverse groups whose influence sustains them. Frequently they lead and are themselves led in conflicting directions."[35] Roger Davidson finds a political virtue where those imbued with the managerial approach might see disorder: "In many respects, the civil service represents the American people more comprehensively than does Congress."[36]

The basic concept behind pluralism within public administration is that since the administrative branch is a policy-making center of government, it must be structured to enable faction to counteract faction by providing political representation to a comprehensive variety of the organized political, economic, and social interests that are found in the society at large. To the extent that the political approach's organizational scheme is achieved, the structure comes to resemble a political party platform that promises something to almost everyone without establishing clear priorities for resolving conflicts among them. Agency becomes adversary of agency and the resolution of conflict is shifted to the legislature, the office of the chief executive, interagency committees, or the courts. Moreover, the number of bureaus and agencies tends to grow over time, partly in response to the political demands of organized interests for representation. This approach to administrative organization has been widely denounced as making government "unmanageable," "costly," and "inefficient,"[37] but, as Seidman argues, it persists because administrative organization is frequently viewed as a political question that heavily emphasizes political values.

View of the Individual

The political approach to public administration tends to view the individual as part of an aggregate group. It does not depersonalize the individual by turning him or her into a "case," as does the managerial approach, but rather identifies the individual's interests as being similar or identical to those of others considered to be within the same group or category. For example, affirmative action within the government service is aimed at specific social groups such as blacks and women without inquiry as to the particular circumstances of any individual member of these broad and diverse groups. Similarly, farmers growing the same crops and/or located in the same national geopolitical subdivisions are considered alike, despite individual differences among them. The same is true in any number of areas of public administration where public policies dealing with people are implemented. This is a tendency, of course, that fits the political culture well— politicians tend to think in terms of groups, for example, the "black" vote, the "farm" vote, labor, and so forth. Indeed, this approach is so strong that some, such as David Truman,[38] consider it the main feature of government in the United States. Theodore Lowi argues that a central tenet of the contemporary American "public philosophy" is that "organized interests are homogeneous and easy to define, sometimes monolithic. Any 'duly elected' spokesman for any interest is taken as speaking in close approximation for each and every member."[39] In this view of the individual, then, personality exists, but it is conceptualized in collective terms.

The Legal Approach to Public Administration

Origin and Values

In the United States, the legal approach to public administration has historically been eclipsed by the other approaches, especially the managerial. Nevertheless, it has a venerable tradition and has recently emerged as a full-fledged vehicle for defining public administration. It is derived primarily from three inter-related sources. First is administrative law. As early as 1905, Frank Goodnow, a leading contributor to the development of public administrative theory generally, published a book entitled *The Principles of the Administrative Law of the United States*.[40] There he defined administrative law as "that part of the law which fixes the organization and determines the competence of the authorities which execute the law, and indicates to the individual remedies for the violation of his rights."[41] Others have found this broad conception of administrative law adequate for defining much of the work of public administrators and the nature of public agencies. For instance, Marshall Dimock writes:

> To the public administrator, law is something very positive and concrete. It is his authority. The term he customarily uses to describe it is "my mandate." It is "his" law, something he feels a proprietary interest in. It does three things: tells him what the legislature expects him to accomplish, fixes limits to his authority, and sets forth the substantive and procedural rights of the individual and group. Having a positive view of his mandate, the administrator considers himself both an interpreter and a builder. He is a builder because every time he applies old law to new situations he builds the law. Therefore law, like administration, is government in action.[42]

Taking a related view, Kenneth Davis argues that public agencies are best defined in terms of law: "An administrative agency is a governmental authority, other than a court and other than a legislative body, which affects the rights of private parties through either adjudication, rule-making, investigating, prosecuting, negotiating, settling, or informally acting."[43]

A second source of the legal approach has been the movement toward the "judicialization"[44] of public administration. Judicialization falls within the purview of Goodnow's definition of administrative law, but tends to concentrate heavily upon the establishment of procedures designed to safeguard individual rights. Dimock succinctly captures the essence of judicialization:

> Before the Administrative Procedure Act [1946] came into existence, decisions were made by the regular administrative staff, with the ultimate decision being entrusted to the head of the agency. Characteristically, it was a collective or institutional decision, each making his contribution and all checking each other. The decisions were made on the basis of statutory law, plus agency sublegislation, plus decided court cases. The system worked, and in most cases worked well. Then the idea arose of using "hearing examiners" in certain cases where hearings were long and technical, as in railroad cases coming under the Interstate Commerce Commission. . . .
>
> When the Administrative Procedure Act . . . was enacted, however, judicialization was speeded up, and now, like a spreading fog, it has become well-nigh universal. It began with hearing officers who were recruited by the U.S. Civil Service Commission and put in a pool, from which they were assigned to various agencies. . . . [T]he idea of courtroom procedure was still further enlarged when Congress created the office of "Administrative Judge," this being one who operates inside the agency instead of outside it, as in the case of the European administrative courts.
>
> . . . In actual practice . . . the longer the system has been in existence, the more frequently the hearing examiner's recommended decision becomes the final decision.[45]

Thus, judicialization brings not only law but legal procedure as well to bear upon administrative decision making. Agencies begin to function more like courts and consequently legal values come to play a greater role in their activities.

Constitutional law provides a third source of the contemporary legal approach to public administration. Since the 1950s, the federal judiciary has virtually redefined the procedural, equal protection, and substantive rights and liberties of the citizenry vis-à-vis public administrators.[46] The old distinction between rights and privileges, which had largely made the Constitution irrelevant to individuals' claims with regard to the receipt of governmental benefits, met its demise. Concomitantly, there was a vast expansion in the requirement that public administrators afford constitutional procedural due process to the individuals upon whom they specifically acted. A new stringency was read into the Eighth Amendment's prohibition of cruel and unusual punishment. Wholly new rights, such as the right to treatment and habilitation, were created, if not fully ratified by the Supreme Court, for those confined to public mental health facilities. The right to equal protection was vastly strengthened and applied in a variety of administrative matters ranging from public personnel merit examinations to the operation of public schools and prisons.

The expansion of the constitutional rights of individuals vis-à-vis public administrators has been enforced primarily in two ways, both of which enhance the relevance of the legal approach to contemporary public administration. The courts have sought to force public administrators scrupulously to avoid violating individuals' constitutional rights by reducing public officials' once absolute immunity from civil suits for damages to a qualified immunity.[47] With some exceptions, public administrators are now liable for damages if they "knew or reasonably should have known" that an action taken abridged someone's constitutional rights.[48] In the Supreme Court's view, this approach "in addition to compensating victims, serves a deterrent purpose"[49] that "should create an incentive for officials who may harbor doubts about the lawfulness of their intended actions to err on the side of protecting citizens' constitutional rights."[50] Consequently, the concept of administrative competence is expanded to include reasonable knowledge of constitutional law. In addition, in suits challenging the constitutionality or legality of public institutions such as schools, prisons, and mental health facilities, the courts have frequently decreed on-going relief requiring institutional reforms that place the judges in the role of "partner"[51] with public administrators. Indeed, in some instances judges clearly become supervisors of vast administrative undertakings.[52]

The legal approach to public administration embodies three central values. One is procedural due process. It has long been recognized that this value cannot be confined to any single set of requirements or standards.[53] Rather, the term stands for the value of fundamental fairness and is viewed as requiring procedures designed to protect individuals from malicious, arbitrary, capricious, or unconstitutional harm at the hands of the government. A second value concerns individual substantive rights as embodied in evolving interpretations of the Bill of Rights and the Fourteenth Amendment. In general, the judiciary views the maximization of individual rights and liberties as a positive good and necessary feature of the United States political system. Breaches of these rights may be tolerated by the courts when, on balance, some essential governmental function requires their abridgment. However, the usual presumption is against the government in such circumstances and, consequently, judicial doctrines place a heavy burden on official administrative action that infringes upon the substantive constitutional rights of individuals.[54] Third, the judiciary values equity, a concept that like due process is subject to varying interpretation. However, in terms of public administration in general, equity stands for the value of fairness in the result of conflicts between private parties and the government. It militates against arbitrary or invidious treatment of individuals, encompasses much of the constitutional requirement of equal protection, and enables the courts to fashion relief for individuals whose constitutional rights have been violated by administrative action.

One of the major features of the values of the legal approach to public administration is the downgrading of the cost/benefit reasoning associated with the managerial approach. The judiciary is not oblivious to the costs of its decisions, but its central focus tends to be on the nature of the individual's rights, rather than on the costs to society of securing those rights. This is especially evident in cases involving the reform of public institutions. As one court said, "inadequate resources can never be an adequate justification for the state's depriving any person of his constitutional rights."[55]

Organizational Structure

As suggested in the discussion of judicialization, the preferred structure of the legal approach to public administration is one that will maximize the use of adversary procedure. The full-fledged judicial trial is the archetypical model of this structure. In terms of public administration, however, it is generally modified to allow greater flexibility in the discovery of facts. Juries are not used and hearing examiners often play a more active role in bringing out relevant information. Although this structure is often associated with regulatory commissions, its general presence within public administration should not be underestimated. For example, it is heavily relied upon in contemporary public personnel management, especially in the areas of adverse actions, equal employment opportunity, and labor relations.[56] It is also common in instances where governmental benefits, such as welfare or public school education, are being withheld or withdrawn from individuals.[57] The precise structure varies from context to context, but the common element running through it is the independence and impartiality of the hearing examiner. As Dimock points out, to a large extent this independence undermines the managerial approach's reliance on hierarchy. Hearing examiners stand outside administrative hierarchies in an important sense. Although they can be told what to do, that is, which cases to hear, they cannot be told how to rule or decide. Moreover, for all intents and purposes, their rulings may be binding upon public agencies. This may introduce serious limitations on administrative coordination as the hearing examiner's interpretation of law and agency rules may differ from that of the agency's managerial hierarchy. Dimock summarizes the impact of the adjudicatory structure as follows:

> The hearing officers and administrative judges are on a different payroll. Moreover, unlike other officials in his department or agency, the executive is expressly forbidden to fire, discipline, or even communicate with the administrative judge except under very special

circumstances, which usually means when the judge submits his proposed order. Under the new system, the judge is isolated in the same manner as a judicial judge, for fear that improper influence will be brought to bear upon him.[58]

To a considerable extent, therefore, this model is at odds with all the values embodied in the other two approaches: It militates against efficiency, economy, managerial effectiveness, representativeness, responsiveness, and political accountability. It is intended, rather, to afford maximum protection of the rights of private parties against illegal, unconstitutional, or invidious administrative action.

View of the Individual

The legal approach's emphasis on procedural due process, substantive rights, and equity leads it to consider the individual as a unique person in a unique set of circumstances. The notion that every person is entitled to a "day in court" is appropriate here. The adversary procedure is designed to enable an individual to explain his or her unique and particular circumstances, thinking, motivations, and so forth to the governmental decision maker. Moreover, a decision may turn precisely upon such considerations, which become part of the "merits" of the case. There are some outstanding examples of this in the realm of public administration. For instance, in *Cleveland Board of Education v. LaFleur* (1974)[59] the Supreme Court ruled that before a mandatory maternity leave could be imposed upon a pregnant public school teacher, she was entitled to an individualized medical determination of her fitness to continue on the job. In *Wyatt v. Stickney* (1971)[60] a federal district court required that an individual treatment plan be developed for each person involuntarily confined to Alabama's public mental health facilities. Emphasis on the individual *qua* individual does not, of course, preclude the aggregation of individuals into broader groups, as in the case of class action suits. However, while such a suit may be desirable to obtain widespread change, it does not diminish the legal approach's concern with the rights of specific individuals.

The Separation of Powers

Reflection upon these opposing approaches to public administration suggests that they cannot be synthesized for the simple reason that they are an integral part of a political culture that emphasizes the separation of powers rather than integrated political action. Thus, it is largely true that each of these approaches is associated with the values embodied in a different branch of government. The managerial approach is most closely associated with the executive. The presidency has taken on a vast number of roles and functions, but a major feature of its constitutional power is to make sure that the laws are faithfully executed. This is largely the role of implementation, which is the focus of the managerial approach's definition of public administration. The political approach, by contrast, is more closely associated with legislative concerns. It views public administrators as supplementary law makers and policy makers generally. Hence its emphasis on representativeness, responsiveness, and accountability. The legal approach is very closely related to the judiciary in its concern with individual rights, adversary procedure, and equity.

As Justice Brandeis pointed out, the founders' purpose in creating the constitutional branches was not simply to facilitate efficiency, coordination, and a smooth functioning of government generally. The purpose was also to create a system that would give each branch a motive and a means for preventing abuses or misguided action by another. This would prevent the "accumulation of all powers, legislative, executive, and judiciary, in the same hands," which, as Madison wrote in *Federalist #47,* the founders considered to be "the very definition of tyranny." But the separation of powers would also create a tendency toward inaction. Not only would each branch check the others, but a system of checks and balances would also serve as a check on popular political passions. Thus, the terms of office and the constituencies of members of the House of Representatives and the Senate differ from each other and from those of the president. The judiciary, being appointive, has no constituency per se and serves at good behavior, subject to removal by impeachment. Changing the staffing of the government as a whole, therefore, is something that can be accomplished only gradually. Altering its policy initiatives and directions drastically requires widespread consensus among the citizenry. Importantly, some actions of the legislature, such as approving treaties, over-riding vetoes, and proposing constitutional amendments, require extraordinary majorities. This can enable a political minority to protect itself from a majority passion.[61] Overall, the government was designed to be responsive slowly to relatively long-term public demands and to require the development of relatively broad agreement among the electorate prior to taking action.

This model of government has not seemed well-suited to public policy aimed at widespread penetration of the economic and social life of the political community. It is weighted in favor of inertia and inflexibility. In answer to this problem, during the past century or so, the United States developed a large administrative apparatus to facilitate specialized, positive, and flexible governmental action.[62] This phenomenon is commonly referred to as the "rise of the administrative state" and is hardly confined to the United States.[63] However, in this country it represents an effort to reduce the inertial qualities of the system of separation of powers. In essence, all three governmental functions have been collapsed into the administrative branch. Thus, public administrators make rules (legislation), implement these rules (an executive function), and adjudicate questions concerning their application and execution (a judicial function). The collapsing of the separation of powers has been well recognized. As Justice White wrote in *Buckley v. Valeo* (1976), "There is no doubt that the development of the administrative agency in response to modern legislative and administrative need has placed severe strain on the separation-of-powers principle in its pristine formulation."[64] This strain has also contributed to a "crisis of legitimacy"[65] in public administration because of the accumulation of legislative, executive, and judicial functions in administrative agencies runs counter to the deeply ingrained desire within the political culture for a system of checks and balances.

In a very real fashion, however, a system of checks and balances has devolved to the administrative branch along with the three governmental functions. Thus, as has been argued in this essay, the values associated with each function have been transmuted into distinctive theoretical approaches toward public administration. These approaches have different origins, stress different values and structural arrangements, and view individuals in remarkably different ways. This is precisely because each stresses a different function of public administration. Consequently, although there may be room for greater synthesis of these approaches, seeking to unify theory by allowing one approach to drive out the others would promote public bureaucracy in the most invidious sense of the term. Rather, the task is to develop a distinctive theoretical core suitable to the political culture by building around the need to maintain values, organizational structures, and perspectives on the individuals that tend to check and balance each other.

Precisely how such theory may be derived is, of course, not immediately evident or predictable. However, a few ideas come to mind. First, public administrative theorists must recognize the validity and utility of each of the approaches discussed here. Perhaps others can be added in the future, but the legitimacy of each of these is beyond question. Consequently, a definition of the field of public administration must include a consideration of managerial, political, and legal approaches. Second, it is necessary to recognize that each approach may be more or less relevant to different agencies, administrative functions, and policy areas. For example, regulation stresses adjudication and, consequently, probably should not be organized primarily according to the managerial or political approaches. Likewise, overhead operations most clearly fall within the purview of the managerial approach. Distributive policy may be best organized according to the political approach. Much more thought and research must be devoted to these matters before any firm conclusions can be reached. But clearly it is an administrative fallacy to try to treat all agencies and programs under a universal standard. This is one reason why the much vaunted "rational" budgeting techniques of PPBS and ZBB failed.[66] Third, as heretical as it will sound to some, public administrative theory must make greater use of political theory. As is argued here, the separation of powers goes well beyond the issues of legislative delegation and agency subdelegation—it reaches to the core of the leading theories of public administration. Finally, attention must be paid to the practical wisdom of the public administrative practitioners whose action is circumscribed by internal considerations of checks, balances, and administrative and political pressures generally. Individual public administrators are often called upon to integrate the three approaches to public administration and much can be learned from their experience.

Notes

1. Robert Parker, "The End of Public Administration," *Public Administration Review* 34 (June 1965): 99; quoted in Richard Stillman, *Public Administration: Concepts and Cases* (Boston: Houghton Mifflin, 1976), p. 3.

2. Frederick C. Mosher, "Research in Public Administration," *Public Administration Review* 16 (Summer 1956): 177; Stillman, *Public Administration*, p. 3.

3. Herbert Kaufman, "Emerging Conflicts in the Doctrines of Public Administration," *American Political Science Review* 50 (December 1956): 1057–1073.

4. James Q. Wilson, "The Bureaucracy Problem," *The Public Interest* 6 (Winter 1976): 3–9.

5. See Gabriel Almond and Sidney Verba, *The Civic Culture* (Boston: Little, Brown, 1965), whose findings provide a useful outline of the values forming the core of the U.S. political culture.

6. Carl Schurz, *The Necessity and Progress of Civil Service Reform* (Washington, DC: Good Government, 1894), p. 3.

7. Woodrow Wilson, "The Study of Administration," *Political Science Quarterly* 56 (December 1941): 481–506 (originally copyrighted in 1887).

8. Ibid., p. 481.

9. Frederick Taylor, *The Principles of Scientific Management* (New York: Harper and Bros., 1917).

10. Leonard D. White, *Introduction to the Study of Public Administration* (New York: Macmillan, 1926), pp. vii–viii. See also Herbert J. Storing, "Leonard D. White and the Study of Public Administration," *Public Administration Review* 25 (March 1965): 38–51.

11. *Papers on the Science of Administration,* ed. by Luther Gulick and L. Urwick (New York: Institute of Public Administration, 1937), p. 192.

12. Robert Simmons and Eugene Dvorin, *Public Administration* (Port Washington, NY: Alfred Publishing, 1977), p. 217.

13. Max Weber, From *Max Weber: Essays in Sociology,* translated and ed. by H.H. Gerth and C.W. Mills (New York: Oxford University Press, 1958), pp. 196–244.

14. Peter Blau and Marshall Meyer, *Bureaucracy in Modern Society,* 2d ed. (New York: Random House, 1971), esp. p. 8. See also Victor Thompson, *Modern Organization* (New York: Knopf, 1961), pp. 58–80.

15. See Harold Seidman, *Politics, Position, and Power* (New York: Oxford University Press, 1970), chap. 1.

16. See Eugene Lewis, *American Politics in a Bureaucratic Age: Citizens, Constituents, Clients, and Victims* (Cambridge, MA: Winthrop, 1977).

17. Weber, *Essays in Sociology,* p. 228.

18. Jay Shafritz et al., *Personnel Management in Government* (New York: Marcel Dekker, 1978), p. 94.

19. Ralph Hummel, *The Bureaucratic Experience* (New York: St. Martin's, 1977), pp. 24–25.

20. See Erving Goffman, *Asylums* (Garden City, NY: Doubleday, 1961), esp. pp. 1–24; *Halderman v. Pennhurst State School,* 244 F. Supp. 1295 (1977); *Holt v. Sarver,* 304 F. Supp. 362 (1970); John Hersey, *The Algiers Motel Incident* (New York: Knopf, 1968).

21. See Amitai Etzioni, *Modern Organizations* (Englewood Cliffs, NJ: Prentice Hall, 1964), chap. 4, for a brief, cogent description of the human relations approach. Victor Thompson, *Modern Organization,* discusses bureaupathology at pp. 152–177.

22. Wallace Sayre, "Premises of Public Administration: Past and Emerging," in Jay Shafritz and Albert Hyde, eds., *Classics of Public Administration* (Oak Park, IL: Moore, 1978), p. 201. Dwight Waldo, *The Administrative State* (New York: Ronald Press, 1948), demonstrates how the basic value choices of managerial public administration are ultimately statements of political preference.

23. Paul Appleby, *Policy and Administration* (University, AL: University of Alabama Press, 1949); see also Theodore Lowi, *The End of Liberalism* (New York: W.W. Norton, 1969).

24. *Myers v. U.S.,* 272 U.S. 52, 293 (1926).

25. David Nachmias and David H. Rosenbloom, *Bureaucratic Government, U.S.A.* (New York: St. Martin's, 1980).

26. The literature here is too vast to cite in its entirety. See Samuel Krislov and David H. Rosenbloom, *Representative Bureaucracy and the American Political System* (New York: Praeger, 1981) for a recent discussion.

27. PL 95–454, sect. 3 and sect. 2301 (b) (1). See also *Givhan v. Western Line Consolidated School District,* 99 S. Ct. 693 (1979), which enunciates constitutional conditions permitting a public employee to act as a "representative" within a public administrative structure.

28. PL 92–463.

29. See William Keefe and Morris Ogul, *The American Legislative Process,* 4th ed. (Englewood Cliffs, NJ: Prentice Hall, 1977), p. 407.

30. See Frederick Mosher, *Democracy and the Public Service* (New York: Oxford University Press, 1968); Ralph Hummel, *The Bureaucratic Experience;* Morris Janowitz, Deil Wright, and William Delany, *Public Administration and the Public* (Westport, CT: Greenwood, 1977); Lowi, *End of Liberalism;* William Morrow, *Public Administration* (New York: Random House, 1975); and Bruce Smith and James D. Carroll, eds., *Improving the Accountability and Performance of Government* (Washington, DC: Brookings, 1982).

31. This was an implicit assumption of the nineteenth-century civil service reformers, who argued that "as the functions of government grow in extent, importance and complexity, the necessity grows of their being administered not only with honesty, but also with trained ability and knowledge." Carl Schurz, *Congress and the Spoils System* (New York: George Peck, 1895), p. 4. See Harry Kranz, *The Participatory Bureaucracy* (Lexington, MA: Lexington Books, 1976); and Samuel Krislov, *Representative Bureaucracy* (Englewood Cliffs, NJ: Prentice Hall, 1974) for discussions of social representativeness and efficiency.

32. Marver Bernstein, *The Job of the Federal Executive* (Washington, DC: Brookings, 1958), p. 30.

33. Ibid., pp. 26–37. See also Herbert Kaufman, *The Administrative Behavior of Federal Bureau Chiefs* (Washington, DC: Brookings, 1981), esp. chap. 2.

34. Seidman, *Politics, Position, and Power,* p. 13.

35. Norton Long, "Power and Administration," in Francis Rourke, ed., *Bureaucratic Power in National Politics* (Boston: Little, Brown, 1965), p. 18.

36. Roger Davidson, "Congress and the Executive: The Race for Representation," in A. DeGrazia, ed., *Congress: The First Branch of Government* (New York: Anchor, 1967), p. 383.

37. See Seidman, *Politics, Position, and Power,* chap. 1.

38. David Truman, *The Governmental Process* (New York: Knopf, 1951); see also Arthur Bentley, *The Process of Government* (Chicago: University of Chicago, 1908).

39. Lowi, *End of Liberalism,* p. 71. See also Grant McConnell, *Private Power and American Democracy* (New York: Knopf, 1966), chaps. 4, 5.

40. Frank Goodnow, *The Principles of the Administrative Law of the United States* (New York: G.P. Putnam's Sons, 1905).

41. Ibid., p. 17.

42. Marshall Dimock, *Law and Dynamic Administration* (New York: Praeger, 1980), p. 31.

43. Kenneth Davis, *Administrative Law and Government* (St. Paul: West, 1975), p. 6.

44. Dimock, *Law and Dynamic Administration,* chap. 10.

45. Ibid., p. 113. According to Charles Dullea, "Development of the Personnel Program for Administrative Law Judges," *Administrative Law Review* 25 (Winter 1973): 41–47, the title "Administrative Law Judge" was created by the U.S. Civil Service Commission.

46. The case law and literature are too voluminous to cite. See David H. Rosenbloom, *Public Administration and Law: Bench v. Bureau in the United States* (New York: Marcel Dekker, 1983).

47. See *Scheuer v. Rhodes,* 416 U.S. 322 (1974). See also Rosenbloom, *Public Administration and Law,* chap. 6.

48. *Wood v. Strickland,* 420 U.S. 308, 322 (1975); *Harlow v. Fitzgerald,* 50 Law Week 4815 (1982).

49. *Carlson v. Green,* 446 U.S. 14, 21 (1980).

50. *Owen v. City of Independence,* 445 U.S. 622, 652 (1980).

51. David Bazelon, "The Impact of the Courts on Public Administration," *Indiana Law Journal* 52 (1976): 101–110.

52. Abram Chayes, "The Role of the Judge in Public Law Litigation," *Harvard Law Review* 89 (1976): 1281–1316; Roger Cramton, "Judicial Lawmaking in the Leviathan State," *Public Administration Review* 36 (1976): 551–555.

53. *Hannah v. Larche,* 363 U.S. 420 (1960).

54. See for instance, *Branti v. Finkel,* 445 U.S. 507, 518 (1980), which requires the public employer

to "demonstrate that party affiliation is an appropriate requirement for the effective performance of the public office involved" when making a patronage dismissal.

55. *Hamilton v. Love,* 328 F. Supp. 1182, 1194 (1971).

56. See Robert Vaughn, *The Spoiled System* (New York: Charterhouse, 1975); Richard A. Merrill, "Procedure for Adverse Actions Against Federal Employees," *Virginia Law Review* 59 (1973): 196–287.

57. *Goldberg v. Kelly,* 397 U.S. 254 (1970); *Goss v. Lopez,* 419 U.S. 565 (1975).

58. Dimock, *Law and Dynamic Administration,* p. 114.

59. 414 U.S. 632 (1974). Argued and decided with *Cohen v. Chesterfield Co. School Board.*

60. *Wyatt v. Stickney,* 325 F. Supp. 781 (1971); 334 F. Supp. 387 (1972).

61. See *Federalist #10.*

62. See Peter Woll, *American Bureaucracy,* 2d ed. (New York: Norton, 1977). Woll is among several scholars with a constitutional focus who argue cogently that the administrative process is far more flexible than government according to the original constitutional scheme could be. See also, Davis, *Administrative Law and Government.* James O. Freedman, *Crisis and Legitimacy* (New York: Cambridge University Press, 1978), chap. 2, provides a brief description of the rise of the contemporary administrative state and the tension between its operation and the founders' concept of the separation of powers.

63. Henry Jacoby, *The Bureaucratization of the World* (Berkeley: University of California Press, 1978).

64. *Buckley v. Valeo,* 424 U.S. 1, 280–281 (1976).

65. Freedman, *Crisis and Legitimacy.*

66. Allen Schick, "A Death in the Bureaucracy," *Public Administration Review* 33 (March/April 1973): 146–156; "Budgeting Expert Calls Carter Plan 'Disaster,'" *Houston Post,* April 8, 1977, p. 14A, quotes Peter Phyrr, originator of zero based budgeting, as calling the federal effort to institute ZBB all-at-once "absolute folly."

CHAPTER 2

PUBLIC ADMINISTRATION, EXECUTIVE POWER, AND CONSTITUTIONAL CONFUSION

JOHN A. ROHR

The purpose of this article is to argue that confusion over the meaning of the constitutional grant of "the executive power" to the President has created considerable confusion over the constitutional role of the public administration in American government. Richard Neustadt captured this ambiguity nicely when he noted that the two great themes that have characterized the American presidency have been "clerkship" on the one hand and "leadership" on the other.[1] There is no easy formula to bring clerks and leaders together to make them march in lock-step, and yet the President is clearly both. Today the tendency is to emphasize his role as leader because imperial pretensions and Nixonian excesses are still relatively fresh in our memories, but this is only a question of emphasis. No one denies that the President is a legally accountable officer who must do the bidding of the Congress. This is the clerkship side of the presidency.

Herbert Storing counsels against any effort to cut the Gordian knot and to try to determine once and for all just what it is the American President is supposed to be: clerk or leader. "The beginning of wisdom about the American presidency," Storing maintains, "is to see that it contains both principles and to reflect on their complex and subtle relation."[2] Following Storing's advice, this article reflects on the inherent ambiguity of the executive power that provides the constitutional foundation for the public administration. This reflection has three parts. The first examines the text of the Constitution and the meaning of executive power at the time of the founding. The second studies the confusion that the U.S. Supreme Court has created in its efforts to draw practical conclusions for presidential personnel management from the constitutional grant of "the executive power" to the President in relation to the removal power. The third examines some of the recent problems of executive power that surfaced in the Watergate scandal and became salient in the important constitutional debate over special prosecutors, those most unwelcome intruders into the inner precincts of the Reagan Administration.

From *Public Administration Review* 49, no. 2 (March/April 1989): 108–114. Copyright © 1989 by American Society for Public Administration. Reprinted with permission.

The Founding Period

"Executive" has two conflicting meanings that account in part for the confusion the word occasions in constitutional law and in other fields as well. Etymologically, it is derived from the Latin verb *exsequi,* meaning to follow through or to carry out. *Sequi* is the root verb meaning to follow, and the prefix *ex-* simply intensifies the meaning of following. Etymologically, then, the executive is a follower, and this clearly favors the clerk side of the clerk/leader conundrum. This meaning was prevalent in the eighteenth century, as the *Oxford English Dictionary* (OED) attests, and it survives to the present day. Corporate executives (at least in principle) carry out the will of the board of directors, and executors of estates follow the wishes of deceased testators. But ancient examples from the OED and contemporary usage as well justify a meaning of executive that is independent of higher authority. Kings have been said to execute their own wills, and God Himself is described as one who "executyth... good & indyfferent justyce... to his creatures."[3] Today, Presidents are said to exercise "executive privilege" when they act in a manner utterly antithetical to that of a mere clerk of the Congress or of the courts. Such an executive is clearly a leader.

At the time of the founding of the Republic, the ambiguity that engulfed the executive was due as much to political expectations as to etymology and usage. The framers of the U.S. Constitution wanted a strong executive for two incompatible reasons. The sad administrative experience under the Articles of Confederation taught them the need for an independent executive whose legal existence would be liberated from the committees of the Continental Congress. This line of argument anticipated that of the Civil Service Reformers who would appear a century later. It was an argument grounded in concern for governmental efficiency. The executive was to be independent in order to enable him (or them—the single executive was quite controversial) to carry out the will of the Congress more efficiently. This theme, arising from the colonial experience, favored an independent executive, but not an executive that was equal to the legislature. This is the origin of the clerkship side of the presidency.

Some framers of the Constitution also wanted an independent executive to check the legislative excesses that they saw in many of the states. If they were about to establish a real government at the national level, there would be need for an authentic legislature with powers far greater than those of the hapless Continental Congress. Steps would have to be taken to keep this new national legislature from oppressing the people and disregarding their rights. To this end an independent executive was an indispensable means. He or they would vindicate the rights of the citizens and would maintain a watchful vigilance against the "excesses of democracy," that notorious failing of all popular governments. This political sentiment grounds the theme of President as leader.

Not surprisingly, these ambiguities in language and political expectations found their way into the text of the Constitution itself. The first sentence of Article II provides that "The executive power shall be vested in a President of the United States." This language contrasts markedly with the opening words of Article I: "All legislative powers herein granted shall be vested in a Congress of the United States, which shall consist of a Senate

and House of Representatives." Champions of a strong executive have always emphasized the absence of the qualifying words "herein granted" in Article II. This absence,
they maintain, means that *the* executive power (presumably all of it) is vested in the
President. Congress possesses all those legislative powers that are granted in the Constitution itself, but it does not possess all legislative power. That is, there are many
areas of life in which Congress may not legislate. It may legislate only in those areas
in which the Constitution permits it to do so. To be sure, Congress possesses all legislative powers in the sense that other institutions created by the Constitution have no
explicit authorization to legislate. But the legislative powers of Congress are confined
to the written document.

The practical import of these exegetical niceties is that they serve as a launching pad
for a constitutional argument in support of *inherent* executive powers that are not confined by the text of the Constitution. This argument sees in the executive power clause a
positive grant of power to the President to do whatever any political executive can do.
Activist Presidents, like Jackson, Lincoln, and Theodore Roosevelt, made skillful use of
this argument. Theodore Roosevelt, for example, used this clause to support the robust
theory of presidential power that led him to conclude that "it was not only his [the
President's] right but his duty to do anything that the needs of the nation demanded
unless such action was forbidden by the Constitution or by the laws."[4] Such an interpretation of presidential power would put an end once-and-for-all to the tension between the President's roles as leader and clerk. The Rooseveltian President is not only
leader of his people, but, like Gilbert and Sullivan's Pooh-Bah, he could also claim to
be "first Lord of the Treasury, Lord Chief Justice, Commander-in-Chief, Lord High
Admiral, Master of the Buckhounds, Groom of the Backstairs, Archbishop of Titipu,
and Lord Mayor."

Critics of presidential power have responded in a variety of ways. One line of argument admits that the President does indeed possess all executive power without qualification, but it maintains that this does not justify the far-reaching conclusions of presidential
apologists. What is executive power, they ask. It is simply the power to execute law. The
President may only execute that which the Congress has legislated. It was perfectly
logical for the framers to omit the "herein granted," qualification from the grant of executive power to the President, because, having provided that the Congress has only
those legislative powers "herein granted," there was no need to repeat the same language
in the article establishing the executive. Executive power cannot outstrip legislative power,
for there would be nothing for the executive to execute. He can only execute what the
Congress can legislate. Hence the limitations on the scope of congressional power necessarily encumber the executive power of the President as well.

This argument is reinforced by explicit constitutional grants of power to the President
to command the armed forces of the nation, to grant reprieves and pardons, to share in
the power to make treaties and to appoint officers, to convene either or both houses of
Congress, to receive ambassadors, and so forth. The fact that these powers are explicitly
granted in the Constitution undercuts the argument that the executive power clause confers inherent executive powers on the President. If the executive power clause did this,

what would be the purpose of spelling out all these other powers that are traditionally associated with the executive? These additional powers would all be redundant. They could all be found in the teeming womb of the executive power clause. Clearly, the argument goes, the framers intended that the "executive power" clause should give the President nothing more than the power to execute laws passed by Congress. Whatever other powers he might possess are explicitly stated in Article II. The President has no powers other than the sum of the powers resulting from these two sources.

Another argument against the presence of inherent executive power in Article II is drawn from the opening words of Article III: "The judicial power of the United States, shall be vested in one supreme court, and in such inferior courts as the Congress may from time to time ordain and establish." Critics of presidential power highlight the contrast between Article II which vests only "the executive power" and Article III which vests "the judicial power *of the United States* (emphasis added). It is the judiciary, not the executive, that enjoys inherent power. There is a judicial power of the United States, the argument runs, and this is the power to apply common law.[5] The grant of this inherent power is signaled by the explicit mention of a judicial power *of the United States.* It is a power that inheres in the judicial system of any nation influenced by the English legal tradition. Article II significantly omits any mention of an executive power "of the United States." Had the framers of the Constitution wished to confer such inherent executive power on the President, they would have used the sort of language they adopted when they created the judiciary.

A final textual response to the expansive view of presidential power is based on sections 2, 3, and 4 of Article II. Here the argument differs from the considerations, just discussed. The previous arguments conceded that the executive power clause does indeed grant complete executive power to the President. Having made this concession, the thrust of the previous arguments was to limit the scope of executive power by confining the meaning of the word to executing the will of the Congress and thereby to deny any additional, inherent powers to the President. The argument here maintains that other sections of Article II cannot be reconciled with the claim that the executive power clause gives *all* executive power to the President—no matter how narrowly one defines executive power.

The most important constitutional clause in support of this position states that the President "shall take care that the laws by faithfully executed, and shall commission all the officers of the United States." This language makes it rather clear that the President himself is not to execute the laws, but is to see to it that others do so; and to assist him in doing just this, the Constitution empowers the President to commission officers. These constitutional provisions are followed immediately by the impeachment clauses which clearly describe the President as a legally accountable officer who "presides" (as a *President* should) over an executive establishment that carries out the laws mandated by Congress. This is the textual basis for the clerkship view of the presidency. It is reinforced by the explicit constitutional provision for "executive departments," each of which will be headed by a single "principal officer."

This constitutional language casts a shadow over the interpretation of the executive power clause that maintains that the framers meant to give the executive power (i.e., all of it) to the President alone. Surely a constitutional provision for a principal officer in each of several executive departments implies that these high officials hold some sort of executive power in their own right. But if they hold any executive power at all, the President cannot hold all of it.

These considerations will suffice to support the point that at the time of the founding of the Republic, there was considerable ambiguity and confusion over the precise nature of executive power. This ambiguity and confusion came from the word "executive" itself and, perhaps more importantly, from the framers' conflicting expectations of a strong and independent executive. Not surprisingly, this ambiguity and confusion spilled over into the text of the Constitution itself and there found a permanent home for the irreconcilable themes of the President as leader on the one hand and clerk on the other. Public administration has established its constitutional dwelling place in this uneasy household whose bewildered inmates have brought forth anomalies, enigmas, and contradictions in their own image and likeness.

The President's Removal Power

Article II provides several ways in which federal officers may be appointed; but, except for the impeachment clause, it is silent on how they may be removed. This constitutional silence prompted an important debate during the first Congress. The debate occurred when the House of Representatives was establishing the Department of Foreign Affairs, the original name for the Department of State. There was no doubt that the Secretary of Foreign Affairs should be appointed by the President with the advice and consent of the Senate, but considerable doubt existed about how he should be removed from office. There were four distinct answers to this question, each of which involved an interpretation of the Constitution. One group maintained that the Constitution vests this power in the President alone. A second group said it was vested in the President and the Senate together—this had been the position of Publius in *Federalist #77*. A third said that Congress had the constitutional authority to vest this power in the President alone or in the President and the Senate together. A fourth group, much smaller than the other three, held that impeachment was the only constitutionally permissible method of removal.[6]

The argument was exceedingly complex and was highlighted by brilliant parliamentary maneuvers by the proponents of the position that the Constitution itself vests the removal of officers in the President alone. The debate consumed over five legislative days in which members of the House participated in three roll-call votes. The upshot of the debate was that the President emerged with the authority to remove the Secretary of Foreign Affairs without interference from the Senate. This outcome was called "the decision of 1789." It was a decision of monumental political significance. The President's power to remove the head of an executive department was at the heart of the most important constitutional crisis of Andrew Jackson's presidency and, even more significantly, at the heart of the effort to impeach President Andrew Johnson. To the present day it remains a crucial element in presidential control over the public administration.

Despite the overwhelming importance of the issue, the Supreme Court of the United States did not get around to addressing it until 1926 in *Myers v. United States.*[7] Myers was a postmaster first class in Oregon who had been appointed by President Wilson in July 1917. He was appointed pursuant to an 1876 statute that provided that postmasters "shall be appointed and may be removed by the President with the advice and consent of the Senate, and shall hold their offices for four years unless sooner removed or suspended according to law." In February 1920, long before the expiration of his four-year term, Myers was removed from office by the postmaster general acting under direction from the President. Although the Senate had consented to Myers's appointment, it did not consent to his removal. Myers therefore maintained that his removal was not "according to law" and brought suit for the salary due him for the remainder of his term.

Myers's efforts were in vain. Chief Justice Taft, writing for a six-member majority, held that "the provision of the law of 1876, by which the unrestricted power of removal is denied to the President, is in violation of the Constitution, and invalid." Taft's opinion was a remarkable paean to the need for strong managerial powers in the hands of the President. It was the sort of opinion that could only have been written by an erstwhile President turned Chief Justice. In the course of his opinion, the Chief Justice relied heavily on "the decision of 1789" as an authoritative declaration of the true meaning of the Constitution by a Congress that included a good number of the framers of the Constitution. In appealing to the action of the first Congress, Chief Justice Taft gave too little attention to the fact that in 1789 Congress was debating the President's removal powers over a Secretary of Foreign Affairs, the closest of the President's advisers in an area that is distinctly presidential. The contrast with an Oregonian postmaster could hardly have been greater. In addition, the *Myers* case raised the question of whether the President could remove an officer with a fixed term of office before the expiration of the term, a matter that simply was not at issue in the decision of 1789. These important factual differences between the decision of 1789 and the *Myers* case prompted Justice Holmes to complain in dissent that Taft's arguments "seem to me spider's webs inadequate to control the dominant facts."

The most startling aspect of Taft's opinion was his confident assertion that the historical record unequivocally supported his sweeping view of presidential removal powers. "[T]here is not the slightest doubt," said the Chief Justice, "after an examination of the record, that the vote [the decision of 1789] was, and was intended to be, a legislative declaration that the power to remove officers appointed by the President and the Senate vested in the President alone." The Chief Justice overstated his case; the record is simply not this clear. Justice Brandeis gave a much more precise account of the 1789 debate, when he argued in his dissenting opinion that it "did not involve a decision of the question whether Congress could confer upon the Senate the right, and impose the duty, to participate in removals." In 1876 Congress did address this question and decided that it could confer this right and duty upon the Senate. It was the constitutionality of the 1876 decision that was before the Court in *Myers,* and this question, Brandeis maintained, could not be settled by appeals to the decision of 1789.

With characteristic precision, Brandeis showed that the decision of 1789 involved "merely the decision that the Senate does not, in the absence of a legislative grant thereof, have the right to share in the removal of an officer appointed with its consent; and that the president has, in the absence of restrictive legislation, the constitutional power of removal without such consent." Thus, for Brandeis, the decision of 1789 upholds the central role of Congress in the removal process. If Congress says nothing by law, the President alone may remove an officer whom he has appointed with the advice and consent of the Senate. For Brandeis, the decision of 1789 did not preclude Congress from providing by law that the Senate must concur in the removal of certain officers. The exercise of such power by Congress could be justified by the explicit constitutional authorization for Congress to make all laws "which shall be necessary and proper for carrying into execution the . . . powers vested by the Constitution on the Government of the United States, or in any Department or Officer thereof." The President is an officer of the United States who is empowered to take care that the laws are faithfully executed. A congressional requirement for senatorial approval of a presidential decision to remove an officer like a postmaster might well be considered a necessary and proper means of assuring that the President does take care that the laws are faithfully executed.

Brandeis's interpretation of the decision of 1789 is more accurate than that of Chief Justice Taft.[8] Nevertheless, it is Taft's opinion that is the law of the land. As Edward Corwin has remarked, "what a judge cannot *prove* he can still *decide*."[9] And Chief Justice Taft decided that, as a matter of constitutional law, the President has unfettered power to remove executive officers whom he or a previous President has appointed with the advice and consent of the Senate. This legal rule cried out for further clarification of just what is meant by an executive officer.

The clarification was not long in coming. Early in his first presidential term, President Franklin Roosevelt removed Federal Trade Commissioner Humphrey from office several years before his seven-year tenure had expired. The statute creating the commission and fixing its members' terms at seven years further provided that commissioners could be removed before the expiration of their terms only for cause. Humphrey had given no cause for removal. Clearly, Roosevelt's action was based on his belief that under the *Myers* decision the statutory restrictions on his removal powers were unconstitutional. Humphrey did not see it that way, and he sued for the salary due him for the remaining years in his term of office. In a unanimous decision the U.S. Supreme Court supported Humphrey's claim.[10]

In his opinion for the court, Justice Sutherland distinguished *Myers* on the grounds that that case and the decision of 1789 involved officers whose functions were "purely executive," whereas federal trade commissioners exercise authority that is only quasi-legislative and quasi-judicial. Sutherland maintained that because of these functions, Humphrey was "an officer who occupies no place in the executive department and who exercises no part of the executive power vested by the Constitution in the President." He further maintained that when the Federal Trade Commission exercises an executive function, the power it exercises is not "executive power in the constitutional sense." Whatever action it takes, "it does so in the discharge and effectuation of its quasi-legislative or quasi-judicial powers or as an agency of the legislative or judicial departments of the government."

This was an astounding line of reasoning. It is difficult to comprehend the distinction between "executive power in the constitutional sense" and some other form of executive power. No less puzzling is the meaning of Sutherland's statement that the Federal Trade Commission is "an agency of the legislative *or* judicial departments of the government" (emphasis added). Sutherland seems to put the commission on a constitutional shuttle between the courts and the Congress depending on whether it happens to be exercising quasi-legislative or quasi-judicial authority. The shuttle, however, must not stop at the executive branch of government—or at least at that branch that exercises "executive power in the constitutional sense." Sutherland's strange language led one commentator to wonder just where the trade commissioner belongs in the Court's constitutional cosmology: "[I]s he, forsooth, in the uncomfortable halfway situation of Mohamet's coffin, suspended twixt Heaven and Earth?"[11]

The heart of the problem is that Sutherland accepted that portion of *Myers* that forbade Congress from limiting the President's constitutional power to remove executive officers appointed by the President with the advice and consent of the Senate. Having made this concession, Sutherland had a strong incentive to remove the "executive" label from any officer he believed might be rightfully protected by the Congress from an unfettered presidential power to remove. The *Humphrey* case gave the Court a chance to admit its error in *Myers* and simply to overrule that unhappy precedent. Unfortunately, the Court closed its eyes to the light at the end of the *Humphrey* tunnel. Instead, it ran in circles after an illusory executive power that is something other than "executive power in the constitutional sense." This will-of-the-wisp has as its sorry progeny the mindless chatter heard over the past half-century about the bureaucracy as a "headless fourth branch of government." Since there are only three constitutional branches of government, fourth branch rhetoric attacks the constitutional legitimacy of administrative institutions.

The problem is not confined to the so-called "independent regulatory commissions," like the Federal Trade Commission. The logic of Sutherland's opinion focuses on the function of an agency, not on its place in the *U.S. Government Organization Manual.* Under Sutherland's reasoning, it would seem that any officer who exercises quasi-legislative or quasi-judicial power could be described as one who "occupies no place in the executive department and who exercises no part of the executive power vested by the Constitution in the President." This would include those officers in the executive departments who exercise rule-making and adjudicatory powers.[12] Perhaps such officers should be exempt from presidential removal; this is especially true for those exercising quasi-judicial functions. It makes no sense, however, to say that such officers do not exercise "executive power in the constitutional sense." If the *Humphrey* Court had overruled *Myers,* it could have avoided the need to use such bizarre language. Had *Myers* been overruled, Congress could have resumed its traditional powers to limit the President's power to remove some officers and to give the President a free hand in removing others. The Congress could do this on an *ad hoc* basis that would consider the particular function of each officer without any constitutional legerdemain about purely executive officers as opposed to those whose duties are quasi-this or quasi-that. The fundamental flaw in *Myers* is that Chief Justice Taft treated the executive branch of government as though it were a managerial enterprise instead of a political institution in which the Congress will always have a legitimate interest, and interest that was bound to grow along with the rise and development of the modern administrative state.

Independent Counsel/Special Prosecutor

Quite recently, the perennial confusion over executive power took a new twist in a Supreme Court decision that resolved the volatile issue of the constitutionality of the office of independent counsel created by the Ethics in Government Act of 1978.[13] Popularly known as "special prosecutors," the independent counsels are appointed by three-judge panels to investigate alleged wrong-doings by high-ranking officials in the executive branch of government. The origin of the independent counsel can be traced to the messy constitutional problems that arose during the Watergate scandal. One of these problems centered on how Special Prosecutor Leon Jaworski, who was presumably an "inferior officer" in the executive branch of government, could defy the wishes of President Nixon, his executive superior, in his relentless (and successful) campaign to force the President to surrender the famous tapes that sealed his doom. The Supreme Court's unanimous ruling in *United States v. Nixon* failed to give an adequate response to this argument; an argument that was urged with the zeal worthy of a better cause by Nixon's brilliant attorney, James St. Clair.

A salient aspect of the problem was the absence of a clear statutory basis for the position and powers of the special prosecutor. The Congress addressed this problem in the Ethics in Government Act of 1978. Under this act, the Attorney General is required to conduct a preliminary investigation of plausible charges against high-ranking officials. After ninety days, he is to report the results of his investigation to a three-judge panel that is called the "special division," a division of the U.S. Court of Appeals for the District of Columbia. The three judges are appointed by the Chief Justice of the United States to serve for a term of two years. If the Attorney General finds "reasonable grounds to believe that further investigation or prosecution is warranted," he must ask the special division to appoint an independent counsel and to define the limits of the counsel's prosecutorial jurisdiction. The statute goes into considerable detail to describe the relationship between the independent counsel and the Department of Justice; but, for purposes here, the most important points are that the independent counsel is appointed by a three-judge panel and can be removed only by impeachment or "by the personal action of the Attorney General and only for good cause, physical incapacity, or any other condition that substantially impairs the performance of such independent counsel's duties."

The policy objectives behind the independent counsel legislation were quite clear. Congress wanted to avoid any repetition of the "Saturday night massacre" of the Watergate era. It was important that the independent counsel should be truly independent. To ensure that this would be the case, Congress provided that the appointment should be made by a judicial panel and that removal could be effected only for cause.

Not surprisingly, these provisions were challenged on constitutional grounds. In the case that reached the Supreme Court, *Morrison v. Olson,* a former Assistant Attorney

General, Theodore Olson, was under investigation by independent counsel Alexia Morrison on charges of having given false and misleading testimony to a congressional subcommittee in 1983 and of having wrongfully withheld certain documents from the House Judiciary Committee at that time. In the course of the investigation, Morrison caused a grand jury to issue subpoenas to Olson and two others who refused to comply on the grounds that the legislation creating Morrison's office was unconstitutional. This refusal led to the litigation that eventually reached the Supreme Court.

In a 7–1 decision, Chief Justice Rehnquist upheld the constitutionality of the unusual appointment and removal provisions for the independent prosecutor. The appointment argument was straightforward. The second section of Article II provides that appointments to federal offices are to be made by the President with the advice and consent of the Senate. The same section then adds the following qualification: "but the Congress may by law vest the Appointment of such inferior Officers, as they think proper, in the President alone, in the Courts of Law, or in the Heads of Departments." The Chief Justice maintained that the independent counsel was an inferior officer and, therefore, that Congress could rightfully vest her appointment in a judicial panel. In a long and vigorous dissent, Justice Scalia argued that the independent counsel was not an inferior officer and, therefore, Congress could not vest her appointment in "the Courts of Law."

Underlying the technical issues concerning the meaning of the term "inferior Officer" was a deeper separation of powers question that became clearer as Rehnquist and Scalia presented their conflicting arguments on the constitutionality of the statutory provision that the independent counsel could be removed only for cause—that is, she could not be removed at the pleasure of the President or of the Attorney General acting on behalf of the President. This issue beat a path back to the *Myers* and *Humphrey* cases. Scalia maintained that "the prosecution of crimes is a quintessentially executive function." Prosecutors, he said, are "the virtual embodiment of the power to 'take care that the laws be faithfully executed'" and therefore should be subject to the broad presidential removal powers announced in *Myers*.

Chief Justice Rehnquist disagreed and, in so doing, gave a new and very restrictive interpretation of *Myers*—an interpretation of considerable importance for public administration professionals. He maintained that "the only issue actually decided in *Myers* was that 'the President had power to remove a postmaster of the first class, without the advice and consent of the Senate as required by act of Congress.'" He then acknowledged that the *Humphrey* court had distinguished the case before it from *Myers* on the grounds that a federal trade commissioner exercised quasi-legislative and quasi-judicial authority, as opposed to the purely executive functions of a postmaster first class. According to the *Humphrey* court, this distinction justified the congressional action that imposed a "for good cause" limitation on the President's power to remove a trade commissioner.

Having rehearsed this history, the Chief Justice then made the following, startling comment:

> But our present considered view is that the determination of whether the Constitution allows Congress to impose a "good cause"-type restriction on the President's power to remove

an official cannot be made to turn on whether or not that official is classified as "purely executive." The analysis contained in our removal cases is designed not to define rigid categories of those officials who may or may not be removed at will be the President, but to ensure that Congress does not interfere with the President's exercise of the "executive power" and his constitutionally appointed duty to "take care that the laws be faithfully executed" under Article II.

The Chief Justice went on to explain that in this and in future removal cases the Court will not focus exclusively or even primarily on the sorts of functions that an officer performs. To be sure, the Chief Justice acknowledged that an analysis of the functions performed would not be "irrelevant." "But the real question is whether the removal restrictions are of such a nature that they impede the President's ability to perform his constitutional duty, and the functions of the officials in question must be analyzed in that light."

This is new constitutional doctrine. In dissent, Justice Scalia stated (correctly, I believe) that the *Humphrey* case "is swept into the dustbin of repudiated constitutional principle." Although Scalia recognized some of the problems in the *Humphrey* opinion, he found the loose standard announced by the Chief Justice far worse. He surmised that the new standard would be "an open invitation to congress to experiment." The experiments would test just how far the Congress could go in protecting purely executive officers from dismissal at the pleasure of the President without impeding "the President's ability to perform his constitutional duty." He conjectured that under this standard, the Congress could provide that an "Assistant Secretary of State, with responsibility for one very narrow area of foreign policy," might be removed "only pursuant to certain carefully designed restrictions." Or the Congress might offer similar protection to an Assistant Secretary of Defense for Procurement. Ominously, Scalia brooded:

> The possibilities are endless, and the Court does not understand what the separation of powers, what "[a]mbition counteract[ing] ambition," *Federalist No. 51* . . . , is all about if it does not expect Congress to try them. As far as I can discern from the Court's opinion, it is now open season upon the President's removal power for all executive officers, with not even the superficially principled restriction of *Humphrey's Executor* as cover.[14]

The public administration community will greet Scalia's predictions with greater equanimity than does the dissenting justice. One might well doubt that the Congress will follow through with the bold experiments Scalia fears. If the Congress were to do so, however, it might not be simply to celebrate the new "open season upon the President's removal power." Congress just might take such actions to encourage administrative professionalism in high-ranking executive officers and to protect them from punitive political reprisals from Presidents who prefer ideological subservience to sound administration. Then it would be the duty of the executives themselves to see to it that the President's rightful place in the constitutional balance of powers is preserved. It would be their responsibility as practitioners of the art and science of public administration to be sure that their protected positions against mischievous presidential whim did not weaken the President's capacity to "take care that the laws be faithfully executed."

Notes

1. Richard Neustadt, *Presidential Power: The Politics of Leadership from FDR to Carter* (New York: Wiley, 1960, 1980), chap. 1.

2. Herbert J. Storing, "Introduction," to Charles C. Thach, *The Creation of the Presidency 1775–1789: A Study in Constitutional History* (Baltimore: John Hopkins University Press, 1923, 1969), pp. vii–viii.

3. *The Compact Edition of the Oxford English Dictionary*, Volume I, A–O (New York: Oxford University Press, 1971, 1976) E, pp. 393–395.

4. Theodore Roosevelt, *An Autobiography* (New York: Putnam, 1913), pp. 388–398.

5. George Anastaplo, "The United States Constitution of 1787: A Commentary," *Loyola University of Chicago Law Journal* 18 (Fall 1986): 129–139.

6. I discuss the removal question in more detail in a forthcoming monograph, *The President and the Public Administration* (Washington, DC: American Historical Association).

7. 272 U.S. 52 (1926).

8. For an extended argument in support of this assertion, see my monograph referenced in Note 6: For a good counter argument, see Peter L. Schultz, "The Constitution, the Presidency, and the Rule of Law," in *University of Kentucky Law Journal* 76, no. 1 (1987–88): 1–14; and "Separation of Powers and Presidential Prerogative: The Case of *Myers v. U.S.* Reconsidered," in Gary L. McDowell, ed., *Taking the Constitution Seriously* (Dubuque: Kendall-Hunt, 1981), pp. 220–231.

9. Edward S. Corwin, *The President's Removal Power Under the Constitution* (New York: National Municipal League, 1927: repr., Ithaca, NY: Cornell University Press, 1981), p. 339.

10. *Humphrey's Executor v. U.S.,* 295 U.S. 602 (1935). Humphrey himself died after Roosevelt removed him; hence the title of the case.

11. Edward S. Corwin, *The President: Office and the Powers, 1787–1984,* 5th ed., (New York: New York University Press, 1984), p. 108.

12. This interpretation follows Corwin, *The President,* p. 108.

13. *Morrison v. Olson,* 108 S. Ct. 2597 (1988).

14. 418 U.S. 683 (1974).

CHAPTER 3

RESPONSE TO JOHN ROHR

ROSEMARY O'LEARY

What does John Rohr's thesis suggest about the future of public administration? Most importantly, the article indicates a need for law to become an integral part of the public administration curriculum again. In the vast majority of programs approved by the National Association of Schools of Public Affairs and Administration (NASPAA) law is not a requirement. There are several reasons why this situation should be remedied.

First, the relationship between law and administration is central to the operation of democratic government, and it has great impact on public policy. As thousands of court cases are decided annually, so are thousands of public-policy and public-administration issues. If the bureaucrats of tomorrow are to have an understanding of how public policy is made and implemented, knowledge of law is essential.

Second, if improvements are to be made in efforts to maintain American constitutional democracy, understanding of by public servants of the U.S. Constitution is necessary. Classwork that helps public administration students understand the constitutional confusion about the proper place and function of public administration and the implications of such confusion, for example, will better prepare future public servants for the challenges of administration. Where ignorance of law may have been acceptable fifty years ago, it no longer is.

Third, American society has increasingly looked to public administrators for resolution of some of its most difficult problems. Many of these problems have been addressed through use of legal processes and application of legal principles. For example, legal principles have been used to assure proper functioning of markets, to assure safety of products and services, to regulate new technologies, to protect the environment, to regulate employment practices, and to protect "entitlements." It is important for public servants to have a thorough understanding of these legal issues.

Finally, much of the literature suggests that federal judges have become increasingly aggressive in the oversight of administrative action. Judges, in some instances, are no longer passive reviewers of actions that affect the public service but are active participants, shaping litigation and its outcomes. If the next generation of public servants is to function adequately in its interactions with the courts, knowledge of law is important. In sum, law as a course requirement in schools of public administration is more than a nicety; it is a necessity.

From *Public Administration Review* 49, no. 2 (March/April 1989): 115. Copyright © 1989 by American Society for Public Administration. Reprinted with permission.

Chapter 4

CITY MANAGERS AND CITY ATTORNEYS

Associates or Adversaries?

Doyle W. Buckwalter and J. Ivan Legler

The city manager–city attorney relationship has received only cursory attention in recent years. Yet this important and complex relationship can have an extraordinary impact on the operational effectiveness of municipal government. This study identifies the perceptions held by city managers and city attorneys about each other's functional responsibilities and interactive patterns. These perceptions are then summarized and synthesized into specific recommendations for improving the city manager–city attorney relationship. The data sources for the study are twenty in-depth interviews of city managers and city attorneys and two recent (1985–1986) nationwide questionnaire surveys of council-manager cities. Out of courtesy to the officials involved and a desire to avoid creating or aggravating potential interpersonal conflicts, attorney questionnaires and manager questionnaires were not mailed to the same cities, except in a small test group. The response rates represented an acceptable, statistical population cross section of council-manager cities in the United States. Fifty-two percent (104 out of 200) of attorneys responded to the first survey; 42 percent (84 of 200) responded to the second survey. City manager response rates were 61 percent (122 of 200) for the first survey, and 70 percent (141 of 200) for the second.

Before examining the survey results, it is useful to note the historical development of the city manager and city attorney in council-manager cities.

Historical Background

The structural framework of municipal government in the latter part of the nineteenth century was insufficient to withstand the pressures of modern machine politics, corruption, and excessive state government interference. Municipal reform began in earnest between 1850 and 1870 as city councils almost uniformly stripped administrative powers from mayors and created overlapping council committees and multiple independent boards.[1] Though the purpose was to eliminate executive corruption and provide more checks and balances, the reform had unexpected consequences:

> There was such an ingenious combination of checks and balances and mingling of power, that nobody could be to blame for anything. It took everybody to do anything, and everybody did it, and everybody said it was you and not I, and everybody was right.[2]

Municipal legal offices functioned in this labyrinthian committee setting. Subsequently, three significant and somewhat inconsistent trends appeared near the turn of the century, all advocating public accountability: the decline of council committees, the ascendance of the absolute executive appointment power, and the long ballot. In this process, several municipal officers began to be viewed as city overseers: comptroller, treasurer, auditor, and city attorney. City attorneys generally were "to attend to all suits and matters and things in which the city is interested," and to fill the additional role of "independent watchdog" over the city.[3]

Shortly, a divergent reform movement began to deal with the same issue of executive corruption, while at the same time streamlining municipal administration. This was the adoption of the council-manager form of government. Cities involved at the developmental stages of this government form included Staunton, Virginia (1908); Lockport, New York (1910); Sumter, South Carolina (1912); and Dayton, Ohio (1914). The National Municipal League published a Model City Charter in 1915, which contained the outlines of the council-manager form.[4] Undergirding this Model Charter were two unambiguous principles: (1) a unification of ultimate legislative and executive power in one elected council, and (2) a delegation of the day-to-day management operation to a professionally trained administrator, protected from daily politics and inappropriate council interference, but ultimately answerable to the council. One important aspect of the management operation so delegated was the power of appointment. Richard S. Childs, known as the "father of the council-manager system," strenuously advocated that membership in the newly established City Managers Association be contingent on the city manager exercising complete appointment powers:

> To insist that the managers must have appointment power over all the administrative departments does not exclude managers in cities where the charter [now] excepts a few of the minor officers from the managers' control such as corporation counsel, a city clerk, assessors or police judge, for these officers are not necessarily integral parts of the administrative establishment. The provision does, however, prevent some future city from hiring a manager of ten years experience from another city and finding that he knows nothing of police problems. Such situations would tend to bring the professional managers into disrepute.[5]

The eventual conflict between these two reform concepts, checks and balances on the one hand and centralized professional management on the other, produced a range of managerial authority in council-manager cities. This is particularly evident in the arrangements for appointing city attorneys. For example, the 1923 Berkeley, California, charter mandated council appointment of the attorney. The 1928 Austin, Texas, charter allowed for city manager appointment of the city attorney, but that provision was adopted only after numerous exceptionally divisive debates.[6] Fort Worth, Texas, in 1940, provided for council appointment and control of the two "independent watchdog officials"—the treasurer and the director of law.[7] One advocate of city manager appointment of the city attorney, Arthur W. Bromage, attributed some early abandonments of the council-manager form of government to defective charters that required extensive council appointments, including appointment of the city attorney.[8] In 1941, one observer lamented that

> a judicially disposed legal advisor, over whom a city executive has no control is not consistent with vigorous and effective management. A legal advisor who simply looks down his nose and says, "no, it can't be done," or smiles wanly and says, "I guess it's all right to go ahead," is not much help to one responsible for the conduct of administration. What is needed is a helpful and cooperative attorney, one who says, "Let's see what you want to do. It looks to me as if you'd have trouble if you take that course. Why not try this or that? And if that won't fill the bill, why, let's draw an act for the next session of the legislature."[9]

By 1957, survey data showed the following distribution of selection processes for the city attorney in council-manager cities:[10] elected, 6 percent; council appointed, 52 percent; council appointed/manager recommendation, 2 percent; manager appointed, 28 percent; manager appointed/council approval, 7 percent; and other, 5 percent.

Many of these selection processes were mandated by state laws. An in-depth analysis of state statutes dealing with municipal attorneys reveals enormous differences between jurisdictions, not only in appointing processes but in attorney responsibilities. Some of these inherited, statutorily mandated appointment processes have undoubtedly had a great deal to do with city manager–city attorney relationships in individual cities. The significant differences in the city attorney appointment processes throughout the country show that the institutional "heritage" of the city manager–city attorney relationship is a lack of consensus on whether the attorney is a member of the "management team" or whether the attorney fills a unique "watchdog" responsibility for the city council.

From 1957 to 1978, observers from both the city management and city attorney professions analyzed the problems in the relationship of these two professionals and pointed up the critical need to remedy the underlying stresses.[11]

Present-Day City Manager and City Attorney Profiles

A brief present-day sketch of these two professionals furnishes the background against which their relationship can be evaluated. While all the city attorneys surveyed possess advanced educational degrees, only 64 percent of the managers surveyed have advanced degrees; 26 percent of the managers surveyed have bachelor's degrees, and 10 percent are without a college degree. On the whole, city attorneys view their city managers as receiving significantly less rigorous college training. Attorneys conclude that the core skills of legal training—issue formulation and case analysis—are the most important skills lacking in management training. The managers, conversely, identify the lack of emphasis on the management skills of administrative integration/coordination and on budgeting as the noticeable weaknesses of legal training.

Slightly more than 80 percent of the city managers selected the city management profession following enrollment in public administration or related classes. Approximately 43 percent of the city attorneys had either some public administration training or some prior experience in local government. Except for a few "range riders," all the managers serve as full-time city employees and are prohibited from additional employment. In critical contrast, about 46 percent of the attorneys are on part-time retainer, and only 48 percent are full-time, in-house. Among this latter group of city attorneys, 45 percent are permitted to engage in outside private practice. . . .

The data suggest a significant and even troublesome tenure difference between city managers and city attorneys. Managers serve about 5.75 years per city, while attorneys serve about double that. Twenty-five percent of the attorney respondents claim the advantage of a long-term policy perspective, saying that they have witnessed "several managers come and go." In the survey, managers and attorneys were asked to characterize their own and the other profession. The results are synthesized and reported in Table 4.1. They confirm that in spite of relational problems, each profession has a fairly accurate perception of the other's general characteristics.

Functional Responsibilities

Whether city managers and city attorneys are associates or adversaries appears to have a great deal to do with their perceptions of each other's functional responsibilities.

City Managers

Regardless of the size of city organizations, writers for the International City Management Association (ICMA) and the National Institute of Municipal Law Officers (NIMLO) and most state and city codes concur that city managers have the following primary responsibilities:

1. to serve as the chief administrative officer;
2. to provide for all aspects of the personnel function;
3. to prepare budget and appropriate financial documents;
4. to serve as the prime law enforcement officer;
5. to attend council meetings; and to provide studies and recommendations for the council.[12]

However, since the mid-1970s, the city management profession has undergone a major metamorphosis as a result of new management expectations in a changing political and economic environment. More and more, city managers are expected to be

Table 4.1

Characterization of Professionals

Managers claim attorneys are

More interested in	Than in
• elusive constitutional rights and processes	• administrative efficiency
• testing ideas/scenarios	• implementing ideas/scenarios
• researching	• brainstorming
• early prioritizing	• "extinguishing fires"
• ideological security	• ideological flexibility
• caution	• willingness to commit resources
• providing behind the scenes input	• achieving visibility
• philosophical concepts	• administrative issues
• avoiding "the can of worms"	• taking chances
• individual professional contributions	• group participation
• preventing liability	• exploring new services

Attorneys claim managers are

More interested in	Than in
• task orientation	• managerial style
• entering politically sensitive areas	• avoiding the political thicket
• challenges	• the status quo
• practicalities	• theory
• expressing optimism	• expressing pessimism
• restraining legal cost	• aggressive preventive law programs
• encouraging employees to accept long-range, cost-cutting standards	• reducing immediate program costs
• achieving a team management status	• supporting individual accomplishments
• creativity and innovation	• perfecting present practices

the "economic entrepreneurial leader" and "mobilizer of community resources"; the "strategic planner" and the "administrative innovator."[13] While city management is a collaborative effort, the manager has primary responsibility to orchestrate the effort, under scrutiny of the council and the public. . . .

City Attorneys

NIMLO and ICMA authors are in essential agreement on the primary city attorney responsibilities:

1. to assure that city operations are constitutional;
2. to provide advice to city officials;
3. to prepare formal legal opinions and other documents;
4. to prosecute state and local misdemeanor violations; and
5. to provide legal representation for the city in civil litigation.[14]

A recognition of broader application of attorney skills has led to some amplification of this list:

> The legal profession is characterized by precision of thought and expression and by analytical skills, qualities that can be put to good use by the skillful administrator who is able to involve the attorney in the city's administration. . . . The legal mind . . . is trained to analyze problems, and to separate critical issues from irrelevant ones. Finally, experienced trial attorneys have devoted their careers to rapidly acquiring extensive knowledge about widely varied subjects. These skills give the administrator who has a good rapport with this attorney an "instant expert" who may master not only the legal aspects of a subject, but often its technical aspects as well.[15]

The historical nonconsensus on whether they city attorney is part of the manager's team or independent council "watchdog" has led to a wide range in state code and city ordinance job descriptions for city attorneys. While some codes elaborate on attorney responsibilities relating to bonds, contracts, and so on, more often than not, the descriptions are unhelpfully brief and general. . . .

To some extent, the image of an "independent" city attorney may draw its impetus from attorney membership in organized bar associations which, in most states, exercise licensing and disciplinary authority over attorneys under the direction of the state supreme court. These organizations propose model rules of conduct that are adopted and enforced by the local courts. Although by law city attorneys scarcely have more of an affirmative obligation to investigate and report wrongdoing within the city organization than do other department heads, attorneys do have unique rules and considerations to follow in reacting to such wrongdoing. If attorneys ignore these rules, disciplinary proceedings may follow. For example, all attorneys owe strict duties of confidentiality to clients, both individual and organizational.[17] Furthermore, attorneys representing organizations must weigh the wrongfulness of acts by employees, officers, and directors against the likelihood of harm to the organization. Actions taken by the attorneys must minimize disruption to the organization.[18] In each case, higher authority is to be consulted, and in the case of cities, "the city council shall have the right to employ or retain special attorneys, if it deems it to be in the best interest of the city."[19]

Generally, city attorneys exercise some prosecutorial authority under state statutes, usually to enforce state and local misdemeanor laws. This may be another basis for the image of the "independent" city attorney. However, most city prosecutors do not perform independent investigations of criminal conduct but work closely with the police, the manager, and the other department heads who exercise code enforcement authority. Except in the rare cases of express statutory authority to conduct independent investigations, city attorneys would necessarily work closely with organizational authorities in any investigation of wrongdoing. To do otherwise, even as a prosecutor, could run afoul of the duties to the "organization as client." In only 2 of the 100 city codes providing for appointed city attorneys studied in this research are references found to "inherent attorney investigative responsibilities." An example of such a reference reads:

> If any citizen has knowledge of the misapplication of funds of the city, or the abuse of its corporate powers, or of the nonperformance of any contract, . . . he may present evidence of the same to the City Attorney who shall thereof investigate such evidence and shall take such legal course as the necessities of the case require.[20]

Whether city attorneys can or should enter the policy-making process is a constant question. Furthermore, practitioners wonder if and when city attorneys may publicly dissociate themselves from policy with which they disagree or which they believe will be harmful to the city organization or to the public. The American Bar Association (ABA) Model Rules of Professional Responsibility require a government attorney to maintain confidentiality of information relating to policy decisions with which the attorney disagrees.[21] On the other hand, an attorney is authorized to give advice not only on the technical law but on relevant moral, economic, social, and political factors as well.[22]

Some have argued that legal practitioners are the "most serviceable instruments of authority" because of their precedent mindset, attention to detail, cold analysis, inquisitiveness, and inclination to attack. This "thinking like a lawyer," and a degree of detachment from city administration, may be a reflection of (1) the expansion of constitutional protection for individuals affected by public administration; (2) the significant rise in public law litigation leading to reforms in public institutions; and (3) the change from absolute to qualified immunity for public administrators. In contrast, municipal administrators often perceive themselves as "professional diplomats," with specialized skills in human relations, negotiation, compromise, and accommodation, and supported by service delivery training with ample authority to achieve the public interest as determined by the council.[23]

Interaction Patterns

Having identified the perceptions of the functions of city managers and city attorneys, we may look at the actual interactions reported. First, however, we should note than Allen Grimes, a long-time student of the city attorney subject, has ranked the city manager as the preeminent municipal officer, followed by the city attorney. He asserts that these two independent officers, often both appointed by the city council, should exercise no administrative control over each other. Organizationally, the manager is the administrative officer, and the attorney is the legal officer.[24] James Banovetz asserts that when the council is involved in appointing the city attorney, it causes the attorney to "feel little direct responsibility to the administrator."[25] The question, then, is whether actual manager-attorney interactions are characterized by this independence and aloofness, particularly in the areas of (a) administrative control, (b) professional relations, and (c) access to the city council.

Administrative Control

Managers and attorneys surveyed were asked to indicate if the manager exercises administrative control over the attorney. Approximately 80 percent of the combined respondents said yes, at least to some extent, regardless of who appoints the attorney. Manager-appointed city attorneys, of course, expect to report directly to the manager and only indirectly to the council. But a surprising number of council-appointed attorneys acknowledge at least some administrative responsibility to the city manager. Twelve percent of the council-appointed attorneys indicate that they report directly to the manager; 64 percent report to the council; and 24 percent claim direct ties to both. Managers' perceptions of administrative reporting by the attorney differs; 18 percent assert that the attorney reports directly to the manager; 42 percent acknowledge a council-attorney line of authority; and 40 percent recognize dual supervision.

Banovetz speaks of "multiple supervision" of the attorney's office: "When appointment review or approval by the Council is combined with the attorney's lawyer-client view of his relationship to the elected council, it will be seen that most legal departments have a dual responsibility to the chief administrator and to the legislative body."[26]

In connection with this issue of administrative control, our survey asked if city attorneys have a "greater public responsibility" than other department heads—a possible basis for a sense of independence from the manager. In cities with council-appointed attorneys, 93 percent of the attorneys and 36 percent of the managers regard attorneys as ultimately having a "greater public obligation" than other department heads. In contrast, in cities with manager-appointed attorneys, 67 percent of the attorneys and just 18 percent of the managers held that attorneys have a greater obligation to the public. . . .

Some managers report an "us versus them" attitude among city attorneys who hold to this sense of "greater public responsibility." One attorney who disapproves of such an attitude has said:

> The theory seems to be that the lawyer . . . had acquired some duty . . . to be the final arbitrator of right and wrong. I cannot agree with this philosophy. . . . I do not believe that the ritual of becoming a member of the bar invests a government lawyer with the power of life and death over the agency he serves. The agency head takes his own oath of office, and he is also subject to the inscrutable forces of public opinion. In carrying out his responsibility to decide policy, the agency head looks to his lawyer's counseling as one of his strongest supports; but the lawyer's counsel can never usurp the decision which must be made by the responsible head of the agency.[28]

David Caylor has said that attorneys have an overarching obligation to assure justice, achieve fairness, and avoid using the economic power of government to harass individuals or groups. Nevertheless, when an attorney is ordered by the council to take illegal or questionable actions, Caylor declares that a single reasonable attempt by the attorney to articulate an opposing position is all that is required. He or she should not attempt to serve as an advocate on behalf of an abstract "public" client against the incumbent city council.[29] Allen Grimes has said in this regard:

> I smile when young lawyers are asked in the examination process for recruitment for duties what they would do if the Council instructed them to prepare an ordinance which they had told the Council was unconstitutional. Almost universally, they will reply that they will refuse to draft it. Well, if they do refuse, they will not continue to be an Assistant City Attorney for long. There is just one course of action unless you are an elected city attorney or you do not want to keep drawing your salary, and that is—do it.[30]

Survey respondents were also asked if they agree with the historical "watchdog" or "whistle-blower" role for city attorneys. In cities with council-appointed attorneys, 88 percent of attorneys and 76 percent of managers say yes. In cities with manager-appointed attorneys, 70 percent of attorneys and only 48 percent of managers acknowledge the role. . . .

Most city codes routinely designate a number of entities and officials (such as the council, the manager, department heads, and city employees) as being served by the city attorney. Therefore, managers and attorneys were asked to disregard their codes and to express their own feelings about who they specifically considered to be the attorney's client. Sixty-three percent of total respondents identify the corporate "city" as the client. . . .

Clearly, the managers and attorneys surveyed share similar perceptions about the level at which the city attorney is functioning and should function. Though a majority of attorneys are now functioning at a high level of activity, 83 percent of the city managers and 60 percent of the city attorneys further state that the city attorney should be a permanent member of the manager's "policy team," so that the city attorney would be regularly used in the policy-making process. Those who advocate this expanded role for the city attorney cite the attorney's extensive knowledge of public case law, problem-solving and analytical skills, and long-term familiarity with city programs.

Paradoxically, some ambiguity about the extent of administrative control over the legal department is acceptable to 96 percent of the managers and 93 percent of the attorneys surveyed. . . .

Professional Relations

Managers and attorneys recognize each other as the ranking, professionally trained municipal officials. However, their evaluations of each other's professionalism show some striking differences. Seventy-one percent of the managers rate attorneys as very high in professional development; 24 percent accord a high ranking; and 4 percent give a moderately high ranking. However, only 48 percent of the attorneys rank the managers very highly professional; 25 percent express a high professional rating; and 24 percent give a moderately high ranking.

Managers appear more disposed to have high confidence in the attorney's professional abilities, despite the fact that 47 percent of the managers also express frustration over attorneys' "it can't be done attitude." Attorneys, on the other hand, appearing somewhat more preoccupied with administrative deficiencies in their manager, simultaneously bristle at any "nay-sayer" label. . . .

Access to City Council

Lay city councils can often become somewhat dependent on the advice and skills of the city attorney. Thus, one of the more emotional issues of the manager-attorney relationship can be the degree to which the manager influences the city attorney's access to the council, collectively and as individuals. Managers and attorneys surveyed are in substantial agreement (85 percent) that the council should have ready access to the city attorney. However, there is less agreement on how best to coordinate council use of the attorney's resources through the manager's office. Attorneys are divided between such manager involvement and regular, independent conferences with the council. Wholesale disagreement exists on whether to limit individual council member's access to the city attorney. Whereas 71 percent of the managers want restricted individualized council member access to the city attorney, only 40 percent of the attorneys favor that restriction. . . .

Conclusions

The short answer to the question posed at the beginning of this article is that city managers and city attorneys are both associates *and* adversaries. Most manager-attorney relationship patterns are characterized by a certain aloofness and independence. Yet, in spite of the institutional frustrations and frictions, the managers and attorneys surveyed feel reasonably positive about their relationships with one another, with the managers being somewhat more positive than the attorneys. Ninety-three percent of the managers rank the relationship in the category of "very good to excellent," while only 67 percent of the attorneys agree with that classification.

The data suggest that the manager-attorney relationship is not unduly volatile, nor is it characterized by extreme territoriality, misinterpretation, status jealousies, insensitivity, or professional mistrust. Rather, it can be characterized as "coexistence by necessity." But therein continues to lie a definite limiting effect and a potentially crippling impact on local government effectiveness. To cope with the urban environment of the 1980s and 1990s, these two professions must resolve the institutional frictions passed on to them from historical municipal reforms and make the relationship a "problem-solving team." The data suggest the following recommendations:

Code Reform

In cases of council-manager cities with appointed attorneys, state and municipal codes may profitably be revised to better delineate the following issues:

a. Who exercises authority to appoint and dismiss city attorneys?
b. What are the supervisory lines and roles, and do attorneys have independent public responsibilities not shared by other department heads?
c. How are attorney services and facilities allocated to the manager, the council, department heads, etc.?
d. What independent investigative powers do the attorneys have, if any, and how may these relate to manager and council powers?
e. When may the council and manager retain special counsel?
f. Who are the ultimate clients of city attorneys, especially in case of conflict?

Interpersonal Expectations

Interviews and the survey results repeatedly emphasize that success of the city manager–city attorney relationship is contingent on achieving a high level of mutual respect, both personal and professional. An appreciation of the expectations of each profession for the other can facilitate that goal.

City attorney expectations of city managers:

1. Understand the nature of legal services, including lead times, other time constraints, ambiguity of precedent, preferability of preventive law over reactive law, and the dual role of the attorney as counselor and advocate; the former role being conservative and the latter role being liberal.
2. Keep the attorney informed on status of projects, contracts, and negotiations to facilitate preventative law.
3. Invite the attorney to all determinative meetings to facilitate discussion and decision making.
4. Involve the attorney earlier in the policy process for his or her assistance and detached perspective.
5. Establish priorities to help the attorney properly allocate legal resources.
6. Support the attorney in providing legal training to departments to help them grasp legal implications of department programs and policies.
7. Develop early agreements on code enforcement philosophy and practices.
8. Channel legal opinion requests from departments through the manager's office, but allow some flexibility for direct council requests.
9. Consult with the city attorney on retainer of special counsel, and keep him or her informed of special counsel activities.
10. Do not discount the priority of an adequate legal department budget during the program budgeting process.

City manager expectations of city attorneys:

1. Appreciate that nonlegal aspects of administrative issues, including financial, organizational, and political aspects, are of equal importance to legal aspects.
2. Function in the "watchdog" capacity only in accordance with the considerations of Rules 1.6 and 1.13 of the ABA Model Rules of Professional Conduct, by working closely with management, where appropriate.
3. Assist in ameliorating the dual-supervision issue by recognizing the need for some management supervision of the legal department.
4. Translate legal competency into team spirit by finding avenues to further council-manager objectives, where possible.
5. Avoid public discussion of the merits of legal and policy issues prior to council consideration.
6. Regularly inform the manager on the status of legal issues.
7. Display interest in policy issues, particularly in requests to aid in the policy process.
8. Limit outside practice to permit quality time and attention to municipal issues.

9. Pursue continuing legal education in municipal law to meet the challenges on the horizon for urban services.
10. Accept some flexibility and ambiguity as part of the policy-making process, rather than insisting on rigid adherence to past precedent or required procedures, at least in the initial stages.

A former city attorney, now turned city manager, touched on the essence of this issue when he said, "To remove the adversarial relationship and develop the associate perspective will require communication, clarification, and cooperation."

Notes

1. Edward Pease Allison and Boies Penrose, *Philadelphia 1861–1887: A History of Municipal Development* (Philadelphia: n.p., 1887), p. 263.
2. Samuel Bowles, "Relation of State to Municipal Government and the Reform of the Latter," *Journal of Social Science* 9 (January 1878): 142.
3. Charles B. Elliott, *The Principles of the Law of Public Corporations* (Chicago: Callaghan and Company, 1898), p. 238. See also Ernest S. Griffith, *A History of American City Government: The Conspicuous Failure, 1870–1900* (New York: Praeger, 1938).
4. Richard S. Childs, "The Theory of the New Controlled Executive Plan," *National Municipal Review* (January 1913): 80.
5. Richard S. Childs, "Professional Standards and Professional Ethics in the New Profession of City Manager," *National Municipal Review* 5 (April 1916): 198.
6. Charles M. Kneier, *Illustrative Materials in Municipal Government and Administration* (New York: Harper and Brothers, 1939), p. 190.
7. Austin F. MacDonald, *American City Government and Administration* (New York: Thomas Y. Crowell, 1946), p. 215.
8. Arthur W. Bromage, *Manager Plan Abandonments* (New York: National Municipal League, 1940), pp. 12–18.
9. Thomas Harrison Reed, *Municipal Management* (New York: McGraw-Hill, 1941), p. 291.
10. Robert H. McManus, "How Should the City Attorney Be Selected?" *Public Management* 39 (January 1957): 4.
11. See Charles S. Rhyne, *Municipal Law* (Washington, DC: National Institute of Municipal Law Officers, 1957), sec. 8–62; Allen Grimes, "The Jobs of City Manager and City Attorney," *Public Management* 41 (February 1959); James M. Banovetz, ed., *Managing the Modern City* (Washington, DC: International City Management Association, 1971); Allen Grimes, *The City Attorney: A Practice Manual* (Washington, DC: National Institute of Municipal Law Officers, 1978).
12. Banovetz, *Managing the Modern City,* p. 96; The National Institute of Municipal Law Officers, *Model Administrative Code,* 1–3–1.1; Albermarle City, North Carolina, *City Charter,* 4.2.
13. See Wayne Anderson, Richard Stillman II, and Chester Newland, *The Effective Local Government Manager* (Washington, DC: International City Management Association, 1983).
14. Grimes, *The City Attorney,* p. 7; Banovetz, *Managing the Modern City,* pp. 404–414.
15. Banovetz, *Managing the Modern City,* pp. 403 and 406.
. . .
17. American Bar Association, *Model Rules of Professional Conduct* (Chicago: American Bar Association, 1983), p. 7, Rule 1.6.
18. Ibid., at p. 15, Rule 1.13.
19. Lewiston City, Maine, *City Charter,* 4.04; ABA Model Rules, p. 15, Rule 1.13.

20. Grand Rapids City, Michigan, *City Code,* 6.7a.

21. ABA, *Model Rules,* p. 7, Rule 1.6.

22. Ibid, at p. 18, Rule 2.1.

23. See Laurin A. Wollan, Jr., "Lawyers in Government—The Most Serviceable Instruments of Authority," *Public Administration Review* 38 (March/April 1978): 105–112; David H. Rosenbloom, "Public Administrators and the Judiciary: The 'New Partnership,'" *Public Administration Review* 47 (January/February 1987): 75–83; Harry C. Shriver, *The Government Lawyer* (Potomac, MD: Fox Hills Press, 1975); David Rosenbloom, *Public Administration and the Law* (New York: Dekker Press, 1985); Karl Llewellyn, *The Bramble Bush* (New York: Oceana, 1960); Richard J. Stillman II, *The Rise of the City Manager* (Albuquerque: University of New Mexico Press, 1974).

24. Grimes, *The City Attorney: A Practice Manual,* p. 61.

25. Banovetz, *Managing the Modern City,* p. 404.

26. Ibid., p. 416.

. . .

28. John K. Carlock, "The Lawyer in Government," in Albert Love and James Saxon, eds., *Listening to Leaders in Law* (Atlanta: Tupper and Love, 1963), pp. 268–269.

29. David Caylor, "Attorney-Client Privilege of City Attorneys," a paper presented at the meeting of the Texas City Attorneys' Association, Austin, Texas (June 30, 1982), p. 95.

30. Grimes, *The City Attorney: A Practice Manual,* p. 18.

CHAPTER 5

RETROFITTING THE ADMINISTRATIVE STATE TO THE CONSTITUTION

Congress and the Judiciary's Twentieth-Century Progress

DAVID H. ROSENBLOOM

[U]nder our system of divided powers, the executive branch of the national government is not exclusively controlled by the President, by the Congress, or by the courts. All three have a hand in controlling it, each from a different angle and each in a different way. (Meriam 1939, 131)

One of the "big questions" of American public administration has been how to retrofit, or integrate, the federal administrative state into the nation's constitutional scheme. The parameters of the problem are well understood. The Constitution's framers could not have anticipated the size, scope, or power of the modern administrative state. American public administration was not organized according to democratic theory and values (Waldo 1948, 1984). The separation of powers collapses into administration as agencies combine legislative, executive, and judicial functions. Administrative agencies threaten the separation of powers because, in the words of former Supreme Court Justice Robert Jackson, they are "a veritable fourth branch of the Government, which has deranged our three-branch legal theories much as the concept of a fourth dimension unsettles our three-dimensional thinking" (*Federal Trade Commission v. Ruberoid,* 343 U.S. 470 [1952]).

The overall problem of integrating federal administration into democratic-constitutional government may not be fully solvable (Waldo 1984, xviii), but its scope should not be allowed to obscure the progress that has been made. One of the great administrative developments of the twentieth century has been the extent to which Congress and the federal judiciary have responded to the rise of the administrative state by infusing it with constitutional values and folding it into the separation of powers. Psychologically, the turn of the century is a time for taking stock. That is the genre and purpose of this article.

From *Public Administration Review* 60, no. 1 (January/February 2000): 39–46. Copyright © 2000 by American Society for Public Administration. Reprinted with permission.

The Orthodox Response: Enhance Presidential Control

American public administrative thought was founded from the 1870s through the 1920s on a variety of propositions that are now regarded as untenable, perhaps even hazardous. In fairness to the nineteenth-century civil service reformers and the progressives who followed them, it should be noted that their public administrative doctrine was developed primarily to serve fundamental political objectives (Rosenbloom 1971, chap. 3; Rosenbloom and O'Leary 1997, 2–6). Nevertheless, the orthodoxy's politics-administration dichotomy has been "confounding" (Golembiewski 1984). Its belief that administrative systems and techniques are freely transferable among political systems has promoted frequent, and sometimes catastrophic, failure (Caiden 1991; Farazmand 1998).

Less well-appreciated, the orthodoxy denied that the development of the large-scale federal administrative state in the 1930s posed significant problems for the constitutional separation of powers. In its view, administration was almost exclusively an executive function that could be managed by the president and an institutionalized presidency. However, "executive-centered" public administrative theory has also proven to be inadequate. Congress and the courts cannot be relegated to minor roles in determining the course of federal administration.

The Constitution clearly provides Congress with considerable authority over federal administration. Funding, staffing, and empowering agencies require legislation. As W.F. Willoughby put it in 1927, Congress is the source of federal administration (115). The role of the courts is less specifically charted by the Constitution. However, in the framers' day judicial power was extensive and could reasonably be assumed to bear broadly on administration (Woll 1963, 91–92). Nevertheless, in the mid-1930s, the orthodoxy argued that the best way to integrate federal administration into the separation of powers was to place it almost entirely under the president's control.

The orthodoxy's most significant call for presidential domination of administration came from the U.S. President's Committee on Administrative Management (PCAM) in 1937. Its membership included three pillars of the public administrative establishment: Louis Brownlow (chair), Charles Merriam, and Luther Gulick (see Karl 1963). Proceeding on the basis that "The President is indeed the one and only national officer representative of the entire Nation," the Committee claimed that only good could come of enhancing his ability to be "the Chief Executive and administrator within the Federal system and service" (PCAM 1937, 1, 2). The "canons of efficiency require[d] the establishment of a responsible and effective chief executive as the center of energy, direction, and administrative management" (PCAM 1937, 3).

Not surprisingly, the committee specified no role in federal administration for the judiciary. The courts were out of favor with New Dealers for their interpretations of the Commerce Clause and the "non-delegation" doctrine. Shortly after the committee issued its report, President Roosevelt introduced what became known as the courtpacking plan and called for other changes in the federal judicial system (Gunther 1975, 167–168). At the time, calling for greater judicial involvement in federal administration was unthinkable (see Pritchett 1948).

The committee was not much more generous toward Congress. It viewed the legislative role as essentially appropriating funds, with no strings attached, and then turning the entire administrative enterprise over to the president: "We hold that once the Congress has made an appropriation, an appropriation which it is free to withhold, the responsibility for the administration of the expenditures under that appropriation is and should be solely upon the Executive" (PCAM 1937, 49–50).

This constitutional theory is worse than dubious: It is patently wrong. In John Rohr's words, "At the heart of the [Committee's] doctrine is a fundamental error that transforms the president from chief executive officer into sole executive officer" (1986, 139).

It was also a major political error. Congress rejected most of the committee's specific recommendations. The committee's report may have been the orthodoxy's high noon (Seidman 1970, 9), but its chief legislative proposal was denounced in Congress as "the dictator bill" (Karl 1963, 24). As Senator Joel Bennett Clark put it, "no member of that committee had any real belief in Congress or any real use for the legislative department of government" (Polenberg 1966, 127). The answer to retrofitting the federal administrative state into the constitutional scheme does not lie in equating administration with the president's constitutional duty to faithfully execute the laws (see Willoughby 1927, 10–11; 1934, 114; *Morrison v. Olson,* 487 U.S. 654 [1988]). The president has substantial authority over administration, of course, but so do Congress and the federal courts.

Congress's Strategy for Retrofitting the Administrative State

In the 1930s, several senators and representatives publicly wondered how Congress should respond to the full-fledged administrative state (Rosenbloom 2000). There was considerable concern that either Congress was allowing itself to be supplanted by the agencies, or that the agencies were usurping its powers. Throughout the New Deal, Congress had delegated legislative authority to the president and administrative agencies on scale without precedent. Sometimes these delegations contained no real standards (*Schechter Poultry Corporation v. United States,* 295 U.S. 495 [1935]). The legislative committee structure was archaic, and Congress was institutionally incapable of exercising anything more than haphazard oversight of the agencies' activities (La Follette 1946). After World War II, some members even asked if Congress was necessary and gave "serious thought to the possibility that Congress might not survive the next twenty years" (Kefauver and Levin 1947, 5).

After intermittently considering how to deal with federal administration for about a decade, in 1946 Congress collectively adopted a lasting institutional strategy for repositioning both itself and the agencies in the constitutional structure (see Rosenbloom 2000). Congress would write the procedures to be used by administrative agencies and exercise "continuous watchfulness" of their operations. In the process, it would begin to retrofit the agencies into the constitutional scheme by mandating that administrative procedures incorporate constitutional values and by subjecting administration to more systematic congressional control. These approaches crystallized during the extensive legislative debates on the Administrative Procedure Act of 1946, the 1946 Legislative Reorganization Act (which included the Tort Claims Act as Title IV), and the Employment Act (1946). Debate often focused on the nature of the separation of powers and the scope of individual rights.

Congressional retrofitting involved two main prongs. Each has served as a platform for the continuing infusion of democratic-constitutional values into federal administration and for the subordination of administration to congressional influence. Together, they do much to integrate federal administration into the constitutional scheme.

Constitutional Values

First, Congress reluctantly agreed that it would perforce continue to delegate its legislative authority to the agencies. However, unlike past practice, it would treat the agencies as *extensions of Congress* for carrying out legislative functions. This would be accomplished primarily by structuring their procedures, especially those regarding rule making and openness. The same general values that informed congressional lawmaking would be imposed on the agencies. As Representative Frances Walter explained, "Day by day Congress takes account of the interests and desires of the people in framing legislation; and there is no reason why administrative agencies should not do so when they exercise legislative functions which the Congress has delegated to them" (U.S. Congress 1946, 5756).

The Administrative Procedure Act (APA) was a major step toward applying legislative values to federal administration. It was hailed by supporters as a statute of constitutional proportions (*American Bar Association Journal* 1946, 377), though, in retrospect, many of its original provisions may appear rudimentary and riddled with loopholes. President Truman readily signed the act despite some doubt in the executive branch as to the wisdom of having Congress specify administrative procedures (Brazier 1993, 318–330).

The APA seeks openness and the opportunity for public participation in rule making (see Kerwin 1999, chap. 2, 5; Warren 1996, chap. 4, 6). Informal rule making involves publishing proposed rules in the *Federal Register* and providing an opportunity for public comment. Formal rule making procedures create an elaborate hybrid between legislative and judicial hearings. The act also calls on agencies to publish and provide information about their operations. Other key features speak to the scope of judicial review and due process in agency adjudication. In some respects, the act was viewed as "a bill of rights for the hundreds of thousands of Americans whose affairs are controlled or regulated in one way or another by agencies of the Federal Government" (Senator Pat McCarran, U.S. Congress 1946, 2149).

Participation and Representation in Rule Making

The APA's rationale for promoting public participation in rule making has served as a platform for three additional statutes that further infuse federal administration with constitutional values: the Federal Advisory Committee Act of 1972 (FACA), the Negotiated Rulemaking Act of 1990 (NRMA), and the Small Business Regulatory Enforcement Fairness Act of 1996 (SBREFA).

FACA was a congressional effort to make the federal advisory committee system more effective and representative. Such committees, which are established and funded by the government, are sometimes considered a "fifth branch" of the federal government (U.S. Senate 1978, 217, 293, 299–300). FACA requires their membership to represent the interests they purport to speak for and their meetings to be open to public scrutiny (see Steck 1984).

In some respects, NRMA is an idealization of the legislative process. It provides for regulatory negotiation in which a committee representing affected interests, including regulated entities, the public, unions, and the agency, openly negotiates the content of a rule. Regulatory negotiation looks toward reducing the adversarial quality of conventional rule making, finding better solutions to real world problems, and reducing the likelihood of litigation after a rule is enacted (see Coglianese 1997). From an orthodox standpoint, the notion that politically neutral administrative experts should negotiate rules with outsiders is, no doubt, startling.

The APA, FACA, and NRMA open agency rule making to public participation. SBREFA takes their logic one step further: It requires agencies to reach out to small entities that might not otherwise be able to comment effectively on proposed rules or have the opportunity to serve on advisory and negotiating committees. Its substantive purpose is to assist agencies in assessing the impact of proposed rules on small businesses and governments.

The SBREFA also provides Congress with greater control over the content of agency rules. It requires that rules be submitted to Congress and the General Accounting Office (GAO) before they can take effect. Major rules are subject to a sixty-day review period in Congress, during which they can be disapproved by a joint resolution. There are a number of exceptions, and such a joint resolution can be vetoed by the president (though potentially reinstated by congressional override). However, if a rule is successfully disapproved by Congress, it cannot be reissued in the absence of specific legislative authorization. This aspect of the SBREFA closes an important link in Congress's delegate-but-regulate strategy for making the agencies' exercise of legislative functions comport more faithfully with constitutional values. It enables Congress, the preeminent representative governmental unit, to reject the agencies' exercise of delegated legislative authority on the grounds that a rule does not comport with legislative intent.

Transparency

The APA's limited provisions for transparency also served as a platform for additional congressional regulation of administrative procedures. The chief statutes here are the Freedom of Information Act of 1966 (FOIA, substantially amended in 1974) and the Government in the Sunshine Act of 1976. Both were congressional initiatives that engendered considerable executive opposition.

FOIA is a disclosure statute that builds on the APAs limited provisions for public information. Its key feature is that an individual does not need to show any particular standing or special need for the information he or she is seeking (see Vaughn 1994 for an evaluation).

The Sunshine Act applies to about fifty federal multiheaded boards and commissions. As a general rule, it requires them to exercise their legislative authority in the open rather than behind closed doors. However, there are a number of exceptions and meetings, or portions of them, that can be closed for a variety of reasons (see May 1997). In an earlier form, the Sunshine bill fully incorporated the view that agencies are extensions of Congress for legislative functions by applying the same requirements for openness to congressional committees. (The provision was dropped in favor of dealing with congressional openness separately.)

FOIA and the Sunshine Act are frequently criticized for encumbering the administrative process and frustrating agency decision making. But such critics miss a key point that was made during the congressional debates over legislating administrative procedures. As Senator McCarran explained in 1946, the Senate Judiciary Committee had "taken the position that the [APA] bill must reasonably protect private parties even at the risk of some incidental or possible inconvenience to, or change in, present administrative operations" (U.S. Congress 1946, 2150). Transparency is a matter of constitutional concern that, for Congress, trumps orthodox administrative values. The Senate's report on FOIA rests much of its case on James Madison's claim that "Knowledge will forever govern ignorance, and a people who mean to be their own governors, must arm themselves with the power knowledge gives. A popular government without popular information or the means of acquiring it, is but a prologue to a farce or a tragedy or perhaps both" (U.S. Senate 1974, 37–38). As administrative law scholar Robert Vaughn (1994, 481) notes, federal information policy is not an "isolated body of law" because "[c]onflicts regarding information policy inescapably participate in major debates about theories of administrative legitimacy and decision-making."

Supervising Administration

The second major component of Congress's strategy for better integrating federal administration into the constitutional scheme was to subject the agencies to more comprehensive legislative supervision. Leading public administrative thinkers from the orthodoxy to contemporary "reinventers" have been wary—if not outright hostile—to such supervision (for example, Brownlow 1949, 116; Gore 1993, 13, 17, 20, 34). Nevertheless, the constitutional logic for congressional oversight is compelling. Agencies are empowered and funded by Congress and, therefore, they should be subject to its scrutiny. As Representative A.S. Mike Monroney explained in 1946, "[O]nly half the job of a standing committee is finished when it passes the legislation. . . . [T]he other half should be in seeing how that legislation is carried out and seeing if the agencies are living up to the mandates of the Congress and living within the restrictions which we provide" (U.S. Congress 1946, 10040).

The Legislative Reorganization Act of 1946 was an initial step toward upgrading congressional oversight of administration. It reorganized the congressional committee structure so that the committees in each chamber would more or less parallel one another and, to an extent, the organization of the federal bureaucracy. Section 136 called on each standing committee "to exercise continuous watchfulness of the execution by the administrative agencies concerned of any laws, the subject matter of which is within the jurisdiction of such committee." Additionally, the act increased and further institutionalized committee staff, in part to assist with oversight.

As in the case of the APA, the 1946 Legislative Reorganization Act provided a platform for extending Congress's role in federal administration. Today, congressional (sub)committees are deeply involved in agency decision making and operations. In some cases congressional action is excessive—even abusive (Gore 1993, 13). Nevertheless, this may be part of the price the United States pays for the separation of powers. As Francis Rourke (1993) has reminded us, constitutionally, federal administration is under the "joint custody" of the president and Congress (and, one should add, the courts as well). Following the PCAM's advice might not have led to "an American form of dictatorship," as Representative Hamilton Fish contended (Polenberg 1966, 50). However, if the checks and balances system is to be balanced, each constitutional branch needs leverage and authority over federal administration, which, by all accounts, is a major center of governmental power.

For the most part, Congress's extension of its supervisory capacity since 1946 is well-known to the public administration community. Its formal oversight mission was strengthened by the Legislative Reorganization Act of 1970, which calls on the committees to "review and study, on a continuing basis, the application, administration, and execution of those laws" under their jurisdictions. The number and quality of committee staff has grown substantially (Rosenbloom 2000). The Congressional Budget and Impoundment Control Act of 1974 strengthened Congress's information and role in the budget process (Joyce 1993, 10). The Inspector General Act of 1978 created congressional "moles" in the agencies (Moore and Gates 1986, 10; Light 1993). The GAO was transformed from an auditing agency into one with great competence in program evaluation (Mosher 1984; Walker 1986). Similarly, the Legislative Reference Service, which was established by the 1946 Reorganization Act, was significantly upgraded in 1970 by its transformation into the modern Congressional Research Service. The Chief Financial Officers Act of 1990 was aimed at improving federal financial management and the quality of information available to Congress about agencies' finances.

The potential for congressional supervision of the agencies took a quantum leap with the enactment of the Government Performance and Results Act of 1993 (GPRA). The act was a congressional initiative that enjoyed the Clinton-Gore administration's support for its promotion of results-oriented administration. It requires agencies to formulate strategic plans with concrete goals and indicators, preferably quantitative, for assessing progress toward them. It specifically requires the agencies to "consult with the Congress" when formulating their strategic plans. Although not actually required by the act, Congress has also claimed "a vital role regarding performance measurement development" (U.S. General Accounting Office 1997, 13).

In practice, the GPRA goes a long way toward enabling congressional committees and work teams to define legislative intent for the agencies and to make sure that it is written into their strategic plans. By most definitions, this gives congressional units a direct role in managerial decision making. The act also looks toward performance budgeting as a means of making sure that Congress obtains the programmatic results it seeks, or at least does not pay for agency activities that do not deliver what it wants (see Radin 1998 for an analysis). It has the potential to strengthen the congressional portion of joint custody immensely.

1946 As a Baseline for Retrofitting

If 1946 is used as a baseline for Congress's effort to retrofit federal administration into the constitutional scheme, it is evident that by the 1990s, considerable progress had been made. Administrative procedures now more closely reflect democratic-constitutional norms for legislating and governing in general. In fact, the entire debate over administrative procedures has shifted. In 1934, the American Bar Association's Special Committee on Administrative Law (1934, 228) voiced a common complaint that agency procedures were haphazard and obscure: "Practically every agency . . . has published its enactments, sometimes in the form of official printed pamphlets, bound or loose-leaf, sometimes in mimeographed form, sometimes in privately owned publications, and sometimes in press releases. Sometimes they exist only in a sort of unwritten law." Today, complaints are much more likely to be about how administrative law aimed at facilitating public participation, representation, and transparency encumbers administrative performance (Sargentich 1997, 136–137; Lubbers 1997, 121).

Similarly, it is clear that Congress has gone a long way toward integrating the agencies into the separation of powers by strengthening its capacity to supervise them. In 1946, Representative Monroney contended that Congress was "trying to do [its] work sitting on an old-fashioned high bookkeeper's stool with a slant-top desk, a Civil War ledger, and a quill pen" and therefore could not do the " . . . fundamental task of supervision that the framers of the Constitution had in mind" (U.S. Congress 1946, 10039). By contrast, today Vice President Al Gore's National Performance Review seeks to "liberat[e] agencies from congressional micromanagement" (Gore 1993, 34).

Evaluations of congressional retrofitting are bound to differ. Perhaps Congress has gone too far or not yet far enough. For the most part, however, its actions have been in keeping with contemporary constitutional theory. Congress lost the legislative veto in *Immigration and Naturalization Service v. Chadha* (462 U.S. 919 [1983]). However, the Supreme Court's language in other cases, notably *Vermont Yankee Nuclear Power Corporation v. Natural Resources Defense Council* (435 U.S. 519 [1978]) and *Morrison v. Olson* (487 U.S. 654 [1988]), endorses very broad congressional involvement in federal administration. In this respect, one of the Court's decisions in 1838 remains good law as we enter the twenty-first century: "[I]t would be an alarming doctrine, that [C]ongress cannot impose upon any executive officer any duty they may think proper, which is not repugnant to any rights secured and protected by the constitution; and in such cases, the duty and responsibility grow out of and are subject to the control of the law, and not to the direction of the President" (*Kendall v. United States,* 37 U.S. 524 [1838]).

Judicial Retrofitting

Retrofitting by the federal judiciary has been extensively analyzed elsewhere and consequently requires only brief review here (see Rosenbloom and O'Leary 1997; Rosenbloom, Carroll, and Carroll 2000). Its thrust is to force constitutional rights, reasoning, and values into public administrative practice at all levels of government. It is best understood as the product of four interrelated steps.

First, beginning in the 1950s and continuing to the present, the federal courts established a vast array of previously undeclared rights for individuals in their encounters with public administrators. For instance, clients or customers gained substantive rights, procedural due-process protections, and far greater equal protection of the laws. Their privacy received protection (albeit modest) under the Fourth Amendment. Public employees were afforded similar rights and protections. Street-level interactions became infused with Fourth Amendment considerations. Prisoners' Eighth Amendment, due process, equal protection, and other constitutional rights were strengthened substantially. Individuals confined to public mental health facilities obtained a constitutional right to treatment or habilitation. Property owners' Fifth Amendment protections against uncompensated takings have been enhanced (see Rosenbloom and O'Leary 1997).

Second, the courts made it easier for individuals to gain standing to sue administrative agencies for violations of their rights. At one point, the threshold for bringing suit in federal court was reduced "to the simple proposition that one who is hurt by governmental action has standing to challenge it" (Davis 1975, 72). Although standing requirements are tighter today than they were in the 1970s, it is probably still easier to challenge agencies in federal court than it was prior to the 1960s (Rosenbloom and O'Leary 1997, 289–291).

Third, the federal courts developed a new type of lawsuit that facilitates their direct intervention in administrative operations as a means of protecting individuals' rights. Such "remedial law" suits enable a single federal judge to control an entire prison, mental health facility, school, personnel, or other public administrative system. Although such suits typically involve state or local governments, federal agencies are subject to them as well (see Rosenbloom and O'Leary 1997, 283–289).

Fourth, the courts vastly increased the liability that most public employees face for violating individuals' constitutional rights. Today, a public employee typically faces personal liability for violations of clearly established constitutional rights of which a reasonable person should have known. Punitive as well as compensatory money damages can be assessed against individual public administrators. Indemnification varies among federal agencies and other governmental units (see Rosenbloom and O'Leary 1997, 265–281).

Liability for constitutional torts (that is, violations of individuals' constitutional rights) gives public employees a strong incentive to know the constitutional law that governs their work. In effect, as the Supreme Court has flatly stated, competence in constitutional law has become a standard aspect of job competence for public administrators at all levels of government (*Harlow v. Fitzgerald,* 457 U.S. 800 [1982]; Rosenbloom, Carroll, and Carroll 2000).

The judicial framework for retrofitting public administration into the constitutional scheme was essentially in place by the mid-1970s. How the courts use it varies among constitutional rights and according to judicial philosophies. For instance, standing requirements have been tightened since the 1970s. The Supreme Court has also tried to rein in the federal district courts' practice of remedial law, though without clear success (Rosenbloom and O'Leary 1997, 287–289). At the same time, the Court has extended First Amendment rights to contractors (*Board of County Commissioners, Wabaunsee County v. Umbehr,* 518 U.S. 668 [1996]; *O'Hare Truck v. City of Northlake,* 518 U.S. 712 [1996]; see Rosenbloom 1999, 160–164). It has applied equal protection more rigorously to governmental contracting than in the past, though whether this expands or reduces constitutional rights depends on one's view of affirmative action (see especially Justice Clarence Thomas's concurring opinion in *Adarand Constructors v. Pena,* 515 U.S. 200 [1995]). In a set of decisions that may have far-reaching implications for governmental outsourcing, the Court strongly reiterated the principle that private parties engaged in "state action" (for example, public functions such as incarceration) are subject to constitutional constraints (*West v. Atkins,* 487 U.S. 42 [1988]; Rosenbloom 1999, 150–155; Gilmour and Jensen 1998). Currently, the potential liability of "private state actors" for constitutional torts is greater than that of public employees (*Richardson v. McKnight,* 117 S. Ct. 2100 [1997]; Rosenbloom 1999, 155–160).

As in the case of congressional retrofitting, judicial imposition of constitutional concerns into public administrative practice is best measured against the baseline of the 1940s. At that time, equal protection analysis still allowed racial segregation in public schools, prisons, and government agencies. It failed to prevent rampant governmental discrimination. Clients' benefits could be denied or terminated without regard to procedural due process or substantive rights, as could public employees' jobs (Rosenbloom and O'Leary 1997, chaps. 4–7). Federal employees were investigated and sometimes dismissed for disloyalty on the basis of behavior that is now clearly protected by the First Amendment (Rosenbloom and O'Leary 1997, chap. 6; Rosenbloom 1971, chap. 6). The Eighth Amendment did not apply to conditions in prison. Even within this framework of limited rights, public administrators generally enjoyed absolute immunity from suit for their constitutional torts. Today, by contrast, public administration is extensively governed by constitutional law.

Conclusion: A Machine That Would Go of Itself?

The Constitution has been likened to "a machine that would go of itself" (see Kammen 1987). However, congressional and judicial retrofitting of the administrative state into the constitutional scheme has been neither automatic nor easy. There has been opposition— much of it concerted—from elected executives, political appointees, and public administrators at many steps along the way (Rosenbloom 2000). Criticism of congressional "micromanagement" and judicial "interference" remains common. Often, the critics and retrofitters talk past one another.

Whether retrofitting has been good or bad for administrative cost effectiveness is not the whole issue. As Chief Justice Warren Burger once noted, constitutional government can seem "clumsy, inefficient, even unworkable," but its purpose is to "preserve freedom" not to maximize convenience or efficiency (*Immigration and Naturalization Service v. Chadha* 462 U.S. 919, 959 [1983]). The larger question is how best to adjust twentieth-century retrofitting to the twenty-first-century challenges that are sure to come. Constitutional government has strong logics. It may even "go of itself" in some sense. But as Constance Homer, former director of the U.S. Office of Personnel Management, suggested some time ago, constitutional government is likely to go much better if the public administrators who inhabit it play a larger role in constitutional discourse (Homer 1988, 14).

References

American Bar Association. 1934. "Report of the Special Committee on Administrative Law." In *Separation of Powers and the Independent Agencies: Cases and Selected Readings,* U.S. House, Senate, Committee on the Judiciary, Subcommittee on Separation of Powers. 91st Congress, 1st Session. S. Doc. 91–49.

American Bar Association Journal. 1946. "The Federal Administrative Procedure Act Becomes Law," Vol. 32: 377.

Brazier, James Edward. 1993. *Who Controls the Administrative State? Congress and the President Adopt the Administrative Procedure Act of 1946.* Ann Arbor, MI: UMI.

Brownlow, Louis. 1949. *The President and the Presidency.* Chicago: Public Administration Service.

Caiden, Gerald E. 1991. *Administrative Reform Comes of Age.* New York: Walter de Gruyter.

Coglianese, Cary. 1997. "Assessing Consensus: The Promise and Performance of Negotiated Rulemaking." *Duke Law Journal* 46(6): 1255–1349.

Davis, Kenneth Culp. 1975. *Administrative Law and Government.* 2d ed. St. Paul, MN: West.

Farazmand, Ali. 1998. "Failure of Administrative Reform and the Revolution of 1978–79 in Iran." *Korean Review of Public Administration* 3(2): 93–123.

Gilmour, Robert S., and L. Jensen. 1998. "Reinventing Government Accountability: Public Functions, Privatization and the Meaning of 'State Action.'" *Public Administration Review,* 59(3): 247–257.

Golembiewski, Robert T. 1984. "Ways in Which 'The Study of Administration' Confounds the Study of Administration." In J. Rabin and J. Bowman, eds., *Politics and Administration,* 235–247. New York: Marcel Dekker.

Gore, Albert. 1993. *From Red Tape to Results: Creating A Government that Works Better & Costs Less.* Washington, DC: U.S. Government Printing Office.

Government Performance and Results Act of 1993. U.S. Public Law 103-62. 3 August 1993.

Gunther, Gerald. 1975. *Cases and Materials on Constitutional Law.* 9th ed. Mineola, NY: Foundation Press.

Homer, Constance Joan. 1988. Remarks on FEI's 20th Anniversary Dinner. Charlottesville, VA: U.S. Federal Executive Institute.

Joyce, Philip. 1993. "The Reiterative Nature of Budget Reform: Is There Anything New in Federal Budgeting?" *Public Budgeting and Finance* 13(3): 36–48.

Kammen, Michael G. 1987. *A Machine That Would Go of Itself: The Constitution in American Culture.* New York: Knopf.

Karl, Barry Dean. 1963. *Executive Reorganization and Reform in the New Deal.* Cambridge, MA: Harvard University Press.

Kefauver, Estes, and J. Levin. 1947. *A Twentieth-Century Congress.* New York: Essential Books.

Kerwin, Cornelius M. 1999. *Rulemaking.* 2d ed. Washington, DC: CQ Press.

La Follette, Robert. 1946. "Congress Wins a Victory over Congress." *New York Times Magazine,* 4 August, 11 ff.

Legislative Reorganization Act. 1946. U.S. Public Law 79-601. 60 Stat. 812. 2 August 1946.

Legislative Reorganization Act. 1970. U.S. Public Law 91-510. 84 Stat. 1140. 26 October 1970.

Light, Paul Charles. 1993. *Monitoring Government: Inspectors General and the Search for Account-ability.* Washington, DC: Brookings Institution.

Lubbers, Jeffrey S. 1997. "Paperwork Redux: The (Stronger) Paperwork Reduction Act of 1995." *Administrative Law Review* 49(1): 111–121.

May, Randolph. 1997. "Reforming the Sunshine Act: Report and Recommendation by the Special Committee to Review the Government in the Sunshine Act." *Administrative Law Review* 49(2): 415–428.

Meriam, Lewis. 1939. *Reorganization of the National Government: Part I: An Analysis of the Problem.* Washington, DC: Brookings Institution.

Moore, Mark H., and M. Gates. 1986. *The Inspectors-General: Junkyard Dogs or Man's Best Friend?* New York: Russell Sage Foundation.

Mosher, Frederick. 1984. *A Tale of Two Agencies.* Baton Rouge: Louisiana State University Press.

Polenberg, Richard. 1966. *Reorganizing Roosevelt's Government: The Controversy over Executive Reorganization 1936–1939.* Cambridge, MA: Harvard University Press.

Pritchett, C. Herman. 1948. *The Roosevelt Court.* New York: Macmillan.

Radin, Beryl. 1998. "The Government Performance and Results Act (GPRA): Hydra-Headed Monster or Flexible Management Tool?" *Public Administration Review* 58(4): 307–316.

Rohr, John. 1986. *To Run A Constitution.* Lawrence, KS: University Press of Kansas.

Rosenbloom, David. 2000. *Framing Legislative Centered Public Administration: Congress's 1946 Response to the Administrative State.* Tuscaloosa, AL: University of Alabama Press.

———. 1999. "Constitutional Problems for the New Public Management in the United States." In R. Carter and K. Thai, eds., *Current Public Policy Issues.* Philadelphia: PrAcademics Press.

———. 1971. *Federal Service and the Constitution.* Ithaca, NY: Cornell University Press.

Rosenbloom, David, J. Carroll, and J. Carroll. 2000. *Toward Constitutional Competence for Public Managers: Cases and Commentary.* Itasca, IL: F.E. Peacock.

Rosenbloom, David, and R. O'Leary. 1997. *Public Administration and Law.* 2d ed. New York: Marcel Dekker.

Rourke, Francis E. 1993. "Whose Bureaucracy Is This, Anyway?" *PS: Political Science and Politics* 26(4): 687–692.

Sargentich, Thomas. 1997. "The Small Business Regulatory Enforcement Fairness Act." *Administrative Law Review* 49(1): 123–137.

Seidman, Harold. 1970. *Politics, Position, and Power.* New York: Oxford University Press.

Steck, Henry. 1984. "Politics and Administration: Private Advice for Public Purpose in a Corporatist Setting." In J. Rabin and J. Bowman, eds., *Politics and Administration,* 147–174. New York: Marcel Dekker.

U.S. Congress. 1946. *Congressional Record,* vol. 92, 79th Congress, 2d session. Washington, DC: U.S. Government Printing Office.

U.S. General Accounting Office. 1997. *Managing for Results: Using the Results Act to Address Mission Fragmentation and Program Overlap.* Washington, DC: U.S. General Accounting Office.

U.S. President's Committee on Administrative Management. 1937. *Report of the Committee.* Washington, DC: U.S. Government Printing Office.

U.S. Senate. 1978. *Federal Advisory Committee Act (Public Law 92-463) Source Book: Legislative History, Texts, and Other Documents.* Committee on Governmental Affairs, Subcommittee on Energy, Nuclear Proliferation, and Federal Services. 95th Congress, 2d session. Washington, DC: U.S. Government Printing Office.

———. 1974. *Freedom of Information Act Source Book: Legislative Materials, Cases, Articles.* Committee on the Judiciary, Subcommittee on Administrative Practice and Procedure. 93rd Congress, 2d session. Washington, DC: U.S. Government Printing Office.

Vaughn, Robert G. 1994. "Federal Information Policy and Administrative Law." In David Rosenbloom and R. Schwartz, eds., *Handbook of Regulation and Administrative Law,* 467–484. New York: Marcel Dekker.

Waldo, Dwight. 1984. *The Administrative State.* 2d ed. New York: Holmes and Meier.

———. 1948. *The Administrative State.* New York: Ronald Press.

Walker, Wallace Earl. 1986. *Changing Organizational Culture: Strategy, Structure, and Professionalism in the U.S. General Accounting Office.* Knoxville: University of Tennessee Press.

Warren, Kenneth F. 1996. *Administrative Law in the American Political System.* 3d ed. Upper Saddle River, NJ: Prentice Hall.

Willoughby, William F. 1934. *Principles of Legislative Organization and Administration.* Washington, DC: Brookings Institution.

———. 1927. *Principles of Public Administration.* Washington, DC: Brookings Institution.

Woll, Peter. 1963. *American Bureaucracy.* New York: W.W. Norton.

PART II

THE RELATIONSHIPS BETWEEN COURTS AND ADMINISTRATORS

Many people equate law with judges and court decisions. Law, viewed from this perspective, plays a role in administration because court decisions directly affect administrative actions and can require changes that become significant factors in an organization's management. Others personify the courts and discuss them as proactive policy makers: *courts* decide to reform social services or review administrative action. Both of these perspectives are founded on incomplete understandings of the relationship between public administration and law. The chapters in this section of the book first illuminate a broader understanding of the role courts and judicial decision-making have on public administration by first providing some comments about litigation and court processes. Second, this section discusses how administrators are the users of court decisions and third, how courts also have administrative roles. Finally, this section considers the debates about how the relationship between courts and administrators can be represented as a partnership.

When government is sued, the litigation is brought by individuals or businesses that claim a grievance and injury caused by government action. Public administrators also bring lawsuits to enforce statutes, rules, and rights. Lawsuits involve claims about facts, circumstances, laws, and implications. Lawsuits are formal and adversarial disputes brought before a neutral decision maker; as such, courts often act as referees to evaluate governmental authority and decisions. Being brought to court is often asserted as an environmental factor that affects how administrators make decisions and take actions. During trials, courts are asked to evaluate and determine the facts of the individual dispute as well as legal issues related to government actions in constitutional, procedural, and substantive legal areas. During the appellate stages, the focus of the case becomes the legal questions. A single case may contain multiple legal questions and practical administrative concerns. As Buckwalter and Legler articulated earlier in Chapter 4, how lawyers and administrators evaluate a case can differ. Lawyers focus on legal and constitutional issues; administrators are more likely to focus on pragmatic concerns. The same type of differing focus may be found in the ways in which courts and public administrators view the same case. Some judges may be more willing than others to consider the administrative ramifications of the decisions reached and rulings made. The case-by-case court review process can result in more or less deference given to administrative discretion in particular types of cases; it may also lead to the assertion of judicial control over the entire administrative process for a governmental organization. The court decree will answer the question of whether the action at hand fits within the structure of the law, but it is less likely that a court decree can authoritatively answer the normative question of whether a government action is good or bad administrative practice.

The political process of developing policy and legislation is known to many. Decision making by leaders is also well known. The use of research studies and reasoned analysis of data is familiar practice to administrators, but there are a number of legal concepts that may be less well known. Some of these legal concepts, such as governmental constitutional responsibilities and individual rights, were introduced in Part I. Constitutional concerns arise in factual issues and judicial constitutional doctrines can change over time. The important constitutional right of due process, as explained in the introduction to Part I, is linked to judicial processes for trials and appeals. The question of what is appropriate adjudicatory procedure, a frequent issue in public law litigation, is the domain of the courts. How the courts interpret constitutional questions is an important and difficult part of understanding the legal environment of public administration. Other legal concepts that are briefly explained here include: precedent, common law, dicta, and legal interpretation.

Precedent is the idea that judicial decisions rest upon prior decisions. The decision made in one case on related legal and factual issues is connected to prior precedent and it becomes precedent for subsequent cases. The judicial decisions on legal and factual issues in one case is called the law of the case and it immediately affects the parties to that case. The decision on the legal issues in an appellate case then becomes legally binding prospectively to similar situations: this is legal precedent. The collection of precedent found in the numerous appellate decisions is called the common law. This common law precedent is considered binding law. Changing precedent requires either a change in statutory law or a reinterpretation of the common law. Trial and appellate court decisions also have another prospective element that may do more to shape the general environment of management in the public sector than the ruling in an individual case. This additional direction—dicta—is often used by public administrators and attorneys to determine how judges might view actions based on similar facts and laws in future cases. The guidance given in the decision may address a number of questions including: What type of administrative action is discretionary or mandatory? What level of immunity from lawsuit does an individual administrator have? How should another case or another statute be interpreted? And, what role should the court play in the administration of public organizations?

Judges are called upon to interpret statutes, rules, and the relevant constitution. In the legal interpretation of statutes, courts begin by looking at the language of the statute; they look to the purpose of the law and what authority it delegates to administrators. They look to see if there is discretion or limited authority granted to administrators. If the language is not clear, courts then look to the intent behind the law, or what the framers intended. Courts may look to similar court decisions on other statutes and reason by analogy to the current statutes. Courts also will consider how the administrators tasked with responsibility interpret their roles. The courts take a similar approach in interpreting the text of contracts when they are in dispute. The final authority on constitutional interpretation is the Supreme Court.

Courts are called upon to answer questions that are based in three types of law: statutes, common law, and constitutional law. All may be raised as authority in a legal action. Common law is built on precedent; statutory law is based on laws passed by legislatures; constitutional law derives from the principles established in state and federal constitutions. When there are no cases that have considered the issue, courts may reason by analogy to prior decisions on similar legal or factual issues. Administrators often use the experiences and development of internal policy decisions and processes to guide their interpretations and implementation of their organizational mission and responsibilities. An example of a recurring important question for both courts and public administrators is what is the balance between precedent and due process in achieving an agency's objectives.

After a decision is reached by the court, administrators then must apply the law and may apply the dicta to decision making in their institutions. Thus, public administrators are the users of court decisions. Two of the chapters in this section consider how administrators use court decisions. An area where there has been extensive litigation is environmental law. In addition to regulating and affecting individuals, federal environmental policy directly affects state and local governments. This area of environmental law may raise federalism or management concerns. A series of cases discussed by Rosemary O'Leary in Chapter 6 addresses the U.S. Supreme Court's application of the Commerce Clause of the U.S. Constitution to prevent local governments from stopping the flow of municipal waste. This has allowed waste management companies a "level playing field" in disposing of materials. Leveling that field, though, has resulted in significant constraints on local governments protecting the public welfare of its residents through controlling land-use decisions. Court decisions about the different treatment of classes of individuals also affect public management practices. In Chapter 7, Heidi O. Koenig shows how court cases developed precedent regarding constitutionally protected free speech and how two classes of workers—government employees and government contractors—are treated differently under court constitutional law decisions.

The extensive use of courts to review government actions and affect government decisions has made courts a factor in the public administration environment; this is the topic of Chapter 8. In a perceptive article from 1976, Roger C. Cramton reviews trends in judicial law making, models of judicial review, and administrative roles of judges. Cramton notes the pressures on the judiciary with the increased filing of lawsuits and he questions the long-term effects of lawsuits seeking the injunctive relief of court supervision of government procedures. Cramton questions the propriety of the role courts are asked to play in day-to-day public administration.

The concerns about court review and administrative actions is long standing. There have been extensive discussions about the relationships between courts and administrators; a predominant approach is to call this relationship a partnership. The final chapters in this section, from 1985, provide two viewpoints about this relationship. In Chapter 9, R. Shep Melnick asserts that public administrators must be aware of the court as a political actor as well as an institutional check on the decision-making processes of government. He evaluates judicial review of administrative action and both legislative and executive political concerns as well. Phillip J. Cooper in Chapter 10 asserts that the common representations of courts in public administration writings are either myths or incomplete. He argues that judicial-administrative conflict should be seen as a source of constructive tension that strengthens democratic governance. Both Melnick and Cooper indicate how many issues about governance are embedded in this partnership debate, and they also demonstrate how thoroughly public administration is affected by the courts.

In all of the chapters in this section, law is perceived as the foundation of public administration. The material presented in these chapters furthers our understanding of the role of courts in public administration by placing it in context. O'Leary notes how state, local, and federal policies are affected by court decisions. Koenig raises ways in which administrative responsibilities and rights of individuals to administrative protections are altered by judicial decision making. Cramton notes that public administrators may be recipients of judicial intervention, and also shows how public administrators may seek to achieve their own ends through use of the courts. For these authors, what courts say becomes an important consideration to be used by public administrators in developing their missions and managing their organizations.

That decisions in trial and appellate cases may have a significant impact on the actions of individuals in society is not a new development. Most public administrators would acknowledge the principle that courts have the right and responsibility to hear cases regarding the work of the government, yet how a particular case affects an administrative agency is often a concern. The following chapters begin to address some of the enduring questions about courts and public administration: Should courts be able to influence the management environment in the same way that the elected legislature and executive do? Do courts have the capacity to act as administrators? Do courts and administrators have the independent responsibility to seek to affect lasting social changes? How these questions are considered shapes the future of how public administrators respond to and incorporate legal decision making into the organizations they manage.

CHAPTER 6

TRASH TALK

The Supreme Court and the Interstate Transportation of Waste

ROSEMARY O'LEARY

Americans generate more domestic waste than any other country in the world. In 1996, for example, we generated an estimated 200,000,000 tons of domestic waste, the equivalent of 875 kilograms per person. That same year, Japan generated an estimated 40,225,000 tons of domestic waste, averaging 288 kilograms per person, while neighboring Canada generated an estimated 12,600,000 tons of domestic waste, averaging 525 kilograms per person. This excessive generation of waste has yielded immense challenges for our state and local governments that must manage waste not only within their own jurisdictions, but also waste from outside their jurisdictions. Some state and local governments seek out waste from outside their state in order to generate tipping, or disposal, fees while other governments shun such waste, in fear of becoming the dumping ground of the nation.

While state and local governments have been ordered by federal, state, and local laws to develop and implement policies aimed at the reduction and proper disposal of waste, current policy regarding the interstate transport of waste limits their ability to do so. Policy in this area has been shaped by the courts and their interpretation of the Commerce Clause of the U.S. Constitution. The Commerce Clause states that "The Congress shall have the power to regulate Commerce among foreign Nations, and among the several states, and with the Indian Tribes" (U.S. Constitution Article I, Section 8, Paragraph 3). In a series of five key cases, the Supreme Court has tied the hands of state and local governments, severely limiting their options in regulating waste. This [chapter] highlights these cases as well as the implications of these judicial decisions for public administrators.

Back to the Future

Current law concerning out-of-state waste stems largely from the 1978 U.S. Supreme Court case, *City of Philadelphia v. New Jersey,* 437 U.S. 617 (1978), where the Supreme

From *Public Administration Review* 57, no. 4 (July/August 1997): 281–284. Copyright © 1997 by American Society for Public Administration. Reprinted with permission.

Court overturned a New Jersey law that limited the transportation of waste into that state. The Court maintained that the New Jersey law fell "squarely within the area that the Commerce Clause puts off limits to state regulation" (*City of Philadelphia v. New Jersey,* 628). Justice Stewart's opinion hinged upon an argument for the "dormant" commerce clause. The dormant commerce clause, a judicially created doctrine, has been utilized by the courts to strike down state legislation in conflict with national commerce policies, and is often evoked by the courts in instances when states unduly infringe upon interstate commerce.[1]

In *City of Philadelphia v. New Jersey,* there were two issues of contention: Whether the interstate movement of waste consists of "commerce" within the meaning of the Commerce Clause, and whether the New Jersey state law limiting interstate transport of waste is an economic protectionist measure or a law directed at legitimate local concerns that has only incidental effects on interstate commerce.

In response to the issue of whether the interstate movement of waste consists of commerce, the Supreme Court held that "all objects of interstate trade merit Commerce Clause protections; none is excluded" (*City of Philadelphia v. New Jersey,* 622). In a previous ruling on the case, the New Jersey Supreme Court found, in conjunction with several prior Supreme Court rulings, that states can prohibit the importation of some objects because they are not legitimate subjects of trade and commerce. However, in *City of Philadelphia v. New Jersey,* the Supreme Court found that the state court had misinterpreted previous case law: "In *Bowman* and similar cases, the Court held simply that because the articles' worth in interstate commerce was far outweighed by the dangers inhering in their very movement, States could prohibit their transportation across state lines. Hence, we reject the state court's suggestion that the banning of 'valueless' out-of-state wastes by . . . [the New Jersey statute] implicates no constitutional protection" (*City of Philadelphia v. New Jersey,* 617, 622). Therefore, under the Court's interpretation, all objects of interstate trade—including trash—fall under the Commerce Clause and are thus subject to constitutional scrutiny.

As to the issue of whether the New Jersey state law was a protectionist measure or a law based upon legitimate local concerns that has minimal effects on interstate commerce, the Court said that the New Jersey law blocked the importation of waste in an obvious effort to saddle those outside the state with the entire burden of slowing the flow of refuse into New Jersey's remaining landfill sites. That legislative effort was found to be clearly impermissible by the Court under the Commerce Clause of the Constitution.

In an angry dissent, however, Justice Rehnquist strongly disagreed: "New Jersey should be free under our past precedents to prohibit the importation of waste because of the health and safety problems that such waste poses to its citizens. The fact that New Jersey continues to, and indeed must continue to, dispose of its own waste does not mean that New Jersey may not prohibit the importation of even more waste into the State" (*City of Philadelphia v. New Jersey,* 632).

Justice Rehnquist's dissent was based upon the premise that the New Jersey state law was a quarantine law, and as such, should not be considered a forbidden protectionist measure despite the fact that it was directed against interstate commerce. Hence, *City of*

Philadelphia v. New Jersey should not be construed as an absolute declaration by the Court that states cannot regulate out-of-state waste at all. The Court instead has decided that a balance must be struck between regulation and commerce. This balance was articulated in *Pike v. Bruce Church Inc.*, 397 U.S. 137 (1970), as follows: "Where the statute regulates evenhandedly to effectuate the legitimate local public interest, and its effects on interstate commerce are only incidental, it will be upheld unless the burden imposed on such commerce is clearly excessive in relation to the putative local benefits. . . . If a legitimate local purpose is found then the question becomes one of degree" (*Pike,* 140). In accordance with this balancing test, if a local or state government regulates with evenhandedness, and if effects on interstate commerce are only incidental, the regulation may be upheld. It is this balancing test that was the subject of two subsequent cases decided in the Supreme Court's 1992 term: *Fort Gratiot Sanitary Landfill, Inc. v. Michigan Department of Natural Resources,* 504 U.S. 353 (1992), and *Chemical Waste Management, Inc. v. Guy Hunt, Governor of Alabama,* 504 U.S. 334 (1992).

Fort Gratiot Sanitary Landfill, Inc. v. Michigan Department of Natural Resources, 504 U.S. 353 (1992)

Fort Gratiot Sanitary Landfill, Inc. v. Michigan Department of Natural Resources, 504 U.S. 353 (1992) concerned a State of Michigan law that mandated that waste generated in another state or county cannot be accepted for disposal unless explicitly authorized in the receiving county's waste management plan. In 1989, St. Clair County denied the application of the Fort Gratiot Sanitary Landfill to accept out-of-state waste at its landfill since the county plan does not give such authorization. Fort Gratiot sued, contending that by allowing the prohibition of out-of-state waste, the Michigan law impinges upon interstate commerce and as such is a violation of the Commerce Clause of the Constitution. Michigan defended its law by maintaining, first, that the law does not treat out-of-county waste from Michigan any differently than waste from other states. Second, the state pointed out that not all Michigan counties ban out-of-state waste. Finally, the state argued that the Michigan Waste Management Act is a health and safety regulation, not an economic protectionist regulation.

In a 7 to 2 decision, the Supreme Court held for the Fort Gratiot Sanitary Landfill in declaring the Michigan law unconstitutional. Reasoning that the law allows each county to isolate itself from the national economy, affording local waste producers complete protection from competition from out-of-state producers seeking to use local disposal sites unless a county acts affirmatively, the Court said that this was clear discrimination against interstate commerce. The Court also said that there were not valid health and safety reasons for limiting the amount of waste a landfill operator could accept from out of the state on the one hand, but not the amount an operator could accept from within the state on the other.

In a compelling dissenting opinion, Chief Justice Rehnquist joined by Justice Blackmun argued that the Michigan statute was neither economic protectionism nor a simple outright ban on out-of-state waste as was seen in *Philadelphia v. New Jersey.* The two

Justices commended the State of Michigan for stepping into this quagmire in order to address waste problems generated by its own population. Pointing out that the Michigan requirements scrutinized by the Court were part of a comprehensive approach, the Justices chastised their colleagues for penalizing the State of Michigan for its good-faith efforts. Rehnquist and Blackmun then predicted that the Court's decision would encourage each state to ignore its own waste problems in the hope that another will pick up the slack.

The *Fort Gratiot* case is significant primarily because the Court held that local governments were subject to the same standards in relation to the dormant Commerce Clause that had been applied to the state of New Jersey in *Philadelphia v. New Jersey*. The court reasserted previous case law finding that discrimination against out-of-state waste is on its face a protectionist measure unable to withstand scrutiny under the Commerce Clause.

Chemical Waste Management, Inc. v. Guy Hunt, Governor of Alabama, 504 U.S. 334 (1992)

The other waste case decided by the Supreme Court in its 1992 term, *Chemical Waste Management, Inc. v. Guy Hunt, Governor of Alabama* 504 U.S. 334 (1992), centered on an Alabama law concerning out-of-state hazardous waste. The Alabama law imposed a fee on hazardous wastes disposed of in-state, but the fee was higher if the hazardous wastes were generated outside the state and then brought into the state. The site in question was the Emelle hazardous waste facility, which received 788,000 tons of hazardous waste in 1989, 90 percent shipped in from out-of-state. Chemical Waste Management, the owner and operator of the Emelle site, filed a lawsuit challenging the law on the basis that it was an unconstitutional burden on interstate commerce under the Commerce Clause. Alabama defended the law maintaining that the extra fee for out-of-state hazardous waste advanced a legitimate local purpose that could not be achieved by other nondiscriminatory means.

In an 8 to 1 decision, the Supreme Court struck down the Alabama law. Using an argument similar to the one put forth in the *Fort Gratiot* decision, the Court held that the differential treatment of out-of-state waste violates the Commerce Clause of the U.S. Constitution. The Court pointed out that there are fewer discriminatory options available to the state, such as applying an additional fee on all hazardous waste disposed of within Alabama, a per-mile tax on all vehicles transporting such waste across state roads, or a cap on the total tonnage disposed of at landfills in the state.

In his dissenting opinion, Chief Justice Rehnquist, referring to the reasoning of the majority, wrote that his colleagues "[got] it exactly backward" and reiterated the points he previously set forth in the *Philadelphia v. New Jersey* and *Fort Gratiot* decisions (*Chemical Waste Management, Inc. v. Guy Hunt, Governor of Alabama*, 350). The commodity at issue is a safe and attractive environment, he wrote, and taxes are a recognized and effective means for discouraging the consumption of scarce commodities. Pointing out that Alabama has chosen to adopt a differential tax rather than an outright ban, Rehnquist argued that nothing in the Commerce Clause requires Alabama to adopt an "all or nothing" regulatory approach to noxious materials coming from outside the state (*Chemical Waste Management, Inc. v. Guy Hunt, Governor of Alabama*, 349). The Court's decision would create "perverse regulatory incentives," he predicted and was in fact rewarding the other thirty-four states that have no hazardous waste facilities whatsoever (*Chemical Waste Management, Inc. v. Guy Hunt, Governor of Alabama,* 350).

Two years later the Court revisited these same questions. In its 1994 term, the Court decided two additional cases concerning the disposal of waste. Both cases have major implications for public administration.

Oregon Waste Systems, Inc. et al., v. Department of Environmental Quality of the State of Oregon et al., 511 U.S. 93 (1994)

In the first of the 1994 decisions concerning out-of-state waste, *Oregon Waste Systems, Inc. et al., v. Department of Environmental Quality of the State of Oregon et al.,* 511 U.S. 93 (1994), the Supreme Court again struck down a state statute that differentiated between in-state and out-of-state waste. In that case, an Oregon statute imposed a $2.25 per ton surcharge on the disposal of waste that originated outside the state, but only an $0.85 per ton charge on the disposal of waste generated in the state. The drafters of the Oregon statute had been inspired by the 1992 Supreme Court case just discussed, *Chemical Waste Management Inc. v. Hunt,* in which the Court indicated that had the statute incorporated a cost-based fee differential, the statute might have been upheld. In fact, the Oregon Supreme Court upheld the Oregon statute precisely for that reason.

In a 7 to 2 decision, however, Justice Thomas wrote that the difference in fees was clearly discriminatory on its face. At the heart of the problem was the fact that Oregon never maintained that it is more expensive to dispose of waste from other states. Nor did Oregon offer health or safety reasons to support its different treatment of in-state and out-of-state wastes.

Chief Justice Rehnquist again dissented along with Justice Blackmun. "Once again," Rehnquist wrote, the Court has tied "the hands of the States in addressing the vexing national problem of waste disposal" (*Oregon Waste Systems, Inc. et al., v. Department of Environmental Quality of the State of Oregon et al.,* 109). The Court's majority continues to "stubbornly refuse" to recognize that a healthy environment, not waste, is the commodity at issue in this case, he lamented (*Oregon Waste Systems, Inc. et al., v. Department of Environmental Quality of the State of Oregon et al.,* 110). The Chief Justice concluded that the Court's decision gives out-of-state producers of waste a competitive advantage over in-state producers because they do not have to deal with state taxes, landfill capacity issues, or the cleanup of leaking landfills. Furthermore, he found that Oregon did state rational health and safety reasons for its differential treatment based on the source of the waste arguing that "the availability of environmentally sound landfill space and the proper disposal of waste strike me as justifiable 'safety and health' rationales for the fee" (*Oregon Waste Systems, Inc. et al., v. Department of Environmental Quality of the State of Oregon et al.,* 112).

Both the *Alabama* case and the *Oregon* case clarify the Court's stance that differential fee structures for the disposal of solid waste based on the political unit (i.e., state or locality) of the waste's origin are unconstitutional violations of the Commerce Clause unless it can be shown that less discriminatory options are unavailable or that it is more expensive to dispose of wastes from other political jurisdictions.

C & A Carbone, Inc. et al. v. Clarkstown, New York, 511 U.S. 383 (1994)

Contrasted to the four cases just discussed, in 1994 the Supreme Court decided a case that was the flip side of those controversies: keeping trash in a specific state or local government boundary and not allowing it to be shipped out for economic reasons. In the case of *C & A Carbone, Inc. et al. v. Clarkstown, New York,* 511 U.S. 383 (1994), the town of Clarkstown agreed to allow a private contractor to construct a waste transfer station within the town limits and to operate the facility for five years. At the end of the five years, the town planned to buy the facility for one dollar. To finance the transfer station's cost, the town guaranteed a minimum waste flow to the facility, for which the contractor charged a tipping fee. In order to meet the waste flow guarantee, the town adopted a flow control ordinance requiring all nonhazardous waste within the town to be deposited at the transfer station. The shipping of nonrecyclable waste out of the city limits to locations that may charge a lesser tipping fee was forbidden.

After discovering that the Carbone company and other haulers were shipping their wastes to out-of-state locations, Clarkstown filed suit in state court seeking an injunction requiring that the waste be shipped to the town's transfer station. The lower court granted summary judgment to the town and the appellate court affirmed. Carbone and other haulers appealed to the U.S. Supreme Court, arguing, among other things, that the flow control ordinance violated the Commerce Clause of the U.S. Constitution.

In a 6 to 3 decision, the Supreme Court reversed the lower courts and held that the ordinance did indeed violate the Commerce Clause. Writing for the majority of the Court, Justice Kennedy reasoned that while the ordinance was a local one, its economic effects were interstate in nature. He held that the Court need not resort to the test articulated under *Pike* in this case and that the flow control ordinance instead would be subject to heightened scrutiny: "Discrimination against interstate commerce in favor of local business or investment is *per se* invalid, save in a narrow class of cases in which the municipality can demonstrate, under rigorous scrutiny, that it has no other means to advance a legitimate local interest" (*C & A Carbone, Inc. et al. v. Clarkstown,* 392). Contrary to the four cases just discussed, the Court also reasoned that the article of commerce here was not so much the waste itself, but the service of processing and disposing of it. Next, the Court pointed out that the ordinance favored certain operators, disfavored others, and squelched competition. Finally, the Court maintained that the town had other avenues through which it could address its local interests. For example, health and safety regulations could be promulgated to address environmental safety concerns, while taxes or municipal bonds could be utilized to subsidize the costs of facility.

Implications for Public Administration

Taken together, the five Supreme Court cases discussed above pose an immense challenge for public administrators, and reflect a fundamental paradox in U.S. waste policy:

what is considered good law by the courts is not good public policy. The attempt of the federal judiciary to create a level playing field for in-state and out-of-state producers and disposal companies is generally logical on traditional legal grounds. From a policy perspective, however, it is unwise, and severely ties the hands of local and state public administrators to implement prudent waste policy.

In an era of limited landfill space, increased incineration of trash, and increased public demands for prudent environmental regulation, it would make sense to give state and local governments greater power and discretion concerning what to do with waste both generated within their jurisdictions and brought in from other jurisdictions. Instead, the Supreme Court has given them less power and discretion than ever before and is in fact encouraging state and local governments to ignore the solid waste problem in direct contradiction to recent federal, state, and local mandates. I agree with Justice Rehnquist that the Court has it "exactly backward" and is exacerbating what is already a waste crisis in some areas of our country.

One solution is for the Supreme Court to adopt a Darwinian view of the Constitution, and realize that since our current trash problems could not possibly have been foreseen by our founding fathers, the Court's interpretation of the Constitution in this area needs to evolve, as our society has evolved, to give state and local governments greater authority to deal proactively with the waste disposal challenge. Another solution is for Congress to act to override the dormant Commerce Clause[2] to allow restrictions on the interstate transport of waste. In recent years such legislation has been proposed in Congress, but has never been signed into law. Unless Congress or the Supreme Court acts, the interstate transport of waste will continue to pose immense challenges for our state and local public administrators for years to come.

Notes

1. For a critique of the dormant Commerce Clause see Amy M. Petragnani, "The Dormant Commerce Clause: On Its Last Leg," *Albany Law Review* 57 (1994): 1215–1253.

2. It is important to distinguish between the positive aspect of the Commerce Clause that is actually stated in the U.S. Constitution and the judicially created dormant Commerce Clause. Because it is a judicially created doctrine, the dormant Commerce Clause functions as common law and is thus subject to congressional review while the positive Commerce Clause is not. See *White v. Massachusetts Council of Construction Employers,* 460 U.S. 204 (1983) in which the Court affirmed the authority of Congress to override the dormant Commerce Clause asserting that "where a state or local government action is specifically authorized by Congress, it is not subject to the Commerce Clause even if it interferes with interstate commerce" (*White,* 213).

CHAPTER 7

FREE SPEECH

Government Employees and Government Contractors

HEIDI O. KOENIG

Public administration is based in law. Practitioners need little reminding of this, as they are faced daily with issues that arise through lawsuits, judicial decrees, new legislation, and intergovernmental relations that are embodied in contracts (Koenig and Kise, 1996). The scholarly literature reflects some of these relationships, with the primary focus being on omnibus litigation and individual cases of flagrant constitutional violations (Koenig, 1996). It is rarer to find analyses of cases that focus on the day-to-day concerns of the public administrator. The analyses of this type that exist (Koenig and O'Leary, 1996; Baldo, 1990) are offered only on a sporadic basis, often in journals not read by professional public administrators. While increasing numbers of articles relate court decisions to the jobs of public administrators, the vast majority of the literature on the practical impacts of judge-made law remains outside the realm of most public administrators. . . .

[This article considers day-to-day administrative concerns found in] two First Amendment cases recently decided by the United States Supreme Court: *Board of County Commissioners, Wabaunsee County, Kansas v. Umbehr* (116 S. Ct. 2342, 2d 1996); and *O'Hare Truck Service, Inc. v. City of Northlake* (116 S. Ct. 2353, 1996).

The promise of freedom of speech is made in the First Amendment to the United States Constitution. The idea of freedom of speech is one that most American citizens respect and believe to be one of the primary benefits of American citizenship. However, not all speech is protected under the First Amendment (*Connick v. Myers,* 461 U.S. 138, 1984), and not every speaker is given the same level of protection. The United States Supreme Court has held that all governments of the United States may at times terminate a contract of employment, even if that termination would serve to limit the expression of First Amendment rights of government employees, if political affiliation is pertinent to the position (*Elrod v. Burns,* 427 U.S. 347, 1976 [plurality opinion], and *Branti v. Finkel,* 445 U.S. 507, 1980). Some of the most notable limitations of First Amendment rights have come when the speech involved is made by an employee of the government and the government has an identifiable interest in not permitting the speech to be heard. The Court, in *Umbehr,* notes, "The First Amendment's guarantee of freedom of speech protects government employees from termination because of their speech on matters of public concern" (2347). If termination occurs for some other reason than the speech in question, the decision to fire the employee will be upheld.

Because of the important interests involved in cases where free speech is the issue, the Supreme Court fashioned a test that enables any court to weigh the competing interests of the government employee interested in engaging in free speech, and the government interested in protecting the work and reputation of the government (*Pickering v. Board of Education of Township High School District 205, Will County,* 391 U.S. 563, 1968).

The *Pickering* test requires that the employee must first prove that the firing decision was based on the exercise of free speech on a matter of public concern. If the employee is successful in showing that the government used the speech in the termination decision, the government may still prevail if it can show by a preponderance of the evidence that the firing decision would have been made regardless of the speech, or if the government can show that its legitimate interests outweigh the right of free speech. If the employee is successful in proving the claim against the government and the government is unsuccessful in asserting a defense, the damages remedy will be mitigated if the government can prove that facts were discovered after the firing decision that would have led to termination of the employment contract and that some mitigation of damages has taken place.

The application of the *Pickering* test mandates weighing competing interests, but ensures that the weighing process will take place in an even-handed manner. It should be noted that the government is not required to prove its interest to the highest level of scrutiny (the compelling interest) but rather to a preponderance of evidence standard. The preponderance of evidence standard is a low level of scrutiny. However, because there is scrutiny used in the *Pickering* test, a fair balancing of the individual's right to free speech and the government's need to present a united front is guaranteed.

The law governing the relationship between the government and its employees is continually being reshaped. As government expands the ways in which its work is accomplished, there is more ambiguity in employment relations. One gray area in public employment relations is the extent of the relationship created in the process of independent contracting.

Independent contractors have been used with increasing frequency by government to provide services. The status of independent contractors in their relationships with government, though, has traditionally been less than clear. Are independent contractors outside the normal employment scope of government or are they in a position analogous to government employees? This question is one of the basic questions answered by the Supreme Court in *Umbehr* and *O'Hare Truck Service.* In these cases the Court was asked to decide two issues. First, was a government's decision to terminate a relationship with an independent contractor following criticism of that government by the contractor sufficient to state a claim of a violation of the independent contractor's First Amendment rights (*Wabaunsee*)? Second, if such a claim has been successfully brought before the Court, should the same law governing relations between the government and its employees rule the relations between the government and its independent contractors?

Board of County Commissioners, Wabaunsee County, Kansas v. Umbehr, 116 S. Ct. 2342, 1996

Umbehr, a trash hauler in Wabaunsee County, Kansas, filed suit against the county following termination of his hauling contract. In his suit, filed under 42 U.S.C. 1983, Umbehr alleged that the county impermissibly limited his First Amendment right to free speech by terminating his contract in retaliation for criticism Umbehr voiced about policies of the county and the Board of County Commissioners. The United States Supreme Court ruled that the unconstitutional conditions doctrine applies to independent contractors. The doctrine requires that the government not place conditions on receipt of benefits guaranteed under the United States Constitution, even if there is no entitlement to the benefit being sought. Here, the benefit was employment through a contract with the county.

Further, the Court adopted and modified the *Pickering* test to fit the independent contractor situation. The only modifications of the *Pickering* test the Court made in Umbehr were to include independent contractors within the range of the test and to alter the role of the government from employer to contractor.

The United States Supreme Court was not asked to rule on the issue of individual liability for the members of the Board of County Commissioners. The district court ruled that no suit could be maintained against the members of the board in their individual capacity. The court of appeals affirmed that ruling, and the issue was not raised in the Supreme Court.

The final action of the Court was to remand the case to the district court for application of the *Pickering* test to the facts.

O'Hare Truck Service, Inc. v. City of Northlake, 116 S. Ct. 2353, 1996

O'Hare Truck Service, Inc. (O'Hare) was removed from the city of Northlake's towing rotation list after the owner of O'Hare refused to make a political contribution to the new mayor's campaign fund, and subsequently made a contribution to the opponent's campaign and advertised for the opponent. The city of Northlake had traditionally removed a towing company from the rotation only for cause. The company and its owner sued, alleging that they had been damaged due to a violation of the owner's First Amendment rights. The only question the Court answered was whether or not the company could sue, given that the company and the city of Northlake had an independent contractor relationship. The Supreme Court ruled that if the city of Northlake did terminate the towing contract with O'Hare solely because of the owner's choice of political affiliation, then the city violated the owner's First Amendment rights.

The Court's analysis was based on the precedents of *Elrod* and *Branti*. Those cases noted that where governments can demonstrate a reasonable relationship between political affiliation and the effective performance of the job involved, the decision to retain or terminate the employee may rest on the exercise of First Amendment rights. The Court in O'Hare made clear that where no such reasonable relationship was shown, the termination decision would be judged by the *Pickering* rule as modified in *Umbehr*.

The final action of the Court was to remand the case to the district court for application of either the *Elrod/Branti* reasoning or the *Pickering* test to the facts as those facts indicated.

The dissenters to these opinions, Justices Scalia and Thomas, focused their criticism of the decisions on the judicial widening of the protections granted by the Constitution, the increased likelihood of litigation following these decisions, and the fact that the majority of the Supreme Court was issuing a series of decisions based on facts that represented only the position of the person who originally filed suit. This last criticism focuses on the point in the district court case from which appeal was sought. Because the district courts failed to recognize the claim of Umbehr or O'Hare Truck Service, Inc., they never made definitive findings of fact between Umbehr and the County Board of Commissioners or between O'Hare and the city of Northlake. As these cases were dismissed before trial, the facts are viewed in the light most favorable to the original plaintiff. In the eyes of the dissent, this type of review clearly provides the setting for the development of hard facts that lead to bad law.

Impact of *Umbehr* and *O'Hare* on Public Administration

The primary impact of these cases on the practice of public administration is the change in status of the independent contractor in relationship to the contracting government. It is no longer the case that governments have clear choices between direct employment and independent contracting; the once bright line has been blurred by these decisions. Governments that have sought flexibility by using independent contractors to avoid the legal protection given to regular government employees will find such flexibility sharply limited.

The possibility of increased levels of litigation following these decisions is raised by both the majority and dissenting opinions. The majority opinions made little of the likelihood of increased levels of litigation, noting that granting additional rights to independent contractors in other settings had only resulted in a small increase in cases. The dissent noted that any increase in litigation is likely to be costly, particularly as the only preventive activity available to governments will be the adoption of complex processes that permit claims of favoritism to be defeated with ease. It is impossible to say which position is correct. The truth of the dissent's argument regarding the increased costs of procedural protections against suit will soon be tested as governments react to these decisions. This increased litigation, then, is the second potential impact of these cases on public administrators.

The role of partisan appointments in government is discussed. The decisions come down strongly against patronage systems. The dissent asserted that there are sufficient protections against patronage-influenced contractual relationships, often contained in codes that prohibit favoritism in the contracting process. While there are fewer and fewer direct patronage systems in the country, the majorities of the Supreme Court in *Umbehr* and *O'Hare Truck Service, Inc.* clearly felt that stronger prohibitions against patronage influences must be put in place. These protections will make the contracting process more complex and cautious. However, public administrators may also benefit from a system in which patronage has been rejected as a way of allocating public funds.

These three effects—decreases in the strength of patronage systems, potential increases in future litigation, and limitations on the ways in which governments accomplish the work of government—are surely not the only changes that will arise from these decisions. It is important, though, to begin the process of understanding how court decisions influence public administration. As public administrators become more conscious of litigation as a source of direct and indirect influence over their positions, the specific impacts of judicial activity will become increasingly clear.

References

Baldo, Anthony. 1990. "Hear Comes the Judge." *Financial World* 159(8): 42–43.

Koenig, Heidi. 1996. "Studying the Court/Public Administration Interaction: Theory for Guidance or Guidance for Theory?" Paper presented at the Public Administration Theory Network conference, Savannah, Georgia.

Koenig, Heidi, and Amy Kise. 1996. "Law and the City Manager: Beginning to Understand the Sources of Influence on the Management of Local Government." *Journal of Public Administration Research and Theory* 6(3): 443–459.

Koenig, Heidi, and Rosemary O'Leary. 1996. "Eight Supreme Court Cases that have Changed the Face of Public Administration." *International Journal of Public Administration* 39(1): 5–22.

CHAPTER 8

JUDICIAL LAWMAKING
AND ADMINISTRATION

ROGER C. CRAMTON

Seventy years ago in St. Paul, Roscoe Pound gave a famous speech on "The Causes of Popular Dissatisfaction with the Administration of Justice." Recently, a prestigious group of lawyers and judges, assembled by Chief Justice Burger, reconvened in St. Paul to reconsider Pound's theme. A surprising conclusion was that, although the professionals —the lawyers and judges themselves—have many problems with the administration of justice, the tide of popular dissatisfaction is at a relatively low ebb.

In contrast to other agencies of the government, the people have confidence in the fairness and integrity of the courts. True, there is continuing complaint over the law's cost and delay. But, apart from this perennial complaint, popular dissatisfaction appears to stem from two perceptions: first, that decisions in criminal cases turn too often upon procedural technicalities rather than upon the guilt or innocence of the offender; and second, that some judges, and especially the federal judiciary, have been too actively engaged in lawmaking on social and economic issues that are better handled by other institutions of government. The layman, on scanning his newspaper or viewing the television screen, discovers to his surprise that judges are running schools and prison systems, prescribing curricula, formulating budgets, and regulating the environment.

Causation is a tricky matter. A student theme has reported that, since Smokey the Bear posters were displayed in the New York subways, forest fires have disappeared in Manhattan. Despite the risks, I hazard the generalization that several fundamental changes in the nature of our society may have altered the role of the judiciary.

Foremost among those changes is that suggested by the title of this article. The Leviathan is upon us, and it has implications for all branches of government, including the judiciary. Government now attempts so much! Every technical, economic, and social issue seems to end up in the hands of government; and the demand for further government action is combined with charges that existing government is inefficient, heavy-handed, and ineffective. This is one field in which the appetite for nostrums does not fade

From *Public Administration Review* 36, no. 5 (September/October 1976): 551–555. Copyright © 1976 by American Society for Public Administration. Reprinted with permission.

with the demonstrated failure of prior cures. Each reformer, after criticizing the failure and inefficiency of government, then concludes that the remedy is more of the same!

But our attitudes about ourselves and about conflict have also changed. The confrontational style of contemporary America assures that social conflict will increase. "Doing your own thing" is the central value of a hedonistic, self-regarding society; and patience is a nearly extinct virtue. Nowadays no one takes "no" for an answer, whether it is a job aspirant or a welfare claimant or a teacher who has been denied tenure. We perceive our society as having grown old; the enthusiastic and venturesome spirit that prompted the uncharted growth of the American past is now suffering from hardening of the arteries. As we experience slower economic development and approach zero population growth, organized groups contend with each other with increasing ferocity for larger shares of a more static pie. There is a declining sense of a common purpose; the prevailing attitude is "what's in it for me?"

These trends give lawyers and judges an even more central role in our society than they have had in the past. The decline of moral consensus and of institutions of less formal control, such as the family and the church, places much more strain on the law as an instrument of conflict resolution and social control. And the increasing contentiousness of groups organized for their own advantage has made conflict resolution a growth industry. If you could buy stock in law firms, I would advise you to do so. Lawyers have a legal monopoly on the conflict resolution industry, and it is the boom industry of today.

To these developments—the increasing reliance on law as an instrument of social control and the rapid growth of group conflict—must be added another factor: the failure of the executive and the legislature to meet the challenge of today's inflated expectations. The public perception that these branches of government have failed—a perception greatly abetted by the debacles of Vietnam and Watergate—has led the people to turn increasingly to the courts for solutions to their problems.

Models of Judicial Review

Consider in the context of the Leviathan State two models of judicial review of administrative action. The traditional model is one of a restrained and sober second look at what government has done that adversely affects a citizen. The controversy is bipolar in character, with two parties opposing each other; the issues are narrow and well defined; and the relief is limited and obvious. Has a welfare recipient been denied a benefit to which he is entitled by statute? Was fair procedure employed by the agency? Were constitutional rights violated?

Judicial review in this model serves as a window on the outside world, a societal escape valve that tests the self-interest and narrow vision of the specialist and the bureaucrat against the broader premises of the total society. Every bureaucracy develops its own way of looking at things and these belief patterns are enormously resistant to change. In time an agency acquires a tunnel vision in which particular values are advanced and others are ignored. An independent judiciary tests agency outcomes against the statutory framework and the broader legal context.

Judicial review in this form is an absolute essential, especially in a society in which the points of contact between officials and private individuals multiply at every point. The impartial and objective second look adds to the integrity and acceptance of the administrative process rather than undermining it. If the administrator is upheld, as usually is the case, citizen confidence in the fairness and rationality of administration is enhanced. In the relatively small number of cases in which the administrator is reversed, the administrator is forced to readjust his narrower view to the larger perspective of the total society.

During the last twenty years the pace of constitutional change, especially in judicial review of government action, has been astounding. The values implicit in general constitutional provisions such as due process, equal protection, and free speech have been given expanded content and new life. Even more important, constitutional rights have been extended to persons who were formerly neglected by the legal system—blacks, aliens, prisoners, and others. One can disagree with the merits of particular decisions. But the general trends—implementation of fundamental values by the courts and the inclusion of previously excluded groups in the application of these values—constitute a great hour in the long struggle for human freedom.

There is, however, a second model of judicial review that is growing in acceptance and authority. This model of the judicial role has characteristics more of general problem-solving than of dispute resolution. Simon Rifkind speaks of a modern tendency to view courts as modern handymen—as jacks of all trades available to furnish the answer to whatever may trouble us. "What is life? When does death begin? How should we operate prisons and hospitals? Shall we build nuclear power plants, and if so, where? Shall the Concorde fly to our shores?"[1]

Thoughtful observers believe that controversies of this character strain the capacities of our courts and may have debilitating effects on the self-reliance of administrators and legislators. At the risk of appearing more reactionary than I am, let me focus not on the achievements of the past but on the possible dangers that arise when the judiciary succumbs to pressures to attempt too much.

The Court as Administrator

The traditional judicial role, earlier described, envisions a lawsuit that is bipolar in character, seeks traditional relief (usually damages), and applies established law to a relatively narrow factual situation. The relief given is backward looking and does not order government officials to take positive steps in the future.

The traditional model still persists in much private litigation and in many routine cases challenging official action, but in many other constitutional and statutory controversies radical changes have occurred. The changes have led Abram Chayes to argue that the basic character of public litigation has changed.[2] In today's public litigation, a federal judge often is dealing with issues involving numerous parties; indeed, everyone in the community may be affected. Moreover, the issues are complex, interrelated, and multi-faceted; and they turn less on proof concerning past misconduct than on complex predictions as to how various social interests should be protected in the future. Since the remedy is not limited to compensating named plaintiffs for a past harm, the judge gets drawn, for example, into coercing school officials to close schools, bus pupils, change curricula, and build new facilities. The federal judge becomes one of the most powerful persons in the community; on the particular issue, he is the one who decides.

Consider the role of one man, Frank Johnson, in the governance of the once sovereign State of Alabama. Johnson, a distinguished United States District Judge in Alabama, is supervising the operation of the prisons, mental hospitals, highway patrol, and other institutions of the state. His decrees have directed the state to hire more wardens with better training, rebuild the prisons, and even extend to such details as the length of exercise periods and the installation of partitions in the men's rooms.

What is the authority of a federal judge to take such far-reaching actions? Why is not the Alabama legislature the proper body to determine what prison or hospital care should be provided, and at what cost, through agencies administered by the state's executive branch? The answer is that all of these actions are designed to remedy violations of the constitutional rights of prisoners, mental patients, and others. And the Alabama legislature and executive have defaulted on their obligation to remedy these violations.

We are caught on the horns of a terrible dilemma. It is unconscionable that a federal court should refuse to entertain claims that state officials have systematically violated the constitutional rights of prisoners, mental patients, or school children. On the other hand, the design of effective relief may draw the court into a continuing role as an administrator of complex bureaucratic institutions. The dangers of the latter choice are worth brief exploration.

First, the judge who assumes an administrative role may gradually lose his neutrality, becoming a partisan who is pursuing his own cause. In one recent class action, a federal judge not only appointed expert witnesses, suggested areas of inquiry, and took over from the parties a substantial degree of the management of the case, but also went so far as to order that $250,000 from an award required of the defendants be paid for social science research on the effectiveness of the decree. That may be good government, but is it judicial justice?

A further problem arises from the tentativeness of our knowledge about such matters as minimum standards in operating a prison or mental hospital. We fervently hope that civilized and humane treatment will be provided to all of those who are confined to public institutions. But is it desirable to take the view of the current generation of experts, especially those self-selected by the plaintiffs or the judge, and to give their views of acceptable standards the status of constitutional requirements, with all that implies concerning their fixed meaning and difficulty of change?

Here as elsewhere, our capacity to anticipate the future or to discern all relevant facets of polycentric problems is limited. Thus, for example, when a federal judge ordered New York City to close the Tombs as a city jail or to rebuild it, the City, faced with an extraordinary financial crisis, opted to close it and prisoners confined to the Tombs were transferred to Riker's Island. The crowded conditions of the Tombs were immediately duplicated on Riker's Island. But a further result was not anticipated: Riker's Island is much less accessible to the families and attorneys of prisoners; and there is reason to believe that the vast majority of prisoners prefer the convenience of the Tombs, despite its problems, to the inaccessibility of Riker's Island.

The underlying truth is that court orders cannot by judicial decree achieve social change in the face of the concerted opposition of elected officials and public opinion. In a representative democracy, the consent of the people is required for lasting change.

The impulse to reform, moreover, is not limited to courts nor to constitutional law. A vigilant press, an informed populace, and the leadership of a committed minority have mobilized forces of change and reform throughout our history. A representative democracy may move slowly, but if we lack patience we may undermine the self-reliance and responsibility of the people and their elected officials.

The danger of confrontation between branches of government is yet another concern. What happens, for example, if Alabama refuses to fund its mental hospitals or prisons at the level required to achieve the standards specified in Judge Johnson's decrees? The next step, Judge Johnson has said, is the sale of Alabama's public lands in order to finance, through court-appointed officers, the necessary changes.

A degree of tension is a necessary concomitant of the checks and balances of a federal system. But in our urge to check we should not forget that balance is involved as well. One of the lessons of the Watergate era is that cooperation, restraint, and patience among the various branches and levels of government are necessary if our system is to survive in the long run. As Ben Franklin said many years ago, we must hang together or we will hang separately.

Pressures for Judicial Action

Why have the courts undertaken these more expansive functions? They have not done so as volunteers desirous of expanding their own powers, but reluctantly and hesitantly in response to public demands for effective implementation of generally held values.

The American people today have little patience or restraint in dealing with social issues. An instant problem requires an instant solution that provides instant gratification. Playing this game under those rules, the executive and legislature have done their best— grinding out thousands of laws and regulations, many of them ineffective and some of them intrusive and harmful. The public, while demanding even more action from legislators and administrators, perceives these bodies as inept, ineffective, and even corrupt. Moreover, issues on which there is a deep social division, such as school busing or abortion, are avoided by elected officials, who view them as involving unacceptable political risks.

Nature abhors a vacuum and the inaction of the executive and lawmaking branches creates pressures for judicial action. A prominent federal judge put it succinctly at the recent St. Paul conference: "If there is a serious problem, and the legislature and executive don't respond, the courts have to act."

And they have done so on one after another burning issue. The mystery is that they have been so successful and that there has been so little popular outcry. The desegregation of

Southern schools, of course, is a success story of heroic proportions. Legislative reapportionment is also generally viewed as a success despite the mathematical extreme to which it was carried in its later years. Organs of opinion, especially the TV networks and major newspapers, support the Court's actions in general and especially in such areas as civil rights and criminal procedure. There is no institution in our society that has as good a press as the Supreme Court. Judicial activism, it appears, has the approval of the intellectual elite who have become disillusioned with the effectiveness of social change by other means. It is more doubtful, however, whether the common man concurs either in the elite's support of judicial lawmaking or of its substantive results.

Long-Term Effects

Neither popular acclaim nor criticism, of course, can answer the long-term question of the appropriate lawmaking role of the judiciary and the desirable limits on the scope of judicial decrees. More fundamental considerations must be decisive.

First, the practical question of comparative qualifications. Do judges, by training, selection, or experience, have an aptitude for social problem solving that other officials of government lack? And are the techniques of adjudication well designed to perform these broader policy-making functions? Professor Abram Chayes of the Harvard Law School has answered these questions with a confident affirmative.[3] I am inclined to disagree.

Second, what will be the long-term effects of this trend on the credibility of the courts and on the sense of responsibility of administrators and legislators?

After completion of this article, my fears on this score received support from an unlikely source—Anthony Lewis in the *New York Times.* After acknowledging, as I do, that the Boston School Case "presented exceptional difficulties," that "a judge could [not] in conscience remit the complaining black families to their political remedy," and that District Judge Garrity's lonely efforts should be viewed with sympathy, Lewis nevertheless concludes that Garrity's involvement in the day-by-day administration of school affairs "has not worked well" and "is a serious philosophical error":

> American judges have to handle many controversial problems with political implications—redistricting, prisons and the like. Their object should always be to nudge elected officials into performing their responsibility. [Excessive intervention by the judge] tends to take responsibility away from those who ought to be seen to bear it.[4]

And finally, as Simon Rifkind has put it, there is "the ancient question, *quo warranto?* By what authority do judges turn courts into mini-legislatures?"[5]

The critical question in a republic is how government by nonelected, lifetime officials can be squared with representative democracy. The magic of the robe, the remnants of the myth that law on these matters is discovered by an elaboration of existing rules (rather than by personal preference), and the prudence of the judiciary in picking issues on which it could command a great deal of popular support—perhaps these factors explain why the judges have been as successful as they have.

I fear, however, that the judiciary has exhausted the areas where broad majoritarian support will sustain new initiatives and that the tolerance of local communities for "government by decree" is fast dissipating. If so, caution is in order lest a depreciation of the esteem in which we hold the courts undermines their performance of the essential tasks that are indisputably theirs and that other institutions cannot perform.

The authority of the courts depends in large part on the public perception that judges are different from other policy makers. Judges (but not elected officials) are impartial rather than willful or partisan; judges utilize special decisional procedures; and they draw on established general principles in deciding individual cases. In short, traditional ideas concerning the nature, form, and functions of adjudication as a decisional technique underlie popular acceptance of judicial outcomes.

While the precise boundaries of the adjudicative technique are flexible rather than fixed, if they are abandoned entirely the judge loses credibility as a judge. He becomes merely another policy maker who, in managing prisons or schools or whatnot, is expressing his personal views and throwing his weight around. When that point is reached, the judge's credibility and authority is no greater than that of Mayor White in Boston or Mayor Rizzo in Philadelphia.

With the credibility of the legislature and executive branches of government in such disrepair, we cannot afford any further depreciation in the judicial currency. General acceptance of the authority of law is a necessary bulwark of our otherwise fragile social order. If it disappears, the resulting collapse of order may put the American people in the mood for that "more effective management" that is likely to characterize any distinctly American brand of authoritarianism.

Opportunities for charismatic and authoritarian leadership, it has been said, derive in considerable measure from the ability to "accentuate [a society's] sense of being in a desperate predicament." If the courts, by overextension and consequent failure, contribute to our growing sense of desperation, our liberties may not long survive. When a people despair of their institutions, force arrives under the masquerade of ideology.

Notes

1. Simon H. Rifkind, "Are We Asking Too Much of Our Courts?" paper prepared for the National Conference on the Causes of Popular Dissatisfaction with the Administration of Justice, St. Paul, Minn., April 8, 1976, p. 5.

2. Abram Chayes, "The Role of the Judiciary in a Public Law System," *Harvard Law Review* (May 1976).

3. Ibid.

4. *New York Times,* May 24, 1976, p. 29.

5. Rifkind, "Are We Asking Too Much of Our Courts?" p. 20.

CHAPTER 9

THE POLITICS OF PARTNERSHIP

R. SHEP MELNICK

In 1971 Chief Judge David Bazelon of the Circuit Court of Appeals for the District of Columbia marked the arrival of "a new era in the long and fruitful collaboration of administrative agencies and reviewing courts" by ordering recalcitrant administrators to initiate proceedings to ban the pesticide DDT.[1] A dissenting judge grumbled that the court was "undertaking to manage the Department of Agriculture."[2] The D.C. Circuit soon had many bureaucrats grumbling as well. All the court's talk about "partnership" and "collaboration" could not hide the fact that this court and many others were overruling agency decisions at an accelerating rate, were criticizing administrators for acting arbitrarily, parochially, and sloppily, and were demanding compliance with complex new rule-making procedures. With partners like this, who needs enemies?

Yet over a decade later it is clear that judicial rhetoric about a court-agency partnership is more than just a clever disguise for judicial usurpation of administrative authority. While a few agencies—most notably the Federal Communications Commission and the Nuclear Regulatory Commission—continued to fight with the courts for years, most adapted to the courts' requirements and have even applauded their efforts. "The effect of such detailed factual review by the courts on the portion of the agency subject to it," wrote one Environmental Protection Agency attorney after careful investigation, "is entirely beneficial."[3] Similar sentiments are frequently expressed by lawyers in other agencies as well.[4]

The Partners' Objectives

What are the objectives of this new partnership? The answer most frequently provided in judicial opinions is "open, fair, and rational decision making." This means most immediately that agencies must present rationales supporting their major decisions and that these rationales must be technically sound. To this end, the courts have read a number of new requirements into the notice and comment rulemaking provisions of the Administrative Procedures Act.[5] When agencies propose new regulations, they must make public the data, methodology, and arguments on which they have relied. Not only must they

Excerpted from *Public Administration Review* 45, no. Special Edition (November 1985): 653–660. Copyright © 1985 by American Society for Public Administration. Reprinted with permission.

invite comment on this material, but they must also respond to all "significant" criticism. Then they must provide a detailed explanation of how they arrived at their final rule. All this information must be compiled in a record that can be reviewed by the appropriate court. The reviewing court will give a hard look at the record, insisting that the agency "articulate with reasonable clarity its reason for decision and identify the significance of the crucial facts, a course that tends to assure that the agency's policies effectuate general standards, applied without unreasonable discrimination."[6] Courts have insisted upon undertaking such searching and careful review even when it requires immersing themselves in highly technical material.

Going hand-in-hand with the goal of assuring adequate analysis is the objective of assuring participation by all affected interests. In part the latter serves the former: when all can speak, more information and alternatives are presented for consideration. But the concerted efforts of the courts to open the door to participation by such non-traditional groups as environmentalists, civil rights organizations, and consumer groups also reflect their concern about the political biases of administrative agencies. In the late 1960s the courts began to complain that administrators were focusing too narrowly on the accepted missions of their agencies, losing sight of the public interest in the process. At best, agencies were unimaginative; at worse, they had been captured by the powerful industrial interests they were created to control. Led by the D.C. Circuit, the courts sought to open up these "iron triangles" by giving a variety of interests the chance to be heard.[7] The "reformation" of administrative law, as Richard Stewart explained, "changed the focus of judicial review . . . so that its dominant purpose is no longer the prevention of unauthorized intrusion on private autonomy, but the assurance of fair representation for all affected interests in the exercise of the legislative power delegated to agencies."[8] Just as the technical components of agency decision making would be scrutinized for accuracy, the more political components would be scrutinized for fairness and breadth of view.

Who could object to this? Certainly not the agencies, which would hardly claim the right to be irrational or unfair. Certainly not Congress, which constantly criticizes bureaucratic myopia. Before long, Congress had written these judicially created procedures into many regulatory statutes.[9] Certainly not the press, for which openness is next to godliness. And certainly not legal scholars, who want nothing more than for government to be as fair and reasonable as the most distinguished members of their profession. To be sure, a few judges complained of the enormous burden this put on the courts; but this was a cross most judges would gladly bear.

Adding Bite to Its Bark

For all this to work, however, judges must be able to spot fair and reasonable policies when they see them—or, more accurately, be able to recognize unfair and unreasonable policies. One factor contributing to the difficulty of this task is the amount of scientific and technical uncertainty that inevitably accompanies public policy making. Another is that on most important public issues even when the facts are undisputed people still disagree strenuously about what is fair and reasonable, with neither side clearly wrong. As agencies dutifully gathered more information, uncertainty seemed to grow rather than diminish. As they listened to more people, they found their options widening rather than converging. Given the fuzziness of the reasonableness and fairness standards, resourceful administrators, it would seem, can easily learn how to jump through all the hoops—and then do whatever they want. What agencies would lose in delay they would gain in improved public relations.

This possibility led one leading commentator, Joseph Sax, to claim in the early 1970s that these judicial efforts would prove futile.[10] He was wrong. The "new era" in administrative law did not fade into procedural irrelevancy because judges were able to devise more specific standards to give bite to their intensified scrutiny. The source of these standards was an agency's enabling statute, or, more precisely, the courts' often creative interpretation of such statutes. It is the statute as interpreted by the court that determines which factors are relevant, and thus what lines of analysis can be considered reasonable.[11]

Statutory interpretation adds a third partner to the policy-making firm: Congress. In Judge Harold Leventhal's words, "the courts are a kind of partnership for the purpose of effectuating the legislative mandate." Added Judge Skelly Wright, "Our duty, in short, is to see that the legislative purposes heralded in the halls of Congress, are not lost in the vast halls of the federal bureaucracy."[12] Judges, of course, have always insisted that administrators comply with explicit statutory requirements that bar them from exceeding their legal authority. In recent years, however, courts have been increasingly willing to second-guess administrators when the meaning of the statute is far from evident. Many a statute, as Justice John Harlan so colorfully put it, "reveals little except that we have before us a child born of the silent union of legislative compromise." Congress frequently "voice[s] its wishes in muted strains and [leaves] it to the courts to discern the theme in the cacophony of political understanding."[13] In the 1970s judges gained confidence in their ability to discern the harmonies of the Muses amid the static emanating from Capitol Hill. As the courts were giving increasing scrutiny to legislative enactments, Congress itself was going through dramatic changes both internally and in its relations with the president. This transformation gave new significance—and additional allies—to judicial activism.

Congressional Resurgence

In the late 1960s when the new administrative law was beginning to take shape, it would not have been inaccurate to make three generalizations about Congress. First, when Congress takes action on major issues, it generally follows the president's lead—"the president proposes and Congress disposes." Second, Congress usually speaks in vague language, using such phrases as "the public interest," "convenience," and "necessity." And third, except in extraordinary circumstances (such as after the 1932 and 1964 Democratic landslides), the conservative coalition of Republicans and Southern Democrats can block passage of important liberal legislation.

By 1975 when the new administrative law hit full stride, these generalizations had become demonstrably false. For more than five years the Democratic Congress engaged in battle with President Richard Nixon on both regulatory and spending matters. Increasingly numerous Northern liberal Democrats broke the hold of the conservative coalition and instituted major structural reform in Congress. The most important reforms were those that increased the number, power, autonomy, and staff of congressional subcommittees. Already a decentralized institution, Congress became even more so. Only this time it was the younger, more activist, and entrepreneurial members, not their more stolid and conservative adversaries, who controlled the subcommittees. Using subcommittee resources, members initiated new programs and revised old ones, challenging the president for the title of "chief legislator." No longer would Congress respond to calls for action by passing vague legislation telling the executive to do something. Now Congress was writing detailed statutes that not infrequently deviated from the president's program. Subcommittees were also using oversight hearings to make sure that administrators paid heed not just to the letter of their legislation, but to its spirit as well.[14]

Efforts to make these powerful subcommittees representative of Congress as a whole were abandoned as each member sought a piece of the action and was allowed to choose the type of action he or she favored.[15] Environmental advocates flocked to subcommittees on environmental protection; those advocating expansion of social welfare programs chose their favorite subcommittees on the Labor and Public Welfare and the Education and Labor committees. The influence of the more cautious "insider" committees—Rules, Ways and Means, and Appropriations—plummeted. As more and more legislation reached the floor, non-committee members had less and less time to scrutinize each enactment. Sensing an imbalance, members attempted to increase party control over legislation and to create a new budget process capable of setting rational budget priorities. But party and budget reform wilted in the face of subcommittee government.[16]

Presidents Nixon, Ford, Carter, and Reagan could hardly ignore these developments. Since 1970 all presidents, Democratic as well as Republican, have tried to reduce federal spending and to limit regulatory demands placed on private enterprise. In doing so they have increased the power of the organization best equipped to translate these presidential directives into legislative and administrative action—the Office of Management and Budget (OMB). The role of the president as budget-cutter and the power of OMB were most apparent in 1981 when Congress adopted the Reagan administration's proposal to reduce annual spending by $35 billion. But Nixon's impoundments, Ford's numerous vetoes of spending bills, Carter's use of the budget act to cut $10 billion from the budget in 1980, and executive-congressional conflicts since 1981 remind us of the institutional causes of continuing differences over the scope of government activity.

A major consequence of this struggle between Congress and the president is that federal administrators frequently find themselves caught between the competing demands of congressional subcommittees on the one hand, and the White House and OMB on the other. OMB cuts agency budget requests; subcommittees condemn administrators for failing to carry out their missions. Subcommittees urge regulators to read statutes broadly; OMB insists that they regulate only when they are sure that benefits will out-weigh costs.

Courts hearing administrative law cases are often forced to resolve these conflicts between subcommittee advocates and lieutenants of the president. The spate of recent cases involving the Reagan administration's efforts to relax regulatory requirements is only the most graphic illustration of this pattern.[17] While few judges or law professors will admit it, administrative law is increasingly becoming a forum for resolving interbranch competition for control of the bureaucracy.

The Real Partners

When put in this political context, the courts' new procedural requirements and tech-niques of statutory interpretation take on new significance. The courts have strengthened congressional subcommittees at the expense of the presidency. One must say subcom-mittee rather than Congress because major administrative law cases seldom, if ever, involve instances in which Congress as a whole has spoken clearly. When courts look to congressional intent to resolve ambiguity, they usually find the intent of the program advocates who dominate subcommittees. The real partners in the new administrative law, to put it bluntly, are the courts, subcommittees, and those administrators who wish to be freed from the influence of OMB and the president.

The most obvious way in which courts increase the influence of subcommittees is by relying heavily on legislative history. Most of the elements of legislative history—reports, floor statements, and hearings—are produced by subcommittee leaders and staff. Subcommittee staff has become adept at creating enormous legislative histories, por-tions of which are carefully designed for later judicial consumption.[18] As legislative histories grow longer (the legislative history of the Clean Air Act compiled by the Con-gressional Research Service runs on for 7,500 pages), it becomes less likely that ordi-nary members of Congress will be familiar with them. Indeed, major components of legislative histories are often manufactured by staff members without any participation by elected members of Congress.[19]

More subtle is reliance on statutory purpose to tilt statutory interpretation to the ad-vantage of program advocates. All statutes combine purposes with constraints. We want to protect the environment, but not put people out of work. We want to aid families with dependent children, but not spend too much money. We want to provide the handi-capped with an appropriate education, but not impinge upon the states' prerogative to control their schools. To the extent that courts increase their emphasis on statutory pur-pose, they strengthen the hands of those who advocate achieving these objectives at the expense of those who seek to impose constraints.[20]

These are, of course, tendencies rather than iron laws. There is far too much play in the joints of statutory interpretation to permit definitive generalization. Statutes differ in their structure; judges in their emphasis; subcommittees in their unity, skillfulness, and single-mindedness; agencies in their loyalty to the president. Indeed it is the difficulty of generalization on statutory construction that has led students of the judiciary to downplay its significance. For this reason it is all the more important to consider how the courts affect relations among members of Congress, administrators, and presidential aides in a variety of policy arenas.

How the courts, led by the D.C. Circuit, cemented an alliance between the Environmental Protection Agency (EPA) and environmental protection advocates in Congress and substantially reduced White House influence over air pollution policy has been explained in detail elsewhere.[21] . . .

Entitlements

For many years federal courts intervened far less frequently in spending programs than in regulatory ones. Not only did judges view spending as an activity most appropriately controlled by the other branches of government, but few federal statutes spelled out in detail who should receive how much money (the old age insurance section of the Social Security Act being the glaring exception). Within Congress the purse strings were controlled not by the authorizing committees that wrote legislation establishing spending programs but by the appropriations committees that put together the annual budget. In deciding how much to include in the budget, the appropriations committees paid much more attention to the recommendations of OMB (then known as the Bureau of the Budget) than to the far higher recommendations of the authorizing committees.

This changed dramatically in the late 1960s and early 1970s. Increasingly aggressive authorizing committees convinced Congress to enact "backdoor" spending measures not subject to annual review by the appropriations committees and OMB. The most important form of backdoor spending is the entitlement, which guarantees the payment of a certain sum (often including a cost-of-living adjustment) to all eligible individuals, regardless of the total cost of such payments. In 1972, 66 percent of the budget was "uncontrollable"; by 1982 this figure was nearly 80 percent.[25] Thus, shortly after the courts altered legal doctrines to open the courthouse doors to recipients of government largess,[26] changes within Congress produced a multitude of detailed spending statutes for judges to interpret. As with regulatory statutes, the members of Congress most involved in writing entitlement laws were those most interested in expanding government programs.

There was, however, an additional complication. Many federal programs do not provide money directly to private individuals but rather funnel the money through the states. Such statutes establish general program guidelines, but they delegate administrative responsibility to the states and offer the states considerable discretion in setting eligibility standards and funding levels. Federal administrators are expected to enforce federal rules by cutting off funds to states that fail to comply "substantially." In practice this means that federal statutory requirements can easily be flaunted, since the penalty can have a devastating effect on program recipients and, consequently, will seldom be employed. Liberalizing reforms approved at the national level can easily be blocked by state legislatures and governors tenaciously guarding the public fisc.[27]

To deal with this problem, the federal courts deployed an arcane but potent judicial weapon, the private right of action. When a court discovers that a federal statute contains or implies a private right of action, it offers alleged beneficiaries the opportunity to bring suit against states or private parties to vindicate their statutory rights—even if a federal agency has been given primary responsibility for assuring compliance with the statute.[28] This means not only that private parties gain control over enforcement mechanisms but also that federal courts gain additional opportunities to determine what benefits statutes promise to private citizens. The private right of action has special significance in joint federal-state spending programs. If an alleged beneficiary could only bring suit against a federal administrator for failing to enforce federal standards, the only relief the court could offer successful plaintiffs would be an injunction cutting off federal funds to the state. In most cases, this would mean that victorious litigants would lose money. But when potential recipients can bring suit against the state for failure to comply with federal requirements, the court can compel the state to pay the plaintiff the money owed. The private right of action, thus, significantly alters the balance of power between the federal government and the states.

It did not take program advocates at the national level long to recognize the advantages of the new regime. Officials of the Department of Health, Education, and Welfare (HEW) began to issue more detailed regulations and joined with private plaintiffs in attacking state practices in federal court. Few judges asked why these administrators were challenging the very programs they had formally approved just months before. Congress responded to this opportunity to expand federal control over joint programs by adding more elaborate eligibility requirements, writing lengthy legislative histories, and passing broad cross-cutting mandates that apply to all state programs receiving federal funds.[29]

Aiding the Handicapped

Nowhere are the political consequences of these institutional and doctrinal developments more evident than in programs for the handicapped. In the 1960s and 1970s, a number of public interest groups and professional associations brought to public attention a multitude of problems facing the handicapped, ranging from lack of adequate transportation to exclusion from public schools to inhumane conditions in state institutions. These groups began to achieve success in Congress just as the potential for using private rights of action was becoming evident. A cohesive subcommittee-agency-court-interest group alliance managed to build strong programs and to pass most of the costs along to the states.

As the problems of the handicapped were brought to the attention of Congress, subcommittees investigating the issue multiplied. Few members of Congress were unsympathetic to the plight of the handicapped. The problem was that relief would cost a great deal of money, and the Nixon and Ford administrations were seeking to avoid large deficits.

One congressional response was to add new mandates without adding more money. Such was the strategy of Section 504 of the Rehabilitation Act of 1973. This section, little noticed at the time of passage, prohibits discrimination on the basis of handicap in any program receiving federal funds, however, it fails to define "discrimination." When the Republican administrations did little to implement this provision, the handicapped went to court. Relying on language inserted in a conference committee report issued one year after passage of Section 504, the federal district court for the District of Columbia ordered HEW to issue and enforce regulations implementing the new federal mandate. After still another suit, a change of administrations, and a sit-in at his office, Secretary Joseph Califano reluctantly published new rules. Many other courts subsequently found an implied private right of action in Section 504. They could not, after all, leave enforcement of the law to administrators who seemed so reluctant to put it into effect. Judicial interpretation of Section 504 helped push the cost of the program into the billions of dollars.[30]

On the issue of education for handicapped children, subcommittees on education and the handicapped in the House and the Senate took a more direct approach. Insisting (erroneously) that federal courts had ruled that all children have a constitutional right to an education, they championed an authorizations bill that would provide billions of dollars to help states meet the judicial mandate. The Nixon and Ford administrations threatened a veto. The subcommittees reduced the authorization levels, and President Ford signed the Education for All Handicapped Children Act into law in 1975. Subsequently the appropriations committees, following the advice of OMB, kept actual funding at only a fraction of authorization levels.

The Education for All Handicapped Children Act is far more than just a funding act. It contains elaborate procedures and guidelines to ensure that all handicapped children receive an "appropriate" education. Local schools must construct an individualized education program (IEP) for each handicapped child. Parents have the right to participate in the formulation of the IEP, and they can appeal any provision in the IEP first to an independent hearing officer and then to the state board of education. While the procedural aspects of the act are elaborate, nowhere does it specify what constitutes a "free appropriate public education." There is logic to this: the major decisions on appropriateness are made by state and local educators who can study each case in detail and who bear responsibility for footing most of the bill.

The Senate bill said little about judicial review of IEPs, and the House bill subjected state and local decisions to a lenient standard of judicial review. However, the conference committee, which reconciled the bills of the two houses quietly but drastically, altered the role of the courts. In the final version of the legislation there appeared a new judicial review provision that enabled parents to challenge IEPs in federal court and required judges to "make an independent decision based on a preponderance of the evidence" and to "grant all appropriate relief." Final authority to decide what constitutes an appropriate education thus was transferred from state and local officials to federal judges. Program advocates on the conference committee had used a seemingly technical change to alter the balance of power between the states and the federal government.[31]

The Education for All Handicapped Children Act has generated scores of federal court cases. While judges have expressed concern about the huge cost of providing an appropriate education for the handicapped, they have nonetheless ordered schools to provide residential care for severely retarded and emotionally disturbed children, prohibited states from limiting the academic year for the handicapped to the normal 180 days, required schools to perform such quasi-medical procedures as catheterization, and even ordered schools to pay compensatory damages for past student misplacements.[32] Before being overruled by the Supreme Court, several circuit courts held that an appropriate education means the best possible education a school can provide.[33] Partly as a result of these decisions, the cost of the act has become enormous. One estimate puts it at $10 billion per year. Federal appropriations have leveled off at about $1.2 billion, far less than was promised to the states in the authorization passed in 1975.[34]

The fact that the federal courts are available to put bite into a vague statutory mandate provides program advocates with two strategic advantages. Most obviously, judicial review creates a mechanism for maintaining the flow of benefits even when federal budgets grow tight. If congressional appropriations committees reduce federal funding, state and local budgets must absorb the differences.[35] A more subtle consequence is that state and local officials then become lobbyists in the appropriations process, protecting the appropriations base and demanding federal spending increases. This strategy has worked: federal spending for education of the handicapped has remained constant while other education programs have sustained major cuts.

The Price of Success

Some writers have characterized policy making for the handicapped as dominated by a new "iron triangle" of subcommittee, agency, and interest group.[36] Given the pivotal role of the lower courts, it is tempting to speak of an "iron rectangle" instead. But the metaphor is probably not worth saving. As Hugh Heclo has pointed out, contemporary "issue networks" of policy advocates inside and outside government tend to be larger and less coherent than classic iron triangles.[37] Subcommittees are too numerous and fickle, public interest groups too varied and transitory, and federal courts too decentralized and unpredictable to move in lock step. Most importantly, the costs of many of these programs have grown too large for outsiders to ignore. The iron triangles of old maintained their autonomy by keeping their programs out of the limelight, either by passing costs along to taxpayers at a time when taxes were relatively low and competition for federal money less intense or by passing them along to consumers in the form of higher prices. Inflation put the political spotlight on rising prices. Huge deficits are doing the same for rising agency budgets.

The very success of the court-agency-subcommittee-interest group partnership can reduce its autonomy by exposing program costs. Exposure can be especially dangerous for those who have ingeniously built extensive programs on narrow political bases—to be more direct, those who have constructed legislative histories in lieu of legislative coalitions.

For the partnership the challenge becomes finding ways to reduce the visibility of program costs without curtailing program operations. In regulatory programs the best way to do this is to ease up on enforcement against existing employers. EPA, Congress, and the courts have all cooperated in giving polluters with established work forces much more time to comply with pollution requirements. At the same time they have increased the burdens on new facilities that have not yet established constituencies.[38] For programs requiring extensive government spending, advocates have increasingly relied on two strategies: spreading costs over federal, state, and local governments and making total spending a function of thousands of individualized decisions that are hard to control from above. Unfortunately, these cost-disguising strategies can have undesirable consequences. Placing heavier burdens on new facilities than on old ones is inefficient and discourages innovation. Relying on individualized decision making, including litigation, for the education of the handicapped, directs disproportionate resources to children of upper middle-class parents and to those requiring expensive residential care.[39]

In sum, behind the judicial rhetoric about a court agency partnership lies a new political reality. The old administrative law evolved during the New Deal when liberal reformers such as Felix Frankfurter could aid their cause from the bench merely by deferring to administrators chosen by Roosevelt to carry out New Deal legislation.[40] By 1970 the presidency had become a threat to liberal reforms now championed by congressional entrepreneurs, often in cooperation with bureaucratic careerists. At this point the courts switched institutional partners, protecting program advocates in the bureaucracy from presidential interference, reading statutes to reflect the intention of subcommittee activists, and substantially increasing federal administrative control over the states. New Deal politics was high visibility, breakthrough politics. Dramatic legislative victories were followed by well-publicized action by self-confident whiz kids. Recent activism is far less at home in the limelight. It is complex, low visibility, administrative politics. As the courts voluntarily became "in a real sense part of the total administrative process,"[41] they simultaneously became part of an as yet poorly understood political coalition. While one cannot tell how long this coalition will survive, it has unquestionably left its mark on the American polity.

Notes

1. *Environmental Defense Fund v. Ruckelshaus,* 439 F.2d 589, 597 (D.C. Cir. 1971).

2. Ibid., p. 598 (Judge Robb, dissenting).

3. William F. Pederson, "Formal Records and Informal Rulemaking," *Yale Law Journal,* vol. 84 (1975), pp. 59–60.

4. William H. Rodgers Jr. discusses the broad acceptance of heightened judicial scrutiny in "A Hard Look at Vermont Yankee: Environmental Law Under Close Scrutiny," *Georgetown Law Journal* 67 (1979): 699. On cooperation between EPA and the courts, see R. Shep Melnick, *Regulation and the Courts: The Case of the Clean Air Act* (Washington, DC: Brookings Institution, 1983), especially pp. 379–383.

5. "Notice and comment" or "informal" rule making is governed by Section 553 of the Administrative Procedures Act. For years the courts applied the lenient "arbitrary and capricious" standard in reviewing informal rule making. Important examples of the more demanding judicial review of informal rule making include *Kennecott Copper Corp. v. EPA,* 462 F.2d 846 (D.C. Cir. 1972); *Portland Cement Assoc. v. Ruckelshaus,* 486 F.2d 375 (D.C. Cir. 1973); and *South Terminal Corp. v. EPA,* 504 F.2d 646 (1st Cir. 1974). The evolution of judicial review is described in Pederson, "Formal Records,"

and Richard B. Stewart, "The Reformation of American Administrative Law," *Harvard Law Review* 88 (1975): 1667.

6. *Greater Boston Television Corp. v. FCC,* 444 F.2d 841, 851 (D.C. Cir. 1970).

7. *Moss v. CAB,* 430 F.2d 891 (D.C. Cir. 1970); *Office of Communications of the United Church of Christ v. FCC,* 425 F.2d 543 (D.C. Cir. 1969); *Calvert Cliffs Coordinating Committee v. AEC,* 449 F.2d 1109 (D.C. Cir. 1971); *Scenic Hudson Preservation Conf. v. FPC,* 354 F.2d 608 (2nd Cir. 1965).

8. Stewart, "The Reformation of American Administrative Law," p. 1712.

9. Examples include the Clean Air Act Amendments of 1977 and the Magnuson-Moss Warranty-Federal Trade Commission Improvement Act.

10. Joseph Sax, "The (Unhappy) Truth about NEPA," *Oklahoma Law Review,* vol. 26 (1973), p. 239.

11. The "relevant factors" language comes from the landmark case, *Citizens to Preserve Overton Park v. Volpe,* 401 U.S. 402, 416 (1971). The importance of aggressive statutory interpretation was obvious not just in this case (especially at pp. 415–416), but also in the equally important case of *EDF v. Ruckelshaus,* 439 F.2d at 593–596. Legal commentators have generally focused on the procedural aspects of these decisions, ignoring their use of "creative" statutory interpretation.

12. *Calvert Cliffs Coordinating Committee v. AEC,* 449 F.2d at 1111. The Leventhal quotation comes from *Portland Cement Assoc. v. Ruckelshaus,* 486 F.2d at 394.

13. *Rosado v. Wyman,* 397 U.S. 397, 412 (1970).

14. There is a huge literature describing these changes in Congress. Most helpful are the following: Lawrence C. Dodd and Bruce I. Oppenheimer (eds.), *Congress Reconsidered,* 3d ed. (Washington, DC: Congressional Quarterly Press, 1985); Thomas E. Mann and Norman J. Ornstein (eds.), *The New Congress* (Washington, DC: American Enterprise Institute, 1981); James Sundquist, *The Decline and Resurgence of Congress* (Washington, DC: Brookings Institution, 1981); and Arthur Maass, *Congress and the Common Good* (New York: Basic Books, 1983).

15. Maass, *Congress and the Common Good,* pp. 99–103.

16. Allen Schick, *Congress and Money: Budgeting, Spending, and Taxing* (Washington, DC: Urban Institute, 1980) (budget); Maass, *Congress and the Common Good,* pp. 54–63; and Lawrence C. Dodd and Bruce I. Oppenheimer, "The House in Transition: Change and Consolidation," in *Congress Reconsidered* (party).

17. Examples include *Chevron v. Natural Resources Defense Council,* 52 U.S.L.W. 4845 (1984); *Motor Vehicle Manufacturers Assoc. v. State Farm Mutual,* 103 S. Ct. 2869 (1983); *ASH v. CAB,* 699 F.2d 1209 (D.C. Cir. 1983); and *Building and Construction Trade Dept. v. Donovan,* 553 F. Supp. 352 (D.C. Cir. 1982).

18. For an example, see Bruce A. Ackerman and William T. Hassler, *Clean Coal/Dirty Air* (New Haven, CT: Yale University Press, 1981), pp. 48–58.

19. Michael Malbin, *Unelected Representatives* (New York: Basic Books, 1980), p. 30.

20. This is particularly clear in aid to families with dependent children (AFDC) cases such as *Lewis v. Martin,* 397 U.S. 552 (1970). For an example of its application to a regulatory statute, see *NRDC v. Gorsuch,* 685 F.2d 718 (1982).

21. Melnick, *Regulation and the Courts.*

. . .

25. Schick, *Congress and Money,* p. 27; and Congressional Quarterly, *Budgeting for America* (Washington, DC: Congressional Quarterly Press, 1982), p. 49.

26. In the legal literature this change goes under the rubric of "the demise of the rights-privilege distinction." *Goldberg v. Kelly,* 397 U.S. 254 (1970) is usually considered the key case, and Charles Reich's article, "The New Property," *Yale Law Journal* 73 (1964): 733, is the classic argument for the change.

27. The best description of the behavior of federal administrators before the transformation of legal doctrines is Martha Derthick, *The Influence of Federal Grants: Public Assistance in Massachusetts* (Cambridge, MA: Harvard University Press, 1970).

28. The leading cases on private rights of action are *Cort v. Ash,* 422 U.S. 66 (1975), and *Maine v. Thiboutot,* 448 U.S. 1 (1980). While court decisions have been changing and inconsistent, it appears that the Supreme Court is becoming less inclined to find implied rights of action in federal statutes, but increasingly is willing to find authority for such lawsuits in 42 U.S.C. §1983, originally passed as part of the Civil Rights Act of 1871.

29. Advisory Commission on Intergovernmental Relations, *Regulatory Federalism: Policy, Process, Impact, and Reform* (Washington, DC: ACIR, 1984), ch. 1.

30. The key decision was *Cherry v. Mathews,* 419 F. Supp. 922 (D.D.C. 1976). The importance of this case was pointed out to me by Robert Katzmann of the Brookings Institution, who is completing a major study of the politics of Section 504 and transportation policy.

31. Senate Report No. 168, 94th Cong.; House Report No. 332, 94th Cong.; and Senate Conference Report·No. 455, 94th Cong. Erwin L. Levine and Elizabeth Wexler, *PL 94–142: An Act of Congress* (New York: Macmillan, 1981) provides a detailed review of congressional activity on education of the handicapped.

32. *Doe v. Anrig,* 692 F.2d 800 (1st Cir. 1982); *Kruelle v. Biggs,* 489 F. Supp. 169 (D. Del. 1980); *Battle v. Commonwealth of Pennsylvania,* 629 F.2d 269 (3rd Cir. 1980); *Crawford v. Pittman,* 708 F.2d 1028 (5th Cir., 1983); *Tatro v. Texas,* 468 U.S. (1984); *Boxall v. Sequoia Union High School Dist.,* 464 F. Supp. 1104 (N.D. Gal. 1979).

33. *Hendrick Hudson Dist. Bd. v. Rowley,* 458 U.S. 176 (1982).

34. John C. Pittenger and Peter Kuriloff, "Educating the Handicapped: Reforming a Radical Law," *The Public Interest* (Winter 1982), p. 72; *Congressional Quarterly Weekly Report,* November 5, 1983, p. 2317.

35. This holds true even for states that refuse federal funds under the act. The Department of Education has ruled that Section 504 incorporates all regulations issued under the act.

36. Levine and Wexler, *PL 94–142;* Pittenger and Kuriloff, "Educating the Handicapped"; Diane Ravitch, *The Troubled Crusade: American Education 1945–1980* (New York: Basic Books, 1983), pp. 305–312. Martin Shapiro uses the act as an example of a "new iron triangle" of agency, court, and interest group, leaving out subcommittees, in "The Presidency and the Federal Courts," in Arnold J. Meltsner, ed., *Politics and the Oval Office* (San Francisco: Institute for Contemporary Studies, 1981).

37. "Issue Networks and the Executive Establishment," in Anthony King, ed., *The New American Political System* (Washington, DC: American Enterprise Institute, 1978).

38. Lester Lave and Gilbert Omenn, *Cleaning the Air: Reforming the Clean Air Act* (Washington, DC: Brookings Institution, 1981), p. 41; and Melnick, *Regulation and the Courts,* ch. 7.

39. Richard A. Weatherley, *Reforming Special Education: Policy Implementation from State Level to Street Level* (Boston: MIT Press, 1972), especially pp. 124–127 and 137–140.

40. See Martin Shapiro, "The Presidency and the Federal Courts," and "The Constitution and Economic Rights," in M. Judd Harmon, ed., *Essays on the Constitution of the United States* (Port Washington, NY: Kennikat Press, 1978).

41. *Greater Boston Television Corp. v. FCC,* 444 F.2d at 852.

CHAPTER 10

CONFLICT OR CONSTRUCTIVE TENSION

The Changing Relationship of Judges and Administrators

PHILLIP J. COOPER

Administrators these days often express frustration, resentment, and anxiety over judicial intervention into administrative operations. The indictment is familiar. Beginning in the late 1960s and early 1970s, the story goes, federal courts began a movement toward greater interference in administrative matters that has become progressively more intrusive. The trend, the argument runs, continues to this day.

It should not be at all surprising that administrators resent judicial rulings limiting their discretion and mandating procedural or substantive policy changes in agency operations. After all, one of the administrator's primary tasks is to anticipate and eliminate contingencies in the organizational environment.[1] Judicial rulings would seem to be just one more troublesome factor constraining administrative flexibility.

However, the courts perform a variety of essential functions required of them by the Constitution and statutes. They must ensure that administrators do not exceed their statutory authority, ignore basic procedural requisites, conduct themselves in a manner that is arbitrary and capricious or an abuse of discretion, make important policy determinations without some kind of reasoned decision based upon a record, or violate the provisions of the Constitution.[2] Neither these functions nor the courts designated to perform them are going to be eliminated.

The problem then is to develop an effective working relationship between judges and administrators. But before such an accommodation can be reached it will be necessary to assess the current relationship between these legal and administrative institutions. The starting point for such a reassessment must be a realization that the federal courts, led by the Supreme Court, have changed the law governing administrative agencies in ways more charitable to administrators. It is not true that there is a continuing trend toward greater interference in administration. Recent cases indicate an increasing judicial sensitivity to management problems and priorities.

This [chapter] examines the premises underlying current tensions between judges and

Excerpted from *Public Administration Review* 45, Special Edition (November 1985): 643–652. Copyright © 1985 by American Society for Public Administration. Reprinted with permission.

administrators. It then turns to a consideration of the various counts in the indictment brought by administrators against the courts indicating the importance of recent federal court rulings. There is one new area of tension developing between courts and agencies, cases in which administrators refuse to act at all or engage in administrative deregulation. Judicial reactions to this problem are also assessed. Finally, the article suggests that law is a discretion-reinforcing agent, a fact that argues for improved judicial-administrative relations and against continued hostility.

Law and Administration: Natural Animosity or Constructive Tension

Two premises are essential to any discussion about law and administration. First, discretion is an essential commodity in modern public administration. Problems are simply too diverse and specialized and the environment too dynamic for legislators to provide more than a moderate amount of guidance to those who must administer public programs. Beyond that, managers must have sufficient flexibility to adapt their organizations and practices to changing conditions in order to perform effectively and efficiently. A lack of discretion would stifle creativity and confine administrators to rigid behavior patterns producing a panoply of bureaucratic dysfunctions long feared by scholars of organizational theory.[3]

The second premise is that law is intended to, and does in fact, limit discretion. Internal checks acquired by careful recruitment and training of promising public servants and the external checks provided by executive supervision and legislative oversight have never been thought adequate substitutes for the opportunity to call an official into court to demonstrate the validity of his or her actions. "No man in this country," the Supreme Court has admonished us, "is so high that he is above the law. No officer of the law may set that law at defiance with impunity. All of the officers of government, from the highest to the lowest, are creatures of the law, and are bound to obey it."[4]

From these two premises it follows that there will inevitably be tension between judges and administrators. Adding to that conflict are the differing perspectives of legally trained professionals and management educated professional administrators.[5]

However, the fact that some tension exists between judges and administrators is not necessarily destructive nor should it transform natural tension into animosity. Such a polarized view of the judicial-administrative relationship would be understandable only if managers could successfully argue that absolute discretion is absolutely good and necessary or if legalists could contend that all discretion is bad. Neither argument has merit. Discretion does not necessarily have a straight-line correlation with efficiency.[7] The relationship is more curvilinear. No discretion would paralyze management. On the other hand, complete discretion may undermine efficiency. Sofaer, for example, found in his study of an agency with extremely wide discretion that broad flexibility can lead to "inconsistency, arbitrariness, and inefficiency."[8] He concluded that "the evidence seemed to refute the hypothesis that discretion results in less costly, speedier administration. . . . The presence of discretionary power seemed throughout the administrative process, disproportionately to attract political intervention."[9] Legalists have the same problem. The relationship between just decisions and discretion is again nothing so simple as a straight-line negative correlation. Absolute discretion would mean a high probability of arbitrary and inconsistent administrative judgments. On the other hand, no discretion would mean rule-bound administration without accommodation for equity or any other consideration of individualized justice.

The challenge, then, is to find useful mixes of discretion and checks on abuses of discretion not only to achieve just decisions and bolster accountability but also to protect necessary administrative flexibility so that managers can administer their organizations efficiently. The most useful approach to thinking about law and administration is not a juxtaposition of law against administration, but development of an understanding of the interaction of courts and agencies as a necessarily ongoing relationship.

Before progress can be made in improving the judicial-administrative relationship, administrators must be made aware of some of the important changes in the law. There are indications in a variety of recent rulings of increased judicial sensitivity to administrative concerns.

Judges Neither Understand nor Care About Administrative Problems: Mythology and Reality in Recent Legal Developments

A common misconception is that a straight-line progression of judicial assumption of authority has occurred, substituting legal judgment for administrative discretion. Examination of administrative law cases over the past decade, however, indicates that part of this management perception is based upon a number of myths or misunderstandings, which are not generally supported by the case law. True, there are important controversies, but the relationship is not as adversarial as it may seem. . . .

1. Courts do not care about costs. There is substantial evidence to the contrary. Consider the development of standards for administrative due process, judicial acknowledgment of the need to avoid supplanting legislative budgeting, and the recognition of fiscal problems faced by administrators in institutional reform litigation.

Even before the important recent changes in the requirements of administrative due process, the Supreme Court acknowledged the need to permit a flexible approach to due process to accommodate administrative circumstances. In a 1976 ruling, *Mathews v. Eldridge,* the court went even further.[10] In *Eldridge,* the court found that Social Security disability recipients were not entitled to a hearing before the termination of their benefits, though they would have an opportunity to be heard at some point later in the process. The significance of this decision lies not in permitting administrators to deny claimants any due process, but in granting flexibility in assessing what process is due under varying administrative conditions. In *Eldridge,* the Supreme Court developed a balancing test for determining how much process is due someone before an administrative agency that specifically recognizes fiscal and administrative burden as a major element of the balance. In order to decide what process is due, the court said, one must consider

> first, the private interest that will be affected by the official action; second, the risk of an erroneous deprivation of such interest through the procedure used, and the probable value, if any, of additional or substitute safeguards; and finally, *the Government's interest, including the function involved and the fiscal and administrative burdens that the additional or substitute procedural requirements would entail.*[11] (Emphasis added.)

The *Eldridge* balancing test has been the controlling due process standard since 1976.[12] The court has consistently rejected calls for expanded administrative due process since that time and has, in fact, relaxed some of the requirements imposed in earlier cases.[13]

This approach to due process overtly considers the problems of financial and administrative burden so important to administrators. There are other indications that judges at both the Supreme Court and lower court levels are increasingly aware that their rulings have substantial fiscal implications for public administration.[14] . . .

Thus, evidence shows that judges are aware of some of the fiscal implications of their judgments and are concerned about the need to minimize these burdens. That does not mean they are willing to accept a budgetary justification for violating constitutional rights, but neither are they oblivious to administrative problems.

Some question exists, however, as to whether administrators have tried in complex litigation to assist judges to understand relevant fiscal dimensions and to work out accommodations where necessary to minimize judicial-administrative tension. For example, in one northern school desegregation case, the state, when called upon by the judge to produce a proposed remedy, sent six plans, recommended none of them, and provided only one witness for the remedy hearing whose only role was to explain what was in the plans.[18] The state provided the judge no help whatsoever in understanding the administrative and fiscal problems involved in implementing any of the proposed remedies. In an Alabama case, state mental health officials were given six months to take action to remedy unconstitutional conditions at state mental health facilities, but they took no action at all. Moreover, the state refused offers of assistance from federal agencies. After indicating his understanding that state administrators may have lacked funds to implement reforms, the judge asked just how that prevented the administrators from producing a plan that could be implemented when funds did become available.[19]

Administrators can improve their relationship with judges in such cases by making careful decisions about when to fight and when to negotiate. They can present detailed and understandable explanations of their concerns about financial and administrative feasibility. They can resist the temptation simply to ignore likely judicial action until it is forced upon them.

2. Courts are increasingly unwilling to defer to the expertise of administrators. Again, there have been a number of opinions, particularly Supreme Court rulings, demanding deference to administrative expertise. The court has issued these admonitions in two types of cases, rulemaking review and institutional reform litigation.

The court's leading ruling on judicial review of administrative rulemaking was the unanimous opinion issued in *Vermont Yankee Nuclear Power Corp. v. United States Nuclear Regulatory Commission.*[20] *Vermont Yankee* warned lower courts against fashioning procedural requirements beyond those contained in the statutes administered by the agency involved. Lower courts are to examine the record prepared by the agency during rulemaking, and, if it is adequately supported and within the statutory authority of the agency, the action is to be affirmed.[21] While there has been disagreement among members of the court as to precisely how much deference is due,[22] the prime forces expanding rulemaking procedural requirements in recent years have been legislation and executive orders, not judicial mandates.

The court subsequently issued a number of rulings demanding lower court respect for and deference to administrative expertise at the state as well as the federal level. . . .

In other cases, the court has held that judges must "design procedures that protect the rights of the individual without unduly burdening the legitimate efforts of the states to deal with social problems"[28] and insisted that *"courts cannot assume that state legislatures and prison officials are insensitive to the requirements of the Constitution or to perplexing sociological problems of how best to achieve the goals of the penal function in the criminal justice system. . . ."*[29]

3. The Supreme Court is continually expanding the authority of federal district courts to issue complex remedial orders obstructing administrative operations. There are two important factors to be considered in assessing the remedial decree cases. First, administrators have often welcomed suits against prisons and mental hospitals as means to pressure legislators for increased appropriations.[30] Thus, it is not always clear that the relationship of court to agency in these cases is primarily adversarial.

In fact, for a decade now the Supreme Court has been moving to make it harder for trial judges to justify issuance of a remedial order,[31] narrowing the scope of such orders[32] and limiting the duration for which district judges may retain supervisory jurisdiction over administrative institutions.[33] In cases involving school desegregation, mental health, and prison conditions, the court has admonished lower courts to avoid unnecessary orders, to carefully tailor those that are necessary to remedy constitutional violations without undue interference in agency operations, and to terminate control over those institutions as soon as possible.

4. The Supreme Court keeps expanding legal protections available to employees at the expense of managers' discretion. An expansion of employee rights did occur in the late 1960s and early 1970s. Once again, however, care must be exercised in judgments about judicial interference with administration. In the first place, many employee rights were created by statute or executive order and not judicial rulings.[34] It is, of course, true that federal courts added protections, particularly in the area of First Amendment free speech and association as well as due process requirements in adverse personnel actions. However, important changes have been made in recent Supreme Court decisions that define employee rights, particularly in the First Amendment and due process fields.

Using the *Eldridge* balancing formula, the court has drawn back from what were some years ago expanding administrative due process requirements in employee terminations concerning which employees are entitled to a hearing[35] and the type and timing of any hearing that is required.[36] These cases have indicated that the court will be reticent to require more elements of due process than are specified in statutes and regulations. Moreover, they have rejected claims by employees that civil servants are entitled to a hearing before they are removed from their jobs rather than some time later in the administrative process.

In the First Amendment field, the court has shifted the burden and increased the level of proof required for the employee to prevail on complaints of unlawful termination in violation of First Amendment free speech protections.[37] The most direct statement of the court's intention to leave managers free of unnecessary judicial involvement in personnel decisions came recently in *Connick v. Myers.*[38]

The *Connick* case arose when Myers, a deputy district attorney in Orleans Parish, Louisiana, got into a disagreement with her supervisor regarding a job transfer. She had been offered a transfer and promotion based upon her performance, but she resisted the step up because it would have required her to prosecute cases in the court of a judge with whom she had been working for some time on an offender diversion program. She saw the move as a conflict of interest. When her supervisor disagreed and insisted upon the move she charged that this was another example of his poor administration of the office. Her criticism alleged a range of administrative problems including attempts to coerce employees into participating in partisan political activities. The supervisor indicated her views were not widely shared within the office. At that, Myers went home and prepared a questionnaire that she circulated to other employees. Her supervisor summoned Myers who was summarily dismissed. The district court awarded damages on grounds that there was no question that she had been fired because of her First Amendment protected speech and there was no showing of significant impairment of organizational operations as defined by previous case law that justified the termination.[39]

The Supreme Court reversed, finding that Myers had not adequately demonstrated the public significance of her speech. In so doing, the court added a new requirement to the existing burden an employee must carry in defending his or her speech against reprisal. It was not, however, merely the court's change of this test regarding when an employee can be disciplined that made the case so important, but it was also Justice White's insistence upon deference to management discretion in such matters.

> When employee expression cannot fairly be considered as relating to any matter of political, social, or other concern of the community, government officials should enjoy wide latitude in managing their officers, without intrusive oversight by the judiciary in the name of the First Amendment. Perhaps the government employer's dismissal of the worker may not be fair, but ordinary dismissals from government service which violate no fixed tenure or applicable statute or regulation are not subject to judicial review even if the reasons for the dismissal are alleged to be mistaken or unreasonable.[40]
>
> We hold that where a public employee speaks not as a citizen, upon matters of public concern, but instead as an employee upon matters only of personal interest, absent the most

unusual circumstances, a federal court is not the appropriate forum in which to review the wisdom of a personnel decision taken by a public agency allegedly in reaction to the employee's behavior. . . .

When close working relationships are essential to fulfilling public responsibilities, a wide degree of deference to employers' judgment is appropriate. Furthermore, we do not see the necessity for an employer to allow events to unfold to the extent that the disruption of the office and the destruction of working relationships is manifest before taking action.[41]

The court's language in *Connick* coupled with its cautions against extensive judicially imposed due process requirements indicates a significant shift toward deference to administrative interests.

5. The Supreme Court has consistently issued rulings that make it easier to bring suit in federal court. It is true that in the late 1960s and early 1970s the Warren court relaxed the rules governing who could bring a suit in federal court permitting a wider range of litigation. However, the Burger court has issued a string of decisions placing significant limits on standing to sue and other procedural standards governing access to federal courts.[42] In fact, it is in the area of court access rules that the Burger court has made some of the most dramatic changes from the Warren court precedents.

The Burger court has sent other signals indicating that groups interested in changing policy should look to arenas other than the federal courts. . . . For several reasons, then, it simply is not true that the trend of the Warren court years to open the doors of the federal courthouse to more lawsuits has been continued by the current court.

6. Federal courts are constantly expanding the threat to administrators from tort liability judgments. The controversy surrounding the vulnerability of officials and units of government to damage claims is considered elsewhere in this symposium [in *Public Administration Review,* special edition 1985]. But since administrators' frustration and anxiety about tort lawsuits is an important part of the conflict between judges and managers, some caveats are worthy of brief mention here.

First, while the Supreme Court has permitted more types of suits for damages over the past decade, it has brought about a kind of trade-off for administrators. At the same time that it has been allowing a wider range of damage suits, it has been limiting broad remedial orders that interfere with ongoing administration.[45] The message to lower courts is to limit interference with current administrative operations, but to let claimants come into court after the fact and collect damages if they can make their case.

Second, recent liability rulings are not unrestricted invitations to sue public officials. Even in the decisions expanding the range of possible damage claims, the Supreme Court has created a series of immunities making it relatively difficult for a plaintiff to win a case.[46] More recently, the court has recognized that its official liability decisions have placed added burdens upon public administrators discouraging initiative and producing time-consuming and costly litigation.[47] In *Harlow v. Fitzgerald,* the court expanded the standard immunity afforded public officials in federal tort suits and instructed judges to guard against unnecessary pretrial discovery and other burdensome procedures.[48]

In sum, the rules and judicial trends affecting the judicial-administrative relationship are not part of a continuing judicial assault on public administration. In a variety of areas the federal courts have demonstrated a sensitivity to the problems administrators must face. That does not mean that they have been willing to serve as rubber stamps for administrative action, but it does give lie to some of the more extreme charges that the courts are about the business of undermining administrators.

Administrative Deregulation and Refusal to Act: A Developing Judicial-Administrative Tension

In one area an increase has recently occurred in judicial-administrative tension. Historically, legal challenges to administrators have primarily concerned efforts to limit overzealous use of administrative discretion. In the administrative environment of the late 1970s and the 1980s, however, attention has shifted to situations in which administrators either refuse to act at all or withdraw from previously developed policies. Although the need to compel administrative action as well as guard against excessive administrative zeal is rarely discussed these days, it is an important issue that was stated by Carl Friedrich more than forty years ago.

> Too often it is taken for granted that as long as we can keep government from doing wrong we have made it responsible. What is more important is to insure effective action of any sort. . . . An official should be as responsible for inaction as for wrong action; certainly the average voter will criticize the government as severely for one as for the other.[49]

The efforts of the Carter and Reagan administrations to deregulate and generally move administrative agencies to less proactive approaches to their work have been the focal point of controversy. It is important in any discussion of administration and law to consider not only limits on the discretion to act but also the legal forces compelling the exercise of discretion. The cases calling for mandatory use of administrative authority have been basically of four types: (1) those objecting to an administrative refusal to launch a fact-finding or policy-making process; (2) agency refusal to issue rules; (3) intentional delay in agency action; and (4) rescission of existing or proposed policies.

Controlling the agency agenda is an important element of administrative discretion. Deciding what problems to address and assigning priorities is often more than a question of efficient management. It may involve a strategic decision. Administrators would frankly prefer to avoid some problems. . . .

While the court will not dictate the outcome or the particular administrative process to be employed, the simple assertion of absolute discretion will be challenged.

Another problem area is the refusal to make rules. The Eighth Circuit Court of Appeals, recently found that the secretary of agriculture had abused his discretion by refusing to issue rules under a statute governing farm loan foreclosure. A family charged that the Department of Agriculture had an obligation under the statute to promulgate rules and provide adequate notice to those affected concerning possible deferments of foreclosures. The government argued that the statute "merely created an additional power to be wielded at the discretion of the agency, or placed in the Secretary's back pocket for safekeeping."[51] The court found the refusal to make rules or institute any kind of process of reasoned decision making a "complete abdication" of responsibility.[52]

In some ways related to the refusal to make rules is the tactic of delaying for as long as possible the issuance of rules required by statute. Here again, courts seem willing to draw a line. Efforts by the Environmental Protection Agency (EPA) to delay implementation of rules required by the Resource Conservation and Recovery Act covering toxic wastes were successfully challenged in a number of lawsuits. Among the remedies sought by the plaintiffs in one of the cases was an award of attorney's fees under the Equal Access to Justice Act. The court awarded the fee finding that the intentional delaying tactics employed by the agency were "exactly the type of arbitrary governmental behavior that the EAJA was designed to deter."[53]

Finally, a number of challenges have been brought against efforts of administrators to deregulate by rescinding existing agency regulations or withdrawing pending rules. The Federal Communications Commission (FCC) efforts to reduce its regulatory control over broadcasting have prompted several such lawsuits. Another recent example is the withdrawal of mandatory automobile passive restraint rules by the Department of Transportation. In both cases, administrators claimed that the decision to reduce regulation administratively was not really policy making and was a purely discretionary matter not subject to judicial examination. The courts rejected that claim in both cases and insisted that a change in policy is a policy decision whether it results in promulgation of a new rule or abandonment of an old one. In fact, a panel of the D.C. Circuit Court of Appeals said, "such abrupt shifts in policy do constitute 'danger signals' that the Commission may be acting inconsistently with its statutory mandate. . . . We will require therefore that the Commission provide a reasoned analysis indicating that prior policies and standards are being deliberately changed, not casually ignored."[54] Having said that, however, the court upheld the FCC deregulation. It cautioned the commission that it was perilously close to violating its statutory responsibility but found enough evidence to say the FCC had met its requirements of reasoned analysis.

The Supreme Court did not find the necessary foundation for the rescission of the passive restraint rule and remanded the matter to the agency. It concluded that an "agency changing its course by rescinding a rule is obligated to supply a reasoned analysis for the change beyond that which may be required when the agency does not act in the first instance."[55] Since a rule was presumably adopted in the first instance on the basis of a careful reasoning process using the agency's expertise and available evidence, there is a presumption in favor of the rule. The court concluded:

> In so holding, we fully recognize that 'regulatory agencies do not establish rules of conduct to last forever, . . . and that an agency must be given latitude to adapt their rules and policies to the demands of changing circumstances. . . .' But the forces of change do not always or necessarily point in the direction of deregulation. In the abstract, there is no more reason to presume that changing circumstances require the rescission of prior action, instead of a

revision in or even the extension of current regulation. If Congress established a presumption from which judicial review should start, that presumption—contrary to petitioner's view—is not *against* safety regulation, but *against* changes in current policy that are not justified by the rulemaking record. (Emphasis in original.)

There is one final problem of what might be termed negative discretion. Administrators often argue that judges should defer to their administrative expertise regardless of the type of policy under consideration. However, judges sometimes doubt that administrators are entitled to such deference when there does not appear to be a policy at all but rather a failure to make any policy or to enforce existing standards. Justice Brennan, for instance, observed that while judges ought to defer to the expertise of correctional administrators, the prison conditions frequently in dispute often arise not from a policy decision based upon administrative expertise but from sheer neglect. "There is no reason of comity, judicial restraint, or recognition of expertise for courts to defer to negligent omissions of officials who lack the resources or motivation to operate prisons within the limits of decency."[57]

In sum, administrators may not assume absolute administrative discretion when they refuse to act as compared to cases where they are alleged to have acted too vigorously. The problem of relating administrative discretion and judicial obligations to ensure accountability is all the more difficult when there is no policy for a given action but an actual departure from stated policy or simple neglect. This concept of negative discretion is an aspect of the judicial-administrative relationship that is very much a developing matter and worthy of attention.

Law as a Discretion-Reinforcing Agent

There are and always will be natural tensions between administrators and judges over the nature and boundaries of administrative authority. Yet there is a simultaneous positive aspect to this law-administration relationship. It is worthwhile to assess the reasons administrators ought to attempt to foster better working relations with judges, notwithstanding the difficulties such a prescription entails.

Knowledge of the legal elements of administration is an enabling force. Formal authority of administrators is derived from a statute or executive order. Care in using such authority supports effective administration. There is an admittedly rough but useful analogy to the budget process. An agency without adequate fiscal resources is in serious trouble. The amount of funds available is a significant factor in the agency's ability to perform. It is both an enabling force and, in a sense, a constraint. The fact that budgetary politics are complex and often disappointing does not indicate that a good manager ought to abandon concern for the subject or cease efforts to improve relationships with appropriations committees. The same is true of law and administration.

An understanding of legal developments is also important as a defensive matter. It can help to avoid liability judgments, prevent the loss of invested time and effort when agency decisions are reversed, avoid loss of control over one's agency to a complex remedial court order, and lead to savings of money as well as time from having to replicate and improve work rejected in judicial review.

Two other key functions are served by enhancing the relationship between administrators and judges. Understanding the relationship provides increased predictability which is critical to any manager. The first task is to understand judicial trends sufficiently to anticipate likely judicial responses to agency actions. An awareness of legal limits on administration provides an ability to predict not only what courts will do with respect to one's own but also to other agencies. Administrators thus informed can manage their operations with some expectation of how other agencies will be able to respond. Administration without attention to law would not mean more efficiency, it would mean chaos.

Finally, administrators need legal support for their claim to legitimacy within government and, perhaps more importantly, within the larger society. There is a certain irony in the fact that administrators busy challenging the legitimacy of judicial involvement in policy making are in danger of being convicted by their own arguments. Many of the charges made against judges can be made in only slightly modified form against administrators. They are not elected. Many cannot be removed from office except for cause. It is extremely difficult to keep them responsive and responsible. They frequently do precisely what the majority of the people do not wish them to do. The list goes on. Beyond that particular threat to legitimacy, however, is the need for assistance in establishing a legitimate place for administrators in the constitutional framework. Our constitutional authority is derivative. We obtain our authority by inference and indirectly.[60] We must always be able to trace our authority back through the chain of statutes and judicial rulings that support us.

Conclusion

This article has assessed common assumptions about the evolving relationship between federal courts and administrators. It has provided evidence that despite the natural tensions between administrators and judges, it is an overstatement to charge that federal judges neither understand nor care about the harm their rulings may cause to management. In fact, legal authorities and opinions, if properly understood, are enabling and protecting forces providing sources of administrative discretion and protecting its use.

Moreover, the federal judiciary, led by the Supreme Court, has in several respects drawn back from intervention in administration in open recognition of the need for managerial flexibility. That good reasons exist for not applauding some of those deferential rulings does not change the fact that they do support more discretion. One rapidly developing area of judicial administrative challenge is likely to remain of importance in the near term at least: the refusal of administrators to use the discretion that they possess.

Good reasons exist for administrators to develop their relationship with courts, reasons of an extremely practical nature and others of wider import, including the need to have law as a support for the legitimacy of public administration. In the final analysis, administrative discretion does not exist for its own sake. Administrators are vested with particular authority to serve public purposes in a society predicated on a rule of law. Natural tension, yes, but necessary as well.

Notes

1. Victor Thompson, *Bureaucracy and the Modern World.* (Morristown, NJ: General Learning Press, 1976), p. 10.

2. 5 U.S.C. §706.

3. See Robert K. Merton, "Bureaucratic Structure and Personality," in Robert K. Merton et al., eds., *Reader in Bureaucracy* (New York: Free Press, 1952).

4. *United States* v. *Lee,* 106 U.S. 196, 220 (1882).

5. It is, of course, understood that many are administrators as a second profession and that a substantial proportion of those managers have not received advanced training in public administration. See Frederick Mosher, *Democracy and the Public Service* (New York: Oxford University Press, 1984).
. . .

7. Phillip J. Cooper, *Public Law and Public Administration* (Palo Alto, CA: Mayfield, 1983), pp. 217–219.

8. Abraham Sofaer, "Judicial Control of Informal Discretionary Adjudication and Enforcement," *Columbia Law Review* 72 (1972): 1374.

9. Ibid., pp. 1301–1302.

10. *Mathews v. Eldridge,* 424 U.S. 319 (1976).

11. Ibid., p. 335.

12. Evidence for this is provided in my study on administrative due process since *Goldberg v. Kelly,* which was reported in "Due Process, the Burger Court, and Public Administration," *Southern Review of Public Administration* 6 (Spring 1982): 65–98.

13. See, for example, *Parham v. J.R.,* 422 U.S. 584 (1979); *Bishop v. Wood,* 426 U.S. 341 (1976); *Paul v. Davis,* 424 U.S. 693 (1976); *Board of Curators v. Horowitz,* 435 U.S. 78 (1978); and *Ingraham v. Wright,* 430 U.S. 651 (1977). The court has spoken of the *Eldridge* balancing formula as "the familiar test prescribed in *Mathews v. Eldridge.*" *Schweiker v. McClure,* 72 L.Ed.2d 1, 9–10 (1982).

14. One federal district judge put it this way: "Subject to constitutional limitations, Arkansas is a sovereign State. It has a right to make and enforce criminal laws, to imprison persons convicted of serious crimes, and to maintain order and discipline in its prisons. This Court has no intention of entering a decree herein that will disrupt the Penitentiary or leave Respondent and his subordinates helpless to deal with dangerous and unruly convicts.

"The Court has recognized heretofore the financial handicaps under which the Penitentiary system is laboring, and the Court knows that Respondent cannot make bricks without straw." *Holt v. Sarver,* 300 F. Supp. 825, 833 (E.D. Ark. 1969). See also Ralph Cavanagh and Austin Sarat, "Thinking About Courts: Toward and Beyond a Jurisprudence of Judicial Competence," *Law & Society Review* 14 (Winter 1980): 408.
. . .

18. See, generally, *Bradley v. Milliken,* 345 F. Supp. 914 (E.D. Mich. 1972).

19. *Wyatt v. Stickney,* 334 F. Supp. 1341, 1344 (M.D. Ala. 1971).

20. *Vermont Yankee Nuclear Power Corp. v. U.S. Nuclear Regulatory Commission,* 435 U.S. 519 (1978).

21. See, for example, *Federal Communications Commission v. WNCN Listeners Guild,* 450 U.S. 582 (1981), and *Office of Communications of the United Church of Christ v. FCC,* 707 F.2d 1413 (D.C. Cir. 1983).
. . .

22. See, for example, *Industrial Union Dept, AFL-CIO v. American Petroleum Institute,* 448 U.S. 607 (1980) and *American Textile Manufacturers Institute v. Donovan,* 452 U.S. 490 (1981).
. . .

28. *Parham,* 422 U.S. at 608, n. 16. This case involved commitment of juveniles to state mental hospitals.

29. *Rhodes v. Chapman,* 452 U.S. 337, 352 (1981), a case challenging conditions at Ohio's principal maximum security prison. See also, *Bell v. Wolfish,* 441 U.S. 520, 539 (1979).

30. Stephen L. Wasby, "Arrogation of Power or Accountability: 'Judicial Imperialism Revisited,'" *Judicature,* vol. 65 (October 1981), p. 213. See also, Stonewall B. Stickney, "Problems in Implementing the Right to Treatment in Alabama: The Wyatt v. Stickney Case," *Hospital & Community Psychiatry* 25 (1974): 454–455.

31. See, for example, *San Antonio Independent School District v. Rodriquez,* 411 U.S. I (1973); *Washington v. Davis,* 426 U.S. 229 (1976); *Personnel Administrator v. Feeney,* 442 U.S. 256 (1979); *Rizzo v. Goode,* 423 U.S. 362 (1976); and *Rhodes v. Chapman,* 452 U.S. 337, 352 (1981).

32. See, for example, *Milliken v. Bradley,* 418 U.S. 717 (1974); *Dayton Bd. of Ed. v. Brinkman,* 433 U.S. 406 (1977); *Columbus Bd. of Ed. v. Penick,* 443 U.S. 449 (1979); *Dayton Bd. of Ed. v. Brinkman,* 443 U.S. 526 (1979); and *Firefighters Local Union No. 1784 v. Stotts,* 81 L.Ed.2d 483 (1984).

33. *Pasadena Bd. of Education v. Spangler,* 427 U.S. 424 (1976).

34. Indeed one purpose of the Civil Service Reform Act of 1978 was to assemble and clarify the various statutory protections for civil servants provided by, among others, the Civil Rights Act of 1964 as amended, the Age Discrimination in Employment Act of 1967, the Fair Labor Standards Act, and the Rehabilitation Act of 1973. 5 U.S.c. §2302(b) (1978).

35. *Bishop,* 426 U.S. 341, and *Paul,* 424 U.S. 693.

36. *Arnett v. Kennedy,* 416 U.S. 134 (1974).

37. Consider the shift from *Pickering v. Bd. of Education,* 391 U.S. 563 (1968), to *Mt. Healthy Bd. of Ed. v. Doyle,* 429 U.S. 274 (1977), to *Givhan v. Western Line Consolidated School Dist.,* 439 U.S. 410 (1979).

38. *Connick v. Myers,* 75 L.Ed.2d 708 (1983).

39. *Myers v. Connick,* 507 F. Supp. 752 (ED La. 1981), aff'd 654 F.2d 719 (5th Cir. 1981).

40. *Connick,* 75 L.Ed.2d at 719–720.

41. Ibid.

42. See *Allen v. Wright,* 82 L.Ed.2d 556 (1984); *Valley Forge Christian College v. Americans United for Separation of Church and State,* 454 U.S. 464 (1982); *Duke Power Co. v. Carolina Environmental Study Group,* 438 U.S. 59 (1978); *Simon v. Eastern Kentucky Welfare Rights Organization,* 426 U.S. 26 (1976); and *Warth v. Seldin,* 422 U.S. 490 (1975).

. . .

45. See, *Rizzo,* 423 U.S. 362. See also, David Rosenbloom, "Public Administrators' Official Immunity: Developments During the Seventies," *Public Administration Review* 40 (1980): 166–173.

46. See, for example, *Butz v. Economou,* 438 U.S. 478 (1978).

47. 457 U.S. 800 (1982).

48. Ibid., pp. 817–818.

49. Carl Friedrich, "Public Policy and the Nature of Administrative Responsibility," in Carl Friedrich and E.S. Mason, eds., *Public Policy,* p. 4. (Cambridge, MA: Harvard University Press, 1940).

. . .

51. *Allison v. Block,* 723 F.2d 631, 633 (8th Cir. 1983).

52. Ibid., p. 638.

53. *Environmental Defense Fund v. EPA,* 716 F.2d 915, 921 (D.C. Cir. 1983). The other key case compelling production of rules was *Illinois v. Gorsuch,* 530 F. Supp. 340 (D.D. Cir. 1981).

54. *Office of Communications of the United Church of Christ,* 707 F.2d at 1425.

55. *Motor Vehicle Manufacturers' Assn. v. State Farm Mutual,* 77 L.Ed.2d 443, 457 (1983).

. . .

57. *Rhodes,* 452 U.S. at 362 (Brennan, J., concurring in part, dissenting in part).

. . .

60. I am indebted for this idea, if not these precise words, to John Rohr.

PART III

GOVERNMENT OPERATIONS AND ADMINISTRATIVE LAW

How government operations and activities are carried out by public administrators is a matter of wide concern. It is often debated in politics, in newspapers, and through court cases. In law, challenges in this area are categorized as administrative law or constitutional law concerns. Public administrators must carry out legislative responsibilities within the agenda of executive policies and missions. Thus, the activities of public administrators may include the challenges of conflicting responsibilities, balancing limited resources, addressing individual stakeholder concerns, and promoting the general public welfare. This section begins with a discussion of the development of administrative law, and then introduces issues and chapters regarding the three major categories of administrative law: rulemaking practices, adjudication processes, and providing public information provisions.

Around 1900 the term "administrative law" was defined broadly: it often included public management, government operations, and administrative practices. The current common definition of administrative law is narrowly viewed as the federal Administrative Procedure Act (APA) and cases arising under it. This historical difference in definitions also reflects, to some degree, changes in perspectives among public administrators and lawyers. Administrative law now concerns legal challenges to administrative action and tends to focus on three types of issues: whether administrative adjudicative actions meet the requirements of the APA; whether the development of a rule is consistent with the APA procedures and the authorizing statute; and whether an administrative action violates a constitutional principle. Most analyses of the APA begin within the legal framework. However, there are many aspects of administrative practices that are not addressed in court decisions or scholarship on administrative law. The chapters in this section consider government operations and the administrators' perspective.

Doing public administration so that practice matches standards of constitutionality would be impossible without principles and guidelines. Providing these guidelines is a primary purpose of administrative law. As Rosenbloom explained in Chapter 5, the development of the modern administrative state included public debates about structure, responsibilities, activities, and checks and balances of the bureaucracy when it developed binding rules and made enforcement decisions. Whether unelected public officials could hold this broad range of authority and powers was widely debated. A series of cases raising these issues of both constitutional law and administrative law came before the Supreme Court in the 1920s and 1930s, giving rise to precedent and guidance about the extent of the administrative state. Another result of the debate was the development of the U.S. Administrative Procedure Act of 1946.

The federal APA provides principles and enforceable statutory requirements for the practice of public administration in making regulations, granting licenses, holding hearings for enforcement, and providing information about government activities and decisions to the public. The APA has been amended and expanded numerous times since 1946 to require public information through open public meetings (often called Sunshine law provisions) and access to government information through the Freedom of Information Act. Several other sections have been added to the APA, including privacy provisions, open advisory committee meetings, congressional review of rulemaking, administrative dispute resolution authority, and regulatory negotiation processes. Many states have similar statutes, and although these state APAs are less frequently studied, many of the concerns of governmental operations and the federal APA apply to other levels of government.

The promise of the APA to the public, for all levels of government, is accessibility, accountability, and fairness in governance. In cases challenging government administration, the courts often address the concern of using legal and consistent procedures for both fairness to the public and for administrative reasons of consistency, accountability, and efficiency. Congress specified the standard for judicial review in the APA. The language of the act in Section 706 states courts can review and set aside agency actions—including rulemaking and adjudications—if they are "arbitrary, capricious, an abuse of discretion, or otherwise not in accordance with law." Thus in reviewing administrative decisions and actions, courts seek support for the agency's actions first in legislative grants of authority, and then examine the records of the actions to see if agencies based their decisions on information and evidence and then explained how they reached their decisions. Although there are differences, the preferred judicial remedy under the APA is to remand decisions that courts find lacking back to the agencies. In addition, courts also consider whether agency actions are consistent with constitutional law. In the discussions of courts and administration, Chapters 8, 9, and 10 addressed some of these judicial review concerns.

Although this introduction can only summarize the focus of administrative law, there are many books and articles that analyze this area of law. A general discussion of administrative law provides a conceptual framework, but the particular practices and requirements of administrative law differ from agency to agency, based on the tasks the agency does and on specific legislative mandates and court decisions. The purpose of the APA is the same for all government agencies: government must provide fair and consistent proceedings.

The APA is divided into three major categories: rulemaking, adjudication, and providing public information. The APA specifies processes and procedures to develop rules and regulations. This is called quasi-legislative authority. The APA provides procedures to develop rules—called legislative rules—that are binding on private activity. The source for the particular topic or substance contained within the rule comes from enabling statutes or other congressional action. The vast majority of legislative rules are "informal rules," which are developed through a notice and comment process. Under the APA, the required steps includes: providing advance and adequate notice of a proposed rulemaking process, issuing a proposed rule, seeking public comment on the rule, and publishing the final rule. When an agency publishes the final rule it must discuss the public comments, but it is not compelled to act on the comments. In formal rulemaking situations such as setting rates, an agency must follow procedures that include holding an evidentiary hearing. Formal rulemaking is less common than informal rulemaking.

An informal or formal government rule can be challenged in court before it goes into effect, and this frequently occurs. Critiques of formal and informal rulemaking raise a variety of issues, including bureaucratic and political processes, types of public input, regulatory capture, time frames, information needed, and the expense and delay from litigation. When the provisions of the APA are viewed from the administrative perspective, different issues arise. One primary public management concern is developing rules consistent with congressional statutory authority and intent. Another primary concern is developing rules consistent with presidential policy initiatives; furthermore there are a number of Executive Orders that impose internal checks and review of rules. Thus, rulemaking involves administrators acting in a political environment. In Chapter 11, William West details the political difficulties faced by the FTC when it decided to develop more consumer-oriented procedures and switch from an adjudicative model to a rulemaking model.

The second major type of administrative function addressed in the APA is administrative adjudication, a type of administrative power also called quasi-judicial authority. Congress recognizes that administrators hold special expertise, but that there should be some type of consistent and fair procedures used in government operations in this area. Thus the APA set forth administrative adjudication provisions. Furthermore, many court decisions expanded the settings where administrative adjudication under the APA is required. Thus, administrative adjudication under the APA is required when administrators enforce laws and regulations, grant or terminate licenses, grant or end public benefits, or when government actions may involve takings under the Fifth or Fourteenth Amendments.

An early concern was whether the adjudicatory powers sections of the APA provided for objective hearing officers in order to avoid conflicts of interest that might favor the government. Court cases found the statutory structure sufficient to avoid conflicts. Another set of issues regarding agency adjudication concerned a possible violation of the constitutional separation of powers which in U.S. Constitution Article III established the Supreme Court. When this issue was addressed by the Supreme Court, it found administrative adjudications are authorized under Article I of the U.S. Constitution, which granted Congress the power to establish specialized courts. In response to these two preliminary and essential questions about administrative hearings, courts have found administrative adjudications permissible as long as they do not violate constitutional protections and the agencies in question follow the statutory procedures.

In general, court decisions regard the process of administrative hearings to be very important. Courts are particularly vigilant when reviewing due process challenges to administrative practices and hearings. In reviewing administrative due process, the courts evaluate individual's due process rights regarding factors such as what is appropriate notice, what type of hearing is needed, and when a hearing must be held. Often these protections for individuals may be balanced with considerations of whether additional administrative practices would provide better protections for individuals.

The due process procedures required in a particular administrative adjudication differ based on factors such as the type of governmental actor, the type of interest at issue, and the type of action the agency is seeking. Thus, the standards for a hearing to remove an individual's eligibility for Social Security benefits, suspend students from public school, terminate a government employee, or seek penalties for environmental violations are different in the particulars. Questions of what are appropriate hearing processes have been raised in many court decisions. Yet, court review of an agency's hearing for one claimant focuses on the effect on the individual and not on the similarity of process between government agencies. In developing procedures, agencies must look to what is fair for the class of affected individuals. Many of the requirements of a trial apply to hearings, yet this is an area where different types of agency actions may require different procedures. Knowing the applicable specific court rulings requires staying current with court decisions and with legal advice developed for the particular agency's actions and responsibilities.

Although administrative adjudication may allow for due process for one group, other groups that are affected by agency actions may not be entitled to a hearing, a concern raised in Chapter 12. In this chapter, Barbara S. Grumet considers a conflict between precedent, due process, and statutory responsibilities. Administrators developed rules to enforce standards for contractual nursing home service providers and sought to decertify non-performing providers. When individual clients of the nursing homes challenged the decertification, the court held those clients did not have a property interest or a due process right to challenge the decertification process. The result—nursing homes losing federal status—presented hardships for those individuals that the regulatory scheme intended to protect, but these beneficiaries could not seek court review of the agency's decisions. Although Grumet's article is from 1982 and the particulars of law may have changed, her study indicates the compelling administrative choices and the limits of judicial review. It also demonstrates how differing groups are affected by legislation, litigation, and administrative practices.

Public participation is one issue in the process of making administrative rules and policies. One way governments limit or control activities is through licensing. In granting licenses federal agencies must comply with the adjudicatory process provisions of the APA. Licensing decisions are also common administrative procedures for state and local governments. The types of hearing practices and public involvement in licensing differ from hearings that affect an individual. These concerns are raised in Chapter 13, where Judy B. Rosener describes the process California required for making land use decisions that affected the coastal environment. Rosener also documents a number of political aspects of licensing, beginning with how California implemented citizen participation processes as a result of a referendum to establish the statute. Rosener considers the relationship between the commissioners, the administrative staff, and public partici-pation on contested permit applications. In her quantitative analysis of hearing deci-sions, Rosener tests the influence of staff expertise and citizen presence on the results of these administrative hearings.

The need for democratic accountability and public information about policies and administrative actions is addressed in the APA through a high standard of openness in administrative proceedings, and through statutory tools such as the Freedom of Informa-tion Act (FOIA) and Sunshine laws. The information provisions in the APA are a source for public accountability and access but at the same time they are sources of administra-tive tensions and expenses. This accountability and transparency under FOIA may come at a high administrative cost, as Lotte E. Feinberg notes in her analysis in Chapter 14. Since the publication of Feinberg's analysis of FOIA in 1986, there have been dramatic changes in information technology and government information access. In 1996, major amendments were enacted; these are known as the Electronic Freedom of Information Act or E-FOIA. With this change, information policy shifted toward internet access and electronic archives of documents. However, many of Feinberg's concerns continue in the electronic age.

Government operations are held in check by the application of administrative law and constitutional challenges. Administrative law operates within the limits set by legisla-tive bodies. Often two concerns are raised in administrative law: the processes by which legislative and binding rules are made, and the use of arbitrary administrative proce-dures. The chapters in this section suggest that when legislative bodies introduce politi-cal agendas into administrative practices that ultimately impact adjudicatory procedures, the outcome of the application of administrative and constitutional protections may be radically different than would occur if only the APA or traditional analysis were used. One can only conclude that the checks created by the Administrative Procedures Act pose practical questions for public administration practices that are often evaluated by the courts.

CHAPTER 11

THE POLITICS OF ADMINISTRATIVE RULEMAKING

WILLIAM WEST

Despite growing concern with statutory implementation, political scientists have shown a notable lack of interest in administrative processes—the formal means or tools by which agencies carry out their mandates. Students of administrative law have, of course, written extensively in this area, but have focused mainly on considerations of "good administration" rather than on the politics of procedural choice. A premise here is that, because administrative processes often have substantive implications, they may also be of strategic importance to those affected by agency policies. Thus, their use may be influenced by and may subsequently affect an agency's relationship with its "political environment."

The following study examines rulemaking by the Federal Trade Commission in the area of consumer protection. Critics of the FTC long advocated that the agency rely on rulemaking as an administratively superior alternative to case-by-case adjudication. Ironically, however, the commission's emphasis on rulemaking in recent years has proved largely unsuccessful, and has brought the agency into disfavor. The FTC's experience and other available evidence suggest several generalizations concerning the political determinants and effects of rulemaking.

Introduction

Rulemaking is the exercise of legislative authority that has been delegated from Congress to an agency. Rules interpret and elaborate on more general goals expressed by the legislature, have only future effect, and are usually legally binding.[1] The obvious function of rulemaking from an administrative perspective is to guide the application of policy in individual situations. In turn, application decisions can take a wide variety of forms, but in regulatory areas legally binding determinations with regard to named individuals are usually reached through adjudication, a trial-like process in which decisions must be based on the facts of the case at hand. Rulemaking is often optional, and can be viewed

From *Public Administration Review* 42, no. 5 (September/October 1982): 420–426. Copyright © 1982 by American Society for Public Administration. Reprinted with permission.

as an alternative to the exercise of discretion through adjudication or other means of case-by-case decision making.

Rulemaking has received considerable attention as an alternative means of implementing statutes. It has frequently been endorsed because of its alleged fairness to affected interests, and its expedience and rationality as a means of developing policy.[2] A few have attacked these claims, arguing that adjudication is preferable to rulemaking in some regulatory contexts, or that substantive differences between the two processes have been oversold.[3] While there is a large (if inconclusive) literature dealing with rulemaking from an "administrative" perspective, scholars have paid little attention to its "political" implications. There has been scant speculation and a near absence of empirical work that bears on the significance of rulemaking in terms of an agency's relationship with its political environment.[4] The perspective here is from the agency, looking outward toward those external actors interested in its operations and able to render support or bring about sanctions.

In the case of the Federal Trade Commission, the politics of rulemaking has stemmed from but has taken precedence over administrative considerations. Trade Regulation Rules (TRRs) have been a potentially more forceful means than adjudication for the FTC to regulate industry; consequently, the use of rulemaking has been of great interest to consumer and business groups, and their supporters in government. The shifting balance of forces in the agency's environment has proved dominant in determining its use of rulemaking over the past twenty years. Also, the repercussions of the commission's emphasis on TRRs illustrate the political difficulties posed by rulemaking within a conflictual environment, and help explain the frequently criticized tendency of regulatory agencies to implement statutes on a case-by-case basis.

Rulemaking in the Federal Trade Commission

The two primary missions of the FTC are antitrust enforcement and consumer protection. The commission has issued rules to prevent "unfair or deceptive practices" in furtherance of both these ends, although consumer protection has been by far the more commonly stated basis for rulemaking. With one exception, the FTC has not issued rules as a means of antitrust enforcement in areas other than deception, such as illegal mergers and anti-competitive pricing.

The Commission's Adoption of Rulemaking Authority

The FTC did not begin issuing Trade Regulation Rules (TRRs) until 1962. Prior to that time, it had relied primarily on adjudication in attempting to protect consumers and industry from deception in the market place. Under adjudication the FTC would bring suit against an individual whom it felt was guilty of an unfair or deceptive practice. Formal, trial-like hearings would be held for the purposes of determining (1) whether or not the party in question did, indeed, engage in the alleged practice, and (2) whether or not the practice was unfair or deceptive. The commission also employed a variety of informal devices in attempting to prevent deception, including consent orders, advisory opinions, and Guides.[5]

The FTC's decision to begin issuing rules was controversial, since it was based on what the agency construed as an implicit grant of authority in its enabling legislation (the FTC Act of 1914). Critics argued that rulemaking authority must be explicitly delegated from Congress to an agency. In addition, they cited evidence from the FTC Act's legislative history indicating that at least some members of Congress specifically did not want the commission to issue rules.[6] The full controversiality of the FTC's assumption of authority to issue rules is perhaps best illustrated by the fact that its rulemaking was subsequently declared illegal by the courts on two occasions, but eventually vindicated upon appeal.

It is understandable, then, that the commission came to its decision with great difficulty. This is evidenced by the fact that the agency's foremost proponents of rulemaking vacillated in their public statements regarding the legality of substantive TRRs. For instance, FTC Commissioner Everette MacIntyre stated in 1961 that the commission was empowered to issue rules having the force and effect of law. Later, however, he retreated, stating before the Miami–Dade Chamber of Commerce that a TRR would establish only a *prima facie* case, and that a respondent could show that a rule should not be regarded as legally binding during an adjudication.[7] Likewise, FTC Chairman Paul Rand Dixon stated that rules that had the "force and effect of law" were authorized by the FTC Act, but later said that the commission had no intention of issuing substantive rules, and that TRRs "would not be law in any sense."[8]

Given the thorny nature of the issue, what explains the FTC's adoption of rulemaking? The most obvious explanation is simply that, in several respects, rulemaking represented a more expedient way for the agency to pursue its regulatory goals. The commission was becoming increasingly frustrated with adjudication as its only legally binding enforcement tool. Often deceptive practices would be widespread throughout an industry, yet the FTC could attack only one violator at a time. Others engaged in the same or similar practices could go on doing so until the commission moved against them. Thus, it might take years to police an entire industry.[9]

A related shortcoming of adjudication was that it had limited substantive scope, since the commission could only proscribe those specific actions named in a suit. Restricted only by their imaginations, businesses were free to adopt new deceptive practices that were often similar to and had substantially the same effects as the old. As a leading student of the FTC has observed, " . . . firms can and do change their advertising messages with great frequency. By the time a complaint—or even an application for a preliminary injunction—is entered, the firm has abandoned the questionable claims and made many others."[10]

The commission saw in rulemaking a much more positive policy-making tool for some areas. TRRs would be general statements of policy that would apply to entire industries or all of commerce, and that could be expressed in such a way as to preclude future inventiveness. Once promulgated they could be used as bases for adjudicatory actions against parties who violated their terms. An essential advantage of rulemaking was that, in an enforcement proceeding, the commission would be burdened only with proving that the accused had engaged in an act that violated a TRR, and not that the act itself was unfair or deceptive. This would not only make adjudicatory proceedings easier, but would, hopefully, deter industry members from "testing" the commission.

The "administrative" consideration of effectiveness, thus, does much to account for the FTC's assumption of rulemaking authority. It is not, however, a complete or fully sufficient explanation. Agency people, as well as other government influentials and scholars, had been aware of the potential advantages of FTC rulemaking for years. For example, the Brownlow Commission had advocated that the FTC issue rules as early as 1937. Yet, despite the apparent utility of rulemaking, the agency waited almost half a century to issue its first TRR.

The controlling explanation for the adoption of rulemaking is that the balance of forces within the commission's political environment shifted, giving the agency sufficient support to take actions that might alienate industry. Consumerism began to "take off" in the late 1950s and early 1960s, and as one of the major consumer-protection agencies, the FTC was encouraged from a number of quarters to strike a more aggressive posture.

Such support had begun to filter through Congress by the late 1950s. In 1957, for example, the House Interstate and Foreign Commerce Committee established a subcommittee that looked into the performance of the independent commissions. According to Congressman John Moss, who served on the subcommittee from 1958–68, the FTC was subject to a good deal of "adverse comment" for its lack of diligence in the consumer protection area. None of the subcommittee's reports explicitly recommended rulemaking. It is safe to assume, however, that a good deal of informal encouragement was given to the commission. As Moss stated in regard to rulemaking: the subcommittee " . . . invited the commission to stop being so timid and to go out and undertake to test the full reach of its powers . . . and to let the courts tell them they had exceeded it (sic), rather than attempting beforehand to tightly circumscribe their own authority." He added that this was virtually a unanimous sentiment among the members.[11]

The FTC's Early Use of Rulemaking

The decision to issue TRRs, then, ultimately resulted from increased political support for consumer protection. The FTC, however, began issuing rules in an atmosphere of uncertainty. This was partially because the legality of rulemaking was very much in question in the early 1960s. In addition, although the commission knew it had some political support for rulemaking, it did not know how much. Because of these doubts, the agency's first rules were token efforts to "test the water" that evoked little opposition from regulated interests.

Most of these initial TRRs were not even substantive additions to FTC policy, since they merely codified principles already established through adjudicatory precedent. At any rate, they proscribed industry practices that would have required little time or effort to prove unfair or deceptive in individual proceedings. For example, the first TRR stipulated that sleeping bag labels and advertisements must reflect the size of the finished product, rather than that of the pre-sewn halves. Pre-sewn measurements obviously over-stated the sizes of bags, and were, therefore, deceptive. There was nothing controversial about this rule, and the sleeping bag industry had little room for complaint.

The commission's first TRR of real consequence was its famous rule requiring health warnings on cigarette packages, promulgated in July 1964. The FTC had attempted to confront deception by cigarette manufacturers through adjudication for thirty years with little success. Relying on the report by the U.S. surgeon general and spurred by pressure from health groups such as the American Cancer Society and the American Heart Association, the cigarette rule involved several controversial issues. First, there was the factual question of whether or not smoking was a health hazard. Second, there was a broad policy question: assuming that smoking was harmful, did the failure of cigarette manufacturers to include health warnings on packages and in advertising fall under the ambit of the FTC's vague mandate to "prevent unfair or deceptive practices"? Third, there was the legal question of whether or not the commission could rely on rulemaking. No one had seriously pressed the issue of rulemaking authority until that point, since previous TRRs had been non-controversial.

As one might expect, the cigarette rule did not go well with the tobacco industry. The reaction by cigarette manufacturers and tobacco growers (to the health warning regulation) was so formidable that Congress soon enacted a statute that nullified the regulation, imposing considerably less stringent standards.[12] This same legislation banned the promulgation of further cigarette rules for a period of four years. Congress's lack of support "burned" the commission deeply, and, as a result, the agency reverted to the issuance of trivial rules. One of the most inane was a TRR specifying that advertisements for extension ladders must reflect true length, and not the length of the two halves (which of course overlap).

The scope and effect of TRRs remained very modest until the late 1960s when the commission encountered a new wave of criticism from consumer activists. In 1969, a group of law students working for Ralph Nader compiled a report on the FTC that was highly critical of the agency's passiveness in the area of consumer protection.[13] The report received considerable attention, and largely because of this, President Nixon asked the American Bar Association to recommend ways in which the structure and activities of the commission could be improved. One of the ABA's suggestions was that the FTC rely more heavily on rulemaking as a consumer protection tool. Shortly thereafter, Miles Kirkpatrick, who had headed the ABA study, was appointed as FTC chairman.

Criticism of the commission and the publicity surrounding it spurred both popular and governmental support for FTC activism. As a result, TRRs issued in the late 1960s and early 1970s were clearly more ambitious than their predecessors, most of which had merely codified precedent that had been developed in individual proceedings. The new rules embraced more significant industry practices and relied on more controversial interpretations of the commission's enabling legislation. Some of the more notable TRRs promulgated during this period regulated the care-labeling of clothing, retail food store advertising, the use of negative option plans, and door-to-door sales.

The Struggle Over Rulemaking Authority

Predictably, the FTC's renewed vigor brought about considerable opposition from regulated industry. In contrast to the trivial rules made previously, some of the new TRRs had significant economic impact. Resistance again led to the curtailment of rulemaking activity, but this time opponents intervened through the courts rather than through Congress. In 1968, a federal district court denied a claim for injunctive relief partially on the theory that the FTC lacked authority to issue rules. Later, in 1971, the National Petroleum Refiners' Association successfully challenged the FTC's octane rule in the U.S. District Court, again on the grounds that the commission did not possess rulemaking authority. This decision was eventually reversed at the Circuit Court level in 1973, but during the interim FTC rulemaking activity almost came to a halt.[14]

During the period of uncertainty over its authority, the commission asked Congress to amend the FTC Act by providing an explicit grant of rulemaking power. Beginning in 1969, a series of bills was introduced proposing such an amendment. Hearings on this legislation provide a lucid illustration of the importance attached to rulemaking by members of the FTC's political environment. A wide array of industry groups (including such "peak organizations" as the National Chamber of Commerce and the National Association of Manufacturers) vehemently opposed the measure, and a fierce battle ensued between consumer advocates and the business community that was drawn out over three Congresses.

Opponents of FTC regulation argued that such an open delegation by Congress in an area as expansive as "interstate commerce" was probably unconstitutional and certainly undesirable. They contended that most other delegations of rulemaking authority were confined to areas where single industries were affected and usually limited agency discretion to more concretely defined goals. In contrast, a statute authorizing FTC rulemaking to "prevent unfair or deceptive practices in or affecting commerce" was a delegation of the vaguest, broadest sort. Relatedly, it was argued that rulemaking would allow the commission to make decisions of great importance to business without the due process guaranteed by adjudication. One group spokesman even went so far as to predict that a grant of such far reaching authority would be tantamount to an "economic death sentence" for American industry.

On the other hand, advocates of strong regulation contended that rulemaking authority was necessary if the FTC was to transcend its role as the "little old lady of Pennsylvania Avenue" and effectively protect consumers. Rulemaking would allow the commission to establish broadly applicable standards more quickly and more economically. In addition, it was argued that rulemaking permitted a qualitatively broader range of policy making. For example, a former FTC staff attorney testified before the House Interstate and Foreign Commerce Committee that the imaginative policy set forth by the octane rule, which specified that gasoline octane ratings be derived by averaging the results of the two currently popular measuring techniques, could not have been established through adjudication.[15]

Advocates of rulemaking enjoyed strong support, and after five years of debate, Congress gave the commission explicit authority to issue TRRs in the Magnuson-Moss Act of 1974. Interestingly, however, this legislation was not without its concessions to business.

The act also required the commission to use trial-like procedures in formulating new rules. Interested parties would be afforded limited rights of cross-examination and rebuttal with regard to the FTC's decisional premises, and final rules would have to be based on evidence contained in a record. Similar procedures (as opposed to the more common "informal rulemaking") had proved to be a considerable source of delay and discouragement for other agencies.[16]

Subsequent Efforts at Rulemaking

The Magnuson-Moss Act seemed pro-consumer and pro-FTC on the whole, and was construed by the commission as a clear signal to begin aggressive rulemaking. In 1976, the FTC's Bureau of Consumer Protection reported to Congress that the proportion of its staff resources devoted to rulemaking had risen to 21.3 percent, as compared with 10.0 percent in 1974. Moreover, the bureau declared its intention to emphasize rulemaking even more heavily in the future.[17]

But a final and revealing twist in the history of FTC rulemaking is that, although the agency has devoted much more energy to developing TRRs since 1974, its actual output has been minimal. Of the more than 20 TRRs proposed since the commission received explicit rulemaking authority, only four have been finally promulgated. This turn of events has had two related causes. First, the decision-making procedures that accompanied the commission's grant of rulemaking authority have caused the agency to be more painstaking in collecting and evaluating evidence, and more circumspect in reaching conclusions.

Second, the wave of ambitious new proposed TRRs has precipitated an intense reaction from the business community. The most frequent criticisms have been that proposed rules go far beyond "legislative intent," and that they would impose undue costs on industry. In turn, Congress has registered this protest. If the legislature was pro-FTC in 1974, its mood has most assuredly changed. For example, contending that the FTC is "out to destroy free enterprise," one congressman has stated: "Back home, the way to kill a rattlesnake is to cut its head off. That is what we ought to do today."[18] Appropriations cuts and a legislative veto requirement (with respect to TRRs) are tangible evidence that sentiment such as this has become widespread. In addition, the legislature has recently limited the commission's mandate to include only "deceptive" practices. Industry reaction to TRRs proposed since the mid-1970s has been so intense that Congress has viewed the concept of "unfair" as being a too sweeping, indefinite, and politically troublesome delegation of authority. The commission has been reluctant to promulgate many proposed rules out of fear that they will provoke further wrath.

The Politics of Rulemaking

TRRs have permitted the FTC to formulate regulatory policy much more expeditiously than it could through adjudication. Because of this, rulemaking has elicited support from advocates of consumer protection, and opposition from anti-regulatory groups and their friends in Congress and the executive branch. Ultimately, the use and non-use of rulemaking has been determined, not by the commission's detached consideration of the administrative advantages and disadvantages of TRRs, but by the push and pull between these two factions within the agency's environment. The initial adoption of rulemaking authority and the subsequent decisions to emphasize TRRs as a means of policing deception have come in response to heightened pressure from consumer advocates, while intervening lulls in rulemaking have come in the wake of intense industry opposition.

Rulemaking (or the prospect thereof) has made the FTC's consumer-protection efforts much more visible and salient to members of its environment, and on balance, the emphasis of rulemaking has brought about reactions against the FTC of unprecedented magnitude. Some might argue that these reactions have been due to the substance of particular TRRs as opposed to the use of rulemaking *per se*. Indeed, several recent proposed rules have taken on powerful groups and have involved controversial interpretations of the commission's enabling legislation. New regulation that proscribes practices already in use is bound to be controversial, however, and rulemaking has clearly been significant as a way of establishing such regulation in a more "precipitous" manner. As Gellhorn and Robinson note:

> . . . the FTC's power to remedy "unfairness" in the marketplace never received as much attention when it was used to shore up adjudicatory complaints against individual advertisements as when it was used to challenge by rule a class of advertising by an entire industry. The greater immediate reach of the rule made the agency appear much more threatening. . . .[19]

The Political Costs of Rulemaking

Students of the administrative process who have puzzled over the failure of regulatory agencies to issue rules have focused on the administrative advantages of rulemaking to the exclusion of its political costs. Rulemaking is a commitment in statutory interpretation, and the FTC's history illustrates the difficulty inherent in making a commitment within a conflictual, unstable environment. (Consider, for instance, that some of the commission's proceedings of the mid-1970s, such as the renowned children's advertising rule, were initiated at the urging of consumer advocates in Congress, but later became a source of rebuke as allegedly going beyond statutory intent.) Although it may have been impossible for the commission to forego rulemaking given the criticism it encountered in the late 1960s and early 1970s, the FTC's difficulties plausibly explain the frequently cited reluctance of other regulatory agencies to issue rules. Lowi's observation that regulation typically occurs within conflictual, unstable environments supports this notion.[20]

Even to the extent regulatory agencies develop standards within conflictual environments, it may be prudent to do so through adjudication. One reason for this is that the case-by-case approach allows policy to be developed incrementally. Individual application decisions do not tend to establish as much policy at any one point in time; therefore, broad regulatory principles established piece-by-piece are likely to evoke less opposition than similar standards established in a single proceeding. Certainly, the FTC has formulated much more policy through case law over the years than it has through rulemaking, yet the latter process has brought about unprecedented opposition from regulated interests.

Two other political considerations may also favor adjudication over rulemaking as a policy-making tool within conflictual, unstable environments. First, policy established through adjudication may be easier to reverse, leaving an agency more flexible to cope with a shifting balance of forces. As Shapiro has argued,

> . . . by eschewing rules in favor of the declaration of [standards] by adjudication, an agency is likely to regard itself as freer, and in fact will be given greater freedom by the courts, to ignore or depart from those [standards] in specific instances without giving sufficient reasons.[21]

Second, adjudication may be perceived as a more legitimate process, and may encounter less resistance from opponents of regulation as a result. Freedman argues that judicial due process has provided the traditional means for reconciling administrative discretion with our seemingly contradictory belief in representative democracy.[22] Interestingly, one of the most frequent complaints from business during the Magnuson-Moss hearings was that non-elected officials would be able to exercise broad policy-making authority without the constraints of cross-examination, rebuttal, and decision making on the record. Opponents of rulemaking contended that these safeguards had ensured sound reasoning, careful attention to evidence, and compliance with statutory intent during adjudicatory proceedings.

Factors That Encourage Rulemaking

It is also appropriate to comment on what might encourage or facilitate rulemaking, since observers generally feel that it is not used frequently enough. The FTC's case history indirectly suggests that agencies should issue rules in stable environments where the members of target groups agree with the ostensible purposes of the statutes being administered. Affected interests may actually favor rulemaking as a quicker and less ambiguous means of achieving desired results in such a context. At least one study supports the hypothesis that environmental harmony and agreement with statutory objectives encourage rulemaking. Freedman states that the Securities and Exchange Commission has often been praised for its articulation of standards through rules, and suggests that this can be explained partially by the fact that the agency operates within a consensual environment. Both buyers and the major sellers of securities benefit from and support SEC regulation.[23]

Of course, there is no way to ensure that everyone agrees with the objectives of a policy being implemented. As a prescription, therefore, the antidote for administrative regulation without standards is the articulation of clear statutory goals. A primary obstacle to FTC rulemaking has been the vagueness of the commission's mandate. One of the most frequent complaints against the FTC in recent years has been that its rules have gone beyond "statutory intent." The inherent controversiality of rules that have construed "unfair or deceptive" past the trivial and obviously illegal has enabled opponents of regulation to intervene successfully through Congress and the courts. The more precise the goals that accompany a delegation of authority, the easier it should be for an agency to issue rules. This is because Congress will have "defused" the controversial issues, making rulemaking less dangerous to an agency in a political sense.

Competing Hypothesis: Rulemaking, Discretion, and Agency Power

The ideas that rulemaking can be an "impolitic commitment" and that there is an inverse relationship between statutory vagueness and the willingness of administrators to issue standards are not new. For instance, Herring stated that:

> The task of interpretation is a continuation of the legislative process. The full implications of this should be faced. Independent commissions are called upon to give substance to a vague congressional mandate by establishing rules and regulations. They are subject to the same pressures that assailed the legislators.[24]

These notions, however, have heretofore received little more than impressionistic support. Moreover, the FTC's experience casts doubt on at least one competing hypothesis concerning the political implications of rulemaking.

Wilson offers an explanation for agency reluctance to issue rules that is quite different from the one developed above. Drawing on Crozier,[25] he argues that administrators are primarily motivated to exert power or control over those they regulate, and that bureaucratic power is, in turn, a function of the ability to behave arbitrarily in making individual decisions. Therefore, rulemaking, which limits case-by-case discretion, is avoided as a vitiation of agency power. Illustrating this with an analogy he states:

> . . . the greater the codification of substantive policy, the less power the agency can wield over any client in the particular case. . . . In a baseball game the umpire has power because he can call me out after three strikes; but his power over me would be much greater if every time I came to the plate he told me that how many strikes I would be allowed depended on how well I swung the bat, or maybe on how clean my uniform was.[26]

Wilson's hypothesis is not borne out by the case of the FTC, where rulemaking has been perceived by the agency as a way to exert more control over regulated interests. Industry has also perceived this, and has opposed rulemaking adamantly. Under Wilson's argument, regulatees desire certainty and stability in their relations with government, and, thus, should favor the issuance of rules. Whatever power the FTC might have derived through the exercise of case-by-case discretion has clearly been outweighed by the substantive breadth and immediate applicability of rulemaking. Of course, it is only fair to add that agencies choose between rulemaking and *ad hoc* discretion within a variety of contexts. Assuming that some power is to be gained through arbitrariness, Wilson's explanation may be more valid in areas such as ratemaking and licensing, where government intervention is, in a sense, a given.

Conclusion

Rulemaking has had important implications for the shape of FTC policy, and because of this, the commission's use and non-use of rulemaking over the past twenty years have been of considerable interest to members of the agency's environment. Despite the popular administrative arguments in favor of rulemaking, it has ultimately been pressure from proponents of forceful regulation that has induced the commission to emphasize TRRs. Similarly, reaction from opponents of regulation has discouraged rulemaking. In general, the FTC's case history illustrates the political costs inherent in a rulemaking approach within a conflictual environment, and suggests why other agencies may be reluctant to issue rules under analogous conditions. As a more precipitous way of developing policy, rulemaking can be impolitic where the balance of forces within an agency's environment is uncertain or subject to change. The commission's experience also suggests, albeit indirectly, that a harmonious environment and the existence of concrete goals in an agency's enabling legislation should encourage rulemaking. The irony of this latter observation is that vague statutory policy makes rulemaking both more desirable from an administrative perspective and less feasible within the context of bureaucratic politics.

Notes

1. "Interpretive rules" do not have the force and effect of law. An agency usually issues an interpretive rule as warning to potentially affected parties that it plans to construe the meaning of a statute in a certain way in future actions. The violation of an interpretive rule, *per se,* is not a violation of the law, however. The practical significance of this is that the agency must still demonstrate the validity of its interpretation in an enforcement proceeding.

2. Rules that refine vague statutory language arguably reduce arbitrariness and capriciousness in the imposition of sanctions and the conferment of benefits. Even in the event like standards might evolve from individual enforcement decisions, rulemaking is said to avoid the problems of "retroactive" policy effects. In making policy, it is presumably more effective and rational to formulate standards in a single proceeding, rather than through a series of application decisions. Also, rulemaking is frequently advocated as a more flexible and sensitive policy-making tool that facilitates planning. This is because rulemaking allows agency decision makers to consider a broader range of affected interests than they can in adjudication, where determinations must be based largely on the facts and circumstances of the case at hand. Kenneth Culp Davis has perhaps been the leading exponent of these views. See, for example, his *Discretionary Justice* (Baton Rouge: Louisiana State University Press, 1969), and *Administrative Law Text* (St. Paul: West, 1972). Also see Warren E. Baker, "Policy by Rule or Ad Hoc Approach—Which Should It Be?" *Law and Contemporary Problems* 22 (1957); Cornelius Peck, "The Atrophied Rule Making Powers of the National Labor Relations Board," *Yale Law Journal* 70 (1961).

3. See David Shapiro, "The Choice of Rulemaking or Adjudication in the Development of Administrative Policy," *Harvard Law Review* 78 (1965); Glen O. Robinson, "The Making of Administrative Policy: Another Look at Rulemaking and Adjudication and Administrative Procedure Reform," *University of Pennsylvania Law Review* 118 (1970); and Antonin Scalia, "Back to Basics—Making Law Without Making Rules," *Regulation* (July/August 1981). It is argued that insufficient knowledge or the need to remain flexible may render broad standards impractical. Also, Scalia argues that rulemaking may "foster decision making in the abstract, outside the context of a concrete, detailed

situation that may serve to clarify both the facts and equities relevant to decision" (p. 26). Shapiro and Robinson have also argued that rulemaking and standard setting are not necessarily coterminous. Rules may be so vague or trivial as to give little guidance to administrators, while individual application decisions may establish important standards. Also, even the plausible contentions that rulemaking avoids retroactivity and that it permits a broader range of decisional input have been attacked. For instance, a rule proscribing an industry practice already in effect may, for practical purposes, impose retroactive economic sanctions. With regard to decisional input, *amicus curiae* briefs may sometimes be used in adjudicatory proceedings.

4. Harold Stein defines an agency's political environment as those external actors that affect or are capable of affecting its operations. "Public Agencies as Political Actors," in Frederick S. Lane, ed., *Current Issues in Public Administration* (New York: St. Martin's Press, 1978).

5. Guides and Trade Practice Rules are interpretive rules (see note 1) and do not have legal force. Consent orders are not voluntary agreements in which accused parties agree to refrain from alleged deceptive practices in return for the commission's promise to drop charges.

6. See Burns Weston, "Deceptive Advertising and the FTC," *The Federal Bar Journal* 24 (1964); and Lee Fritschler, *Smoking and Politics* (Englewood Cliffs, NJ: Prentice Hall, 1975).

7. Weston, "Deceptive Advertising and the FTC," pp. 550 et. seq.

8. Ibid.

9. Fritschler, *Smoking and Politics,* p. 75 et. seq.

10. Alan Stone, *Economic Regulation and the Public Interest: The Federal Trade Commission in Theory and Practice* (Ithaca, NY: Cornell University Press, 1977), p. 233.

11. Representative John Moss, Statement before the Subcommittee on Commerce of the House Interstate and Foreign Commerce Committee, March 30, 1973.

12. Fritschler, *Smoking and Politics*, pp. 115–139.

13. Edward F. Cox, Robert C. Fellmeth, and John E. Schultz, *The Nader Report on the Federal Trade Commission* (New York: Barron, 1969).

14. *Bristol Meyers Corp. v. FTC*, 284 F. Supp. 745 (D.D.C. 1968). On appeal the D.C. Circuit reversed in favor of the FTC, but avoided the question of the legality of rulemaking. *National Petroleum Refiners' Association v. FTC*, 482 F.2d 672, 690 (D.C. Cir., 1973) *cert denied*, 415 U.S. 951 (1974).

15. Mark Silbergeld, attorney for the Consumers Union of the United States. Statement before the Subcommittee on Commerce and Finance of the House Interstate and Foreign Commerce Committee. Hearings on H.R. 20 and H.R. 521, "Consumer Warranty Protection," Comm. Ser. No. 93–17.

16. See, for example, Robert W. Hamilton, "Procedures for the Adoption of Rules of General Applicability: The Need for Procedural Innovation in Administrative Rulemaking," *California Law Review*, 60 (1972).

17. Margery Smith, Statement before the House Judiciary Committee, March 1977.

18. Representative James H. Quillen (R-Tenn.) before the House Rules Committee. Hearings concerning the transfer of temporary funds to pay FTC employees, March 25, 1980. Quoted from *Congressional Quarterly Weekly Report*, March 29, 1980, p. 873.

19. Ernest Gellhorn and Glen Robinson, "Rulemaking 'Due Process': An Inconclusive Dialogue," *University of Chicago Law Review* 48 (1981): 260.

20. Theodore Lowi, "Four Systems of Policy, Politics, and Choice," *Public Administration Review* 32 (1972): 70.

21. Shapiro, "The Choice of Rulemaking or Adjudication," p. 951.

22. James O. Freedman, *Crisis and Legitimacy: The Administrative Process and American Government* (Cambridge, UK: Cambridge University Press, 1978).

23. Ibid.

24. Pendleton Herring, *Public Administration and the Public Interest* (New York: McGraw-Hill, 1936), p. 218.

25. Michael Crozier, *The Bureaucratic Phenomenon* (Chicago: University of Chicago Press, 1964).

26. James Q. Wilson, "The Dead Hand of Regulation," *The Public Interest* 25 (1971): 51.

CHAPTER 12

WHO IS "DUE" PROCESS?

BARBARA S. GRUMET

A major concern that administrators of human services programs face is that of reconciling the needs of setting and maintaining standards with the needs of the clients for receiving services. When services are provided through a contract with a qualified provider, the recipients of the services are considered to be "indirect" beneficiaries of the contractual relationship between an agency and a qualified provider.

If a provider fails to meet the required programmatic, eligibility, fiscal, or other standards, the program administrator must take action. The options open to the administrator usually range from informal consultation with the provider, up to refusal to renew an ongoing contract, or cancellation of an existing agreement.

Numerous due process protections for the provider of services are available in the event that a government agency chooses to end its arrangement with a provider. Pre-termination conferences, post-termination administrative proceedings, and, ultimately, court action, are mandated before a government agency's decision becomes final.

In the midst of the controversy between agency and provider rest the clients—the beneficiaries of the agency program. What rights, or protections, are they afforded? Obviously, the clients have an interest in the outcome of a decertification proceeding, because they will no longer be able to receive services from that particular provider.

A third interest at stake is that of the public. In an era of shrinking tax dollars and increased concern for accountability, taxpayers are demanding tighter agency controls over expenditures.

In recent years, courts have been asked to decide whose interests are at stake when a government agency does its duty, and refuses to renew a contract with a provider of services. In reconciling the competing needs of the agency, the provider, the client, and the general public, the client, as recipient of services, has been found to have the least amount of "interest" in the decertification process.

The Case—Providers vs. Recipients

In the 1980 case, *O'Bannon v. Town Court,* the U.S. Supreme Court held that the residents of a nursing home do not have a due-process right to a hearing before the home is

From *Public Administration Review* 42, no. 4 (July/August 1982): 321–326. Copyright © 1982 by American Society for Public Administration. Reprinted with permission.

decertified as a Medicare-Medicaid provider for noncompliance with federal regulations.[1] The case has ramifications for beneficiaries of other government programs.

The O'Bannon case arose from actions taken by the U.S. Department of Health, Education and Welfare (now Health and Human Services) in 1976 to decertify Town Court Nursing Center, a 198-bed nursing home in Philadelphia, Pennsylvania as a qualified provider of services to Medicare patients. Shortly thereafter, the Pennsylvania Department of Public Welfare decertified Town Court as a Medicaid provider. While administrative procedures for reconsideration of these actions were pending, the nursing home and six of its patients filed an action in federal district court, alleging that both the home and its patients were entitled to an evidentiary hearing before decertification and loss of Medicaid benefits. The district court ruled in their favor.

On appeal, the U.S. Court of Appeals, Third Circuit, held that the HEW procedures for decertification, which include informal pre-termination proceedings and a formal, post-termination evidentiary hearing, did not violate any due-process rights of the Town Court nursing home. It decided, however, that the patients had a constitutionally protected property interest in continued stay at Town Court, which required a hearing before it could be terminated.[2]

The Pennsylvania Department of Public Welfare appealed the decision. On appeal, the U.S. Supreme Court reversed the lower courts, holding that nursing home patients do not have a constitutional right to participate in proceedings to decertify a provider of nursing home benefits paid on their behalf by the government.

The court's majority opinion hinged upon two factors: (1) an interpretation of the Medicare and Medicaid laws and their regulations; and (2) an analysis of the nature of the interest(s) afforded beneficiaries of Medicare and Medicaid.

With regard to the first point, the court noted that while the Medicare statute "gives recipients a right to choose among a range of qualified providers . . . (it does not) confer a right on a recipient to continue to receive benefits for care in a home that has been decertified." While regulations restrict a nursing home's right to transfer a Medicaid recipient, they "do not purport to limit the government's right to make a transfer necessary by decertifying a facility." Moreover, a Medicaid recipient forced to transfer to another provider because of the decertification of a provider is not having his or her benefits terminated or reduced (which would require a pre-termination hearing). As the court noted in this regard: "While a patient has a right to continued benefits to pay for care in the qualified institution of his choice, he has no enforceable expectation of continued benefits to pay for care in an institution that has been determined to be unqualified."[3]

The second rationale for the court's holding involved an analysis of the nature of the government benefit involved. The court made a distinction between direct benefits, which are "essentially financial in character" and indirect benefits, which "involve the government's attempt to confer an indirect benefit on Medicaid patients by imposing and enforcing minimum standards of care on facilities. . . ."[4] In the O'Bannon case, the effect of decertification was "an indirect and incidental result of the government's enforcement (which) does not amount to a deprivation of any interest in life, liberty, or property." The court has traditionally taken the view "that the due process provision of the Fifth Amendment does not apply to the indirect adverse effects of governmental action."[5]

The Statutory Scheme

Medicare and Medicaid are the popular names for Title XVIII and Title XIX of the Social Security Act.[6] They were enacted to provide financial assistance for medical care for the elderly, some chronically disabled, and the indigent. Both programs provide reimbursement, or direct payment, for costs of inpatient care, physicians' services, laboratory and X-ray services, prescription drugs, and skilled nursing facility care.

Nursing homes are residential health care facilities that provide twenty-four-hour skilled nursing care. The first nursing homes were established as part of public alms houses, or by religious or charitable organizations. They provided room and board and minimal amounts of nursing or custodial care. The Social Security Act of 1935 included a provision allowing the assignment of Social Security benefits to nursing homes or similar institutions. This led to considerable expansion of the number of beds. Medicare and Medicaid, which allow for the direct payment for nursing home services, led to a further expansion of the nursing home "industry." At present, there are approximately 1.4 million nursing home beds in the United States.[7] Nursing homes are operated by proprietary groups or individuals, by nonprofit organizations, or by governmental units. Most nursing homes are run as profit-making institutions.[8]

When Medicare and Medicaid were first enacted, opponents who feared that these programs would lead straight down the path to socialized medicine, or total federal control over the provision of health care raised tremendous concern. Partially to allay these fears, one of the first clauses in the Medicare act assures that: "Nothing in this subchapter shall be construed to authorize any federal officer or employee to exercise any supervision or control over the practice of medicine or the manner in which medical services are provided. . . ."[9] The patient's freedom of choice in providers is assured in the provision that "any individual entitled to insurance benefits under this subchapter may obtain health services from any institution, agency, or person qualified to participate under this subchapter. . . ."[10]

The federal government promulgated regulations that defined the criteria for eligibility as providers of services under Medicare and Medicaid. For physicians' services, few requirements were made other than licensure to practice medicine in the state where care was provided. For hospital services, licensure by the state and accreditation by the Joint Commission on Accreditation of Hospitals, were sufficient criteria to be qualified providers. The joint commission requirements were adopted as suitable criteria for two basic reasons: (1) the commission had developed comprehensive criteria for accreditation on a voluntary basis, and was recognized as a nationwide standard for hospitals to strive for and adhere to; and (2) the joint commission, with representation from the American Medical Association, American Hospital Association, American College of Physicians, and American College of Surgeons, was an established peer group rather than a potentially threatening federal agency or interest group.

No such standards were available for nursing homes, however. The Joint Commission on Accreditation of Hospitals had developed standards for accreditation of nursing homes, but virtually no homes were accredited, in part because of lack of agreement concerning what standards were necessary for a home to be accredited. Thus, the joint commission, which focused on acute care hospitals, had never exerted much influence on the long-term care segment of the health care system. It was left to the federal government to develop standards for nursing homes that wished to be "qualified providers" under Medicare and Medicaid. These standards, known as conditions of participation, cover details such as organization and administration, staffing, services provided, and structural requirements.[11] Responsibility for conducting inspections of facilities was delegated to state governments. After inspection, a report of findings and a recommendation for certification were forwarded to the federal government. If approved, a provider agreement was signed between the facility and the federal government.

If a home is found to be deficient in any of the conditions of participation, the facility must submit a plan of correction, which indicates how and when it plans to come into compliance. If numerous deficiencies are found, or the home refuses to come into compliance, steps may be taken by the federal government to terminate the provider agreement.

All findings of inspections, and reports of deficiencies, are discussed with the facility before filing with the federal government. The plan for corrections usually results from negotiations between the provider and the state and/or federal governments. If a provider agreement must be terminated, the facility receives thirty days notice, with opportunity for a post-termination hearing.[12]

During the early years of the program, the federal government and most participating state governments were more concerned with the quantity rather than the quality of providers. Members of the health professions were still quite suspicious of "government interference" with health care delivery. In order to assuage these suspicions, and obtain general acceptance from providers, conditions of participation were leniently applied, with frequent waivers.

During the early 1970s, two phenomena occurred that led to a revision of government policy. First, costs of providing care under Medicare and Medicaid, especially nursing home care, mushroomed beyond the wildest expectations of all concerned with the program. Second, a number of scandals regarding poor care, exploitation of patients, kickbacks, and fraud were uncovered around the country.[13] In response to these two factors, a number of amendments were enacted to Medicare and Medicaid, focusing on fraud and abuse; new conditions of participation were enacted; and a number of states tightened up their own statutes and surveillance procedures.

The Constitutional Issues

In analyzing the impact of the *Town Court* decision on the nursing home patients, as opposed to the nursing home itself, a comparison with other "entitlement" issues is useful. Generally speaking, Medicare and Medicaid benefits fall under a broad category of human services benefits to which eligible recipients are "entitled." Once an individual becomes entitled to benefits from such a program, he or she acquires a "property interest" in continuing to receive these benefits. Such interests, along with life and liberty, are protected by the due process clause of the United States Constitution, and cannot be withdrawn without the protections of due process. In deciding what constitutes "due process" when such benefits are withdrawn, courts have tended to focus on the following factors:

1. The nature of the interest
2. The impact of the decision on the beneficiary
3. The danger of risk or error

Each of these will be discussed in turn.

Nature of the affected interest. The court has attempted on numerous occasions to distinguish the effects of governmental action (or inaction) as having direct, or indirect, consequences upon a third party. If a governmental decision is directed specifically toward a particular individual, then it is considered to have a direct impact upon that individual, and certain due process rights must be afforded that person. For example, if a particular individual is to have his or her welfare benefits terminated, the recipient must be given a pretermination hearing. Due process protections, including notice, confrontation, introduction of evidence, cross examination, and representation by counsel must be given.

If a governmental action is not specifically directed against a particular individual, then it is termed to have indirect or consequential effects, and the individual is considered as a third party to the action. In such situations, even though the individual is clearly affected by the outcome of the decision, he or she does not have a right to participate in the decision-making process. Examples of this third-party effect occur in the context of decertification, suspension or revocation of licenses or operating permits, non-renewal of grants and contracts, or decisions to terminate a particular government program. Thus, if a physician's license to practice medicine is suspended or revoked, his or her patients may be deprived of the benefits of that particular physician's services; however, they have no right to participate in the suspension or revocation process. Similarly, if a government grant establishes a new service for the elderly (such as free transportation to shopping malls, doctors' offices, and so forth) and the grant expires, the recipients of the program have no right to a hearing on the question of the government's refusal to renew funding for the program.

The direct-indirect benefit analysis is complicated when the question of entitlement arises. Entitlement theory emerged during the "welfare rights" movement of the late 1960s.[14] The theory basically means that the granting of certain benefits creates an entitlement to them that cannot be withdrawn without full due process protections, including notice of the contemplated action, an informal hearing, right to present evidence on one's own behalf, and representation by counsel. These due process protections must be provided before the government benefit is withdrawn. In the 1970 case of *Goldberg v. Kelly,* the U.S. Supreme Court declared that a "fair hearing" process after termination of welfare benefits violated the recipient's due process rights because the "termination of aid pending resolution of a controversy over eligibility may deprive an *eligible* recipient of the very means by which to live while he waits."[15] The right to a pre-termination hearing was extended to other government benefits, including the termination of electricity furnished by a municipal power plant and suspension from public school.[16] In other situations, involving the withdrawal of benefits, the court has decided that a hearing after the government action is sufficient protection. For example, a post-termination hearing is adequate protection for a former recipient of disability payments.[17]

Impact on the affected individual. One of the major arguments that the plaintiffs in the original O'Bannon case raised, and that the Third Circuit Court of Appeals accepted, was that removal of the patients from Town Court would seriously endanger the lives or health of the patients. It is well-known in the field of geriatrics that a syndrome known as "transfer trauma" affects some elderly patients who are moved from familiar surroundings into a new environment. The symptoms of "transfer trauma" may range from confusion, disorientation, or depression to serious physical or mental illness, and even death. It is difficult, if not impossible, to predict which patients will develop transfer trauma, or its severity in any given patient.[18] The risk of transfer trauma to the patient must also be balanced against the risk of maintaining patients in a nursing home that has demonstrated that it is providing substandard care, or poses a safety threat to the patients.

The plaintiffs argued that the harm to the patients would result in interference with their health or very lives, akin to a deprivation of liberty, or even life. Thus, a liberty or life interest, mandating protections of the due process clause of the U.S. Constitution, would be created. The Supreme Court, however, found the plaintiffs' argument of transfer trauma "unpersuasive" in establishing a life or liberty interest for the patients. The court chose to focus on the nature of the interest at stake (i.e., a contractual relationship between a provider and the federal government), rather than its impact upon parties deemed to be "indirect" to the contractual interest. The court termed the impact on the plaintiffs "an indirect and incidental result of the government's enforcement action."[19]

In another nursing home decertification case, the Second Circuit Court of Appeals noted that a nursing home operator's expectation of continued participation in Medicare and Medicaid must be placed "in proper perspective with regard to the health and safety expectations of the patients, which . . . the Secretary (of HHS) has a valid interest in protecting."[20] The court held that a post-decertification hearing provided sufficient protections for the nursing home.

The Supreme Court has dealt with the direct-indirect distinction in the context of change of providers in other situations, and established similar results. In a case with similar allegations (i.e., government action will produce emotional and/or physical trauma), the court decided that foster parents do not have a due process right to a hearing before foster children are removed from their care. The court decided that the foster parents' interests were created by state law and contract, and were sufficiently protected by pre-removal conferences, and post-removal "fair hearing" procedures. The foster parents argued that one of the reasons that a full adversarial hearing should be held before the child is removed from a foster home is the possibility that the child will suffer a "grievous (emotional) loss" due to "disruption of the stable relationship needed by the child." The court rejected this argument by stressing that the *nature* of the interest involved (i.e., the statutory and contractual nature of the foster parent-child relationship), rather than its *weight* (i.e., any feelings of love and affection, psychological trauma arising from severing the ties), governs the question of whether any due process rights attach. Neither the foster parents nor the foster child had any protected liberty interest in the relationship. The court thought that the existing procedures, including a pre-removal conference, an informal pre-removal hearing, and a formal post-removal hearing, provided sufficient protections.[21]

The nursing home patients in Town Court had similar interests: a statutory and contractual relationship with a particular provider. The patients, like the foster children, are in a third-party relationship to the provider of services. The patients' possibility of suffering "transfer trauma" due to removal from the nursing home is similar to the trauma suffered by a foster child who is removed from foster parents with whom he or she has established emotional ties. Yet, the courts focus on the *nature* of the interest (i.e., a contract with the provider), rather than its weight (i.e., significance to a third-party beneficiary).

Risk of error. A third factor considered by courts when deciding whether full hearing rights must be afforded before withdrawal of benefits is the concern of risk of error. If the government erroneously removes a beneficiary from a particular program, irreparable harm may result. It was this risk of irreparable harm that led the U.S. Supreme Court to decide that hearings must be held before welfare benefits are terminated, or a student is suspended from school. In *Town Court,* however, numerous opportunities were presented for the nursing home to demonstrate to the state that it had come into compliance with the conditions of participation.

Unfortunately, the risk of error in the enforcement of standards in nursing homes is more likely to lie on the side of not decertifying an ineligible provider, rather than the other way around. The nature of the Medicare-Medicaid enforcement process, coupled with a shortage of nursing home beds in many parts of the country, is responsible for this situation. Seventy-five percent of the nursing homes in the country are certified as Medicare and/or Medicaid providers.[22] The nursing homes must adhere to what are concededly minimal standards to qualify as providers. The incentive to comply with these standards is eligibility for payment on behalf of Medicare and Medicaid patients. The threat of removal of this eligibility theoretically will require a home to keep its operations at the minimal level of federal standards.

The state, as inspector, has a dual interest: upholding minimal quality of providers, and assuring an adequate supply of nursing home beds. In many areas of the nation, nursing home beds are in short supply. If a home falls below minimal standards, and the provider agreement is terminated, the state must assist in finding new placements for patients who are cared for at public expense. In most cases, the state wants to avoid relocation, at almost any cost. Decertification is a last-ditch remedy, when all attempts at less drastic sanctions have failed.[23] The Town Court home, for example, was originally certified as a Medicaid provider in 1967. During 1967–73, the home was found to have numerous deficiencies, but was permitted to remain open under plans of correction. The provider agreement was initially terminated in October 1974. Then in April 1976, a new agreement was executed. In July 1976, after HEW received reports that a special grand jury was investigating the home, they resurveyed the facility. In November, and again in December, the state surveyed the facility. Town Court remained open under a plan of correction. In March 1977, another survey uncovered numerous deficiencies. In May 1977, HEW notified the facility that the provider agreement would not be renewed, effective June 18, 1977. Thus, a home that had a ten-year history of violations and deficiencies remained, with an eighteen-month exception, as a provider of nursing home care to Medicare and Medicaid patients. This pattern is not atypical of the history of provider agreement enforcement in other areas of the nation.

The dual realities of multiple pre-termination reviews, coupled with a strong incentive to avoid relocating numerous patients on short notice, mean that the dangers of erroneous termination of a provider agreement are very slight.

Summary and Conclusions

The Supreme Court treated the *O'Bannon* case as posing a fairly straight-forward due process issue; namely, the recipients of services derived from a contract between the government and a provider do not have a right to participate in proceedings concerning the termination of the contract. The fact that the provider is furnishing services to which the recipient is entitled under a government benefit program is irrelevant, for due process purposes. The recipient's interest is indirect to the property interest of the contractor.

The current fiscal climate for administrators of government programs assures that many benefit programs, particularly in health and human services, will be diminished, if not eliminated entirely. Services targeted for reduction or elimination include welfare, food stamps, public housing, Medicaid, day care, preventive services, alcoholism and drug abuse treatment, education, services for the elderly, and mental health programs. Recipients of these benefits will have their benefits diminished or eliminated. Many programs that are not slated for elimination will be consolidated into block grants, with responsibility for setting priorities and administration delegated to state governments. The resulting shifts in services will require adjustments by administrators, providers, and recipients alike.

The increasingly conservative fiscal and political climate is also creating new interest in accountability. Demands for increasing scrutiny of eligibility for benefits, monitoring of service delivery, and evaluation of programs are designed to weed out ineligible beneficiaries and inefficient or ineffective providers. Increased surveillance will undoubtedly result in more recipients and providers declared ineligible or unqualified. The Town Court case demonstrates the principle that an individual recipient's "right" to receive uninterrupted services from a particular provider may not be absolute—or even existent. This principle can be applied to other governmental services as well.

For the administrator, who is trying to balance the needs and interests of government, taxpayer, provider, and recipient, this case reaffirms the view that the recipients' wishes are perhaps the least crucial aspect to consider when making programmatic changes—at least from the standpoint of the due process clause. The implication for administrators is that when making programmatic changes due to cutbacks in funding, decertification of a provider of services, or termination of a contractual agreement, the due process clause *may* apply to the provider of services, but does *not* apply to the recipient of those services.

The U.S. Supreme Court has ruled that the recipient's interests are "incidental" to the contract between the funding agency and the provider. Therefore, the ultimate beneficiaries of the contract have no "interest" that requires protections of due process. When making decisions about terminating a contract with a particular provider, the program administrator does not have to involve the recipients of service in the decision-making process.

Notes

1. *O'Bannon v. Town Court Nursing Center, Inc.,* 447 U.S. 773, 100 S. Ct. 2467, 65 L.Ed.2d 506 (1980).

2. *Town Court Nursing Center, Inc., v. Beal,* 586 F.2d (CA 3 1978).

3. *O'Bannon,* 100 S. Ct. 2475.

4. Ibid.

5. *O'Bannon,* 100 S. Ct. 2476–77.

6. 42 U.S.C. Subchapter XVIII, "Health Insurance for the Aged and Disabled" (Medicare); 42 U.S.C. Subchapter XIX, "Grants to States for Medical Assistance Programs" (Medicaid).

7. U.S. Department of Health, Education and Welfare, *Health, United States* 1979, p. 154.

8. Ibid.

9. 42 U.S.C. 1395.

10. 42 U.S.C. 1395a.

11. 42 CFR §405, 1101–1137 (Medicare Conditions of Participation). 42 CFR Part 442 (Medicaid Standards).

12. For a detailed discussion of the inspection and decertification process, see Nancy Jones, "Termination of Skilled Nursing Facility Medicaid Provider Agreements: Procedural Due Process Requirements" *American Journal of Law and Medicine* 6 (1981): 451.

13. See, for example, Mary A. Mendelson, *Tender Loving Greed: How the Incredibly Lucrative Nursing Home "Industry" Is Exploiting America's Old People and Defrauding Us All* (New York: Knopf, 1974); Frank E. Moss and Val J. Halamandaris, *Too Old, Too Sick, Too Bad: Nursing Homes in America* (Germantown, MD: Aspen Systems Corp., 1977); and N.Y. State Moreland Act Commission on Nursing Homes and Residential Facilities, *Long Term Care Regulation: Past Lapses, Future Prospects,* 1976.

14. See Charles A. Reich, "Individual Rights and Social Welfare: The Emerging Legal Issues," *Yale Law Review* 74 (1965): 1245.

15. *Goldberg v. Kelly,* 397 U.S. 254, 90 S. Ct. 1101, 25 L.Ed.2d 287 (1970).

16. *Memphis Light, Gas & Water Division v. Craft,* 436 U.S. 1 (1977); *Goss v. Lopez,* 419 U.S. 565 (1975).

17. *Matthews v. Eldridge,* 424 U.S. 319, 96 S. Ct. 893, 47 L.Ed.2d 18 (1976).

18. Anson B. Levitan, "Nursing Home Dilemma? Transfer Trauma and the Noninstitutional Option: A Review of the Literature," *Clearinghouse Review* 13 (1979): 653.

19. *O'Bannon,* 100 S. Ct. 2476.

20. *Case v. Weinberger,* 523 F.2d 602 (CA 2, 1975).

21. *Smith v. Organization of Foster Families,* 431 U.S. 816 (1977).

22. U.S. Department of Health, Education and Welfare, *Health, United States,* 1979, p. 154.

23. Patricia Butler, "Assuring the Quality of Care and Life in Nursing Homes: The Dilemma of Enforcement," *North Carolina Law Review* 57 (1979): 49–50.

CHAPTER 13

MAKING BUREAUCRATS RESPONSIVE

A Study on the Impact of Citizen Participation and
Staff Recommendations on Regulatory Decision Making

JUDY B. ROSENER

Conventional wisdom tells us that participation in public hearings is often ineffective; and that part-time regulators "rubber stamp" the recommendations of their staffs. The implication of this conventional wisdom is that regulators listen to citizens, but take their signals from staff.[1] When this notion is coupled with the private sector cry for less regulation and less citizen participation, it is not surprising that there is a move to minimize both.[2] What is surprising is that while the effectiveness of regulatory requirements has been studied and analyzed, there has been little systematic analysis of the effectiveness of citizen participation in regulatory proceedings.[3] The few studies that have generated reliable data tend to focus on who participates, how many people participate, and why people participate. They monitor participation rather than measure its influence. Similarly, there is very little hard data on whether or not regulators "rubber stamp" staff recommendations.[4] There are some case studies that suggest that they do, and one or two attempts to show that they do, but there is insufficient data to support a theory.

Having served eight years as a commissioner on the California Coastal Commission, a state regulatory agency with far-reaching land use authority, I observed that citizens who participated in public hearings to influence the commission's voting behavior appeared to be effective, that is, they achieved their participation goals. I also observed that the commissioners tended to follow the recommendations of the staff in a selective fashion, that is, when they recommended approval of permits, but not so when they recommended denial. In an attempt to determine whether or not my personal observations were accurate, I conducted a study of three regional California Coastal Commissions over a three-year period. The purpose of the study was to ascertain in a quantitative manner whether or not citizens who participated in regulatory public hearings influenced voting outcomes, and whether or not there was evidence to support the belief that regulators "rubber stamp" staff recommendations, using the commissions as a test case.

From *Public Administration Review* 42, no. 4 (July/August 1982): 339–345. Copyright © 1982 by American Society for Public Administration. Reprinted with permission.

The California Coastal Act of 1972 and Coastal Commissioners

The California Coastal Act of 1972 was created in response to a demand for coastal resource protection. After three years in which the California legislature failed to enact coastal protection laws, citizens circumvented their elected representatives and passed a statewide initiative that created a strong regulatory agency, the California Coastal Commission. The commission was composed of one state commission and six regional commissions. Commissioners were part-time appointees, and had the responsibility and authority to approve or deny all developmental projects (from the erection of a fence to the construction of a shopping center) in an area designated as the "coastal zone." They had veto power over all local land-use decisions.[5]

The Coastal Act has was written by environmentalists and legislators who had championed the need for coastal resource protection. For this reason, strong citizen oversight provisions were included in the act. These provisions were designed to serve as a check on the use of the discretionary authority provided the commissioners. One of these provisions required that an individual public hearing be held for each permit that might have an "adverse environmental impact" on coastal resources. It was assumed that citizens would take advantage of opportunities to participate in these hearings, and that they would be able to influence voting outcomes.

Some comments about the commissioners and their staffs are necessary in order to understand the focus of the study that follows. Regional commissions consisted of six locally elected officials (members of city councils and county board of supervisors) and six "public members," two appointed by the governor, two by the speaker of the State Assembly, and two by the State Senate Rules Committee. This appointment "mix" was written into the act at the request of local officials who threatened to oppose passage of the initiative unless they had equal representation on the commissions with what were expected to be environmentally oriented "public members." The voting behavior of commissioners reflected their concern.[6] The "public members" (who identified with the environmental purpose of the act) voted to deny projects much more often than did the local officials who identified with home rule.

Each commission had its own staff, whose prime responsibility was to make permit recommendations. The Coastal Act was a unique law. There were no precedents for the kind of decisions being made. Commissioners had wide discretion in deciding what constituted an environmental impact. In addition, the commissions, as noted, were split ideologically. Thus, it is easy to see that developing staff recommendations was fraught with difficulties. For the same reasons, it would not be surprising to find citizen participation influencing voting outcomes. It is the author's contention that participation did influence voting behavior (perhaps because of the discretion granted the commissioners) and that it did so independent of staff recommendations. It is also the author's contention that measuring the influence of citizen participation and staff recommendations in a quantitative fashion enhances our ability to understand the role they play in regulatory decision making.

The Study

The study consists of an analysis of 1,816 development permits for which individual public hearings were held. These permits represent approximately 70 percent of all the permits processed by the six regional commissions, although only three of the six commissions were studied.[7] Moreover, this study does not include permit decisions made on the consent calendars or permits issued on the basis of administrative or emergency actions. Each hearing represents one permit application. These 1,816 hearings constitute the total universe of hearings for the three commissions during the period between April 1973 and December 1975. The hearing data represent the votes of thirty-six commissioners. The number of permits processed by the three commissions not included in the study is so small that their inclusion would not materially affect the findings.

The decision environment was as follows: The commission staff would process a permit application, write up an analysis of the project, and make a recommendation for approval or denial. The applicant, interested parties, and commissioners would receive the staff report prior to the scheduled public hearing. Usually one public hearing was held, at which time the staff would make its recommendation, the permit applicant would speak, those in opposition to the permit would speak, the commissioners would ask questions of the staff or participants, and a vote would be taken.

While it is impossible to know whom a commissioner may have talked to outside the hearing, it must be assumed that, for the most part, it was the staff recommendation and discussion that took place in the hearing that influenced the voting outcomes. The reasons for this assumption is that most of the commissioners had regular jobs, and the time they spent outside the meetings on commission business was limited. On an occasional permit, a commissioner might attempt to learn more about a project than he or she might otherwise, but, in general, *ex-parte* communications were frowned upon, and most of the influencing took place in the context of the public hearings. While the ideological predisposition of the commissioners to resource protection and citizen participation may have played a part in their decision making, these two factors are considered to be constants, and were not included in the study.

The Hypotheses and Methodology

As was noted above, there is a dearth of reliable data on whether, or how citizens influence voting behavior in the context of the public hearing, and whether or not part-time regulators "rubber stamp" staff recommendations. In order to generate data, the following hypotheses were tested:

1. The denial rate of permits will increase when there is a staff recommendation to deny them.
2. The denial rate of permits will increase when citizens oppose them in a public hearing.

Table 13.1

Staff Recommendations and Commission Decision

		Commission decision		
		Decision to approve	Decision to deny	
Staff recommendations	Approval	93% (1,290)	7% (99)	77% 1,389
	Denial	45% (186)	55% (228)	23% 414
		82% 1,476	18% 327	N = 1,803

Level of association: phi = .52
Level of significance: phi < 0.0001

3. The denial rate of permits will increase when citizens oppose them in a public hearing, irrespective of the staff recommendation.

The dependent variable used in the analysis was the percentage of permit denials. A denial or "no" vote was seen as an environmental decision, since the Coastal Act said that a project should be approved *only* if it could be shown that it would not cause an adverse environmental impact under the provisions of the act. Thus, to deny a project meant that it would cause an adverse environmental impact.

Although commissioners were given wide latitude in deciding whether or not to deny a permit, and the intent of the Coastal Act was to make sure that no projects were permitted that were not protective of coastal resources, relatively few projects were denied.

Only 25 percent, or 1,816, of the total permits processed by the three commissions studied necessitated an *individual* public hearing, the other 75 percent having been put on a consent calendar or included as administrative or emergency permits. Of the 25 percent of the permits for which an individual hearing was held (the subjects of the study), the denial rate was 18 percent (see Table 13.1). While this may appear to be a high denial rate, it must be remembered that this rate refers only to permit applications that, under the provision of the Coastal Act, had the potential of having a negative impact on coastal zone resources. Given the purpose of the act, which was to protect these resources, the fact that 82 percent of the permits processed were approved indicates that the denial rate was less than might have been expected.

There are a number of reasons why the denial rate was rather low given the mandate of the act. One reason was that it was difficult for commissioners to tell those applying for a permit in a face-to-face situation that they could not build their dream house or subdivide their land. While it is clear that the voters of California were supportive of the Coastal Act, asking individual property-owners and developers to bear the cost of reaching coastal resource protection goals was not easy. Also the provisions of act were vague.

For instance, it was difficult for commissioners in exercising their discretionary authority, to decide what constituted an "adverse impact."

Since it was assumed to be more difficult for commissioners to deny permits than to approve them, attention was focused on permit denials, the rationale being that if participants influence commissioners to deny projects, they can probably influence commissioners to approve them.

The independent variables used in the analysis were the presence or absence of participation in opposition to permits, and the staff recommendations to commissioners for the approval or denial of permits. The rationale for choosing them was similar to that used in choosing the denial rate as the dependent variable. Each permit had a supporter (the applicant) who participated in the public hearings. Not every permit had an opponent. Therefore the variation in participation can most clearly be seen by looking at those who participated in opposition to the permits.

Non-parametric statistical techniques were used to test the hypothesis. The test for determining the level of association was phi. Since most of the data used in the analysis were nominal, and because the investigation was exploratory, the author used conservative measures of association.

Findings

Public hearings were mandated under the California Coastal Act because they were required as a condition of receiving funds from the federal government (under the Federal Coastal Zone Management Act), and because the authors of the coastal initiative thought that the hearing would provide citizens with an opportunity to make commissioners and their staff responsive. It was assumed that citizens, particularly environmentalists, would take advantage of the opportunity to participate, and that their participation would remind commissioners of their responsibility. Strong public hearing provisions in the act were to favor the interests of the environmentalists who fought for its passage. This view is consistent with the notion that expanded participation opportunities serve those interested in "public goods."[8] Put differently, it was assumed that given the evidence that regulator agencies tend to favor the interests of those they regulate (their clients) the opportunity for citizens to influence regulators was needed to prevent "client capture."[9] The findings shed light on these assumptions.

Staff Recommendations

A casual observer might come away from commission hearings sensing a high correlation between staff recommendations and commission decisions. Indeed, most of the time staff recommendations and commission decisions seem to coincide, and commissioners appear to be "rubber stamps" of their staffs. But is this the case? As Table 13.1 indicates, when the commission staff recommended approval of the permits, 93 percent of the time the commission approved them. On the other hand, when staff recommended denial, commissioners followed the staff recommendations only 55 percent of the time. So while

Table 13.2

Presence or Absence of Opposition and Commission Decision

		Commission decision		
		Decision to approve	Decision to deny	
Presence or absence of opposition	No opposition	89% (987)	11% (127)	66% 1,114
	One or more in opposition	66% (387)	34% (197)	34% 584
		81% 1,374	19% 324	N = 1,698

Level of association: phi = .27
Level of significance: phi < 0.0001

there was a strong relationship between the staff recommendations and commission decisions when viewed in the aggregate, this is not the case when permit recommendations were "decomposed," with the citizen participation variable included in the analysis (see Tables 13.3 and 13.4).

Citizen Participation

Data on the relationship between participation of citizens who opposed permits and the commission denial rate are seen above [in Table 13.2].

When there was no opposition to permits, the denial rate was 11 percent. When citizens participated in opposition to the permits, the denial rate went up dramatically, to 34 percent. Viewed in the context of the denial rate of 19 percent, the 34 percent figure seems important. It suggests that participation was effective in changing the voting behavior of commissioners. Because commissioners relied on both the staff recommendations and the effect of participation in making their decisions, however, it is necessary to view participation in terms of specific staff recommendations.

Citizen Participation and Staff Recommendations

One might expect that there would be an association between those permits for which the staff recommended denial and the presence of opponents in the public hearings. It is plausible that the staff would recommend denial on "questionable" permits, and that those would be the same permits that citizens would choose to oppose. Therefore, we need to look at the relationship between opposition to permits while controlling for the staff recommendation. That relationship can be seen in Tables 13.3 and 13.4.

The data in Table 13.3 show that when the staff recommended approval on permits and there was no opposition, the denial rate was quite low. The staff was overruled by commissioners only 4 percent of the time. When the staff recommended approval and

Table 13.3

Presence or Absence of Opposition and Commission Decision, for Permits Whose *Approval* **Was Recommended by Staff**

		Commission decision		
		Decision to approve	Decision to deny	
Presence or absence of opposition	No opposition	96% (876)	4% (40)	71% 916
	One or more in opposition	84% (312)	16% (59)	29% 371
		92% 1,188	8% 99	N = 1,287

Level of association: phi = .20
Level of significance: phi < 0.0001

Table 13.4

Staff Recommendations and Commission Decision, for Permits Whose *Denial* **Was Recommended by Staff**

		Commission decision		
		Decision to approve	Decision to deny	
Presence or absence of opposition	No opposition	56% (110)	44% (87)	49% 197
	One or more in	34% (72)	66% (137)	51% 209
	opposition	45% 182	55% 224	N = 406

Level of association: phi = .21
Level of significance: phi < 0.0001

there was opposition, the denial rate increased to 16 percent. The staff was overruled four times as often. While the absolute number of permit denials is small in comparison to those permits that were approved, it seems reasonable to assume that the presence of participants did have an influence, given the fact that the total number of denied permits is relatively small.

The data in Table 13.4 show that when the staff recommended denial on permits and there was no opposition, the denial rate was 44 percent. It jumped to 66 percent when there was opposition, indicating that even though there was a tendency for commissioners to overrule the staff on recommended denials and vote approval, they did so much less often when citizens appeared in the hearings to oppose those permits.

Discussion

The data suggest a number of things. They show that most of the time citizens did not participate in public hearings held by the Coastal Commission, although when they did, they were effective in increasing the denial rate. Whether their participation or its influence was desirable in terms of the protection of coastal resources is not at issue here. What is at issue, is the fact that citizens, participating in public hearings, influenced voting outcomes, and their influence was measured quantitatively. Should the influence of participation and staff recommendations in other kinds of regulatory hearings be measured in a similar manner, we could begin to accumulate the knowledge needed to evaluate the conventional wisdom about effectiveness of participation and commission staff recommendations.

The data show that while commissioners followed staff recommendations for approval 92 percent of the time, this was not the case when it came to recommended denials. Almost half the time (45 percent), commissioners overruled staff recommendations for denial. This is an important finding because it indicates that looking at staff recommendations in an undifferentiated manner is deceiving. Yet that is how most researchers have viewed the commissioner/staff recommendation relationships.

The data show that participation influenced voting outcomes independent of staff recommendations. It appears that while it may have been difficult for commissioners to say no to permit applicants when there was a staff recommendation for approval, it may also have been difficult to say no to environmentalists when they appeared to plead that permits should be denied. While commissioners overruled staff recommendations for denial 56 percent of the time when there was no citizen opposition, that figure dropped to 34 percent when citizens opposed them. This is an important finding because if the two variables (participation and staff recommendation) had not been analyzed separately, it would not have been possible to show that participation had a force of its own.

Finally, the data show that a recommendation for denial, together with participation in the public hearings, constitute a strong predictive variable. When there was a staff recommendation for denial *and* citizen participation, the denial rate was 66 percent, a far cry from the overall denial rate of 19 percent, as shown in Table 13.2.

How can the findings be explained? The relatively low participation rate (34 percent), which remained constant over the three-year period of the study, is similar to the 32 percent rate found in a study of planning commission decisions in Atlanta, Georgia.[10] The obvious explanation of this finding is that citizens tend to participate only when strongly motivated to do so, and most of the time they are not motivated. In the case of the Coastal Commissions, even though the costs of participation were low, there were costs, for example, time, baby-sitting, xeroxing, travel expenses, and so forth. It must be assumed that citizens tended to oppose only those permits perceived as having a major environmental impact. Interestingly, the perception of which permits those were was different depending on who was doing the perceiving. The data show that 49 percent of the time, permits received staff recommendations for denial when there was no citizen opposition, and 29 percent of the time they received recommendations for approval when there was citizen opposition. What this says is that if citizens and staff members did not agree on which permits should be denied, commissioners must also have had problems making up their minds. One commissioner explained the dilemma this way: "When there is no one out there objecting, I think there is nothing objectionable, even though the staff says there is. When there is someone objecting, it makes me think there is something objectionable, but I have to weigh it against the staff recommendation." The findings seem to suggest that the staff recommendation for denial was a necessary, but not a sufficient condition for a permit denial.

One might ask why, when there was a staff recommendation for denial *and* citizen opposition, did commissioners still approve 34 percent of the permits? One explanation is that commissioners used their discretionary authority to make their job easier, to approve rather than deny permits. (It is always easier to say yes than no.) Another explanation might be that many commissioners (most often the local officials) were not strong supporters of the Coastal Act, and they chose to apply the law "loosely." The two reasons offered are not mutually exclusive, and probably both contributed to the fact that commissioners tended to approve rather than deny permits, even when citizens opposed them and staffs recommended they be denied.

The fact that commission staffs recommended denials on many more permits than were denied suggests that the staffs may have been "leading" the commissioners. In other words, they recommended denial on more permits than they thought would be denied. Many of the staff members were environmentalists, and consciously or unconsciously they may have hoped to convince commissioners to deny permits that could have gone either way. In this regard, it seems possible that staff members viewed citizen participants as a constituency, and recommended denials based on the anticipation that citizens would support their recommendations. Conversations with staff personnel indicate this was often the case. This possibility is intriguing since it is widely held that regulators tend to become "captured" by their clients. These findings suggest that perhaps the participants "captured" the commission staffs. These data on the influence of citizen participation are similar to findings of Sabatier and Mazmanian in their study of the commissions.[11] While participation was not the main focus of their study, they found it to be a factor in explaining the variance in the voting behavior of California coastal commissioners.

Summary and Conclusions

It was postulated that at the outset that there is a need to evaluate the influence of citizen participation and staff recommendations on the voting behavior of regulators in the context of public hearings. To do this, three hypothesis were tested using data from California Coastal Commission hearings. The findings support all three hypothesis: (1) staff recommendations influenced the behavior of the regulators; (2) citizen participation influenced the behavior of the regulators; (3) citizen participation influenced the behavior of the regulators independent of the staff recommendations. Furthermore, the data suggest that the relationship between staff recommendations and voting behavior is more complex than has been assumed; that staff recommendations need to be "decomposed" if a true picture of their impact is to be seen. The data indicate that regulators tend to follow staff recommendations when "yes" votes are called for, and to overrule when "no" votes are recommended, a behavior pattern that, while easy to understand, seems worthy of further study. The findings also suggest that there may be an association between citizen participation and staff recommendations related to the way staff members "lead" regulators. It seems that the anticipation of participation in opposition to permits may influence the development of staff recommendations for denial.

Perhaps the most important finding is that the combination of a staff recommendation for denial and citizen participation in opposition to a permit significantly increases the probability that a permit will be denied. While this finding may seem to be stating the obvious, it is the first quantitative measurement of the influence of these two factors on the voting behavior of regulators.

Taken together, the findings suggest that the conventional wisdom concerning citizen participation and staff recommendations in regulatory hearings needs to be reexamined. While this study does not provide the data necessary to prove the conventional wisdom incorrect, it does suggest a need for a systematic evaluation between citizen participation, staff recommendations, and regulatory decision making in the context of public hearings.

Notes

1. Barry Checkoway, "The Politics of Public Hearings," *Journal of Applied Behavioral Sciences* 17, no. 4 (1981); Paul Sabatier and Daniel Mazmanian, "Relationships Between Governing Boards and Professional Staff, Role Orientations and Influence on the California Coastal Commissions," *Administration and Society* (Fall 1981); Irving Schiffman, "The Limits of Local Planning Commissions," Institute of Government Affairs, University of California Davis (1975); Debra W. Stewart, "Full Time Staff and Volunteer Commissioners: A Comparative Study of Staff-Commissioner Relationships on Local Commissions on the Status of Women," paper delivered at the 1978 Annual Meeting of the Political Science Association, New York, Aug. 31–Sept. 3, 1978.

2. Many of the provisions for the holding of public hearings are embedded in the regulatory policies and laws of the late 1960s and 1970s which are presently under attack on all levels of government.

3. Nelson Rosenbaum, *Citizen Participation: Models and Methods of Evaluation,* Center for Responsive Governance, Washington, DC (February 1977).

4. See, Sabatier, and Mazmanian, "Relationships"; Schiffman, "The Limits of Local Planning Commissions"; Stewart, "Full Time Staff and Volunteer Commissioners."

5. Regional commission permit decisions could be appealed to the state commission, however very few of them (8 percent) were appealed, making the regional decisions the most appropriate sample.

6. Judy B. Rosener, "Environmentalism vs. Local Control: A Study of Voting Behavior of Some California Coastal Commissioners." Unpublished manuscript, University of California, Irvine, 1977.

7. The South Coast Regional Commission processed more permits than all of the other commissions combined. The other commissions included in the study were the San Diego Commission and the Northcentral Commission. Paul Sabatier, UC Davis, collected the data from the Northcentral Commission

files. These three commissions were representative of the different political cultures of the California coastal area included in the coastal zone.

8. Mark Goldberg, "Small Business and Participation in the Regulatory Process," *Citizen Participation,* July/August (1981).

9. Paul Sabatier, "Social Movements and Regulatory Agencies: Toward a More Adequate—and Less Pessimistic—Theory of Client Capture," *Policy Sciences* 1, no. 3 (1975).

10. George Rupnow, "An Analysis of Zoning Problems in Atlanta: Policy Practices and Community Acceptance and Their Problem Solving Applications," in Frank X. Stegert, ed. Report prepared for the Department of Housing and Urban Development, March 1972.

11. Paul Sabatier and Daniel Mazmanian, *Can Regulation Work? The Implementation of Public Policy* (Santa Monica, CA: Goodyear, 1982).

CHAPTER 14

MANAGING THE FREEDOM OF INFORMATION ACT AND FEDERAL INFORMATION POLICY

LOTTE E. FEINBERG

The Department of Defense processed 83,173 FOIA [Freedom of Information Act] requests in 1985; Health and Human Services had 105,687 requests, with 45,953 to the Food and Drug Administration; Treasury had 23,217 and the Department of Energy, 5,723. An estimated 91 percent of all requests were completely filled. Requests are wideranging. A research assistant at a California college and a newspaper reporter in Oregon asked the Department of Energy for detailed information on the Nuclear Emergency Search Team (NEST). A Maryland-based consulting firm asked the Navy for copies of procurement contracts. A Japanese firm in Kyobashi wanted a copy of an application for a drug dealing with antiarrythmia. An inmate in a mid-western prison asked the Army for instructions on making a bomb and advice on where to place it to blow up Denver. A hospital in Massachusetts requested a Quality Assurance Profile conducted by the FDA.[1]

The management of FOIA and the way we think about information have both changed during the past twenty years. Government information in the 1980s has become a tangible commodity with a dollar value. "Information Management" is being defined as a multi-faceted process involving the collection, processing, storage, transmission, and use of information. Each facet is governed by different regulations. Businesses have become major requesters; submitters of information are seeking new protections for their data; the costs of providing information have been significantly higher than Congress anticipated. The Executive branch and a number of legislators are advocating that requesters pay for the records they receive as well as their value. For example, the proposed Senate bill to amend the FOIA (S.150) would permit agencies to charge a "fair value fee" or royalties for government records containing "commercially valuable technological information." But there is little guidance on how to price the future value of information. Some argue that too much government information is being released harming government decision making and intelligence gathering as well as private sector competition. Others claim that access to government information is being sharply curtailed, damaging scientific exchange, research, and democratic processes.

From *Public Administration Review* 46, no. 6 (November/December 1986): 615–621. Copyright © 1986 by American Society for Public Administration. Reprinted with permission.

The focus of this discussion is the management of FOIA, but this is inextricably entwined in the larger question of information policy. The historical context out of which FOIA evolved is sketched first. Next, the way in which FOIA has been implemented and managed, is examined, with attention to how selected agencies have balanced the conflicting demands of Congress and the executive branch against their own goals and interests. Last, key statutes and regulations that shape current information policy are outlined.

The History of FOIA

Signed into law by a reluctant President Johnson, awkward product of compromise, the FOIA uneasily rests on four broad, often incompatible, premises. It is based on belief that: an informed electorate is essential to safeguard democracy; publicity is one of the best protections against the potential for official misconduct; privacy is a fundamental right and corresponds with a need to restrict government's intrusions into people's lives; and secrecy is endemic to bureaucracy and perhaps facilitates organizational efficiency.

The FOIA evolved from three laws. A "housekeeping" statute, originally passed in 1789, gave the head of each federal department authority to "prescribe regulations for the government of his department," set up filing systems, and keep records.[2] The Administrative Procedure Act (APA) of 1946, which the FOIA subsequently amended, required that agencies publish information about their organization, powers, procedures, and substantive rules in the *Federal Register*. Final opinions or orders in adjudicated decisions were to be published or made available for public inspection.[3] Third, in 1958, a single sentence was added to the "housekeeping" statute to prevent agencies from using it to withhold information.[4]

The executive branch, beginning with George Washington, argued that the President had the prerogative for safeguarding agency records for "the public good." This precedent remained largely unchallenged. The courts regarded agency heads as "political or confidential agents of the President, their acts being only politically, not judicially examinable."[5] As late as 1927, one court expressed concern that if a citizen were allowed to exercise his right to inspect records, this "might lead to demands of inspection by other citizens and the disadvantage of conduct of the records office."[6]

Until the rise of the "administrative state" and World War I, federal agencies did not have much interest in compiling records. De Tocqueville reported that public officials gave him original documents to keep. "There is a sense in which public administration is oral and traditional. Nothing is written . . . no archives are formed; no documents are brought together. . . ."[7] With the turn of the century, this changed. As federal government activities expanded so did the volume, scope, and variety of records kept. By the 1940s two management issues, executive secrecy and federal regulation, converged. Secrecy, justified by the war and foreign relations considerations, spilled over into all aspects of agency administration. Federal agencies had multiplied and vastly expanded their regulatory functions, bringing complaints of "agency tyranny." The 1946 APA was the response. It was " . . . drawn upon the theory that administrative operations and procedures are public property which the general public, rather than a few specialists or lobbyists, is entitled to know or to have the ready means of knowing with definiteness and assurance."[8]

To the extent that agencies developed regulations in the *Federal Register* and made information available for public inspection, some of the APA goals were achieved. Overwhelmingly, however, citing two justifying phrases from the APA, agencies kept tight reign on their records. They determined which people were "properly and directly concerned" and what information should be "held confidential for good cause found."[9] The result was "a veritable cave of winds of official discretion."[10] The FOIA of 1966 was the next congressional attempt to address the problem. In many ways, enactment signified not the end of the struggle to manage government information, but the beginning.

Several important similarities characterize the APA of 1946 and the FOIA of 1966. Both took over a decade to enact and were in response to what Congress and interest groups believed was a need to protect citizens from "arbitrary and biased" administrative actions. In each case, organized groups lobbied for change. People affiliated with these groups staffed the congressional subcommittees that researched questions of information policy and wrote the legislation. The American Bar Association took the lead for the APA; the American Society of Newspaper Editors, for the FOIA. Both Acts were attempts to make information available to the public on request. Both relied on agency discretion through rule making and required that regulations be published in the *Federal Register*. Significantly, each statute contained language that was sufficiently flexible as to permit agencies to reinterpret congressional intent.

Oversight

All three branches of government have actively shaped agency management of FOIA. Congress has not only held hearings and commissioned studies, but committee leaders have at times gone directly to agency administrators to seek explanations for specific information decisions, countermand executive branch guidance, or respond to published notices of proposed changes in FOIA regulations. For example, after the Department of Health and Human Services proposed changes in its FOIA regulations in the *Federal Register,* Glenn English, Chairman of the House Subcommittee on Government Information, Justice and Agriculture, wrote to HHS "strongly" objecting to "several features" of their proposals. While noting that the department "had always had a good reputation for its FOIA operations," the Congressman stated that the proposed regulations "are inconsistent with the letter and spirit" of the Act and explained his objections point-by-point.[11] Administrators in several agencies suspect that certain members of Congress have given constituents agency documents that either would not have been released under FOIA or would have had a substantial fee charged.

Executive branch guidance also has taken many forms. Between 1966 and 1983, five Attorneys General prepared memoranda of varying detail to guide agencies in managing FOIA.[12] The Department of Justice publishes updates on the law, consults on difficult cases, and determines whether it will support an agency in court. Training is provided by Justice and the Office of Personnel Management. Executive Orders, Directives, and Office of Management and Budget Circulars have impacted on FOIA management. Studies by the Administrative Conference of the U.S. have recommended changes in the management of the Act. In addition, officials have contributed to the legislation and written congressional reports accompanying the legislation.[13]

Informally, agency personnel have been encouraged, with varying degrees of subtlety, to foster Executive branch goals through the exercise of discretion. FOIA offices have been moved from easily accessible to more obscure locations, and some FOIA positions have been eliminated. *Privacy Times* reported, in winter 1986, that the Public Affairs/FOIA office at HHS had been moved from its ground floor room designed for public use to a fourth floor room hidden behind a bank of elevators.

The courts have taken a steadily growing number of information cases arising from the administration of FOIA with mixed results for administrators. Justice cited a total of 2,278 such judicial decisions by 1985; 19 were issued by the Supreme Court.[14] While some aspects of law have been clarified, the circuits at other times have split on interpretation. Congress has also on occasion stepped in to reestablish its intent in light of Supreme Court decisions.

Agency response to all this guidance can be divided loosely into three phases. During the first (1966–74), agencies tended to use their discretion to ignore the FOIA and to restrict that information they had to release. Some continued to cite the 1789 statute as justification for withholding information. Between 1967 and 1972, congressional oversight was limited. No hearings were held; the House provided informal guidance to requesters and made suggestions about procedures.

Extensive congressional hearings in 1972 and 1973 led to the amendments of 1974 and a marked change in the way agencies responded to FOIA requests. Requesters now had only to "reasonably describe" records, not identify them precisely. The definition of "agency" was expanded. Some exemptions were tightened. The use of *de novo* and *in camera* review by the courts was also clarified. Time limits were set for processing requests. Penalties could be assessed against agencies and employees for failure to comply with the statute. Congress assumed a proactive role; since 1972, both Houses have conducted oversight as have their support agencies. Although there was still a lack of enthusiasm at some agencies, a number of career civil servants felt a professional commitment to carry out the provisions of the Act. The American Society of Access Professionals, formed in 1980, provided additional support for "access professionals."

Since 1978, a perceptible shift has occurred in the way agencies interpret the FOIA.[15] Although still adhering to the requirements of the statute, many agencies, encouraged by executive branch leaders, have begun to find and reassert their discretionary capabilities. For example, by exercising their right to waive fees or charge for information, many agencies have, in effect, returned to the old APA standard of releasing information to those "properly and directly concerned." Agencies are judging such factors as the professional and intellectual qualifications of the requester, the likely use to which the information will be put, and the public interest of the documents as conditions for granting fee waivers. Many requesters, faced with a choice of either paying hundreds or thousands of dollars for documents or taking an agency to court, forgo the request.

Managing the FOIA

During the past twenty years, agencies, requesters, and submitters have all become more sophisticated. Procurement specialists, for example, note that proposals and bids are better written and better organized. Large corporations have achieved a measure of success in their efforts to protect their commercial or financial information that is "privileged or confidential." Since the 1979 landmark Supreme Court decision (*Chrysler Corp. v. Brown*), submitters have been permitted to file "reverse FOIA" suits under the APA. Many agencies have rewritten regulations to routinize notification of submitters when questions exist about releasing information that might be exempt. Submitters can then make a case for withholding. The House has prepared a bill to institutionalize these changes in all agencies.

New businesses have developed. In addition to law firms and publications that specialize in FOI and privacy, there are also "information businesses." FOI Services, Incorporated, makes FOIA requests from FDA and other agencies and sells the information to subscribers. One FDA access professional suggests that this has, in the past, actually saved the agency the costs in time and money of replicating requests.

Administering the Act is in many ways a discretionary task that continues to present two challenges largely ignored by statutory and case law, directives and regulations, and personnel practices despite a twenty-year history. The first emanates from the nature of information as a product; the second, from defining the position of "access professional."

Information is a fragile, time-sensitive commodity. What is secret one week may easily be in the marketplace the next, a result of deliberate choice, serendipitous events, or error. While certain records are routinely released or withheld under the Act, many must be examined case-by-case, word-by-word. Typically, on these, only a portion is judged releaseable. The decision often depends on the timing of the request and the position, background, and training of the people exercising discretion. Procurement specialists may side with a contractor to protect perceived commercial interests while agency attorneys argue that a denial cannot be defended in court; people in public affairs may argue that the information is public while agency attorneys may claim release will harm the deliberative process.

Surprisingly, there is still no *typical* "access professional." Also, no uniform job description or consistently identifiable career path exists. Even the term "access professional" is inadequate to describe the jobs of many employees who participate in deciding whether to release information. Some position series permit movement from GS-5 to GS-15; others offer no such path.[16]

What many FOIA practitioners share is that they became access professionals by chance, not choice. Many stayed because they enjoyed the work and perspective. A clerical worker at FDA liked "the diversity, challenge, and autonomy"; a senior attorney found that FOI "keeps me in touch with every component of the agency."[17]

Lack of a uniform position description has led to an especially diverse group of people expected to perform similar kinds of jobs throughout government. Among the broad categories that have been identified are: former public information and public affairs experts; attorneys and paralegals; investigators and inspectors; management analysts; and records and information specialists.[18] Agency personnel who work with the records, such as procurement specialists or scientists may also participate in FOIA decisions. Inevitably and frequently, people with such differing backgrounds and professional training disagree over whether certain documents should be released. Some requesters have taken advantage of this by making identical requests either to several field offices or to several agencies.

These differences add tension to the work of many FOI officers who feel that their jobs are particularly difficult since they are subject to criticism from requesters, submitters, politically appointed officials of their own agencies, as well as from colleagues with different views. Senior FOI officers also frequently express fear of making errors, such as finding documents after having certified their nonexistence.

Many employees deal directly with requesters and submitters, learning a remarkable amount of personal information about requesters, especially as they seek to determine fee waivers. Although requests and responses are all in writing, many agencies telephone requesters and submitters to negotiate for more time to review records or to suggest how requests can be narrowed.

FOI in the 1980s

According to an experienced staffer in the executive branch, the Reagan administration's approach to information differs substantially from previous administrations. "There was a convergence of belief of the bad effects of too much disclosure . . . [and a fear that] by providing information about what they were doing, they would provide critics with an opportunity to shoot at them."[19]

No president has yet eagerly embraced the FOIA, but the Reagan administration, in the absence of congressional action, has been the most successful in reinterpreting legislative intent. Regulations and guidelines; Executive Orders; and management of the bureaucratic reward structure have been the major techniques. In addition, an ongoing effort has been made to have the private sector manage and sell what has historically been public information.

Plans for action were laid out in *Mandate for Leadership,* the Heritage Foundation's "road map to help the . . . Reagan administration steer the nation."[20] Although the extent to which members of the Administration systematically follow the Foundation's suggestions may be arguable, many of the techniques used to redirect information policy parallel the advice. Specifics for dealing with FOIA are brief but precise, reflecting discomfort with releasing information. The report recommends that the policy of broad discretionary disclosure "should be explicitly reversed by Executive Order in the field of intelligence agency and investigative information and in the area of trade secrets." As a "general rule" government should exercise "its discretion against disclosure, whenever authorized to do so by statute."[21]

More general guidance is also proposed. Executive Orders are described as "one of the major powers which a President can exercise immediately . . . without the necessity for Congressional action."[22] Political executives are told to "discover discretion . . . lucrative 'targets of opportunity' for policy change." The goal is to change administrative procedures or regulations to accomplish the President's "broad agenda" without "significant political cost."[23] They are also told to use "normative control" and "cooptation," as part of their management techniques. For example, an executive is to "refuse to sign documents, make decisions, and approve budgets" unless these further his "political agenda."[24]

Managing the reward system is the most difficult to observe. Even when examples are mentioned, they are almost always off the record and not for attribution, hence the extent to which they have been applied is not measurable. However, interviews suggest that career bureaucrats are sensitive to the prevailing political winds and the power of rewards and punishments.

Executive Order 12356 on Security Classification is one application of the Foundation's advice.[25] Although its primary purpose is to establish procedures and criteria for creating official secrets, an attorney testifying at hearings before the House Subcommittee on Government Information in 1984, said that this Order was used as an exemption by the FBI to reduce what he received from his FOIA request. Before the EO, the documents "though often severely redacted," contained information that was meaningful and useful. After this Order took effect, over two-thirds of the documents received were "completely censored, including their dates, authors, recipients and routing notations. . . ."[26]

The most effective use of regulations and guidelines to change FOIA policy is the 1983 Justice Department Memo providing guidelines for fee waivers.[27] Prior to this, a number of agencies had developed their own criteria to determine whether requester and request merited a fee waiver. Since the Memo, agencies have been amending their regulations to conform more closely to the memo. The guidelines illustrate how a phrase, "in the public interest," can become the Heritage Foundation's "target of opportunity" for the "discovery of discretion" and be administratively used to reinterpret a statute.

Setting fees permits agencies to exercise considerable discretion. People who make FOI determinations are concerned about the costs of complying with the Act which includes time searching for records, analyzing their content to determine what can be released, and reproduction. Congress has never allocated additional funds to administer the Act. Program officers often feel that FOIA review keeps them from doing their "real" jobs. FOI officers are particularly sensitive to what is seen as abuse of the law by corporations and individuals who profit from the information. Typical is the view of a senior career bureaucrat who manages FOI and strongly supports the Act: "We're providing millions and millions of dollars of research free for profit-oriented ventures; this bothers me deeply."[28]

The 1974 amendments were the last time Congress voted on the question of fees. After considerable debate, it was agreed that charges were to be assessed only for search and reproduction, not for administrative time spent in determining what should be released. Fees were to be reduced or waived, "in the public interest because furnishing the information can be considered as primarily benefiting the general public." And, "[t]his public interest standard should be liberally construed by agencies."[29] In general, between 1974 and 1982, requesters and agencies agreed that agencies followed this approach.

According to several staffers who participated in the process, the Reagan administration adopted the premise that "fees are barriers" and that "a free flow of information is not the same as the flow of free information or the flow of information for free."[30]

The Justice guidelines of 1983 reiterate the statutory goal, but shift the emphasis. Not only must agency personnel judge whether the waiver will be "primarily benefiting the general public" but they must "safeguard the public treasury," a standard not found in the statute or its legislative history. Fees can be waived if five criteria are met. These include "genuine public interest" in the subject, the value of the "records themselves," and the requestor's identity and qualification—for example, "expertise in the subject area and ability and intention to disseminate the information to the public." The information must be unavailable in the public domain and the agency must compare "the magnitude of personal interest" with any "discernible public interest."

Requests for waivers are handled case-by-case and require exchange of lengthy, detailed letters between agency and requester. Several examples demonstrate, at least anecdotally, the way agencies make judgments about such factors as the capabilities of the requester and the public interest in the documents.

The Better Government Association, working with United Press International, requested from the State Department copies of Inspector General audits for five U.S. embassies in Western Europe and a fee waiver. The waiver was denied on the basis that there was "no heightened interest in the expenditures of funds by large Embassies abroad," even though, two weeks previously, UPI had issued a story of excessive costs of officials visiting certain foreign embassies.[31] BGA filed suit. Justice reconsidered the case, approved a fee waiver, and said the case should be dismissed since the issue was moot. However, BGA citing an exception to the "mootness doctrine" argued that this policy of granting a fee waiver only after a requester files suit, permits an agency to repeat the process but avoid review. The D.C. Court of Appeals agreed to hear the case.

In a second example, the fee waiver decision turned on an assessment of the public value of "the records themselves." In this case, a department that receives thousands of requests annually, waived the fee for one small portion of records. These pages, though containing deletions, had an index and explanatory paragraphs that were considered "of value." The remaining, much larger and heavily excised portion, had only "titles, headings, and bits of fragmented sentences." The agency billed the requester at the standard ten cents per page for these almost blank pages since they contained "no useful information."[32]

At a third agency, fee decisions rested primarily on a combination of the requester's identity and qualifications and "discernible public interest." A graduate student was denied a waiver for militarily sensitive records on the grounds that "almost all the information you seek is classified. . . . Congress and other appropriate bodies have already been provided all the information, including classified material. . . . your research will be of no additional value to these bodies." The charge for fulfilling the request was estimated at $5,000.

A 50 percent reduction was given to a non-profit organization that published information received through FOIA. Since the foundation charged a fee for its publication to defray costs, the agency ruled that, "it is reasonable to require the Foundation to defray a portion of the government's cost. . . ." The estimated reduced charge was $50; the actual, $29.

The last case, in which an Ohio citizens' group was granted a full fee waiver, on appeal, was decided before the Justice Memo was issued. It suggests that Justice elaborated on and legitimized the way a number of agencies were making decisions. Besides acknowledging that the group was "a *bona fide* public interest group," there was "current public interest," and the organization had "limited financial resources," the Appeals Officer also noted that the head of the organization "often contributes funds to the organization from her limited personal financial resources."[33]

In the 1980s, FOIA officers have been moving toward a more restrictive interpretation of the Act. There has been an increase in the use of the fifth exemption protecting deliberative privilege, attorney-client privilege and attorney work-product privilege. Agency people who handle FOIA requests ask how they can best use the exemptions to withhold information. The time it takes for a requester to receive documents has lengthened as the agencies require more information from requesters which in turn increases the number of letters exchanged. Agencies are developing more complete administrative records to defend their actions. More people are reviewing decisions. In some procurement departments, between ten and thirty-five people may review a request. In the 1970s, review was primarily on requests that were to be denied. In the 1980s, review is also often for information that will be released. Impressionistically, in the mid-1970s, it was the requester who was more willing to take the agency to court, in the 1980s it is the agency that is more willing to risk going to court.

The Contours of Policy

The FOIA, in many ways, is the centerpiece of federal information policy—visible, publicized, used as a model in a number of states as well as in Canada and Australia. In reality, however, it is but one vector in a much larger geometry. While Congress has sought to insure public access to government decision making through FOIA, other statutes and the actions of the executive branch provide equally strong guidance for restricting information and access. The sum of these forces is "information policy." Between 1966 and 1986, beginning with FOIA, Congress enacted four major statutes addressing broad segments of federal information policy.[34] Information control is an integral component of several other statutes. Information-related provisions have been appended to a multitude of other laws.

The Privacy Act of 1974, coming little more than a month after the FOIA was amended, permits individuals to review records the federal government keeps on them, limits the number and kinds of records agencies keep on individuals, protects people from having their records released to others without their knowledge or permission, and establishes criminal penalties for agency officers and employees who willfully maintain a system of records without proper notification or disclose prohibited information. In addition, the Act changes some of the assumptions made in FOIA. Longer and more detailed, it defines "records" and narrows the population protected from "any person" to an "individual" (U.S. citizen or alien lawfully admitted for permanent residence).[35]

The Government in the Sunshine Act (1976) requires that government agencies, with a number of exceptions, insure that "every portion of every meeting" be "open to public observation."[36]

The Paperwork Reduction Act (1980), gives OMB responsibility for managing federal information policy including reduction of federal paperwork by setting standards and developing guidelines for the way the federal government handles all aspects of data: automatic data processing, telecommunications, as well as paper records.[37]

Information control spreads to all areas of government business. For example, it can be found in a most unlikely place—export legislation. The Arms Export Control Act (1976) and the Export Administration Act (1979) each consider information ("Technical Data") a resource to be licensed and governed by agency regulations.[38] Under the Export Administration Act, technology is "the information and know-how that can design, produce, manufacture, utilize, or reconstruct goods, including computer software and technical data, but not the goods themselves."[39] In both Acts "export" occurs when American citizens travel abroad, when information is released "orally or visually to foreign nationals in the U.S. or abroad," or when information is disclosed to foreign visitors or students through academic instruction, symposia, or publication.[40]

As further illustration of the widespread, ad hoc, information control practices, a 1983 survey of forty agencies identified a total of 135 statutory provisions that they claimed as justification for withholding information from FOIA provisions.[41]

In addition to statutes, information policy directives have increased. For example, President Reagan's EO on Security Classification, 12356, has, among other changes, reversed Carter's approach to classification, overturning "If in doubt classify at the lowest level" and substituting "If in doubt classify at the highest level."[42]

OMB Circular A-130 requires that agencies obtain OMB approval for the generation or collection of all forms of new information. To win approval, agencies must demonstrate that the information is required or permitted by law or is essential for accomplishing their missions and prior to collecting information must plan for its dissemination, if any is to occur.[43]

The release of information developed through government contracts and government-sponsored research is also being renegotiated, with a "trend toward including pre-publication review clauses in government-sponsored university-based research contracts . . . even those involving only unclassified information."[44]

"Information Policy" is an emerging field: fragmented, rapidly changing, responding to technological leaps that have outpaced prediction or popular imagination, to competing political and philosophical values, and to the disparate, often contradictory needs of society. Congressional and executive branch responses reflect these contradictions. This overview of the central pieces that are forming federal information policy calls attention to the countervailing trends and conflicts in values in managing information.

The debate over what should be public, private, confidential, and officially secret; who should make these determinations; and how and when, has always been a source of tension fundamental to the nature and practice of American democracy. There is no reason to expect this debate to end, and the conflict it exposes may even be salutary in helping to clarify values and determine the tradeoffs to be made. What is essential is comprehensive, thoughtful, analytic discussion of the issues and their consequences and a resulting policy that reflects government's administrative capabilities and the balance of society's values.

Notes

1. Statistics are from annual reports submitted by each agency to Congress during 1986; estimates of requests completely filled is based on approximations from Congressman English's office. Sample FOIA requests were selected from DOD, DOE, and FDA.

2. 5 U.S.C. 22 (1964).

3. 5 U.S.C. 1002, 3 (1964); recodified as section 552.

4. Amendment to 5 U.S.C. 22 (1964); recodified as 5 U.S.C. 301 (1970). "This section does not authorize withholding information from the public or limiting the availability of records."

5. Harold L. Cross, *The People's Right to Know* (New York: Columbia University Press, 1953), p. 200.

6. Ibid., see *United States ex. rel. Stowell v. Deming et al., Civ. Serv. Commissioners,* 19 F. 2d 697 (App/ D.C. 1927).

7. Alexis de Tocqueville, *Democracy in America,* translated by George Lawrence, edited by J.P. Mayer (New York: Doubleday, 1969), p. 207.

8. Francis E. Rourke, *Secrecy and Publicity* (Baltimore: Johns Hopkins Press, 1961), p. 57. Reprinted from Administrative Procedure Act, 79th Cong., 2d sess., Senate Document No. 248 (July 26, 1946), p. 198.

9. 5 U.S.C. 1002 (1964).

10. Cross, *The People's Right to Know*, p. 239.

11. Letter from Glenn English, chairman, Government Information, Justice, and Agriculture Subcommittee of the Committee on Government Operations, U.S. Congress, to The Honorable Otis R. Bowen, Secretary of Health and Human Services, June 3, 1986.

12. Comprehensive implementation memos were prepared by Attorneys General Ramsey Clark (June 1967) and Edward H. Levi (February 1975). AGs Griffin Bell (May 1978) and William French Smith (May 1981) on "demonstrable harm"; Smith reversed this, relying on agency judgment of the appropriate use of exemptions. Assistant Attorney General Jonathan C. Rose dealt with fee waivers (January 7, 1983).

13. For example, in 1966, the House let the White House write the House report accompanying the FOIA as a condition for President Johnson's support. In 1980, Attorney General Civiletti proposed amendments to FOIA; many of these were subsequently incorporated into the Senate bill prepared during the Reagan administration.

14. Pamela Maida, ed., *Freedom of Information Case List*, September 1985 edition, (Washington, DC: U.S. Government Printing Office, 1985); for analysis of the role of the courts see paper by Phil Cooper in this symposium [in *Public Administration Review*, Nov./Dec. 1986].

15. It is difficult to pick a precise year for change. During the Carter administration there was support for both increased access to information (e.g., National Security) and increased restrictions (e.g., FOIA). The Justice Department, beginning under Attorney General Bell (1978), completed a study of FOIA in December 1980. Attorney General Civiletti transmitted the proposed FOIA reforms to OMB. Many were subsequently incorporated into S. 774. See, for example, Letter from Benjamin R. Civiletti to James 1. McIntyre, Jr., Director of OMB, December 12, 1980 and proposed amendments and supporting memoranda. A career bureaucrat who had helped write the 1966 House FOIA report, said his impression was that President Carter's rhetoric favored FOIA but his behavior did not.

16. "Proper Positions for Access Professionals—The Impossible Dream?" Report of the Professional Standards Committee, American Society for Access Professionals, November 1981.

17. Interviews, June 13, 1985; June 19, 1985.

18. "Proper Positions for Access Professionals."

19. Interview, June 20, 1985.

20. Charles L. Heatherly, ed., *Mandate for Leadership: Policy Management in a Conservative Administration* (Washington, DC: Heritage Foundation, vol. 1, 1981; vol. 2, 1984). The quote is from vol. 2, foreword, p. 1.

21. Ibid., vol. 1, p. 1089.

22. Ibid., vol. 1, p. 1077.

23. Ibid., vol. 2, p. 514.

24. Ibid., p. 525.

25. 47 *Federal Register* 14874, Executive Order 12356, "National Security Information," April 2, 1982.

26. Testimony of Douglas Mirell, U.S. House, Hearings before a subcommittee of the Committee on Government Operations, 98th Cong., 2d sess., May 24, 30, June 20, August 9, 1984, pp. 571–575.

27. Memorandum from Jonathan C. Rose, Assistant Attorney General, Office of Legal Policy, Department of Justice to Heads of All Federal Departments, January 7, 1983.

28. Interview, June 25, 1985.

29. Letter from Chairman Glenn English, U.S. House, Government Information, Justice and Agriculture Subcommittee to Heads of all Departments and Agencies, February 22, 1983. Reprinted in U.S. House, *Hearings on S. 774*, p. 1017.

30. Interview, June 27, 1985.

31. U.S. House, *Hearings on S. 774*, pp. 230–231; information on current status is from conversation with Cornish Hitchcock, attorney representing Better Government Association, July 24, 1986.

32. Interview, June 26, 1986.

33. Agency correspondence, April 24, 1985; November 22, 1985 (the Justice Department has raised questions about this); March 16, 1982.

34. The amendments of 1974 were sweeping and affected all agencies. In 1976, a technical amendment was included in the Government in the Sunshine Act to reverse the 1975 Supreme Court decision in *FAA Administrator v. Robertson* (422 U.S. 255, 1975) by reducing agency discretion and clarifying what Congress considered a (b)(3) exemption. In 1984, the Central Intelligence Agency Information Act was passed as Sec. 2(a) of the National Security Act of 1947. It gives the Director of Central Intelligence discretion to exempt certain operational files from the provisions of FOIA.

35. 5 U.S.C. 552 (a).

36. 5 U.S.C. 552 (b).

37. 44 U.S.C. 3501.

38. 22 U.S.C. 2751 et. seq.

39. 50 U.S.C. App. 2401 et. seq.

40. Mary M. Cheh, "Government Control of Private Ideas," in Harold C. Relyea, ed., *Striking a Balance: National Security and Scientific Freedom* (Washington, DC: American Association for the Advancement of Science, May 1985), p. 9.

41. "The (b)(3) Project: Citations by Federal Agencies (1975–1982)," American Society of Access Professionals (Washington, DC, 1984).

42. Carter Administration, EO 12065, Executive Order on Security Classification, December 1, 1978 (43 *Federal Register* 28949). Reagan Administration, EO 12356, Executive Order on National Security Information, April 2, 1982. For discussion see, *Security Classification Policy and Executive Order 12356*, 29th Report, Committee on Government Operations, August 12, 1982, H. Report 97–731 (Washington, DC: U.S. Government Printing Office, 1982).

43. OMB Circular A-130.

44. John Shattuck, "Federal Restrictions on the Free Flow of Academic Ideas" (Cambridge, MA: Harvard University, July 1985), revised paper.

PART IV

ADMINISTRATORS AND
CONFLICT RESOLUTION

Public administrators are involved in internal conflicts and external conflicts. Many administrative actions produce conflicts. These may arise from internal management concerns, such as employee supervision, developing budgets, or coordinating policy between agencies. External conflicts may arise between agencies and the individuals or interest groups that government actions affect. Promulgating rules, developing procedures and standards, and enforcing legislation and rules may produce conflict. Certainly not all differences of positions or conflicts result in adversarial proceedings or litigation. Yet the threat of adversarial proceedings is real.

Public agencies adjudicate disputes. Public administrators sue and are sued. Therefore, conflict resolution is an important skill for public administrators. This section summarizes the context of dispute resolution. Adversarial practices, particularly litigation, have been widely criticized. This has led to innovations in dispute resolution, one of which is alternative dispute resolution.

During the 1980s there was a national movement away from litigating adversarial conflicts toward more consensual and cooperative approaches to conflict resolution. The primary approaches include arbitration, negotiation, mediation, and mini-trials. Collectively, these are called alternative dispute resolution (ADR). Proponents emphasize five benefits of ADR: it lowers costs; is less time consuming; allows for creative solutions; improves relationships; and encourages participation of affected individuals and citizens. One assumption underlying ADR is that both parties desire and agree to use the ADR process. Another assumption is that ADR can be private and so it is preferable to the delay, expense, and publicness of court hearings.

Early attempts at developing systematic alternatives to courts resolving disputes provided a set of arguments that were used to develop the administrative adjudication provisions of the APA. Administrative adjudication was linked to the desire to avoid litigation and courts. Some of the reasons given to support administrative hearings are court cases are slow, expensive, and dominated by attorneys. In addition, judges are well-educated generalists who carefully considered the data and arguments presented to them by advocates. Thus, the judges hearing the cases are not experts in the questions they are asked to decide; administrators are subject matter experts. Similar rationales were recently used to promote adopting ADR in public administration settings.

Initially, ADR developed as new methods and procedures for resolving disputes in the commercial and the private sectors, but soon ADR was advocated for administrative agencies and governments. However, some analysts questioned whether there was clear and sufficient statutory authority for administrators to use ADR techniques, while others argued that the use of ADR techniques was within the discretionary authority of the bureaucracy. In response to these debates, in 1990 Congress passed legislation that expressed a clear preference for developing and using ADR in government. The two purposes cited by Congress for adopting ADR were lower costs and time savings—two traditional efficiency rationales. In addition, presidents have supported using ADR through Executive Orders.

During the 1990s new types of administrative roles were developed adapting alternative dispute approaches to investigating and evaluating possible conflicts. One type of role was the inspectors general, or process auditors, who look at internal management processes, procedures, and problems. Ombudsmen were another administrative role that developed as a type of trouble shooter. Ombudsmen investigate questions and complaints from the public or from within an agency and they often serve as neutral investigators who can make suggestions on improving government procedures. These process auditor and ombudsman roles in an organization systematically encourage the investigation and development of information-based attempts to resolve misunderstandings before they become full-blown conflicts.

How ADR is used in government varies by the context and type of process adopted. Interest-based negotiations, arbitration, and mediation have been used in public sector personnel management. These three methods were developed in private sector labor relations in the twentieth century and have been extended to the public sector. The use of ADR in public labor negations is also perceived as beneficial. As David G. Carnevale shows in Chapter 15, several ADR innovations promote ongoing relationships and interest-based approaches to public sector labor relations. This chapter looks at a partnership approach aimed at improving performance, and thus it shows how ADR techniques are related to changing models of management-employee relationships.

The frequent critiques of administrative development of regulations, plans, and policies raise issues about the lack of public participation and governmental accountability. The desire is to move to a more open, cooperative, and responsive process. ADR practices are often proposed to provide greater participation and better accountability. Nancy J. Manring, in the second chapter in this section, considers how these new ADR processes can be implemented and evaluated. Note how Manring uses the concerns of administrative autonomy, responsiveness, and organizational setting to evaluate the case of development of Forest Use Plans.

ADR has also been introduced into administrative rulemaking when Congress provided authority to agencies to develop alternatives to legislative rulemaking using the traditional notice and comment regulation. This shift in regulatory rulemaking from the traditional authoritative model is toward a collaborative consensus-based process of negotiating regulations, which is often called "reg-neg." Critics of negotiated rulemaking raise issues such as whether all interests of the affected public will be included in the process; whether this type of negotiated rulemaking is part of the iron triangle of regulatory capture; whether it will reduce litigation that often arises to challenge regulations; and whether it is a practical and more efficient alternative to notice and comment rulemaking.

Although the examples in the chapters in this section are from the federal level, the dispute resolution reforms have clearly added to the techniques and procedures administrators must understand and use at all levels of government. In the final chapter in this section, Zhiyong Lan synthesizes the broader conflict resolution perspective, including its impact, nature, strategic uses, and actors involved. A number of unanswered issues about ADR remain for public administrators: first, how will agencies train administrators in the use of different dispute resolution methods; second, how do we evaluate the effectiveness of ADR processes; and finally, are there occasions when ADR may not be good policy for promoting democratic values of openness and governmental accountability.

CHAPTER 15

ROOT DYNAMICS OF ALTERNATIVE DISPUTE RESOLUTION

An Illustrative Case in the U.S. Postal Service

DAVID G. CARNEVALE

Conflict in organizations is inevitable. A common source arises in formal employee relations systems when labor and management confront each other during the negotiation and administration of collective bargaining agreements. In response to this problem, American industry, government, and unions have initiated a first generation of conflict-reduction strategies that encourage employee involvement, cooperation, information-sharing, and joint-problem solving (U.S. Department of Labor 1991).

A collaborative dispute mechanism receiving increased notice is a method broadly known as alternative dispute resolution (ADR) where the goal is not for one party to achieve "victory" over the other but to produce mutually acceptable settlements that participants can live with (Bowers 1980; Conti 1985; Goldberg and Hobgood 1987; American Arbitration Association 1987).

Employers and unions are interested in alternative dispute approaches because, theoretically, they lead to (1) higher grievance settlement rates short of arbitration, (2) lower costs, (3) reductions in the time it takes to get complaints decided, (4) achievement of better overall results because the parties themselves have a greater hand in working out their own problems, (5) appreciative attitudes toward collaboration, and (6) positive spillover effects in other areas of the relationship between participants. Stated differently, advantages of ADR plans include: lower transaction costs (time, money), increased learning about problem solving, and the advancement of skills helpful to the maintenance of mature, continuing relationships (Goldberg 1989).

Arbitration

A grievance is an employee or union complaint originating out of some question of rights in the employment relationship, as specified in a bargaining agreement. By all accounts, a plurality of grievances is settled at the earlier steps of the procedure. However,

From *Public Administration Review* 53, no. 5 (September/October 1993): 455–461. Copyright © 1993 by American Society for Public Administration. Reprinted with permission.

Box 15.1
The Study and Methodology

This article reports the results of a study of an experimental form of alternative dispute resolution known as Union Management Pairs (UMP), which has been applied in the U.S. Postal Service (USPS). UMP are teams usually consisting of one representative from the National Association of Letter Carriers (NALC) union and one designated management agent. They work with front-line supervisors and union stewards to settle contract differences or violations at the lowest possible organizational level.

The subject of this investigation is the UMP experiment currently operating in the greater Oklahoma City, Oklahoma, area. Data were collected in three ways: (1) interviews with union and management officials experienced in using the UMP process, such as members of the UMP team, the USPS Field Director for Human Resources, and the NALC's National Business Agent; (2) responses from more than fifty front-line supervisors and stewards who answered structured queries concerning what they liked best and least about the program as well as how they would improve it if they could; and (3) training videos and official records prepared by management and labor. The data are qualitative and typical responses were used to illustrate common themes. The research problem was twofold: to evaluate the effects of ADR in this case and to discover underlying properties.

---

those that are not worked out end up in rights arbitration. Nine out of ten of all union-management negotiated grievance procedures contain an arbitration clause that customarily provides that third parties acceptable to both sides hear disputes and impose final and binding decisions (Herman, Schwarz, and Kuhn 1992; Kearney 1984; Aaron, Najita, and Stern 1988).

Grievance arbitration has several advantages over such alternatives as strikes or taking day-to-day employee issues into court. In recent years, however, the process has become increasingly expensive, time-consuming, and legalistic. In total, the best part of a year can pass before the process exhausts itself (Allen and Keaveny 1988). Arbitration is also costly. In addition to time and money, the traditional grievance arbitration process takes a toll on participants.

All of the above characteristics of arbitration may increase transaction costs while lowering the satisfaction of the parties (Herman, Schwarz, and Kuhn 1992). The objective of alternative dispute resolution methods is not to replace arbitration, but to supplement it with devices that magnify satisfaction by granting factions greater direct voice in fashioning more timely settlements.

Labor Relations in the U.S. Postal Service

The Postal Service has a history of contentious employee relations and acrimonious bargaining (Tierney 1988). Effective November 9, 1988, the UMP program was introduced in the NALC/Oklahoma City Division which, like most other jurisdictions, had its share of employee relations problems, the most notable being the shootings in Edmond, Oklahoma, on Wednesday, August 20, 1986, in which a disgruntled postal employee killed fourteen co-workers.

UMP

The UMP program is an innovation that came out of the St. Louis area field office and was part of a strategy to improve labor-management relations in the greater Oklahoma City (OKC) area following the Edmond tragedy.

The procedure follows certain steps. For example, in a case where a supervisor believes a union member should be disciplined for just cause (Figure 15.1):

1. No discipline may be issued until the UMP process is utilized.
2. The proposed disciplinary situation must be discussed between the supervisor and union steward. The steward and the supervisor must jointly investigate the facts surrounding the case. All documentation and information relevant to the case are shared and discussed in an effect to reach an appropriate remedy. The steward and the supervisor fill out and sign a worksheet which demonstrates how they defined the issue, the facts and reasoning used in the matter, "offers" of settlement made by each side, supporting documents relevant to the case, and, if applicable, the nature of the resolution of the problem.
3. If a mutually agreeable solution is not found, the steward will meet with higher levels of management, where the "discovery" process of joint fact-finding is repeated. If no resolution is forthcoming, the UMP team is called.
4. The UMP team reviews the particulars of the case, insures that the steward and appropriate levels of management made a good faith effort to determine the details of the situation and worked reasonably to fashion a settlement. Suggestions can be made by the UMP team, which functions simultaneously as fact-finders and mediators. Moreover, it can impose settlements if it cares to or forward unusually difficult problems to management's Field Director of Human Resources and the union's National Business Agent (NBA) for action.
5. If no agreement is reached, Step 1 of the formal grievance procedure comes into effect which, up to this point, has been waived. Since the grievance process has been held in suspension, no adverse action has been taken against an employee. Therefore, management does not have to defend against back pay and other "make whole" restitution. Neither does it have to engage in "penalty escalation," that is, inflating the initial sanction against an employee in anticipation that an arbitrator will reduce it later. It is free to back away without the appearance of backing down, because UMP is a "predisciplinary" or "pregrievance procedure."
6. Although there are no time limitations on the UMP process, every effort is made to settle issues in a "timely manner," which means within five working days at

Figure 15.1 **UMP Process in Action**

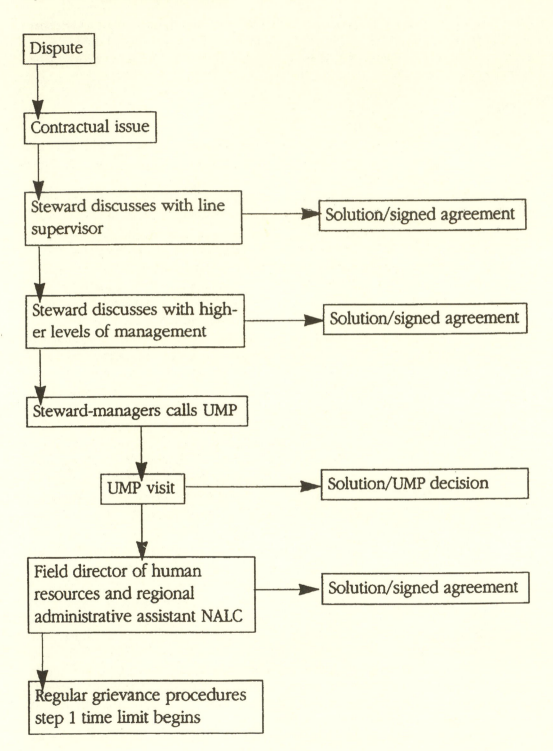

Table 15.1

Effects of UMP Process on Grievance Activity

Fiscal year	Oklahoma City	Oklahoma City MSC*
1986	401	1,302
1987	348	1,148
1988 to UMP	166	483
1988 since UMP**	2	2
1989**	1	1
1990	6	6
1991 (9–23–91)	4	4

Source: USPS, Oklahoma City.
Notes: *MSC means management section center and incorporates the OKC facility, 24 other stations, 306 associate officers, and 21 contract postal units covering approximately 3,500 workers.
**These three grievances are postal inspector cases not eligible for the UMP program.

the unit level and sometimes up to a month at the UMP stage, if the team needs to engage in extensive research (NALC/Oklahoma City Division, UMP Agreement 1988, 1–3).

A category of problems called "exemptions" is not appropriate for UMP. These are Inspection Service cases that involve use of drugs or alcohol, pilferage, or instances where retaining an employee on duty may result in injury to USPS property, loss of mail or funds, or where the employee may be injurious to self or others. Fair questions arise why these circumstances are outside of the UMP process and what proportion of overall incidents of alleged employee misconduct they represent. In other words, is UMP dealing only with a minority of issues and relatively insignificant matters at that? The answer is that these exemptions constitute a slight number of employee impropriety cases (Turner 1992). Moreover, postal inspectors are police officers. The exemptions they handle involve potential criminal activity, and the investigation of such incidents falls outside the kind of investigatory conventions typical of grievance processing.

One UMP team member each is appointed by the union and management to represent them in the process. In both instances, the persons selected are knowledgeable about the national agreement, have credibility with their principals, and can be trusted to be cooperative without being co-opted. All participants in the UMP process receive joint orientation prior to participating.

How Well Does It Work in Practice?

In 1987, more than 100 cases were awaiting arbitration and 200 more were on the way in the St. Louis division when the program was first introduced. Results were immediate and dramatic. The UMP team was able to resolve all of the issues except two. In little more than three years in Westchester, New York, where an UMP system is in effect, only 1 of 677 grievances has gotten to Step 3 in the grievance procedure (Winston 1992). Similar results have been achieved in the greater Oklahoma City area (Table 15.1).

Table 15.1 shows the effect of UMP on the grievance process in both Oklahoma City and the greater Oklahoma City operations area for the years 1986 to 1990 and part of 1991. Additional data collected for this study on UMP activity for the latter part of 1991 show that approximately 85 cases were handled. Of these, decisions were written on 42, 35 were mediated at the station level, and only 7 were sent to the next step unresolved. The results are obvious.

Studies show that the per diem rate for arbitrators rose from $84 in 1951–1952 to more than $400 in 1985. In another study, the costs of arbitration were valued at approximately $2,000 per day for each side (Sigler 1987). In the Central Region of the USPS, $500,000 was spent in 1987 on arbitration and 37,000 grievances were pending. Prior to the implementation of UMP in 1986, 60–70 percent of all grievances in the Oklahoma City area went to arbitration. The OKC area NALC representative said that the arbitration file had over 200 cases awaiting resolution before UMP. At the time of the interview for this study, in late 1991, none were pending. The numbers in Table 15.1, then, suggest significant economies realized with the new procedure. Notably, dollar savings are just part of the story. Lost time and negative effects on the relationship between the parties are influenced as well.

What Makes It Work?

To understand what makes the UMP policy work, one first has to appreciate the dynamics of what can go wrong when conflict arises and is not properly addressed. At the heart of the problem is the fact that the parties to a dispute cease communicating with one another in ways that focus on solving a problem rather than winning a battle. Trust degenerates as the principals escalate the conflict and engage in defensive behavior (Figure 15.2).

Once a grievance complaint is issued, the potential for damaging conflict arises. If the difficulty cannot be resolved quickly, positions harden, information is exchanged in an increasingly competitive manner, and considerable pressure is exerted to spread the dispute to other sections of the workplace as the parties cast about for support and power. Bystanders are urged to take sides. Each bloc begins to distort and stereotype the position of the other to gain advantage. Intensity evolves into anger. As the conflict spirals, it becomes increasingly difficult to agree on the definition of the problem and generate options for settlement. Finally, the dynamics are psychologically draining for those directly involved (Carpenter and Kennedy 1988).

A "better" system is one in which (1) confrontations are settled quickly at the local level, (2) disputants are satisfied with outcomes, and (3) the long-term effect promotes better communication and problem-solving ability on a day-to-day basis (Ury, Brett, and Goldberg 1988). To achieve these results an effective dispute resolution process must be structured to engender face-to-face communication and thorough fact-finding that generates multiple options for settlement in an atmosphere where individuals bear the ultimate responsibility for deciding their own controversies. UMP achieves these results by (1) fostering participation, (2) improving communication, (3) providing timely decisions, and (4) building trust.

Figure 15.2 **Spiral of Destructive Conflict**

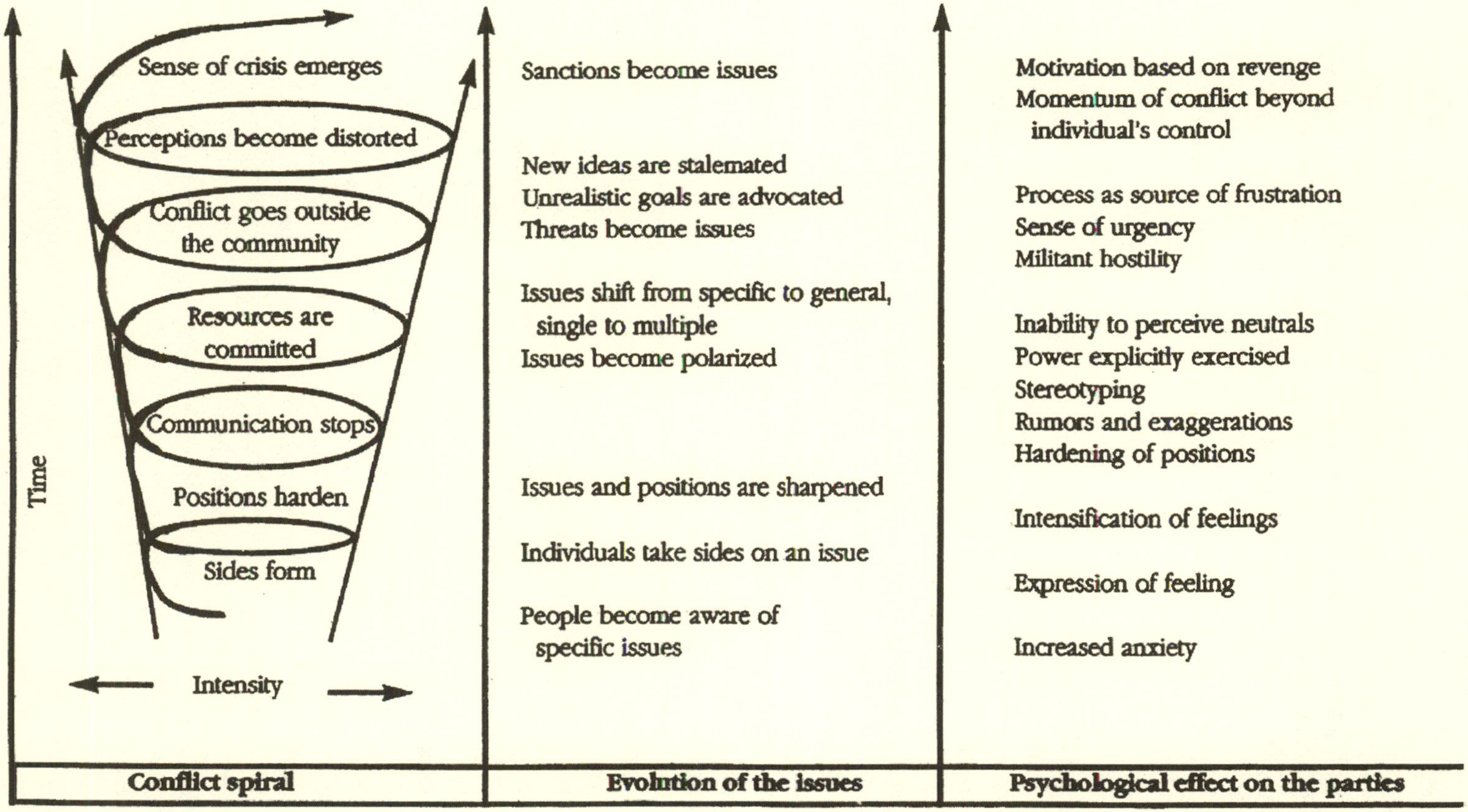

Conflict spiral	Evolution of the issues	Psychological effect on the parties
Sense of crisis emerges	Sanctions become issues	Motivation based on revenge
Perceptions become distorted		Momentum of conflict beyond individual's control
Conflict goes outside the community	New ideas are stalemated	
	Unrealistic goals are advocated	Process as source of frustration
Resources are committed	Threats become issues	Sense of urgency
		Militant hostility
	Issues shift from specific to general, single to multiple	
Communication stops	Issues become polarized	Inability to perceive neutrals
		Power explicitly exercised
		Stereotyping
Positions harden		Rumors and exaggerations
	Issues and positions are sharpened	Hardening of positions
Sides form		
	Individuals take sides on an issue	Intensification of feelings
		Expression of feeling
	People become aware of specific issues	Increased anxiety

Time

Intensity

Source: Adapted with permission. S. Carpenter and W. Kennedy. *Managing Public Disputes*, Jossey-Bass, Inc. Copyright © 1988. Reprinted by permission of John Wiley & Sons, Inc.

Participation

Innovations in workplace practices rely more and more on increasing employee participation. There is growing recognition, for instance, that reducing dysfunctional organizational conflict depends upon high levels of employee participation and labor-management cooperation (Piore and Sabel 1984; Kochan, Katz, and McKersie 1986; Kochan, Cutcher-Gershenfeld and MacDuffie 1989).

In the UMP program, participation is a key feature. At all times, the parties to the conflict are involved with what is done and how it is accomplished. In other words, the UMP approach gives disputants high process and outcome control, which differs markedly from arbitration procedures where a third party governs decisions but not processes and pure mediation policies where a third party regulates processes but not decisions.

Persons who have to live with the decisions are directly involved in the UMP process and clearly prefer it to arbitration because problems are resolved more often at the local level, and the foundations of decisions are better understood as a result of direct participation by the parties.

For example, one respondent characterized the arbitration process as "a huge puppet show" that led to "total frustration, a little bit of hatred, and a whole lot of anger." Several of those interviewed hoped that UMP "would put arbitrators out of business." Arbitrators were seen as outsiders who did not know as much about the postal service or its operations as those who worked there. They were also seen as "part of the bureaucracy." A supervisor felt the best feature of the program was that it "gives the opportunity to settle the problems at the local level. Even if the problem can not be settled at the local level, the UMP are familiar with how an operation should be run and they give more reasonable decisions than arbitrators." Yet another respondent signified that the "greatest feature of UMP is the authority for problems to be resolved at the lowest levels before they become grievances." Still another individual felt that UMP "has created the need for me to research previous decisions as well as the contract and manuals to a far-reaching extent rather than passing this responsibility on to another party." Overwhelmingly, the chance to solve problems at the local level was what supervisors and stewards liked best about UMP. One person simply saw the procedure as a "grass roots movement." Finally, an individual declared that "the best feature of the UMP program is that it enhances the participative management program."

An additional result of increasing direct participation of disputants at the local level was that the reasoning underlying decisions was better comprehended. One union official complained of receiving a thirty- to forty-page arbitration decision and not being able to understand the logic of the determination. In fact, that person protested that the case that the finding was supposed to address was not recognizable. A supervisor echoed the same point when explaining that the "why" of an arbitrator's ruling was less understandable than the rationale behind an UMP settlement because the UMP process allowed more personal involvement.

Experience with participatory schemes suggests that people feel greater ownership of their problems and magnified commitment to implementation of agreements when they have a voice in working them out. Further, the greater the process control (how decisions are made) and outcome control (the nature of the decisions themselves) that individuals have in deciding controversies, the more likely they will judge both the procedures and outcomes as fair (Thibaut and Walker 1975, 1978; Leventhal 1980; Leventhal, Karuza, and Fry 1980; Lind, Lissak, and Conlon 1983).

A companion benefit of increasing participation is that inclusive practices provoke better communication.

Communication

The UMP design significantly improves communication between the parties. It is the key to making the mechanism operate. Of course, that is an objective of traditional griev-ance systems. However, in the old scheme, communicants are often less interested in having a shared understanding of the difficulty than winning a point. In the negotiating or confrontational model of communication featured in traditional grievance operations, information confers advantage and is guarded. The strategy is much like playing poker. The contenders try to gauge the hands of the others while revealing as little as possible about their own. The ambition is to win. Open communication suffers as a result.

Stewards and supervisors, in this case, identified improved communications as a major outcome of the UMP policy. One supervisor's remark that "union and management must communicate with one another rather than engage in avoidance and denial" was typical. The common theme was that "the lines of communication have opened up." A steward said that UMP made it possible to "sit down and discuss a problem and perhaps work it out to satisfy both parties without alienating one or the other from the beginning by standing firm on a platform where things are viewed as either black or white. There is a lot of gray out here." Another union official stated that a new type of steward was emerging because of the approach. Those that communicated more openly and were problem-solvers were displacing unyielding confrontational types. A manager stated simply that UMP "took a lot of poison out of the system" through better communications. Another individual liked the fact that the process produced dialogue that led to "less hostility."

Sustaining communication reduces stereotyping, reliance on power, distorted percep-tions, militant hostility, and the sharpening of positions, all of which obstruct opportuni-ties for settlement and sustain the spiral of destructive conflict.

Speed

Another tenet of grievance processing is that disputes ought to be resolved as quickly as possible before the momentum of conflict escalates out of control. UMP is designed to reach accords in five working days or less. Rather than spend lengthy time awaiting an outcome in the expensive and acrimonious arbitration process, the parties can expect swift solutions.

One respondent to the survey, when asked what feature of UMP was best, indicated "quick." The same person, when asked how to improve the process, answered "quicker." While more succinct than most, the response was representative.

Historical data show that, prior to UMP, a disciplinary case would be moved to the front of the line for arbitration and would still take the best part of a year before a decision could be expected. Following UMP, the typical decision takes about thirty days to decide. Occasionally, a case will take three to four months prior to being settled, but that is rare, and four months is the absolute outside date for resolution (Turner 1992). In short, the program is designed to reduce the time dimension, which prevents disputes from intensifying, and this feature is widely appreciated by stakeholders.

Trust

Trust is a significant factor in the effectiveness of social systems (Carnevale and Wechsler 1992; Blau 1964). High-trust groups are more competent in problem-solving situations (Zand 1972). Trust is also a necessary precondition to participation (Miles and Ritchie 1984), open communication (Mellinger 1956) and labor-management cooperation (U.S. Department of Labor 1991). Employee involvement and alternative dispute methods can not succeed without mutual confidence.

Reciprocal trust is not easily achieved. Historically, each side has been conditioned to be cynical about the motives of the other. Some management officials see collaboration with labor unions as a mark of weakness, a loss of legitimate authority, and a diminution of discipline. Union representatives perceive joint determination initiatives as management manipulation in another guise.

One supervisor indicated that "it seems when the union has erred, it is swept under the carpet and covered up. It's almost like they deny that they ever do wrong." Another feels that "too many employees have a chip on their shoulder . . . and should be glad they have a job . . . and I would like a labor representative that conveyed this to employees." Other supervisors felt that subordinates "were not disciplined as they should be" or "given too many second chances." Distrust is evident among the union representatives, too. One indicated that "some supervisors don't view stewards as equals and have hidden agendas." Another complained that "you can't get information when you ask for it." The UMP team comes in for special criticism. The common complaint from both supervisors and stewards is that each group worries that their representative on the UMP team is too sympathetic to the needs of the other side.

These views underscore that overcoming suspicion is not simple. However, the number of positive comments indicating that UMP has created conditions of trust clearly dominated. Nonetheless, the climate of trust is fragile. It is clear that both sides carefully monitor the UMP process to determine who and what to trust, and under what circumstances. The procedure is always on trial.

Conclusion

The UMP program is a form of alternative dispute resolution applied to grievance processing based on the idea of a labor-management partnership. It differs substantially from adjudicative conflict models like arbitration. The parties themselves work to resolve problems with great dispatch at the lowest organizational level. The mechanism's strongest feature is that it requires on-going, open communication between front-line actors who have to live with the decisions that the system produces. Further, the greater control disputants have over both process and outcome issues strengthens their working relationship and leads to greater satisfaction with the results. Because the method produces timely responses to difficulties, the opportunity for conflict to intensify and reel out of control is greatly reduced. Transaction costs are significantly diminished.

It is important to note that, while UMP may be an alternative to traditional arbitration, it is likely that the scheme would not succeed if the arbitration alternative did not exist. In a sense, arbitration becomes a BATNA or "best alternative to a negotiated agreement" (Fisher and Ury 1981). The participants are encouraged to negotiate, employ integrative problem solving, and seek mutual gain because the alternative is much more costly. It is probable that a large measure of the good faith found in the UMP process exists because of the more costly dispute resolution mechanism that awaits if collaborations fails.

This study has focused on data gathered from stewards, supervisors, and other union and management officials. An important consideration is how grievants themselves feel about the process. Although grievants were not directly surveyed for this analysis, records show that only four cases have been filed, since the beginning of UMP, alleging that the union failed to perform its duty of fair representation under the law. All four cases were dismissed as being without merit by the National Labor Relations Board (Turner 1992). Nonetheless, future studies should deal directly with grievant satisfaction with outcomes of alternative dispute methods like UMP.

An additional research issue is to determine whether or not UMP is growing. There is evidence that it is. UMP enabling agreements typically contain an opt-out provision where either party can abandon the effort if not satisfied. According to officials interviewed for this study, they know of no situation where that option has been exercised. More reports on the diffusion of this innovation would be useful. Perhaps even more important is the need to compare UMP programs with traditional grievance processing plans on a wide range of outcome measures.

Recent incidents of violence throughout the USPS signal that deep, fundamental problems exist in the organization and how it is managed. These create the sort of obstacles to teamwork faced by postal officials in the Oklahoma City area after the Edmond shootings. The fact that a successful, cooperative innovation like UMP could be put into operation in this jurisdiction augers well for what the parties might be able to do to dramatically reduce destructive conflict in other situations.

Finally, ADR should be viewed as an extension of "interest based" problem-solving of the "win-win" type receiving so much attention in the negotiation of labor agreements. The movement toward a more cooperative approach toward collective bargaining needs to be extended to the administration of contracts. Grievance settlement mechanisms are an extension of the bargaining process. Adversarial grievance processing should not militate against everything that has been learned about collaboration and realizing mutual gains in labor relations. For these reasons, principled approaches to grievance processing, like the UMP method, merit additional attention.

References

Aaron, B., Najita, J.M., and Stern, J.L. 1988. *Public Sector Bargaining,* 2d ed. Washington, DC: Bureau of National Affairs.

Allen, R.D., and Keaveny, T.J. 1988. *Contemporary Labor Relations,* 2d ed. Reading, MA: Addison-Wesley, pp. 565–566.

American Arbitration Association. 1987. *Alternative Dispute Resolution in the United States: A Bibliography.* New York.

Blau, P.M. 1964. *Exchange and Power in Social Life.* New York: Wiley.

Bowers, M.H. 1980. "Grievance Mediation: Another Route to Resolution." *Personnel Journal* 59: 132–136.

Carnevale, D.G., and Wechsler, B. 1992. "Trust in the Public Sector: Individual and Organizational Determinants." *Administration and Society* 4: 471–495.

Carpenter, S.L., and Kennedy, W.J.D. 1988. *Managing Public Disputes.* San Francisco, CA: Jossey-Bass.

Conti, A.J. 1985. "Mediation of Work-Place Disputes: A Prescription for Organizational Health." *Employee Relations Law Journal* 11: 291–310.

Fisher, R., and Ury, W. 1981. *Getting to Yes: Negotiating Agreement Without Giving In.* New York: Penguin.

Goldberg, S.B. 1989. "Grievance Mediation: Successful Alternative to Labor Arbitration." *Negotiation Journal* 5: 9–15.

Goldberg, S.B., and Hobgood, W.P. 1987. *Mediating Grievances: A Cooperative Solution.* Washington, DC: U.S. Department of Labor, Bureau of Labor-Management Relations and Cooperative Programs.

Herman, E.E., Schwarz, J.L., and Kuhn, A. 1992. *Collective Bargaining and Labor Relations,* 3d ed. Englewood Cliffs, NJ: Prentice Hall.

Kearney, R.C. 1984. *Labor Relations in the Public Sector.* New York: Marcel Dekker.

Kochan, T.A., Katz, H.C., and McKersie, R. 1986. *The Transformation of American Industrial Relations.* New York: Basic Books.

Kochan, T.A., Cutcher-Gershenfeld, J., and MacDuffie, J.P. 1989. "Employee Participation, Work Redesign and New Technology: Implications for Public Policy in the 1990s." In *Investing in People: A Strategy to Address America's Workforce Crisis. Background Papers,* vol. 2. Commission on Workforce Quality and Labor Market Efficiency, Washington, DC: U.S. Department of Labor, pp. 1893–1949.

Leventhal, G.S. 1980. "What Should Be Done With Equity Theory?" In K.J. Gergen, M.S. Greenberg, and R.H. Willis, eds., *Social Exchange: Advances in Theory and Research,* pp. 27–55. New York: Plenum Press.

Leventhal, G.S., Karuza, J., and Fry, W.R. 1980. "Beyond Fairness: A Theory of Allocation Preferences" In G. Mikula, ed., *Justice and Social Interaction,* pp. 167–218. New York: Springer Verlag.

Lind, E.A., Lissak, R.I., and Conlon, D. 1983. "Decision Control and Process Control Effects on Procedural Fairness Judgments." *Journal of Applied Social Psychology* 13: 338–350.

Mellinger, G.D. 1956. "Interpersonal Trust as a Factor in Communication." *Journal of Abnormal Social Psychology* 52: 304–309.

Miles, R.E., and Ritchie, J.B. 1984. "Participative Management: Quality Versus Quantity." In D.A. Kolb, I.A. Rubin, and J.M. McIntyre, eds., *Organizational Psychology,* 4th ed., pp. 430–440. Englewood Cliffs, NJ: Prentice Hall.

NALC/Oklahoma City Division, U.M.P. Agreement, 1988. November 9.

Piore, M., and Sabel, C. 1984. *The Second Industrial Divide.* New York: Basic Books.

Sigler, J.C. 1987. "Mediation of Grievances: An Alternative to Arbitration?" *Employee Relations Law Journal* 13: 267–285.

Thibaut, J., and Walker, L. 1975. *Procedural Justice: A Psychological Analysis.* Hillsdale, NJ: Lawrence Erlbaum Associates.

———. 1978. "A Theory of Procedure." *California Law Review* 66: 541–566.

Tierney, S.T. 1988. *The U.S. Postal Service: Status and Prospects of a Public Enterprise.* Dover, MA:
    Auburn.
Turner, J.P. 1992. Interview. Labor Relations, United States Postal Service.
Ury, W.L., Brett, J.M., and Goldberg, S.B. 1988. *Getting Disputes Resolved: Designing Systems to Cut
    the Costs of Conflict.* San Francisco: Jossey-Bass.
U.S. Department of Labor, Bureau of Labor-Management Relations and Cooperative Programs. 1991.
    Labor-Management Cooperation: 1990 State-of-the-Art Symposium. Washington, DC: U.S. Gov-
    ernment Printing Office.
Winston, E. 1992. "Labor Partnership Speeds Grievances." *Federal Times* 28 (March 23): 14.
Zand, D.E. 1972. "Trust and Managerial Problem Solving." *Administrative Science Quarterly* 17:
    229–239.

CHAPTER 16

ADR AND ADMINISTRATIVE RESPONSIVENESS

Challenges for Public Administrators

NANCY J. MANRING

In recent years, alternative dispute resolution (ADR)[1] has received a great deal of attention at the federal level. The Administrative Conference of the United States (ACUS), whose mission is to promote improvements in the efficiency, fairness, and adequacy of federal agency operating procedures, held conferences, conducted research, and published recommendations promoting the use of ADR by federal agencies throughout the 1980s. This interest in ADR stems from the observation that dispute resolution techniques can eliminate delays, reduce demands on government, and produce more cost-effective and more satisfying results than traditional administrative procedures or litigation (Susskind, Babbitt, and Segal 1993; Dukes 1993). A diverse set of agencies and departments—some in response to ACUS's urging and some on their own initiative—have used ADR approaches such as negotiation, mediation, fact finding, and minitrials to resolve a wide variety of controversial public issues.[2]

Congress responded to this growing interest in ADR by passing the Negotiated Rulemaking Act (Public Law 101-648) and the Administrative Dispute Resolution Act (Public Law 101-552) in 1990. The Negotiated Rulemaking Act establishes a structure for using consensus-based negotiations to develop federal regulations. The Administrative Dispute Resolution Act (known as the federal ADR act) is more comprehensive in scope. It directs each agency to: designate an in-house dispute resolution specialist; provide ADR training for agency personnel; review all programs for ADR opportunities; adopt dispute resolution policies; and examine grant and contract language to identify means of promoting ADR over litigation (Madigan 1992; Susskind, Babbitt, and Segal 1993).

The successful implementation of the Administrative Dispute Resolution Act faces a number of challenges. The act provides no budgetary support for ADR, and existing budgeting procedures often encourage the use of litigation (Susskind, Babbitt, and Segal 1993). Although ACUS has provided guidance, agency officials will have to learn a number of new skills including identifying disputes that are potential candidates for

From *Public Administration Review* 54, no. 2 (March/April 1994): 197–203. Copyright © 1994 by American Society for Public Administration. Reprinted with permission.

ADR, selecting the appropriate ADR process for specific situations, and choosing third-party neutrals who can work with the disputants. Although ACUS recommendations and the Administrative Dispute Resolution Act address the important issues of confidentiality, representativeness, and accountability, federal officials will have to grapple with the reality of these challenging aspects of ADR (Amy 1990; Hamilton 1991; Susskind 1981).

Successfully implementing the Administrative Dispute Resolution Act also will involve confronting deeper issues associated with the traditional practice and context of public administration and the culture of professionalism. Stephenson and Pops (1991) have questioned whether administrators have the capacity—in terms of education, training, and role—to participate effectively in ADR. In recent years, numerous federal agencies have provided ADR training in specialized workshops or as part of more broadly focused leadership development programs. However, more challenging than providing training and technical assistance will be overcoming the barriers of professionalism: the resistance generated by traditional norms and role expectations. Professionally trained government officials may find it difficult to reconcile ADR—often perceived as political bargaining—with their existing norms and procedures for technical or scientific decision making. Negotiating with members of the public may be viewed as being unprofessional (Freemuth 1989; Manring 1993; Stephenson and Pops 1991). Public officials also may fear that ADR will mean a loss of decision-making authority (Bingham 1986; Meeks 1985; Susskind and Cruikshank 1987). In this article, I examine one such issue that inevitably accompanies the use of ADR but receives little direct attention: the relationship between ADR and administrative responsiveness.

Viewing the U.S. Forest Service's experiences with ADR as a microcosm of the challenges faced by the larger world of public administration, I examine how the use of ADR invokes often unresolved issues associated with administrative responsiveness.[3] Specifically, I discuss the ways individual Forest Service managers try to reconcile their own competing needs for professional autonomy and administrative responsiveness in a context where economy and efficiency are still highly valued and rewarded.[4] The analysis is based on case studies of four national forests that used ADR approaches to resolve administrative appeals of forest plans.

Administrative Responsiveness and ADR

Administrative responsiveness needs to be understood within the larger framework of administrative accountability. Public administration accountability refers to the ways that public agencies respond to and manage the diverse set of expectations generated both internally and externally. Accountability can take several forms including bureaucratic, legal, professional, and political accountability (Romzek and Dubnick 1987). Political accountability is characterized by responsiveness to the policy preferences of constituents. Thus, public administrators' reactions to public involvement in decision making is of central relevance to administrative responsiveness and ultimately ADR.

Box 16.1
Research Design, Sampling, and Data Collection

Research Design

In 1988, four national forests that used alternative dispute resolution approaches (ADR) to resolve administrative appeals of forest plans were selected to explore (1) key bureaucratic interests and incentives associated with the adoption of ADR, and (2) congrucence between organizational and individual interests and incentives to use ADR.

Sampling

Because the research was based on the grounded theory method of qualitative research, theoretical sampling was employed (Glaser and Strauss 1967). Two Forest Service regions that already had been examined by agency policy analysts to assess the outcomes of negotiated appeals were selected for this study. Within these two regions, four forests that used ADR to resolve forest plan appeals were chosen as comparison groups; direct experience with ADR comprised the key theoretical criterion for sampling. The available cases were screened to insure voluntary, face-to-face, consensus-based discussions, often among multiple stakeholders, with or without a third party mediator. Two of the four forests used an external environmental mediator; the other two relied upon unassisted negotiations between agency officials and appellants. On two of the forests, negotiations involved environmental appellants and agency officials; the commodity interests were informally apprised of the progress and content of negotiations. Negotiations on the other two forests involved a balanced set of stakeholders (although the timber interests did not enter negotiations until late in the process on one of these forests).

Data Collection

Thirty-one, in-depth personal interviews were conducted with line officers and key staff members. Interviewing line officers proved a systematic way to obtain information from key decisions makers at all levels in the agency. More specifically, in each region and on the corresponding forests and districts, the regional forester, deputy regional forester, regional director of planning, regional appeals and litigation coordinator, forest supervisor, forest planner, and district ranger were interviewed. At both the regional and forest levels, interviews also were conducted with key staff who had been integrally involved with negotiations and were in a position to provide vital background information. Due to the somewhat sensitive nature of the inquiry, informants were guaranteed complete anonymity; thus the forests and regions are not identified, and the informants are referred to only by title or in general terms.

The interviews were guided by an "Interview Guide" that consisted of open-ended and focused questions. Most of the analysis is based on interview data, giving credence to the interpretations and experiences of the Forest Service officials in the sample (Hummel 1991). Both internal and external agency documents also were collected to augment the interview data. However, because of strategic concerns associated with negotiated appeals, the researcher was told that most of the more important internal analyses and communications purposely were not put in writing to avoid potential disclosure under the Freedom of Information Act.

As with many federal agencies, the U.S. Forest Service operates under myriad statutes that mandate public involvement in agency decision making. The National Forest Management Act of 1976 (NFMA) mandated extensive public involvement in the drafting of land management plans for each national forest.[5] Over the course of about ten years as forest plans were being developed, the agency literally spent thousands of hours and millions of dollars engaged in a variety of traditional public involvement activities to solicit comments from interest groups as well as the public at large. In spite of their best intentions (and largely owing to the limitations of traditional forms of public involvement), disputes over forest management escalated (Blahna and Yonts-Shepard 1987; Wondolleck 1985). By the late 1980s, the agency was faced with hundreds of administrative appeals of forest plans, timber sales, oil and gas leases, and grazing permits. According to the U.S. General Accounting Office (1993, 1), "Nationwide, the number of Forest Service appeals filed annually more than doubled between fiscal years 1983 and 1988, from 584 to 1,298. . . ." According to the *Federal Register* ("Appeal of Decisions" 1989, 3342), the agency received 1,609 appeals in fiscal year 1988 alone; 306 were appeals of forest plans.

Because of the seeming failure of the agency's traditional public involvement activities, the Forest Service turned its attention to ADR. In 1989, the agency revised its administrative appeal regulation,[6] placing an explicit emphasis on negotiations between forest officers and appellants.[7] In an effort to resolve the mounting number of administrative appeals, the Forest Service began using consensus-based negotiations and mediation to try to resolve forest plan appeals on a case-by-case basis.[8]

As Arnstein (1969) pointed out in her classic work, "A Ladder of Citizen Participation," there are "significant gradations" of citizen participation. ADR represents a particularly intense form of public involvement. In a typical dispute resolution process, external stakeholders participate in face-to-face negotiations—sometimes with the aid of an external mediator—with government officials; thus, it is characterized by shared decision making. The agency retains formal and final authority for all decisions; government officials are accountable to the broader public as well as to legal mandates. However, the practical reality of ADR is that external stakeholders participate in annual decision making. Thus, ADR belongs on the upper rungs of Arnstein's ladder where empowered citizens have an authentic voice in decision making as opposed to merely advisory, symbolic, or token forms of participation. The significance of this increasing reliance upon ADR is that now, more keenly than ever, agency officials must somehow come to terms with the demands of administrative responsiveness. Agency officials who participate in ADR processes must grapple with their own conflicting needs for professional autonomy and good faith responsiveness.

Administrative Responsiveness and Professional Autonomy

Coming to terms with administrative responsiveness requires that traditional notions of professional autonomy be re-examined. For public officials, autonomy means the ability to exercise their professional discretion in making decisions within their delegated spheres of authority. Traditional forms of public involvement typically are designed to protect this independence in decision making (Berry, Portney, and Thomson 1989). For example, as one Forest Service official noted, "Traditionally we've taken the viewpoint that we will ask for public comment way over here. It comes into the agency, into an autonomous decision-making process. We will sort and digest and analyze. We isolated the public involvement process from the decision making process." It is typically assumed that directly involving external stakeholders in decision making—as is the case with ADR—will reduce agency officials' professional autonomy because they are not making decisions independently. However, closer scrutiny of this traditional assumption is warranted; conclusions depend upon the larger context for administrative behavior and the meaning of professional autonomy.

The Role of the External Organizational Environment

Notions of professional autonomy cannot be meaningfully understood without reference to the external environment of the organization and its influence on day-to-day administrative behavior. In other words, more is at stake than the micro decision-making environments faced by individual agency managers; larger organizational implications also need to be carefully considered.

The Forest Service historically has had a high degree of organizational autonomy and independence (Clarke and McCool 1985; Robinson 1975). As one forest ranger in the sample observed, "You know, Woody, a ranger back in the thirties, he did anything he wanted. Hell, we were gods. Nobody questioned us." However, the traditional autonomy of the Forest Service has been threatened in the past decade. Both the National Environmental Policy Act of 1969 and NFMA substantially increased the involvement of the public as well as other government agencies in forest planning. The level of conflict associated with forest management also has risen dramatically as the nation's environmental constituency has grown and mobilized, and as unresolved wilderness issues have continued to smolder in many states (Wondolleck 1988).

The escalation of conflict poses a threat to the Forest Service in that the agency can lose its jurisdiction over forest management issues through judicial and congressional intervention. When administrative appeals of forest plans or specific management actions are reviewed, Forest Service reviewing officers uphold the decisions of lower level line officers 70 percent of the time (Appeal of Decisions 1988, 17313). In other words, the formal decision on an appeal may not resolve the actual conflict; the appellants may seek legal or legislative recourse that can diminish the agency's autonomy. Thus, the agency no longer has the near-unfettered autonomy that it once enjoyed. As one forest officer emphasized, "The day of complete autonomy is history." Instead, the agency appears to experience what Thompson (1967) refers to as "conditional autonomy." The conditions of the Forest Service's current autonomy include legislative prescriptions outlined in NFMA, the expanded role of the courts in forest decision making, and increased involvement of the public so that constituency dependence is now necessary to accomplish larger organizational goals (Selznick 1953; West 1982).

Coming to terms with administrative responsiveness necessitates that Forest Service officials understand the reality of the agency's conditional autonomy and the corresponding implications for their own professional autonomy. Under circumstances of conditional autonomy, agency officials do not have the independence that they once had. As one forest officer emphasized, "I'd prefer to operate with negotiation where I still make decisions. I may not have the broad scope of decision-making authority that I possibly once had; it may be somewhat restricted. But I'd rather be in that situation than have all my decisions made for me by Congress." A forest supervisor emphasized, "The hard line answer is, if you don't go through negotiation, and the administrative appeal process runs its course, and then you go to court, then you let some judge decide what you're going to do to manage the national forests . . . or the legislature responds and prescribes to you how you'll manage. Would you rather have that, or would you rather have the latitude to manage here in this local setting? Of course it is preferable in the local setting."

Forest Service officials who have participated in ADR are beginning to understand that in order to protect the autonomy of the larger organization and ultimately their own professional autonomy, they must respond to their constituents through meaningful negotiations. They recognize that often their "best alternative to a negotiated agreement" (Fisher and Ury 1981) is not unrestricted, autonomous decision making, but rather stymied decision making that occurs in the shadow of potential judicial or congressional intervention.

The autonomy of the agency as well as individual Forest Service officials is inextricably linked with obtaining public consent for policies and management programs. The professional autonomy of individual Forest Service managers can be seriously constrained by lack of public consent; unresolved conflict can thwart the implementation of management activities. While administrative appeals are pending, Forest Service managers may be constrained from using certain practices in particular areas of the forest. For example, clear-cutting operations often have had to be suspended in order to avoid aggravating the controversy; similarly, agency officials have been enjoined by court order from using certain management practices such as chemical brush control. Conversely, responding to constituents through the use of ADR and gaining acceptance and support for Forest Service programs can enable agency officials to resume management activities that may have been thwarted by unresolved conflict and appeals. As one forest officer noted, "Through conflict resolution, you can get out there and really manage." In other words, building public consent through responsive negotiations enhances Forest Service officials' autonomy by allowing plan implementation to proceed.

Given the realities of the external organizational environment, utilizing ADR as a means of responding to their constituents' concerns actually strengthened the professional autonomy of Forest Service officials. As one forest officer explained, ". . . if the plan is set within a consensus with the public, within that, you really have much more autonomy." Similarly, another added, "Negotiation gives you a great deal of autonomy; by being responsive, you make decisions that the public sees as important, that they can live with." Thus, the conventional assertion that responsiveness through authentic public involvement in decision making will inhibit government officials' professional autonomy rests on a limited view of the managerial situation that excludes consideration of the nature of the organization's external environment. Under circumstances of conditional autonomy where policy making is often characterized by conflict and gridlock, direct negotiations with stakeholders can enhance public officials' professional autonomy.

Professional Autonomy: Process or Outcomes

Coming to terms with administrative responsiveness also involves re-examining the meaning of professional autonomy. Is the real measure of autonomy based on process or outcomes? In many cases, Forest Service officials are able to make decisions; however, they are restrained from implementing their decisions by unresolved conflict. As one forest officer explained, "So are you really autonomous in the sense that you can make a decision and cause something to happen that you want to happen? Just making a decision that doesn't lead to anything doesn't mean much . . . if your decisions as a deciding officer cannot be carried out on the ground—if they don't result in any change out there in the environment—you really aren't accomplishing anything." This suggests that realistic professional autonomy is linked with the ability to accomplish desired objectives. As the same forest officer stressed, "Without consensus you can make decisions on paper that mean nothing, but that's not autonomy."

Again, conventional wisdom would suggest that responsiveness through shared decision making reduces the professional autonomy of public administrators because they are not acting independently. However, evidence suggests that notions of autonomy that focus only on the process of making decisions are flawed. The professional autonomy cannot be viewed simply in terms of the process of making decisions, divorced from the ability to accomplish intended objectives.

Redefining professional autonomy in terms of accomplishment raises issues associated with the meaning and sources of bureaucratic power. For the Forest Service officials in the study, reassessing the meaning of autonomy has gone hand-in-hand with revising their notions of professional power. Rather than defining the sources of their power in traditional, autocratic terms, they have come to see power also in terms of accomplishment. As one forest officer emphasized, "Our ability to implement the plan in the political climate is a measure of our effectiveness and our power. If we're successful in implementing, then we have increased power." This view echoes Kanter's (1979, 66) assertion that, "Power in organizations . . . is the ability to mobilize resources . . . to get things done. The true sign of power, then, is accomplishment."

Internal Autonomy

Professional autonomy is multi-faceted and involves internal organizational dimensions as well. The effect of responsive management on agency officials' internal autonomy also needs to be considered. Informants emphasized that using ADR to resolve forest plan appeals enhanced the internal autonomy of line officers. For example, one forest officer observed, "Negotiation increases your autonomy if you are able to negotiate yourself at your level. This means you are more autonomous as a decision maker."

The alternative to negotiating appeals is to utilize the formal appeal process, where issues are elevated to higher levels in the organization.[9] Thus, the original deciding officer loses his or her jurisdiction over the issues in question and is unable to tailor his or her own solutions to problems. Professional autonomy is further reduced in that the affected line officers must live with the ongoing effects of decisions made at higher levels in the organization, instead of making their own decisions to resolve difficulties that emerge in implementing an appeal decision. In contrast, ADR gives lower level line officers the opportunity not only to devise their own solutions to problems but also to adapt and fine tune agreements over time as needed. This flexibility in decision making enhances autonomy. Responsive management through ADR also enhances the autonomy of line officers by providing the opportunity to expand their normal influence and jurisdiction over management decisions. The forest supervisor or district ranger who is able to negotiate appeals as well as other more informal disputes may be given more latitude in running programs over the long run.

Finally, ADR can enhance the internal autonomy of line officers by enabling land managers to adapt national policy to local circumstances and needs. It can be difficult for Forest Service managers to abide by national policy while simultaneously trying to accommodate local or regional pressures. Current forest management consists of an ongoing tension between national policy and local and/or regional circumstances and interests (Wilkinson and Anderson 1985). However, in negotiations, line officers and their constituents are able to design agreements that suit their particular interests and local circumstances.[10]

Organizational Barriers to Administrative Responsiveness

Coming to terms with administrative responsiveness has not come easily for Forest Service employees. It has been difficult to surrender traditional attitudes, reinforced by the culture of the organization (Frome 1984; Kaufman 1960; Robinson 1975), that interfere with the acceptance of ADR and authentic responsiveness. Agency officials have struggled to overcome professional arrogance and a fondness for "winning." In 1966, R.W. Behan, a prominent observer of the Forest Service, wrote an article aptly entitled "The Myth of the Omnipotent Forester." Although Behan's views of professional forestry diverge sharply from the "omnipotent forester" (1990), he succinctly captured the agency's proud tradition in this earlier work: "We must have enough guts to stand up and tell the public how their (sic) land should be managed. As professional foresters, we know what's best for the land" (1966, 398).

It can be difficult to reconcile the newer norms of responsive management with traditional notions of professional autonomy, power and winning. For example, one forest officer expressed his ambivalence about ADR as follows:

> And sometimes it's just good to win—no I'm, serious—it's just good for the whole organization. You can get kicked around and kicked around—it's like a child, you never win anything and before you know it, you're a loser. There's just a value in winning, there just

is! But again, negotiation is an avenue of winning. And a lot of people can't see that. They see it as a cop-out. . . . It takes a man to negotiate. It takes anybody to knock you on the ground; anybody can do that. But to negotiate takes a person that is well developed.

The changes in attitude that have occurred in recent years have been largely the result of external pressures on the organization.[11] Agency officials have had to struggle to integrate new forms of political accountability with more traditional systems of professional and legal accountability (Romzek and Dubnick 1987). Their experiences with ADR—by definition, a form of genuine responsive management—have pushed them to re-examine the premises of professional autonomy.

The difficulties faced by agency officials are exacerbated by the fact that they are operating in an administrative environment that still values and rewards economy and efficiency (Tipple and Wellman 1991). Informants emphasized that responsive negotiations required a great deal of time and effort; therefore, decision making is not as efficient. As one forest officer stated, "It's more difficult when you really take the time to involve people; it's tough to meet targets. . . . That cut doesn't come as easy as it used to . . . it takes more time." A critical issue for enduring administrative responsiveness and ADR concerns the organizational response to these changes. Informants suggested that key policy makers in the Washington office of the Forest Service did not understand the demands of ADR. One forest officer said, "Negotiation is not a recognized cost of doing business." Similarly, another emphasized:

So with these negotiated appeals, the Washington Office doesn't necessarily understand the price tag. They still expect all the same things to get done; that makes it rough. We're still expected to do the same degree of everything else you do before you got into negotiation— and do this too, like there is all this flexibility in time and we are only working two hours a day . . . so the Washington Office doesn't have a sympathetic appreciation of the challenges on the ground yet.

Perhaps more important than whether Washington Office staff understand the demands of negotiation is the fact that organizational mechanisms have not yet been instituted to accommodate this form of responsive management. Work loads have not been adjusted to incorporate the time it takes to build consensus so that projects can be successfully implemented. Similarly, standard organizational reward structures have not yet been altered to include positive recognition for successful, responsive negotiations. As one forest officer lamented, "You get rewarded for meeting time frames and deadlines and targets; you don't get rewarded for holding everything up. Negotiations and discussions hold things up. And, if you say, 'I processed fifteen appeals on time,' that's more meaningful than, 'I didn't process any appeals but I got results through discussions.'"

Preliminary evidence suggests that some top agency officials are beginning to take formal organizational steps to address the demands of ADR. For example, several regional foresters are incorporating conflict management skills in the performance evaluations of their lower level line officers and staff. One regional forester mentioned that he uses "cash awards if it has been a very difficult negotiation." However, these localized mechanisms will need to be incorporated within formalized organizational policy and procedures throughout the organization in order to be truly effective. It is important to question how long agency officials will continue to use ADR without changes in organizational policies and reward systems to facilitate this more modern style of responsive management.

Conclusion

The implementation of the Administrative Dispute Resolution Act will involve a variety of challenges. Chief among these will be coming to terms with the relationship between ADR and administrative responsiveness: ADR demands genuine responsiveness on the part of public officials. It appears that the future of ADR depends upon several factors. First, public administrators need to be guided by a realistic understanding of the larger administrative context: the nature of the external organizational environment needs to receive more critical attention. Conventional wisdom suggests that involvement of the public in decision making tends to decrease public officials' professional autonomy. However, traditional assertions ignore the sociopolitical dimensions of the external organizational environment. Where public involvement is insufficient to block agency action, no doubt, negotiation would decrease professional autonomy. However, for agencies that experience such a significant degree of outside interference in policy making (Gortner 1977) such that decision making is characterized by frequent stalemate,[12] authentic public involvement through responsive management can enhance professional autonomy. In other words, public officials need to understand that in a context of conditional autonomy, ADR can protect the autonomy of the larger organization as well as actually enhance their own professional autonomy. Second, public officials need to understand both the external and internal dimensions of their professional autonomy and the effects of administrative responsiveness on both dimensions. They need to recognize that ADR can enhance the internal autonomy of line officers. And finally, it is vital that organizational procedures and reward structures be modified to incorporate the realities of ADR. Traditional notions of economy and efficiency need to be supplanted with a more modern calculus that values and accommodates the pace of administrative responsiveness.

Notes

1. Section 581(3) of the Administrative Dispute Resolution Act defines ADR as follows: "Alternative means of dispute resolution means any procedure that is used in lieu of an adjudication . . . to resolve issues in controversy, including settlement negotiations, conciliation, facilitation, mediation, fact finding, minitrials, and arbitration, or any combination thereof."

2. Federal agencies and departments that have used ADR or offered dispute resolution training to their employees include the Federal Highway Administration, the Federal Deposit Insurance Corporation, the Coast Guard, the Army Corps of Engineers, the U.S. Environmental Protection Agency, the General Services Administration, Securities and Exchange Commission, Office of Personnel Management, and the Departments of Interior, Agriculture, and Justice, to name a few (Madigan 1992; Susskind, Babbitt, and Segal 1993).

3. Widespread use of ADR in public policy making raises questions about other dimensions of political accountability including representativeness and access as well as issues associated with power (see Amy 1987; Crowfoot 1980). However, my intent is to focus on issues of central relevance to public administrators that previously have been neglected in the literature.

4. For an excellent discussion of the Forest Service's transition from primary emphasis on the administrative values of economy and efficiency to more recent requirements for responsiveness and representativeness in decision making, see Tipple and Wellman (1991).

5. Forest planning is arguably one of the most ambitious planning efforts ever undertaken by a federal agency. NFMA mandated that each national forest conduct a comprehensive inventory of forest resources, then develop its land management plan based on complex calculations of biological, economic, and social opportunities, constraints, costs and benefits. Unlike some fields where planning is only tangentially related to action, forest planning specifically prescribes what will be done and how it will be accomplished on the national forests.

6. The Forest Service recently revised its appeal regulation for projects and activities that implements land and resource management plans (i.e., forest plans). The final rule (36 CFR Parts 215 and 217) became effective on November 4, 1993 (58 FR 58904). The appeal regulation for forest plans (36 CFR Part 219) currently is under review.

7. At 36 CFR Part 217.12, under Resolution of Issues, the appeal regulation states: (a) When a decision is appealed, the Deciding Officer may discuss the appeal with the appellant(s) and intervenor(s) together or separately to narrow issues, agree on facts, and explore opportunities to resolve the issues by means other than review and decision on the appeal. . . . Reviewing Officers may at the request of the Deciding Officers, or on their own initiative, extend the time periods for review and specify a reasonable duration to allow for conduct of meaningful negotiations.

8. Throughout the rest of this article, the terms "ADR" and "negotiation" are used interchangeably for simplicity and readability. However, negotiation refers to the consensus-based negotiations typical of ADR.

9. Like many federal resource agencies, the Forest Service is a decentralized hierarchy. Agency officials work at the district (the lowest level of the organization), forest, or regional levels, or in the Washington office. Although forest plans are developed at the forest level, regional foresters are the officers of record for forest plans. When a forest plan is appealed, it is first appealed to the Chief of the Forest Service (the reviewing officer for forest plans) in Washington, DC. If a second level of review is necessary, it moves up to the Secretary of Agriculture.

10. Tailoring negotiated agreements to the concerns of local constituents invokes questions about the broader dimensions of political accountability: the Forest Service is accountable to the general public as well as to local interests. Negotiations with local constituents that resulted in major changes to forest plans could raise questions about the agency's professional and legal responsibilities to the broader public. In the study, the Forest Service was able to negotiate agreements that resolved the administrative appeals of the forest plans without making major amendments to the plans that could be construed as the result of capture by local interests (Culhane 1981).

11. Attitude changes in the Forest Service also have been the result of diversifying the work force by adding other professionals such as landscape architects, wildlife biologists, and archeologists as well as women and minorities to the agency ranks. Younger employees who grew up with the modern environmental movement also have added new perspectives on resource management (Frome 1984; Wondolleck 1988).

12. In fact, ADR does not become a viable option until a stalemate exists between the affected interests (Cormick 1980; Susskind and Weinstein 1980).

References

Amy, Douglas J. 1987. *The Politics of Environmental Mediation.* New York: Columbia University Press.
———. 1990. "Environmental Dispute Resolution: The Promise and the Pitfalls." In Norman J. Vig

and Michael E. Kraft, eds. *Environmental Policy in the 1990s,* 211–234. Washington, DC: Congressional Quarterly Press.

"Appeal of Decisions Concerning the National Forest System, Proposed rule." 1988. *Federal Register* 53, no. 94 (16 May).

"Appeal of Decisions Concerning the National Forest System, Final Rule." 1989. *Federal Register* 54, no. 13 (23 January).

Arnstein, Sherry R. 1969. "A Ladder of Citizen Participation." *Journal of the American Institute of Planners* 35 (July): 216–224.

Behan, Richard W. 1966. "The Myth of the Omnipotent Forester." *Journal of Forestry* 64 (6): 398–400, 407.

———. 1990. "Multiresource Forest Management: A Paradigmatic Challenge to Professional Forestry." *Journal of Forestry* 88 (April): 12–18.

Berry, Jeffrey M., Kent E. Portney, and Ken Thomson. 1989. "Empowering and Involving Citizens." In James L. Perry, ed., *Handbook of Public Administration.* San Francisco: Jossey-Bass.

Bingham, Gail. 1986. *Resolving Environmental Disputes: A Decade of Experience.* Washington, DC: Conservation Foundation.

Blahna, Dale J., and Susan Yonts-Shepard. 1987. "Preservation or Use: Confronting Public Issues in Forest Planning and Decision Making." Paper presented for Policy Studies Organization Symposium on Outdoor Recreation Policy, Pleasure and Preservation: An Outdoor Recreation Policy Dilemma. Greenwood Press.

Clarke, Jeanne Nienaber, and Daniel McCool. 1985. *Staking Out the Terrain.* Albany: State University of New York Press.

Cormick, Gerald W. 1980. "The 'Theory' and Practice of Environmental Mediation." *The Environmental Professional* 2: 24–33.

Crowfoot, James E. 1980. "Negotiations: An Effective Tool for Citizen Organizations?" *The NRAG Papers* 3(4): 24–44.

Culhane, Paul J. 1981. *Public Lands Politics.* Baltimore: Johns Hopkins University Press for Resources for the Future, Inc.

Dukes, Frank. 1993. "Public Conflict Resolution: A Transformative Approach." *Negotiation Journal* 9 (January): 45–57.

Fisher, Roger, and William Ury. 1981. *Getting to Yes: Negotiating Agreement Without Giving In.* Boston: Houghton Mifflin.

Freemuth, John. 1989. "The National Parks: Political Versus Professional Determinants of Policy." *Public Administration Review* 49 (May/June): 278–286.

Frome, Michael. 1984. *The Forest Service,* 2d ed. Boulder, CO: Westview Press.

Glaser, Barney G., and Anselm L. Strauss. 1967. *The Discovery of Grounded Theory.* New York: Aldine.

Gortner, Harold F. 1977. *Administration in the Public Sector.* New York: John Wiley & Sons.

Hamilton, Michael S. 1991. "Environmental Mediation: Requirements for Successful Institutionalization." In Miriam K. Mills, ed., *Alternative Dispute Resolution in the Public Sector,* 164–187. Chicago: Nelson-Hall Publishers.

Hummel, Ralph P. 1991. "Stories Managers Tell: Why They Are as Valid as Science." *Public Administration Review* 51 (January/February): 31–41.

Kanter, Rosabeth M., 1979. "Power Failure in Management Circuits." *Harvard Business Review* 57 (July/August): 65–75.

Kaufman, Herbert. 1960. *The Forest Ranger: A Study in Administrative Behavior.* Baltimore: Johns Hopkins University Press for Resources for the Future.

Madigan, Denise R. 1992. "Update on ADR in the Federal Government." *The Practitioner's Notebook.* Cambridge, MA: MIT-Harvard Public Disputes Network, no. 1.

Manring, Nancy J. 1993. "Reconciling Science and Politics in Forest Decision Making: New Tools for Public Administrators." *American Review of Public Administration* 23 (4): 343–359.

Meeks, Gordon, Jr. 1982. *Managing Environmental and Public Policy Conflicts.* Denver: National Conference of State Legislatures.

Robinson, Glen O. 1975. *The Forest Service.* Baltimore: Johns Hopkins University Press for Resources for the Future.

Romzek, Barbara S., and Melvin J. Dubnick. 1987. "Accountability in the Public Sector: Lessons from the Challenger Tragedy." *Public Administration Review* 47 (May/June): 227–238.

Selznick, Philip. 1953. *TVA and the Grass Roots.* Berkeley, CA: University of California Press.

Simon, Herbert. 1957. *Administrative Behavior.* New York: Free Press.

Stephenson, Max O., Jr., and Gerald M. Pops. 1991. "Public Administrators and Conflict Resolution: Democratic Theory, Administrative Capacity, and the Case of Negotiated Rule-Making." In Miriam K. Mills, ed., *Alternative Dispute Resolution in the Public Sector,* 13–25. Chicago: Nelson-Hall.

Susskind, Lawrence E. 1981. "Environmental Mediation and the Accountability Problem." *Vermont Law Review* 6: 1–47.

Susskind, Lawrence E., Eileen F. Babbitt, and Phyllis N. Segal. 1993. "When ADR Becomes the Law: A Review of Best Practice in Federal Agencies." *Negotiation Journal* 9 (January): 59–75.

Susskind, Lawrence E., and Jeffrey Cruikshank. 1987. *Breaking the Impasse: Consensual Approaches to Resolving Public Disputes.* New York: Basic Books.

Susskind, Lawrence E., and Alan Weinstein, 1980. "Towards a Theory of Environmental Dispute Resolution." *Environmental Affairs* 9(2): 311–357.

Thompson, James D. 1967. *Organizations in Action.* New York: McGraw-Hill.

Tipple, Terence J., and J. Douglas Wellman. 1991. "Herbert Kaufman's Forest Ranger Thirty Years Later: From Simplicity and Homogeneity to Complexity and Diversity." *Public Administration Review* 51 (September/October): 421–428.

U.S. General Accounting Office. 1989. Resources, Community, and Economic Development Division. 1989. *Information on the Forest Service Appeals System.* Briefing Report to the Honorable Max Baucus, U.S. Senate. Washington, DC: Government Printing Office, February (B-233613).

West, Patrick C. 1982. *Natural Resource Bureaucracy and Rural Poverty: A Study in the Political Sociology of Natural Resources.* Ann Arbor: University of Michigan, Natural Resource Sociology Research Lab, Monograph no. 2.

Wilkinson, Charles F., and H. Michael Anderson. 1985. "Land and Resource Planning in the National Forests." *Oregon Law Review* 64: 7–373.

Wondolleck, Julia M. 1985. "The Importance of Process in Resolving Environmental Disputes." *Environmental Impact Assessment Review* 5, no. 4: 341–356.

———. 1988. *Public Lands Conflict and Resolution: Managing National Forest Disputes.* New York: Plenum.

CHAPTER 17

A CONFLICT RESOLUTION APPROACH
TO PUBLIC ADMINISTRATION

ZHIYONG LAN

Public administration literature has dealt extensively with how to execute the will of the people effectively and efficiently (Wilson 1992; Gulick and Urwick 1937; Brownlow, Merriam, and Gulick 1937); how to deliver public services entrepreneurially and innovatively (Savas 1987; Osborne and Gaebler, 1992); and how to be accountable and responsive to the public in general (Waldo 1948; Ostrom 1973; Goodsell 1986; Rourke 1992; Ingraham and Romzek 1994). However, the field has had much less emphasis on conflict resolution, although sporadic studies have described the conflictual nature of public administrators' work or addressed microlevel (individual and organizational) conflict resolution in public organizations (Simon 1957; Lipsky 1980; Vizzard 1995).

The Civil Justice Reform Act of 1990 (28 U.S.C. sec. 471 et seq.), the Administrative Dispute Resolution Act of 1990 (Public Law 101–552), and the Negotiated Rulemaking Act of 1990 (Public Law 101-648) explicitly expressed support, outlined methods, or stated requirements for federal agencies and departments to implement alternative strategies to resolve their administrative disputes (Madigan 1992; Susskind, Babbit, and Segal 1993; Manring 1994; Deavel 1994).[1] These acts are Congressional responses to the incredible growth in costs of civil litigation and delays that contribute to those costs.[2] They send out a strong message that conflict resolution is an indispensable component of contemporary public administration and that it is time the field started paying serious attention to it.

Indeed, moving into the 1990s, the conflicts public administrators confront are much more complex, multifaceted, and intense. Besides the typical interpersonal and interorganizational conflicts, such as personnel grievances, labor disputes, and organizational jurisdiction disputes, many institutional-level conflicts have also surfaced or intensified. Such conflicts include economic development versus environmental protection; rising public interest concerns versus the call for more dependence on private methods; decentralization of power versus the need for coordinating larger tasks of high technology development and global competition; increased social wealth versus the

From *Public Administration Review* 57, no. 1 (January/February 1997): 27–35. Copyright © 1997 by American Society for Public Administration. Reprinted with permission.

enduring problems of poverty and crime; shaken public confidence in government versus increased need for confidence in the nation's economy; uncompetitive compensation versus the requirement for high-quality public service personnel; organizational uncertainty versus increased reliance on employee loyalty to public service; high-level national debt versus increased pressure for public spending on social and environmental programs; postmodern democratic demands versus modern quests for efficiency and effectiveness; special interests versus the general public interest; national homogeneity versus cultural diversity claims; need for cooperation versus tensions among ethnic groups and between genders; nationalism versus internationalism; and promotion for free international markets versus new tariffs to protect domestic industries. The length of this list, which is by no means exhaustive, underscores the message that today's public administrators cannot manage well without adequate understanding of, and skills in, conflict resolution.

Nonetheless, today's public administration literature is still shy of systematic efforts in the understanding of conflict resolution and its relevance to public administration. In eight mainstream public administration journals in the three years between 1992 and 1995, only four articles specifically addressed the issue of conflict resolution.[3] Among them, three are about alternative conflict resolution (Manring 1993, 1994; Carnevale 1993), and one is about the impact of agenda conflict on policy formulation and implementation (Vizzard 1995). All are case-study based. A small number of books have also been published in the past decade addressing conflict resolution in public administration. However, they generally address specific conflict resolution issues or target specific audiences. Such books include Miriam K. Mills's edited book *Alternative Conflict Resolution in the Public Sector* (1991) and Julia M. Wondolleck's book *Public Lands Conflict and Resolution: Managing National Forest Disputes* (1988).

The paucity of literature on conflict resolution in today's mainstream public administration research calls for more attention to be focused on conflict studies on the part of public administration scholars and practitioners. This paper is an effort to answer this call. It provides an initial road map into the labyrinth of conflict resolution studies and demonstrates how a conflict resolution perspective can be relevant to public administration, not only at the level of practice but also at the level of theory-building.

The Conflict Resolution Perspective

Conflict resolution has been an area of study in sociology, international relations, labor relations, psychology, economics, political science, and organizational development for quite some time. Its variant form, alternative dispute resolution, is now capturing the attention of those in the public and private sectors (Goldberg and Hobgood 1987; Stephenson and Pops 1991; Mills 1991; Manring 1993, 1994; Carnevale 1993; Susskind and McKearnan 1994).

Various definitions of conflict exist. Some regard the overt hostility (exchange of negative sanctions) among two or more parties as conflict (Blalock 1989). Others argue that conflict exists when there is a manifest purpose in the struggle for status, power, and

Table 17.1

The Conflict Resolution Approach

Impact of conflict	- Identity clarification - Self-study - Stabilizing effect - Actual freedom of choice

Nature of conflict	- Subjective conflict
	- Objective conflict
	    pure competition
	    pure cooperation
	    mixed types

Conventional strategies for resolution of conflict	- Litigation and executive orders - Punitive sanctions on conflictual behavior - Avoiding conflict escalation
Alternative dispute resolution strategies	- Common goal establishment - Consensus building - Joint problem-solving - Negotiation - Informal arbitration - Mediation - Nonbinding minitrials - Conflict enlargement - Conflict containment - Partnering - Outlets for emotions
Roles of actors in the conflict	- Observers - Arbitrators - Parties to conflict

resources (Himes 1980). Brickman (1974, 1) defined conflict as a "situation in which parties must divide or share resources so that, to some degree, the more one party gets, the less others can have."

Conflict occurs in many different situations: between and among members of a family; between labor and management; in political parties, religious groups, formal organizations, and nations; and even within a single mind ("Editorial" 1957, 1–2). The actors in a conflict can be individuals, social groups, formal organizations, or political and social institutions. In this sense, conflicts can be divided into microlevel and macrolevel conflicts. Microlevel conflicts are interpersonal and interorganizational and are often dispute-specific, while macrolevel conflicts are less dispute-specific and are typically at the institutional level. Regardless of the level of conflicts, the foci of conflict studies, however, generally fall into one of the following categories: the study of the impact of conflict, the nature of the conflict, the types of the conflict, conflict resolution strategies, and roles of conflict resolvers. Table 17.1 presents the different foci of conflict studies and their general analytical framework.

The Relevance of a Conflict Resolution Perspective to Public Administration Practice and Theory Building

In this section, I shall discuss how the foci of conflict studies and their related analytical framework are relevant to contemporary public administration practice and theory building.

The Impact of Conflict

Scholars differ in their views about the impact of conflict. One view regards conflict as having potentially destructive effects. According to this view, the most important task of conflict study is to search for reasonable means to ameliorate or remove the causes of conflict (Osgood 1962; Rapoport 1962; Fisher 1964; Frank 1968; Pruitt 1971). Another view regards conflict as inevitable with either positive or constructive potential (Coser 1956; Lorenz 1966). It argues that conflict has at least the following positive effects. One, conflict helps establish group and personal identities. External conflict often fosters internal cohesiveness and loyalty within the group. Two, conflict forces one to test and assess oneself. It stimulates interest and curiosity in others and promotes innovation, change, and progress in groups that are driven to seek a competitive advantage in the conflict. Three, conflict is likely to have stabilizing and integrative functions for relationships in loosely structured societies. Four, conflict is a useful condition for particular individuals to enjoy freedom to choose their own courses of action. This freedom derives from the inability of either side in the conflict to enforce its value system in its entirety (Coser 1956; Deutsch 1973; Brickman 1974).

One telling example of the positive use of conflict involves the recent call for reinvention in public administration. Since the 1980s, antigovernment sentiment has been widespread. Tension between the public and the providers of public service has been high. Public employee morale has dropped to an all-time low (Heclo 1986; Palmer 1986; Levine 1990; Lan 1994). Innovative public administrators called for a reinvention of government as opposed to joining the crowd and continuously bashing bureaucrats (Osborne and Gaebler 1992). While details of the reinvention principles could be further discussed and perhaps "reinvented," the positive attitude of the reinvention initiative toward conflict has offered an opportunity to reinvigorate American public administration. In this sense, a greater awareness of the possible impacts of conflict can help public administrators turn destructive conflicts into constructive efforts.

The positive opportunities that conflict provides are also discussed in the literature on alternative dispute resolution. In her recent studies of the conflict resolution cases in the U.S. Forest Service, Nancy Manring (1993) found that conflict, when resolved through alternative dispute resolution techniques such as negotiation and consensus building, may accentuate the need for sound scientific information and a broadened knowledge base. Conflict is not necessarily a threat. It also provides opportunities for better management. The sensitivity of public administrators to the opportunities provided by conflict could make a difference in the outcome of the conflicts.

The Nature of the Conflict

Conflict resolution literature classifies conflict into subjective conflict and objective conflict. Subjective conflict refers to conflict that is not real but is nonetheless perceived by the parties to a conflict. Objective conflict refers to conflict that actually exists, but may or may not be recognized (Brickman 1974).

If the conflict is subjective, explanations and facilitated communications can help alleviate the problem. One example Susskind and his colleagues described has to do with a conflict involving the Minnesota Department of Natural Resources, environmental groups, and the manufacturers of forest products over the use of aerial spraying of herbicides in 1987 (Susskind and McKearnan 1994). The chemicals have long been used for controlling the growth of underbrush around commercially valuable pine trees. But the environmental groups argued that the chemicals are dangerous and aerial spraying magnifies the danger. The Department of Natural Resources assessed and affirmed the safety of the herbicide, but that did little to assuage the concerns of the environmental groups. The groups threatened to take legal action against the agency. In this scenario, the conflict is subjective. Communication, provision of scientific information, consensus-building, and rapport-building can effectively contribute to the resolution of the conflict.

When the conflict is objective, however, the conflict resolution strategies listed above may not be enough. Objective conflict can be broken down into three categories: pure cooperation (or pure coordination), pure competition, and mixed motives. Pure cooperation refers to a situation in which the rewards and punishments that can accrue to each party are similar or noncompetitive. Pure competition refers to a situation in which one party cannot be better off without harming the interests of the other. The mixed motives situation is one in which conflicting parties may gain by cooperating around some common interests while competing for resources that come only at the expense of the other (Brickman 1974).

In pure cooperation conflict, the conflict disappears when the situation is understood. When all citizens want a civic center in a downtown area, all that is left is to work out the details of how to get it built. Citizen participation, empowerment, partnerships, coordination, information-sharing, common goal establishment, and prioritization of opportunities are ideal methods for solving the problem.

Pure competition conflict, however, is entirely different, especially when the conflict involves serious stakes. The more the party that may suffer a loss understands the issue, the less likely that party will cooperate in facilitating its resolution. Historically, the approaches used to resolve these conflicts are war, oppression, deception, rationalization of opportunities for the future, or compensation, which may turn pure competition into mixed motives. For example, slavery and other types of authoritarian societies endure not only because they use force, but also because they create widely accepted myths and stories that obscure the conflict (Brickman 1974, 3). Recent advances in information technology have made thousands jobless, including many midlevel managers. However, the conflict between the owners of the new technology and the now obsolete workers is alleviated through society's massive belief in the opportunities that the new technologies can provide in the future. Because of this belief, few at-risk employees attempt to destroy new technologies in the 1990s as many workers did in the early years of the industrial revolution.

The approach used to alleviate conflict is dependent upon the primary concerns of the society or the parties to conflict (stability versus conflict resolution). Sometimes it is advantageous for the society or the parties to a conflict to keep the conflict dormant; other times it is advantageous to activate conflict by awakening the awareness of the parties to the conflict. In scenarios of pure competition conflict, alternative dispute resolution techniques such as negotiation, information-sharing, consensus building, and participation may not be the best way out.

Most of the conflicts that public administrators encounter are of the mixed type, or they can be turned into the mixed type by offering alternative compensation for the losing party. In this scenario, conflict resolution techniques such as clarification of benefits and costs, negotiation, mediation, arbitration, bargaining, and alternative choice provision can be used (Manring 1993, 1994; Carnevale 1993; Susskind and McKearnan 1994).

Types of Conflict

Conflicts can be grouped into four types: unstructured, partially structured, fully structured, and revolutionary conflicts. In unstructured conflicts, the parties are not bound by any rules. Their choices can be impulsive and emotional. In fully structured conflicts, the conflicts are clearly defined; the parties are fully bound by rules, social norms, and ethical standards. In partially structured conflicts, the parties constrain certain behaviors but leave others to the free choice of the parties. Revolutionary conflict is an extreme case of unstructured conflict. It represents conflict on a massive scale not bound by rules, timelines, culture, myth, or shared conceptual paradigms.

The structured conflicts in public administration are normally resolved through the rule of law administered in court, or by way of organizational policies upheld by the chief executive. Many cases of violation of affirmative action law, obstruction of justice, violation of citizens' rights (such as the right to freedom of speech, association, access to information, etc.), or violation of organizational policies are resolved in this manner. Many of the budget allocation conflicts within the executive branch, within the legislative branch, or between the executive and the legislative branches are also structured conflicts. The norms, rationale, processes, decision power, and voting privileges are defined in advance. The parties to conflict know how, where, and when to seek the resolution of the conflict. Deadlines and budget processes are prescribed by law to ensure that impasses are reduced to a minimum; this is a way to ensure the normal operation of the government. For example, in the case of the fierce budget debate that began in late 1995, "President Clinton and Republican congressional leaders had to agree to put their broader differences aside and work on a limited agenda of spending cuts and tax credits to end their long standoff." As a Republican congressional strategist said, "The Republicans need to demonstrate they can get some things done and Clinton needs to show he can walk the walk" (Devroy and Pianin 1996).

A great number of public administration issues fall in between the fully structured and unstructured category, with norms, rules, and regulations constraining some of the behaviors in conflict resolution while leaving others to the free choices of the individuals. For example, in a case described by Manring (1994), there is an understanding that authority of forest management generally lies with the Forest Service. However, the National Environmental Policy Act of 1969 and the National Forest Management Act of 1976 mandated extensive public involvement in forest planning. The procedures for resolving forestry planning and management-related conflicts thus became less binding. Appellants may seek judicial or legislative intervention if they are not happy with the resolution proposed by the Forest Service. The Forest Service could thus lose its jurisdiction over forest management issues to the court or to the legislature. In such conflict situations, politics become pervasive and innovative. Deals of unconventional nature are made.

Unstructured conflicts arise due to impulses or nonrational behaviors; thus, agreed-upon rules for their resolution are often lacking. For example, high public expectations for government services, and citizens' limited willingness to pay taxes are two sides to a conflict in which public administrators have a stake. Yet, the appropriateness of the level and areas of services and the necessary level of revenue support have never been articulated and agreed upon. The intensity of such conflict varies from time to time depending on a number of variables, including socioeconomic factors as well as the political mood of the public. There is no defined method, rule, or timeline for the resolution of such conflict. The lack of structure of this conflictual relationship makes its resolution a difficult undertaking. Extreme events may be required to create the change of perception necessary for its resolution. For example, the depression of the 1930s confronted the United States with its greatest crisis since the Civil War. The depression seriously impaired the public's confidence in business leadership. The distrust of large businesses opened up the road to success for Roosevelt's introduction of massive governmental intervention.

In the 1980s, the Reagan administration swung the pendulum to the other extreme. The New Deal ideology was turned completely upside down (Palmer 1986). Tax cuts, privatization, and devolution became the norm (Savas 1987; Osborne and Gaebler 1992). Even a few years after the Clinton administration entered the White House, public administrators, politicians, the general public, and even the president himself often had to start their discussion of the positive features of the government by first criticizing the existing government (Clinton 1993; Gore 1993, 1994).

A *Washington Post* article stated: "The Republican freshmen—73 in the House and 11 in the Senate—have brought a heavy load of angry antigovernment populism with them from home. . . . For one thing, many don't look to politics as a career path. They just want to dismantle government and go home" (Taylor and Dewar 1995, 3).

At the orientation one Congressional freshman said, "There are only three or four among us with a progovernment bias and we know who they are" (Taylor and Dewar 1995, 10). The relationship between the government and the public has become perceptually antagonistic instead of cooperative. Bureaucrat-bashing has become the norm. In terms of how big or how small a government should be, or when and to what extent the downsizing effort should stop, there is no bottom line.

The conflict over the role of government stems from a combination of political values, personal experiences, and understanding of reality. The fact that different people have different experiences and understand their experiences differently further complicates the situation. The resolution of this conflict, which underlies the health of American public service, requires not only knowledge, technical skills, and ideological principles, but also political wisdom, public relations skills, media cooperation, and the art of governing—which were exemplified by the framers of the Constitution in the years of the American Revolution.

In the face of revolutionary conflict, parties to conflict often resort to war or other forms of violence. By means of extreme force, resources and social power are redistributed and a new social order achieved. Due to the oppressive and destructive nature of violence, the democratic world has reached an agreement that peaceful methods are preferred forms of conflict resolution (Rostow 1971; Locke 1963; Rousseau 1973). De-escalation, compromise, deterrence, and even deception are often used to minimize revolutionary conflict.

Strategies for Conflict Resolution

Strategies for conflict resolution are perhaps the most extensively discussed topic in the conflict resolution literature. Conventionally, conflict resolution relies upon the court of law or chief executive arbitration. The rule made by the court or the decision made by the chief executive, within the guidelines of the law or organizational policy, is final. Such a method relies on the expertise and discretion of the judges and administrators, and it is efficient, effective, and often economical. Arbitration, punitive sanctions on conflictual behavior, and conflict containment (control, management, and escalation) are typical tools of traditional conflict resolution. Administrative courts, hierarchy of offices, and unity of command are mechanisms designed for resolving conflict in such a manner. The extensive use of courts and lawyers in recent decades, however, has dramatized the costs of litigation. The costs have forced individuals and organizations to search for alternative ways to resolve conflicts. Alternative dispute resolution methods such as consensus-building, joint problem-solving, negotiation, informal arbitration, mediation, nonbinding minitrials, partnering, outlets for emotions, enlargement of conflicts to include more players, increasing the stakes, and so on, have begun to dominate the conflict resolver's agenda.

In spite of their popularity and universality, these methods are not without problems. First, methods such as arbitration and mediation require a third party's participation. In many cases, such third parties are independent contractors, consulting firms, or law firms. When a public agency has a dispute with its employee, or with a group of citizens (e.g., the cases of the U.S. Forest Service and the Department of Natural Resources), a private corporation will be invited to be a resolver. This is what is known as the privatization of public functions. The decisions concerning public affairs will no longer be made by trained experts, who are supposed to be responsible for the public welfare, or by the court, which is supposed to uphold the principles of law and justice, but by negotiation experts whose primary interest is to make a deal and get compensated for the work. In so doing, public administration de facto authorizes "private parties to perform agency decision-making powers" (Deavel 1994, 5).

Second, alternative dispute resolution methods are about bargaining and negotiation, not about fairness or social justice. The method can displace the social and administrative objectives that aim at achieving fairness, due process, and social justice. The constitutionality of alternative dispute resolution is often questionable, and it has a tendency to favor those who are in better bargaining positions, such as those who have money, power, or the capacity to endure a long process or even the total loss of a dispute. Past studies have revealed that "a [conflict] player's intransigence, or unwillingness to retreat to fallback positions, generally works to his/her advantage" (Brams and Doherty 1993).

Third, in the long run, alternative dispute resolution is not necessarily more efficient or less costly. If such methods become the norm, parties to conflict will use them in every single dispute in the hope of winning "something extra," even if quicker resolutions could have solved the problem.

Fourth, due to the informal binding feature of alternative dispute resolution, even after the arbitrator has helped the parties achieve an agreement, the losing parties may feel cheated when they realize their losses. Filled with regrets, they may start the whole process over, increasing instead of reducing the costs of conflict resolution.

Because of such problems, public administrators cannot simply adopt existing conflict resolution strategies without thought. Patterns of conflict resolution do have major administrative ramifications.

Actors in the Conflict

Conflict resolution literature pays close attention to the different roles played by actors in a conflict. It categorizes the actors in three groups: (1) interested audience to the conflict—observers or onlookers, either sympathetic or unsympathetic; (2) parties to the conflict; and (3) conflict resolvers—arbitrators, mediators, or facilitators (Deutsch 1973; Deavel 1994). Interestingly, these categories correspond to various perspectives on the nature of public administrators' work.

The observer's role is analogous to the neutral competency role defined by one school of public administration theorists. In this role public servants execute the will of the people from their nonpartisan stance (Wilson 1992; Goodnow 1900; Rourke 1992). They do not participate in disputes. If they are asked by either party in a conflict to pass something on or hand something over, they do it quickly, faithfully, and with no biases against either party to the conflict. Other than that, they watch the process and wait for the outcome, with either a sympathetic or unsympathetic heart. While the observer's role "reinforces the powerless, alienated, 'office boy' image of the bureaucrat that is destructive of the self-respect so necessary for mature moral growth" (Rohr 1978, 63), it is often a more appropriate role for public administrators than other possible alternatives. In areas where governmental presence is not particularly called for or areas that lie outside of public administrators' jurisdictions, public administrators should stick to their observer's stance in spite of temptations to intervene. The observer's role blends well with the political culture of small and hands-off government. In terms of public administration ethics, the observer's role is somewhat equivalent to John Rohr's "low-road approach to public administration" (Rohr 1978), in which administrative discretion is reduced to adherence to agency rules.

Public administrators also often assume the role of arbitrator. This role is analogous to public administrators' role as the governor of the state. A group of public administration theorists view public administration as "part of the governing process, of deciding what is to be done and who shall carry the burden" (McCurdy 1985, 8). To them, public administration is a technology for human cooperation. It emphasizes rationality, organization, and management in the pursuit of cooperation (Waldo 1948). When the duties of public administrators call them to act as arbitrators, they work to seek a resolution that will reflect justice, public interest, regime values, trustworthiness, and righteousness, or at a minimum, a resolution that will be accepted by the parties to the conflict. The arbitrator's role gives public administrators the position and power to make use of strategies such as persuasion, arbitration, value assertion, and value inculcation to resolve the conflict in favor of the desired goals of the community or the society.

A third role, the role of a party to conflict, is equivalent to the political role of public administrators. This role can hardly be denied but is less willingly asserted. The political role of public administrators fits with the democratic notion of checks and balances in government. Public administrators often represent different political forces by way of active and passive representation (Krislov 1974). When public administrators have strong opinions or stakes in a conflict, and it is within the boundaries of law for them to address their concerns, they should rightfully identify themselves as a party to the conflict and exercise their legal, positional, and constitutional rights to seek a resolution in their favor.

Scholars of public administration have searched through the Constitution for public administration's constitutional legitimacy, only to find that the most salient values of the Constitution are separation of powers, checks and balances, citizens' rights (recognition of organized interest), and individual liberty, not efficiency and effectiveness (Fairfield 1966; Spicer 1995). The administrative power of the executive official needs to be checked by legislative, judicial, and organized interest powers.[4] Similarly, the powers of the politicians, interest groups, and judges must be checked by public administrators. It is not efficiency, effectiveness, or economy, but the ability of the governing structure to prevent abuse of powers by a selected few that makes a great democratic society. In this sense, public administrators have a larger role to play than what is popularly expected of them.

In a way, the conflict resolution perspective captures the three distinctive traditions of public administration literature described by Rosenbloom (1983): the managerial, the legal, and the political (see Table 17.2). It views administrative practice as a set of methods to resolve social and organizational conflicts in favor of long-term stability and harmony. It legitimizes all three roles of the public administrators and gives these three roles a unified purpose—conflict resolution.[5] Under the conflict resolution framework, public administrators can legitimately play different roles on the basis, not of the classi-

Table 17.2

The Rosenbloom Framework: Existing Perspectives of Public Administration

	Managerial approach	Political approach	Legal approach
Values	economy efficiency effectiveness	representation responsiveness accountability	constitutional integrity procedural due process substantive rights
Proposed structure	ideal-type bureaucracy	pluralism	judicial trial and adversary procedure
View of individual	impersonal case	member of group	individual with equal rights
Cognitive approach	scientific	public consensus	legal and case analysis

Notes: See Chapter 1, this book, and David Rosenbloom (1989), *Public Administration: Understanding Management, Politics, and Law in the Public Sector,* 2nd ed. (New York: Random House) for a more detailed explanation.

Table 17.3

Roles of Public Administrators

Traditional approaches to public administration studies as summarized by Rosenbloom (1989)	Roles of public administration from the conflict-resolution perspective
Managerial approach	Observers of conflict
Legal approach	Arbitrator in conflict resolution
Political approach	Parties to conflict

fication of their job titles (e.g., legal counsels, managers, policymakers), but on the basis of the nature of the work with which they are dealing. Table 17.3 illustrates the relationships of the two approaches.

The unique contribution of the conflict resolution perspective, however, is that it is sensitive to conflict and prone to conflict resolution. In a post-industrial age in which cultures clash, political groups contend, gender and ethnic awareness awaken, and citizens' expectations of the government rise while willingness to pay for its services declines, a conflict resolution perspective gives us a conceptual tool to help with the task of "reconciling the irreconcilable." This, as concluded by Rosenbloom (1983), is destined to be the mission of public administrators.

Conclusion

American public administration in the 1990s has been particularly characterized by the amount of conflict with which it deals (Deavel 1994, note 2). The mixed functions of public administrators as conflict resolvers, observers, and parties to conflict often confuse public administrators themselves as well as complicate the public's expectations of them.

What is worse is that many public administrators have not been adequately exposed to the skills and rationales of conflict resolution. Formal public administration programs have very limited course offerings in conflict resolution.[6] As a matter of course, many public administrators adopt a decision rule of conflict avoidance. Rather than actively identifying and analyzing conflicts and seeking strategies to resolve them, many have actually forfeited their constitutional responsibility, which includes seeking social justice and being an active player in the checks-and-balances system to prevent the abuse of power by unworthy power players.

Conventional public administration studies either emphasize the technical rational approach or the political approach (policymaking) to public administration. They fail to highlight public administrators' role as conflict resolvers—those who seek to reconcile the irreconcilable in favor of social harmony and long-term public interests.

Lindblom's "muddling through" argument has provided a philosophical underpinning for and a realistic description of public administration practice. However, it is not much of an analytical tool for improving understanding of real life political, economic, and social conflicts. The conflict resolution literature, however, highlights the conflictual reality in a democratic society. It provides a way of analyzing and resolving problems. It adds an analytical tool to assist contemporary public administrators to muddle through their world of conflicts with sensitivity and self-awareness. It offers new possibilities for public administration theory-building. The field can greatly benefit by incorporating conflict studies into its teaching and research.

Notes

1. The Civil Justice Reform Act explicitly expressed support for the use of a variety of forums, including mediation and nonbinding minitrials to expedite the process of litigation in the court systems. The Negotiated Rulemaking Act established a structure for using consensus-based negotiations to develop federal regulations. The Administrative Dispute Resolution Act went a step further by requiring each federal agency to adopt a policy that addresses the use of alternative dispute resolution and case management.

2. By 1990 there were over 220,000 civil cases pending in the United States. Over 100,000 of these suits involved a federal question, and in more than 55,000 cases the federal government was a party (Deavel 1994).

3. *Public Administration Review, Journal of Public Administration Research and Theory, Administration and Society, American Review of Public Administration, Public Productivity and Management Review, Public Budgeting and Finance, Review of Public Personnel Administration, and Journal of Policy Analysis and Management.* For more detailed description of the content analysis, see Lan and Anders (1996).

4. People familiar with American political science literature know well the term iron triangle, in which agencies, politicians and interest groups join to influence public policy in their favor. "Interest groups staff thousands of bodies that advise the federal government on their own behalf (e.g., the National Rifle Association). Some such advisory groups (or lobbyists) are empowered by law and others act unofficially. . . . For each policy area there is a network of persons in office, in think tanks, in consulting firms, in universities, in law firms, and so on" (Levine, Peters, and Thompson 1990, 52). Interest group politics has provided a check on bureaucratic politics, and in turn, interest groups themselves need to be checked.

5. Public administration's lack of legitimacy has been a serious concern for many public administration scholars in the past few decades (Spicer 1995).

6. According to a survey conducted in 1991, only nine of the 994 courses listed in the seventeen carefully selected major public administration programs throughout the country are about negotiation and contracts (Lan 1991). All seventeen programs offer doctoral degrees. They are: Arizona State University, Carnegie Mellon University, Cleveland State University, George Washington University, Golden Gate University, Harvard University, Ohio State University, Princeton University, SUNY at Albany, SUNY at Brockport, Syracuse University, University of California at Berkeley, University of Georgia, University of Maryland, University of North Carolina at Chapel Hill, University of Southern California, Virginia Polytechnic Institute and State University

References

Blalock, Hubert M., Jr. 1989. *Power and Conflict: Toward a General Theory.* Newbury Park, CA: Sage.

Brams, Steven J., and Ann E. Doherty. 1993. "Intransigence in Negotiations." *Journal of Conflict Resolution* 37(4): 692–708.

Brickman, Philip. 1974. *Social Conflict: Readings in Rule Structures and Conflict Relationships.* Lexington, MA: D.C. Heath.

Brownlow, Louis, Charles E. Merriam, and Luther Gulick. 1937. *President's Committee on Administrative Management in the Government of the United States.* Washington, DC: Government Printing Office.

Carnevale, David G. 1993. "Root Dynamics of Alternative Dispute Resolution: An Illustrative Case in the U.S. Postal Service." *Public Administration Review* 53(5): 455–461.

Clinton, William Jefferson. 1993. *A Vision of Change for America.* Washington, DC: Government Printing Office.

Coser, Lewis A. 1956. *The Functions of Social Conflict.* New York: Free Press.

Deavel, R. Philip. 1994. "Rethinking Civil Litigation: The Potential for Alternative Dispute Resolution in the Air Force." *The Reporter* 21(2): 19.

Deutsch, Morton. 1973. *The Resolution of Conflict: Constructive and Destructive Process.* New Haven, CT: Yale University Press.

Devroy, Ann, and Eric Pianin. 1996. "Clinton and GOP Agree to Disagree." *Washington Post,* 25 January, A-1.

"Editorial." 1957. *Journal of Conflict Resolution* 1(1): 1–2.

Fairfield, Roy P., ed. 1961. *The Federalist Papers.* 2d ed. Garden City, NY: Anchor Books.

Fisher, Roger D. 1964. "Fractionating Conflict." In Roger Fisher, ed., *International Conflict and Behavioral Science,* 91–109. New York: Basic Books.

Frank, Jerome D. 1968. *Sanity and Survival: Psychological Aspects of War and Peace.* New York: Random House.

Goldberg, Samuel. B., and William P. Hobgood. 1987. *Mediating Grievances: A Cooperative Solution.* Washington, DC: Bureau of Labor-Management Relations and Cooperative Programs, U.S. Department of Labor.

Goodnow, Frank. 1900. *Politics and Administration.* New York: Russell and Russell.

Goodsell, Charles. 1986. *The Case for Bureaucracy: A Public Administration Polemic.* 2d ed. Chatham, NJ: Chatham House.

Gore, Albert. 1993, 1994. *Creating a Government That Works Better and Costs Less: Report of the National Performance Review.* Washington, DC: Government Printing Office.

Gulick, Luther, and Lyndall Urwick, eds. 1937. *Papers on the Science of Administration.* New York: Augustus M. Kelley.

Heclo, Hugh. 1986. "Reaganism and the Search for a Public Philosophy." In John Palmer, ed., *Perspectives on the Reagan Years,* 31–61. Washington, DC: Urban Institute Press.

Himes, Joseph. 1980. *Conflict and Conflict Management.* Athens, GA: University of Georgia Press.

Ingraham, Patricia W., and Barbara S. Romzek. 1994. *New Paradigms for Government: Issues for the Changing Public Service.* San Francisco: Jossey-Bass.

Krislov, Samuel. 1974. *Representative Bureaucracy.* Englewood Cliffs, NJ: Prentice Hall.

Lan, Zhiyong. 1991. "Training, Practice, and Field Development in Public Administration." Proceedings of the 14th National Conference on Teaching Public Administration. Knoxville, Tennessee, 377–393.

———. 1994. "Reaganism and the Public Choice Theory in American Public Administration." *Journal of Political Science and International Studies* 8(1): 36–44.

Lan, Zhiyong, and Kathleen Anders. 1996. "Paradigms That Govern Public Administration Research: An Empirical Test." Paper presented at the Ninth National Symposium on Public Administration Theory. 18–19 February. Savannah, Georgia.

Levine, Charles H. 1990. "The Federal Government in the Year 2000: Administrative Legacies of the Reagan Years." In Patricia W. Ingraham and Donald F. Kettl, eds., *Agenda for Excellence: Public Service in America,* 162–186. Chatham, NJ: Chatham House.

Levine, Charles H.B., Guy Peters, and Frank J. Thompson. 1990. *Public Administration: Challenges, Choices, Consequences.* Glenview, IL: Scott Foresman.

Lipsky, Michael. 1980. *Street Level Bureaucracy: Dilemmas of the Individual in Public Services.* New York: Russell Sage Foundation.

Locke, John. 1963. *Two Treatises of Government.* New York: Cambridge University Press.

Lorenz, Konrad. 1966. *On Aggression.* New York: Harcourt, Brace and World.

Madigan, Denise R. 1992. "Update on ADR in the Federal Government." *The Practitioner's Notebook.* No. 1. Cambridge, MA: MIT-Harvard Public Disputes Network.

Manring, Nancy J. 1993. "Reconciling Science and Politics in Forest Service Decision Making: New Tools for Public Administrators." *American Review of Public Administration* 23(4): 343–359.

———. 1994. "ADR and Administrative Responsiveness: Challenges for Public Administrators." *Public Administration Review* 54(2): 197–203.

McCurdy, Howard E. 1985. *Public Administration: A Bibliographic Guide to the Literature.* New York: Marcel Dekker.

Mills, Miriam K., ed. 1991. *Alternative Dispute Resolution in the Public Sector.* Chicago: Nelson-Hall.

Morrison, Samuel Eliot, Henry Steele Commager, and William E. Leuchtenburg. 1977. *A Concise History of the American Republic.* New York: Oxford University Press.

Osborne, David, and Theodore Gaebler. 1992. *Reinventing Government: How the Entrepreneurial Spirit Is Transforming the Public Sector.* Reading, MA: Addison-Wesley.

Osgood, Charles E. 1962. *An Alternative to War and Surrender.* Urbana: University of Illinois Press.

Ostrom, Vincent. 1973. *The Intellectual Crises in American Public Administration.* University: University of Alabama Press.

Palmer, John. 1986. "Philosophy, Policy and Politics." In John Palmer, ed., *Perspectives on the Reagan Years,* 175–203. Washington, DC: Urban Institute Press.

Pruitt, Dean G. 1971. "Indirect Communication and the Search for Agreement in Negotiation." *Journal of Social Issues* 1: 205–239.

Rapoport, Anatol. 1962. "Rules for Debate." In Quincy Wright, William M. Evan, and Morton Deutsch, eds., *Preventing World War III: Some Proposals.* New York: Simon and Schuster.

Rohr, John A. 1978. *Ethics for Bureaucrats.* New York: Marcel Dekker.

Rosenbloom, David. 1983. "Public Administration Theory and the Separation of Powers." *Public Administration Review* 43(3): 219–227.

———. 1989. *Public Administration: Understanding Management, Politics, and Law in the Public Sector.* 2d ed. New York: Random House.

Rosenbloom, David, Deborah D. Goldman, and Patricia W. Ingraham. 1994. *Contemporary Public Administration.* New York: McGraw-Hill.

Rostow, W. Whitman. 1971. *Politics and the Stages of Growth.* New York: Cambridge University Press.

Rourke, Francis E. 1992. "Responsiveness and Neutral Competence in American Bureaucracy." *Public Administration Review* 52(6): 539–546.

Rousseau, Jean-Jacques. 1973. *The Social Contract and Discourses.* Translated by G.D.H. Cole. London: J.M. Dent and Sons.

Savas, Emanuel S. 1987. *Privatization: The Key to Better Government.* Chatham, NJ: Chatham House.

Simon, Herbert. 1957. *Administrative Behavior.* New York: Macmillan.

Spicer, Michael W. 1995. *The Founders, the Constitution, and Public Administration: A Conflict in Worldviews.* Washington, DC: Georgetown University Press.

Stephenson, Max O., Jr., and Gerald M. Pops. 1991. "Public Administrators and Conflict Resolution: Democratic Theory, Administration Capacity and the Case of Negotiated Rule-Making." In Miriam K. Mills, ed., *Alternative Dispute Resolution in the Public Sector,* 13–25. Chicago: Nelson-Hall.

Susskind, Lawrence E., Eileen F. Babbitt, and Phyllis N. Segal. 1993. "When ADR Becomes the Law: A Review of Best Practice in Federal Agencies." *Negotiation Journal* 9 (January): 59–75.

Susskind, Lawrence E., and Sarah McKearnan. 1994. "Enlightened Conflict Resolution." *Technology Review* 93(3): 70–72.

Taylor, Paul, and Helen Dewar. 1995. "Outsiders on the Inside: The House and Senate Have Never Seen Anything Quite Like the GOP Freshman Class of 94." *Washington Post National Weekly Edition,* 17–23 July, 3–10.

Vizzard, William J. 1995. "The Impact of Agenda Conflict on Policy Formulation and Implementation: The Case of Gun Control." *Public Administration Review* 55(4): 341–347.

Waldo, Dwight. 1948. *The Administrative State.* New York: Ronald Press.

Wilson, Woodrow. 1992. "The Study of Administration." In Jay M. Shafritz and Albert C. Hyde, eds., *Classics of Public Administration.* 3d ed., 11–24. Belmont, CA: Wadsworth.

Wondolleck, Julia M. 1988. *Public Lands Conflict and Resolution: Managing National Forest Disputes.* New York: Plenum.

PART V

THE ROLE OF LAW
IN PUBLIC ADMINISTRATION

Many different concepts about law and public administration have been identified and illuminated in the first four sections of this book. This section draws together these concepts into a coherent view of the impact of law on public administration activity. Law applies to everything public administrators do; constitutions constrain everything public administrators do. While not every action taken by public administrators will be defined within federal or state constitutions, every time a public administrator acts, that person is using the power of government to accomplish some discrete purpose. However, the intersection between public administration and law is more than the application of constitutional requirements. Additional points of intersection include public administrators as executors of the law and public administrators as quasi-judicial actors. The final tie is seen when public administrators and the courts act separately or in concert to promote the fundamental goals of our society, including social equity.

The preceding sections have shown that the role of law in public administration is part of governance and management. Public administrators act under the rule of law set forth in state and federal constitutions. The concept of governance is based on both principles and actions that are intertwined with law. In the first section, both Rohr and Rosenbloom argue that the two main sources for law are legislation and common law court decisions. The responsibility and authority to execute the law is delegated to administrators to exercise in the public interest. The inquiries of what is delegated and what is the extent of discretion are practical and situational.

Often law has been presented as legal context, litigious confrontations, or judicial constraint. Some of these representations reflect negative attitudes, and many hold grains of truth. Judicial review and constraints are an important part of the democratic checks and balances—hence the metaphor of administrators and judges as partners. Judicial review allows for disclosure, transparency, accountability, and change. Substantive legislation and executive polices set goals and responsibilities for administrators. The Administrative Procedure Act and court cases have both established procedures and boundaries for the modern administrative state.

Court cases have repeatedly dealt with delegation, discretion, deliberation, and deference. These themes are interrelated, and as previous chapters have shown, the constitutional norms of disclosure and accountability based on facts and established principals are part of judicial decisional rationality and administrative practice. Judicial deference to administrative authority and expertise is often balanced against constitutional concerns about individual and civil rights.

Conflict resolution alternatives to traditional litigation have been proposed and developed. There has been experimentation and development of a wide array of techniques, but a common critique raises concerns about the power relationships. That is, the way that law develops and changes is either through legislative action or through appellate court decrees. When disputes are removed from these two public spheres and reassigned to ADR, the concern becomes whether administrative actions subjected to ADR become private, situational, inconsistent, and non-reviewable. This raises issues of power and justice. The question becomes: Does the administrative expedience and efficiency that result from using ADR undermine democratic values?

Although law may be conceptually articulated as foundation, context, structure, and function for governance, this is an incomplete view. Law is not distinct from democratic values; it is part of them. The courts often consider constitutional rights such as due process when deciding what a just and fair government should be both in its principles and in its actions. The role of law in public administration includes issues of equity, equality, and justice. As the last three chapters here show, ethics is part of the role of law and public administration.

Law connects social equity and public administration as H. George Frederickson shows in Chapter 18. Frederickson argues that it is the job of public administrators to ensure that social equity is achieved—that public administrators occupy a unique position in the structure of government and therefore have the capacity to act for the greater good of all citizens. Ultimately, for Frederickson, the line between courts and public administration is blurred allowing public administrators more active roles in determining the course of civil rights and social justice.

The use of public law litigation to challenge discrimination, illegal administrative practices, or unconstitutional administration was discussed in some of the earlier chapters. Since the 1954 decision of *Brown v. Board of Education,* elimination of segregation and other discriminatory government practices has become a frequent issue before the courts. While seeking changes in policies to promote social justice has been a concern of the executive, legislative, and judicial branches, it is a challenge for administrators. Litigation has become a dominant technique to promote social change in the last fifty years.

Court decisions influence the behavior of public administrators. Articles in each section of this book offer examples of different ways in which change can be exerted on an organization. Whether being party to a lawsuit, interpreting judicial decisions, or reacting to changes in their environment, public administrators are clearly subject to court influence. There are, of course, differing degrees of influence. Being under the court's supervision is clearly more invasive than being a party to a lawsuit, which in turn is more invasive than incorporating judicial decision making into the practices of the organization after reviewing a court ruling on issues raised by others.

The use of injunctive powers of courts to require changes in administrative practices has been debated, but an important analysis presented here considers how court supervision of a public service—primary education—entails problems of administration, leadership, cooperation, and supervision. In Chapter 19, from 2003, Charles R. Wise and Rosemary

O'Leary summarize the effects of the termination of judicial supervision of the Kansas City school system. Their central premise is that once courts begin the process of administering public services, extracting themselves from this role presents difficulties for all parties involved. Blurring the line between ruling on questions of law and the execution of those rulings may be necessary in specific instances to ensure equality of opportunity, but Wise and O'Leary prefer that public administrators implement policies rather than courts. As Wise and O'Leary document the confusion and unintended consequences of the struggle to develop equity in school systems, they also suggest that long-term judicial supervision creates problems of administration that muddy the roles of courts, policymakers, and administrators.

Law is essential to public administration. It is more than a foundation, context, challenge, or constraint. The art and practice of public administration includes the law. It is part of the philosophy of democratic government. Principles matter. In the closing chapter of this book, Ronald C. Moe and Robert S. Gilmore articulate why we cannot neglect law: law is the source of the principles of public administration. Thus, public administration in a democratic constitutional government is bound to the execution of law and the proposed new public management reforms that ignore this legal foundation lack legitimacy.

This, then, is the primary message of this book: Law matters to public administration and public administration matters to the application of law. Balance and partnership are the hallmarks of this relationship. Legislative and judicial mandates, constitutional values, and administrative practices must be balanced. There are partnerships among all the actors whose decisions result in government mandates and whose actions enforce the laws. At times the partnership may seem unbalanced toward one party and at times the partnership may seem to have failed. Yet this fundamental tenet remains true: *Law provides the basis for and legitimation of public administration in our society.* If we do not understand the role of law in public administration, we cannot understand the foundations and future of public administration.

CHAPTER 18

PUBLIC ADMINISTRATION AND SOCIAL EQUITY

H. GEORGE FREDERICKSON

It was 1968. Inequality and injustice, especially based on race, were pervasive. A government built on a Constitution claiming the equal protection of the laws had failed in that promise. Public administrators, those who daily operate the government, were not without responsibility. Both in theory and practice public administration had, beginning in the 1940s, emphasized concepts of decision making, systems analysis, operations research or management science, and rationality. In running the government the administrator's job was to be efficient (getting the most service possible for available dollars) or economical (providing an agreed-upon level of services for the fewest possible dollars). It should be no surprise, therefore, that issues of inequity and injustice were not central to public servants or to public administration theorists.

To remedy what seemed a glaring inadequacy in both thought and practice, I developed a theory of social equity and put it forward as the "third pillar" for public administration, holding the same status as economy and efficiency as values or principles to which public administration should adhere.[1]

... Researchers, especially in the public policy fields, began to analyze variations in the distribution of public service by income, race, and neighborhood, and eventually by gender. The concept of equity was included in the first adopted Principles for the American Society for Public Administration (ASPA), which later became the Code of Ethics. ...

In the past twenty years the phrase social equity has taken its place as a descriptor for variables in the analytic constructs of researchers in the field, as a concept in the philosophy of public administration, and as a guide for ethical behavior for public servants. ...

This review of the place of social equity in public administration begins, as it should, with philosophical and theoretical developments. That is followed by a consideration of the especially important relationship between social equity and the law and what has transpired in the last generation. Following that, developments in analysis and research are reviewed.

Philosophical and Theoretical Developments

Public administration, it has been said, is the marriage of the arts and sciences of government to the arts and sciences of management.[5] Efficiency and economy are primarily

---

Excerpted from *Public Administration Review* 50, no. 2 (March/April 1990): 228–237. Copyright © 1990 by American Society for Public Administration. Reprinted with permission.

theories of management while social equity is primarily a theory of government. In the early years of modern American public administration the marriage, particularly in the conceptions of Woodrow Wilson, was balanced.[6] Theories of business efficiency were routinely mixed with theories of democratic government, the argument being that a government can and should be efficient and fair. . . .

Initial attempts to return to the marriage questions of equity and fairness were simplistic and superficial. Willbern, in his splendid review of the early literature on social equity and the so-called new public administration, observed that critics were "not very precise in defining the goals or values toward which administration and knowledge must be arrived."[7]

So the task was clear, social equity needed flesh on its bones if it was to be taken seriously as a third pillar for public administration. The process was begun with a symposium on "Social Equity and Public Administration," which appeared in the *Public Administration Review* in 1974. . . . [T]hat symposium is illustrative of theory building in public administration.

First, the subject is parsed, in this case, into considerations of social equity: (1) as the basis for a just, democratic society; (2) as influencing the behavior of organization man; (3) as the legal basis for distributing public services; (4) as the practical basis for distributing public services; (5) as operationalized in compound federalism; and, (6) as a challenge for research and analysis.[9]

Second, the subject having been taken apart, good theory building suggests putting it back together. Looking back, it is now clear that considerable progress has been made in thinking about, understanding, and applying various parts of the subject. But it has yet to be put back together.

Third is the arduous task of definition. In this case, it was appropriate to turn to the theories of distributive justice for definition. The phrase social equity and the word equality were essentially without definition in the field. As Rae and his associates have said: "Equality is the simplest and most abstract of notions, yet the practices of the world are irremediably concrete and complex. How, imaginably, could the former govern the latter?"[10] Yet, social equity was advanced in the 1960s and 1970s as an essential third pillar of public administration.

When ideas such as social equity or the public interest or liberty are suggested as guides for public action, the most compelling definitions are often the most abstract. And so it was in this case. The initial attempts to define social equity as it applies to public administration were fastened to John Rawls's *A Theory of Justice.*[11] The Rawlsian construct as an ideal type addresses the distribution of rights, duties, and advantages in a just society. Justice, to Rawls, is fairness. To achieve fairness the first principle is that each person is guaranteed equal basic liberties consistent with an extensive system of liberty for all. The second principle calls for social and economic inequalities to be managed so that they are of greatest benefit to the least advantaged (the difference principle); it seeks to make offices and positions open to all under conditions of *fair* equality of opportunity.

For much of the last two decades perspectives on Rawlsian justice have occupied the intellectual high ground of concern for social equity. While philosophical and scholarly interest in Rawlsian theory has been strong, and certainly the objectives of fairness through justice are compatible with the social equity perspective on public administration, the theory has thus far been of limited use in the busy world of government.

This analysis turns, then, to a more descriptive theory for both greater definition and more likely applicability to the theories and practices of public administration. Following Douglas Rae and Associates, a rudimentary language and a road map are set forth for the notion of equality, with attendant definitions and examples.[12] I label this the Compound Theory of Social Equity. This Compound Theory serves as the basis for later considerations of legal and research perspectives on social equity in public administration.

Simple Individual Equalities

Individual equality consists of one class of equals, and one relationship of equality holds among them. The best examples would be one person–one vote and the price mechanism of the market, which offers a Big Mac or a Whopper at a specific price to whoever wishes to buy. The Golden Rule or Immanuel Kant's Categorical Imperative are formulas for individual equalities.

Segmented Equality

Any complex society with a division of labor tends to practice segmented equality. Farmers have a different system of taxation than do business owners, and both differ from wage earners. In segmented equality, one assumes that equality exists within the category (e.g., farmers) and that inequality exists between the segments. All forms of hierarchy use the concept of segmented equality. All five-star generals are equal to each other as are all privates first-class. Equal pay for equal work is segmented equality. Segmented equality is, in fact, systematic or structured inequality. Segmented equality is critically important for public policy and administration because virtually every public service is delivered on a segmented basis and always by segmented hierarchies.

Block Equalities

Both simple individual and segmented equalities are in fact individual equalities. Block equalities, on the other hand, call for equality *between* groups or subclasses. The railroad accommodations for Blacks and whites could be separate, so long as they were equal in *Plessy v. Ferguson* (1889).[13] *Brown v. Board of Education* (1954)[14] later concluded that separation by race meant inequality; therefore, the U.S. Supreme Court required school services to be based upon simple individual equality rather than block equality, using race to define blocks. The claims for comparable worth systems of pay for women are, interestingly, block egalitarianism mixed with equal pay for equal work, which is segmented equality.

The Domain of Equality

How does one decide what is to be distributed equally? The domain of equality marks off the goods, services, or benefits being distributed. If schools and fire protection are to be provided, why not golf courses or recreational facilities? Domains of equality can be narrowly or broadly defined, and they can have to do with *allocations* based on a public agency's resources or they can be based on *claims*—claimants' demands for equality. Domains of equality constantly shift, aggregate, and disaggregate. Certain domains are largely controlled by the market such as jobs, wages, and investments, while others are controlled primarily by government. It is often the case that the governmental domain seeks equality to correct inequalities resulting from the market or from previous governmental policies. Unemployment compensation, Aid to Families with Dependent Children, college tuition grants, and food stamps are all kinds of governmental compensatory inequality to offset other inequalities outside of the governmental domain of allocation but within a broader domain of claims.

Domains can also be intergenerational, as in the determination of whether present taxpayers or their children pay for the federal debt built up by current deficits.

Equalities of Opportunity

Equalities of opportunity are divided into *prospect* and *means* opportunity. Two people have equal opportunity for a job if each has the same probability for attaining the job under conditions of prospect equality of opportunity. Two people have equal opportunity for a job if each has the same talents or qualifications for the job under conditions of means-equal opportunity. Examples of pure prospect equality of opportunity are few, but the draft lottery for the Vietnam War is very close. In means equality of opportunity, *equal rules,* such as Intelligent Quotient (I.Q.) tests, Standard Achievement Test (SAT) scores, equal starting and finishing points for footraces, and so forth define opportunity. "The purpose and effect of these equal means is not equal prospect of success, but legitimately unequal prospects of success."[15] Aristotle's notion that equals are to be treated equally would constitute means-based equality of opportunity.

In any given society not all talent can be equally developed. Following John Schaar: "Every society has a set of values, and these are arranged in a more or less tidy hierarchy. . . . The equality of opportunity formula must be revised to read: equality of opportunity for all to develop those talents which are highly valued by a given people at a given time."[16] How else, for example, can one explain the status of rock musicians in popular culture?

The Value of Equality

The value of equality begins with the concept of *lot equality* in which shares are identical (similar housing, one vote, etc.) or equal. The advantage of lot equality is that only the individual can judge what pleases or displeases him or her. Lots can also be easily measured and distributed, and they imply nothing about equal well-being. The problem, of course, is that lot equality is insensitive to significant variations in need. To remedy this, Rae and associates suggest a "person equality" in which there is nonarbitrary rule-based distribution of shares based on nonneutral judgments about individuals' needs. A threatened person may require more protection (and police officials may so decide) merely to make that person equal to the nonthreatened person. The same can be said for the crippled as against the healthy child, the mentally retarded as against the bright. Person-regarding equality is often practiced in public administration to "make the rules humane."

It is clear that any universal scope for equality is both impossible and undesirable. Rather than a simple piece of rhetoric or a slogan, the Compound Theory of Social Equity is a complex of definitions and concepts. Equality then changes from one thing to many things—equalities. If public administration is to be inclined toward social equity, at least this level of explication of the subject is required. In the policy process, any justification of policy choices claiming to enhance social equity needs to be analyzed in terms of such questions as: (1) Is this equality individual, segmented, or block? (2) Is this equality direct, or is it means-equal opportunity or prospect-equal opportunity? (3) What forms of social equity can be advanced so as to improve the lot of the least advantaged, yet sustain democratic government and a viable market economy? The Compound Theory of Social Equity would serve as the language of the framework for attempts in both theory building and practice, and it would serve to answer these questions.

Social Equity and the Law

Marshall Dimock made this dicta famous: "Public administration is the law in action." It should be no surprise, then, that the most significant developments in social equity have their genesis in the law. "Local, state and national legislators—and their counterparts in the executive branches—too often have ignored, abdicated or traded away their responsibilities. . . . By default, then, if for no other reason, the courts would often have the final say."[17] The courts are the last resort for those claiming unequal treatment in either the protection of the law or the provision of service. Elected officials—both legislators and executives—are naturally inclined to the views and interests of the majority. Appointed officials—the public administrators—have until recent years been primarily concerned with efficiency and economy, although effectiveness was also an early concern, as noted by Dwight Waldo in *The Administrative State*.[18]

Employment

The most important legal influences resulting in more equitable government are in the field of employment, both public and nonpublic. The legal (not to mention administrative) questions are: who ought to be entitled to a job, what are the criteria, and how ought they to be applied?

The Civil Rights Act of 1964 as amended and the Equal Employment Act of 1972 were designed to guarantee equal access to public and private employment. This was done by a combination of block equalities (whereby persons in different racial categories could be compared and, if found subject to different treatment, a finding of violation of law would be made) and a means-equal opportunities logic (whereby fair measurements of talent, skill, and ability would determine who gets jobs). The landmark case was *Griggs v. Duke Power,* in which the U.S. Supreme Court held that job qualifications that were not relevant to a specific job and that on their face favored whites over Blacks were a violation of the law.[19] The Court clearly rejected the idea of prospect equality, but because it upheld the idea of equality by blocks or, to use the words of the law, "protected groups," a strong social equity signal was sent. Race-consciousness as an affirmative action was to be based upon equality between Blacks and whites both in the work cohort and between the work cohort and the labor market—a kind of double application of equality.

John Nalbandian, in a recent review of case law on affirmative action in employment, observed that cases subsequent to *Griggs* have systematically limited "affirmative action tightly within the scope of the problem it was supposed to solve." The case law has sought to limit negative effects, such as unwanted inequality befalling nonminorities as a result of these programs.[20] *The University of California Regents v. Bakke* was the most celebrated example of judicial support for black equality to bring Blacks up to an enrollment level equal to whites, while at the same time protecting a nonminority claimant who would likely have qualified for admissions in the absence of a protected c l ass.[21]

Government Service

In 1968 Andrew Hawkins, a Black handyman living in a neighborhood called the Promised Land, an all-Black section of Shaw, Mississippi, gathered significant data to show that municipal services such as paved streets, sewers, and gutters were unequally distributed. Because these services were available in the white section of Shaw, Hawkins charged that he and his class were deprived of the 14th Amendment guarantee of equal protection of the law. The U.S. District Court disagreed, saying that such a distribution had to do with issues of "municipal administration" that were "resolved at the ballot box."[27] On appeal, the decision of the District Court was overturned by the U.S. Court of Appeals, in part based on this amicus curiae brief from the Harvard-MIT (Massachusetts Institute of Technology) Joint Center for Urban Studies:

> . . . invidious discrimination in the qualitative and quantitative rendition of basic governmental services violates an unyielding principle . . . that a trial court may not permit a defendant local government to rebut substantial statistical evidence of discrimination on the basis of race by entering a general disclaimer of illicit motive or by a loose and undocumented plea of administrative convenience. No such defense can be accepted as an adequate rebuttal of a prima facie case established by uncontroverted statistical evidence of an overwhelming disparity in the level and kind of public services rendered to citizens who differ neither in terms of desire nor need, but only in the color of their skin.[28]

While the appellate court ruled in Hawkins's favor, it construed the issue of equal protection so narrowly as to all but preclude significant court intervention in service allocation decisions where *intent* to discriminate cannot be conclusively demonstrated.

Desegregation of public schools following *Brown v. Board of Education* has resulted in varied and creative ways to define and achieve equality. Busing is a means of achieving at least the appearance of block equality. Busing has, however, been primarily from the inner city out. Magnet schools are an attempt to equalize the racial mix via busing in the other direction. Building schools at the margins of primarily white and primarily Black (or Hispanic) neighborhoods preserves the concept of the neighborhood school while achieving integration. The major problem has been jurisdictional or to use the language of equality, domain. The familiar inner city, primarily non-white school district surrounded by suburban, primarily white school districts significantly limits the possible equalizing effects of *Brown v. Board of Education.* This is especially the case when wealth and tax base follow white movement to the suburbs. State courts have in many places interpreted the equality clauses of state constitutions to bring about greater equality. Beginning with *Serrano v. Priest* in California, state equalization formulas for school funding have in many states required the augmentation of funding in poor districts.[29] Ordinarily this is done on a dollar-per-student basis. This procedure broadens the domain of the issue to the state, and it is also a simple formula for individual equality. It does, of course, bring about this equality by race-based inequality.

From the point of view of competing concepts of equality, the Kansas City Missouri School District desegregation cases may be the most interesting. After *Brown v. Board of Education* determined that separate but equal schooling was in fact unequal and unconstitutional, two questions remained. Was it sufficient for school districts and state departments of education to stop segregating? Or, was it necessary to repair the damage done by a century of racially separate school systems? In *United States v. Jefferson City Board of Education* the Court of Appeals declared that school officials "have an affirmative duty under the Fourteenth Amendment to bring about an integrated unitary school system in which there are no Negro schools and no white schools—just schools. . . . In fulfilling this duty it is not enough for school authorities to offer Negro children the opportunity to attend formerly all-white schools. The necessity of overcoming the effects of the dual school system in this circuit requires integration of faculties, facilities and activities as well as students."[30]

Later in *Swann v. Charlotte-Mecklenburg Board of Education* the U.S. Supreme Court stated that "the objective today remains to eliminate from the public schools all vestiges of state imposed segregation."[31]

Two conditions pertain in Kansas City, Missouri. First is a dual housing market resulting from an interaction between private and governmental parties in the real estate industry, resulting in racially segregated residential areas. This has resulted in racially segregated schools roughly mirroring the segregated neighborhoods. Originally segregated all-Black schools are now schools of mostly Black students and teachers. The eleven suburban school districts surrounding Kansas City have almost all white students and teachers.

In *Jenkins v. Missouri* in 1984 the trial court under Judge Clark found the Kansas City

Missouri School District and the State of Missouri liable for the unconstitutional segregation of the public schools.[32] The problem, of course, was the remedy. It is one thing to identify inequality; it is another to achieve equality. The School District tried and failed to secure passage of tax levies and bond issues to comply with Judge Clark's order.

Following the *Liddell* and *Griffin* cases, Judge Clark ordered both tax increases and bond issuances to cover the remedies sought in 1986.[33] The court also held that 75 percent of the cost of the plan was allocated to the State of Missouri for funding. The appellate court sustained all of Judge Clark's remedies with the exception of a 1.5-percent surcharge on incomes earned in Kansas City by nonresidents and instructed the state and the district to proceed with the remedies.[34]

If the majority of the citizens had turned down bond issues and had refused higher taxation to enable the school district to meet its desegregation objectives, how could the judge justify imposing those taxes as a matter of law? He said:

> A majority has no right to deny others the constitutional guarantees to which they are entitled. This court, having found that vestiges of unconstitutional discrimination still exist in the KCMSD, is not so callous as to accept the proposition that it is helpless to enforce a remedy to correct the past violations. . . . The court must weigh the constitutional rights of the taxpayers against the constitutional rights of the plaintiff students in this case. The court is of the opinion that the balance is clearly in favor of the students who are helpless without the aid of this court.[35]

From an equality point of view, there are several examples of competing views of fairness. *First,* with the individual definition of equality, each vote is equal to each other vote, and the majority wins in a representative democracy. The court here clearly said that a majority cannot vote away the constitutional rights of a minority to equal schooling. *Second* is the dimension of time or intergenerational equality. The century of inequality in schools for Black children was to be remedied by a period of inequality toward nonminorities to correct for the past. *Third* is the question of domain. To what extent should the issue be confined to one school district? Because schools are constitutionally established in the State of Missouri, Judge Clark concluded that the funding solutions for desegregation were ultimately the responsibility of the state. Indeed, Arthur A. Bensen II, an attorney for the plaintiff, argued persuasively that it was fully within the authority of Judge Clark not only to impose either state or areawide financing to solve school desegregation but also to reorganize the school districts to eliminate the vestiges of prior discrimination.[36] The judge chose not to go that far.

Many more examples of equality can be traced to the courts, including equalizing funding for male and female student athletes in schools and colleges.

An especially interesting and relevant interpretation of the relationship between social equity and law as they have to do with public administration is provided by Charles M. Haar and Daniel W. Fessler. They suggest that the basis for equality in the law is less likely to be found in the United States Constitution and federal statutes and more likely to be found in state constitutions and statutes. "Recognizing the growing practical difficulties in relying on the equal protection clause, we assert the existence—the convincing and determinative presence—of a common law doctrine, *the duty to serve,* as an avenue of appeal that predates the federal Constitution."[37] More than 700 years before the Constitution, judge-made law in the England of Henry VII held "that, at a fundamental level of social organization, all persons similarly situated in terms of need have an enforceable claim of equal, adequate and nondiscriminatory access to essential services; in addition this doctrine makes such legal access largely a governmental responsibility."[38] All monopolies—states, districts, utilities—are in the common law "clothed with a public interest" and obligated to the "doctrine of equal service."[39] If Haar and Fessler are right and if the state-based school funding equalization cases are illustrative, social equity will emerge at the grass roots rather than be imposed by the federal courts.

Social Equity and Analysis

Consequent with the development of theories of distributive justice and the law of equality has been the emergence of policy analysis. Over the past twenty-five years many of America's major universities have established schools of public policy that specialize in the interdisciplinary study of policy issues. In addition, many existing schools and departments of public administration have started to emphasize the policy analysis perspective. Virtually every policy field—health care, transportation, law enforcement, fire protection, housing, education, natural resources and the environment, national defense— is now the subject of regular review and analysis. Generalized scholarly journals as well as journals specializing in some policy fields are now available, and virtually every issue has articles dealing with some form of equity.[40]

Both the ideological and methodological perspectives in policy analysis have been dominated by economics. Although governments are not markets, market-model applications are widely used in policy analysis. The logic is simple. If, in economic theory, both individuals and firms maximize their utilities, their citizens and government bureaus do the same. This perspective has been especially compatible with popular contemporary governmental ideas such as deregulation, privatization, school vouchers, public-private partnerships, cut-back management, and the minimalist or so-called "night watchman" view of American government. While the economic model has been a powerful influence on policy analysis, it has been tempered, especially in recent years, by use of measures of both general and individual well-being that are more compatible with governmental goals. Longstanding and powerful governmental concepts, such as justice, fairness, individual rights, and equality, are now being measured and used in analysis. Broad collective measures, the so-called social indicators such as unemployment and homelessness, are now more often used in policy analysis. Measurements of variations in the distribution of public services by age, race, gender, income, and the like are relatively routine. Social equity concepts are used not only as theory or as legal standards but as measures or variables in research. The problem, of course, in social equity analysis, as in the use of social equity in law or theory, is the compound character of equality.

At the level of the individual, data and findings are now available that map, in at least a rudimentary way, personal views and preferences regarding equality. Jennifer Hochschild has determined that people have contradictory views of equality.[41] These contradictory views are not determined so much by income level or political ideology as by more subtle distinctions. People have varied opinions about equality depending on what domain of life is being considered and how equality is being defined. Using three different domains, *social* (including home, family, school, and community), *economic* (including jobs, wages, taxes, and wealth), and *political* (including voting, representation, and law), and using two conceptions of equality first, equal shares and equal procedures, and second, differentiation (a combination of segmented equality and means-based equality of opportunity) Hochschild's findings are as follows.

In the social domain people hold strongly to norms of equal shares and equal procedures. Equal treatment of children, one spouse, equal sacrifice for the family, and equal treatment in the neighborhood mark the general views of the poor, the middle class, and the rich. In schools, equal or fair procedures are important to just determination of grades. In schools, families tend to move somewhat away from strict individual equality toward a differentiation based upon investment, such as the handicapped child's needing more, an example of Rawlsian justice. And there is evidence of a differentiation of investment for the more gifted or those with greater potential. People are not, however, equally happy with the egalitarian character of social life. If they feel they have some control over their fate and are able to act on the principles of equality, they are more happy. If not, they are bitter and unhappy.

These same people endorse differentiation or means-based equality in the economic domain. People, in other words, want an equal chance to become unequal. Productivity should be rewarded, the poor feeling this would produce more equal incomes, the rich believing it would result in less equal incomes. Private property is deeply supported. Accumulated wealth is not generally opposed by poor or rich, and both strongly oppose inheritance taxes. And both partially abandon their different views when it comes to poverty, feeling that "something should be done."

In the political domain these people are egalitarian again. Political and civil rights should be distributed equally to all. "They want tax and social welfare policies mainly to take from the rich and give to the poor and middle classes. Their vision of utopia always includes more equality."[42] There is deep resentment over perceived unfairness resulting from loopholes in the graduated income tax because it treats people unequally. Many people endorse tuition subsidies for the poor, housing subsidies, and even a national health insurance.

Yet, with all of this, Hochschild found ambivalence. People recognize that their views are sometimes inconsistent or that they are confused. And there is some helplessness and anger over whom to blame for inequality or how to make things better.

As the different domains of people's lives best explain how they feel about equality, they also generally conform to the compound conception of social equity set out [previously]. Both in the theoretical model and in people's outlooks, equality splits into equalities depending on domains, dimensions of time, jurisdictions, abilities, effort, and luck.

Field research on the distribution of local government service is filled with implications for social equity and public administration. Much of this research tests the "underclass hypothesis." If one accepts that hypothesis, it follows that the distribution of libraries, parks, fire protection, water, sewers, policy protection, and education services follows power, wealth, and racial variations. The findings of research on municipal services generally indicate that the underclass hypothesis does not hold.[43] Fixed services such as parks and libraries exhibit "unpatterned inequalities" that are not correlated with power, wealth, or race. These inequalities are more a function of the age of the neighborhood and the condition of housing. Mobile services such as police and fire protection tend to be distributed relatively equally, and such variation as can be determined is not associated with race or wealth. On the burden side, evidence indicates that property tax assessments are unequal in the direction of lower proportionate assessments for minorities and the poor and higher proportionate assessments for the rich and the white.[44]

Both interdistrict and intradistrict school funding variations have tended, on the other hand, to confirm the underclass hypothesis. In the past twenty years, primarily as a result of court cases, more than half of the states have undertaken school-finance reforms designed to equalize funding between schools within districts or between districts. When compared to nonschool-finance reform states, the reform states now evidence greater equity in per-student funding.[45]

Why has the underclass hypothesis not been demonstrated in field research, except in the case of schools? Robert Lineberry and others argue persuasively that urban and state bureaucracies, following patterned decision rules or service delivery rules, have distributed public services in such a way as to ameliorate the effects of poverty and race. The effects of municipal reform, including city managers, merit-based bureaucracies, at-large elections, nonpartisan elections, and the like, have strengthened the public services at the local level. The public services are routinized, patterned, incremental, and predictable, following understood or accepted decision rules or service delivery rules. Police and fire rules require decentralization and wide discretion in deployment of staff and equipment. Social services tend to respond to stated demands. Each service has some basis for its service delivery rules.[46]

What is most significant here is that it is bureaucracy, professional public administration, particularly in larger cities, that distributes public services either generally equally or in the direction of those especially in need. The point is that public administration understands and practices social equity. Social equity is understood or given, in the same way as efficiency or economy, in general public administration practice.

What explains school funding inequities? School bureaucracies have virtually no control over interdistrict funding levels. What explains Shaw, Mississippi, and other glaring examples of race-based service inequity? Often it is the lack of a genuinely professional public service.

Conclusions

This article first reviewed the suggestion made in 1968 that social equity should be the third pillar for the theory and practice of public administration. Theoretical, legal, and analytical developments of the last twenty years were then assessed.

While the more abstract theories of distributive justice were found to be intellectually challenging, the theories that hold the most promise for both empirical verification and practical application to social equity and public administration are those that dissect the subject and illuminate the complexity of equality as an idea and a guide. That theory, coupled with the methodological tools of policy analysts, facilitates examination of the distribution of burdens and benefits so as to make informed decisions that are fair. Legally, equality issues probably reached their zenith in the latter stages of the Warren Court. Both the Burger and Rehnquist Courts have narrowed the emphasis on affirmative action, equity in service distribution, and the like.

For social equity to be a standard for policy judgment and public action, analysis must move from equality to equalities and equity to equities. A compound theory of social equity that details alternative and sometimes competing forms of equality will serve to better inform the practice of public administration. It will always be the task of public servants to balance the needs for efficiency, economy, and social equity—but there can be no balance if public servants understand only the complexities of economy and efficiency but cannot plumb the details of fairness and equality. . . .

Most important in these conclusions is the research that indicates that public administration tends to practice social equity. This is no surprise to those who are in public management at the local level. Public administrators solve problems, ameliorate inequalities, exercise judgment in service allocation matters, and use discretion in the application of generalized policy. Fairness and equity have always been common-sense guides for action. Some are concerned that this seems to put bureaucracy in a political role.[50] No doubt exists that public administration is a form of politics. The issue is, what theories and beliefs guide public administrators' actions? As it has evolved in the last twenty years, social equity has served to order the understanding of public administration and to inform the judgment necessary to be both effective and fair.

Notes

1. H. George Frederickson, *The New Public Administration* (University: University of Alabama Press, 1980).

. . .

5. Dwight Waldo, *The Administrative State* (San Francisco: Ronald Press, 1948).

6. Woodrow Wilson, "The Study of Administration," *Political Science Quarterly* 56 (December 1941; originally copyrighted in 1887).

7. York Willbern, "Is the New Public Administration Still With Us?" *Public Administration Review* 33 (July/August 1973): 376.

. . .

9. David K. Hart, "Social Equity, Justice and the Equitable Administrator," *Public Administration Review* 34 (January/February 1974): 3–11; Michael M. Harmon, "Social Equity and Organization Man: Motivation and Organizational Democracy," *Public Administration Review* 34 (January/February 1974): 11–18; Eugene B. McGregor, Jr., "Social Equity and the Public Service," *Public Administration Review* 34 (January/February 1974: 18–29; Steven R. Chitwood, "Social Equity and Social Service Productivity," *Public Administration Review* 34 (January/February 1974: 29–35; David O. Porter and Teddie Wood Porter, "Social Equity and Fiscal Federalism," *Public Administration Review* 34 (January/February 1974: 36–43; Orion J. White, Jr., and Bruce L. Gates, "Statistical Theory and Equity in the Delivery of

Social Services," *Public Administration Review* 34 (January/February 1974): 43–51.

10. Douglas Rae and Associates, *Equalities* (Cambridge, MA: Harvard University Press, 1981), p. 3.

11. John A. Rawls, *A Theory of Justice* (Cambridge, MA: Harvard University Press, 1971).

12. Much of what appears in the following page is taken from Rae and Associates, *Equalities*.

13. *Plessy v. Ferguson,* 163 U.S. 537 (1896).

14. *Brown v. Board of Education of Topeka,* (I) 3/4/47 U.S. 483 (1954).

15. Rae and Associates, *Equalities,* p. 66.

16. John Schaar, "Equality of Opportunity and Beyond," in J. Rowland Pennock and John W. Chapman, eds., *NOMOS IX: Equality* (New York: Atherton Press, 1967), pp. 231. See also Schaar, "Some Ways of Thinking About Equality," *Journal of Politics* 26 (November 1964): 867–895.

17. Charles M. Haar and Daniel W. Fessler, *Fairness and Justice: Law in the Service of Equality* (New York: Simon and Schuster, 1986), p. 18.

18. Waldo, *The Administrative State.*

19. *Griggs v. Duke Power Company,* 401 U.S. 424 (1971). The U.S. Supreme Court in 1989 stepped considerably back from the Duke Power requirement that employees must demonstrate that the hiring requirements do not discriminate. In *Wards Grove Packing v. Antonio,* in a five-to-four decision, the U.S. Supreme Court now requires a plaintiff to prove employment discrimination. See *New York Times* (June 7, 1989), pp. 1 and 11. *Wards Grove Packing v. Antonio,* Doc. No. 87-1387, 5 June 1989.

20. John Nalbandian, "The U.S. Supreme Court's 'Consensus' on Affirmative Action," *Public Administration Review* 49 (January/February 1989): 38–45.

21. *University of California Regents v. Bakke,* 438 U.S. 265 (1978).

. . .

27. *Hawkins v. Town of Shaw,* 303 F. Supp. 1162, 1171 (N.D. Miss. 1969).

28. Haar and Fessler, *Fairness and Justice,* p. 14.

29. *John Serrano, Jr., et al. v. Ivy Baker Priest,* 5 Cal. 3d584. See also Richard Lehane, *The Quest for Justice: The Politics of School Finance Reform* (New York: Longman, 1978).

30. *Green v. School Board,* 391 U.S. 430, 437–38 (1968).

31. *Swann v. Charlotte-Mecklenburg Board of Education,* 402 U.S. 1 (1971).

32. *Jenkins v. Missouri,* 593 F. Supp. 1485 (W.D. MO 1984).

33. *Liddell v. State of Missouri,* 731 F. 2D 1294, 1323 (8th Cir. 1984), and *Griffin v. School Board of Prince Edward County,* 377 U.S. 218, b233, 84 S. Ct. 1226, 1234, 12 L.Ed.2d 256 (1964).

34. *Jenkins v. State of Missouri,* 855 Fed. R. 8th Circuit 1297–1319.

35. *Jenkins v. State of Missouri,* 672 F. Supp. 412.

36. Arthur A. Bensen II, "The Liability of Missouri Suburban School Districts for the Unconstitutional Segregation of Neighboring Urban School Districts," *University of Missouri at Kansas City Law Review* 53 (Spring 1985): 349–375. Bensen's argument was counter to case law based on *Milliken v. Bradley,* 418 U.S. 717 (1974), in which the U.S. Supreme Court found that jurisdictional boundaries are not barriers to effective segregation, except desegregation under certain conditions. Bensen claims that the Kansas City case satisfies those conditions.

37. Haar and Fessler, *Fairness and Justice,* p. 43.

38. Ibid., p. 21.

39. Ibid.

40. See especially, *Policy Studies Journal,* the *Policy Studies Review,* and *Journal of Policy Analysis and Management.*

41. Jennifer L. Hochschild, *What's Fair? American Beliefs About Distributive Justice* (Cambridge, MA: Harvard University Press, 1981). Much of this page summarizes *What's Fair?*

42. Ibid., p. 181.

43. See Robert L. Lineberry, *Equality and Urban Policy: The Distribution of Municipal Services* (Beverly Hills, CA: Sage, 1977) for a thorough review of the literature as well as a full presentation of the "decision rules" hypothesis.

44. Ibid.

45. Leanna Stiefel and Robert Berne, "The Equity Effects of State School Finance Reform: A Methodological Critique and New Evidence," *Policy Sciences* 13 (February 1981): 75–98.

46. Lineberry, *Equality and Urban Policy,* and Bryan D. Jones, Saadia R. Greenberg, Clifford Kaufman, and Joseph Drew, "Service Delivery Rules and the Distribution of Local Government Services: Three Detroit Bureaucracies," *Journal of Politics* 40 (May 1978): 333–368.

. . .

50. Rodney E. Hero, "The Urban Service Delivery Literature: Some Questions and Considerations," *Polity* 18 (Summer 1986): 659–677.

CHAPTER 19

BREAKING UP IS HARD TO DO

The Dissolution of Judicial Supervision of Public Services

CHARLES R. WISE AND ROSEMARY O'LEARY

In our 1991 *Public Administration Review* article, we examined the implications of the U.S. Supreme Court's *Missouri v. Jenkins* (494 U.S. 33 [1990]) decision for American public administration. In that case, the Court affirmed a federal district court order that imposed local property tax increases for Kansas City, Missouri, residents as a means of raising funds for the local school district's desegregation efforts. Our 1991 article concluded that the decision had empowered and legitimized actions by school administrators, in addition to enhancing the resources available to the school system. The decision, however, severely limited local administrators' ability to set priorities and to control the implementation of many administrative initiatives, from contracting the construction of new facilities to hiring new personnel. New management challenges, particularly in the areas of interorganizational relations and accountability, posed constant demands. The article also concluded that by sanctioning court-ordered taxation, *Missouri v. Jenkins* may also have expanded the new partnership between the courts and public managers—a bipolar relationship—into a "new triumvirate" that includes legislative bodies, but with the courts retaining the senior partnership position.

More than a decade later, this analysis of the Kansas City situation and the *Missouri v. Jenkins* case is presented with two purposes in mind: first, to study how the impact of the decision has changed in the intervening years, with a particular emphasis on policy termination as the district court has attempted unsuccessfully to remove itself from the case; and second, to glean any new lessons for public administration by taking a longitudinal look. Based on interviews with school district personnel, a former school board member, a former member of the court-appointed desegregation monitoring committee, and residents—supplemented by legal and archival research—we conclude that, once begun, a policy of judicially mandated federal court supervision of public institutions is not readily terminated, even pursuant to the expressed wish of the U.S. Supreme Court. We also conclude that the management implications of long-term judicial control of public institutions are more significant than previous authors have realized.

Excerpted from *Public Administration Review* 63, no. 2 (March/April 2003): 177–191. Copyright © 2003 by American Society for Public Administration. Reprinted with permission.

Policy Termination

The question of whether and when judicial supervision of public services should be terminated has not been treated extensively in academic research, nor has the legal doctrine surrounding termination been comprehensively developed. The U.S. Supreme Court has begun to address the issues recently, however, in the school context.

The process of termination does not involve just the courts, but involves other actors in what has been referred to as the "new partnership." Federal appeals court judge Bazelon coined the term "new partnership" to signify the federal courts' increasing involvement in the administration of public programs, and he called for judges and administrators to work collaboratively to assure fair implementation of public policies (Bazelon 1976). As we discussed in our previous article, it may be more accurate to refer to a "new triumvirate" that also includes legislatures in the partnership (O'Leary and Wise 1991, 325). The termination of federal court supervision is a complex process that fully involves the "new triumvirate," as well as a more complex policy network of entrenched political interests.

The literature of public administration and policy has focused more extensively on policy initiation and design—the front end of the cycle—than it has on policy termination—the back end of the cycle (Jones 1997; deLeon 1978, 279; Cameron 1978, 301). While termination has been recognized as an important component of policy making and administration, researchers have termed it "the neglected butt of the policy process" (Behn 1978, 413) and "a wrongly underattended issue" (Biller 1976, 133). "Clearly we know much more about how to get government going than we do about how to get it stopped," Jones concludes (1997, 238). This lack of focus is mirrored in the legal literature, which focuses more on the fashioning of remedial decrees affecting public institutions (Retell 1996; Friedman 1992; Roach 1991; Cooper 1988) than it does on ending them.

Nonetheless, in the context of institutional reform decrees issued by the federal courts, it is important to consider the process by which court-mandated reform programs could be ended. This is significant unless the legal and political system is willing to countenance a permanent change in our system of government, in which the federal courts would become the permanent executive supervisors of many state and local government programs. The U.S. Supreme Court, for one, has proclaimed that it is not willing to see this happen. For example, in the school desegregation case *Board of Education v. Dowell* (498 U.S. 237 [1991]), the Supreme Court, in overturning an appeals court decision, rationalized that the appeals court's criteria for decree termination ". . . would condemn a school district, once governed by a board which intentionally discriminated, to judicial tutelage for the indefinite future," and it concluded that the Fourteenth Amendment did not require such a "Draconian result" (*Dowell* at 245).

In public administration, "Termination refers to the adjustment of policies and programs that have become dysfunctional, redundant, outmoded, and/or unnecessary" (Brewer 1978, 338). However, the study of policy termination cannot be disconnected from the study of preceding actions, and therefore it should be viewed as a process, not a single, sudden act of closure (Jones 1997; deLeon 1978). In addition, at the end of the process, what remains is unlikely to be the total absence of the policy. Instead, " . . . termination is frequently only the replacement of one set of expectations, rules, practices with another. In this sense, termination signals a beginning as much as it does an end" (Brewer 1978, 339). This "replacement of one set of expectations" is not likely to be guided by evaluative elegance, but by political factors, and, in general, a policy's natural political defenses are likely to be formidable. Thus, successful termination—even under the best of circumstances—is the most problematic of political activities (deLeon 1987, 193–194). Policy inertia is a key inhibitor of termination, but it can be overcome if policy makers identify and counter the antitermination forces (Frantz 1992). The goal of termination is to alter policies and programs that are dysfunctional or outmoded, to facilitate an organization's achievement of its primary policy objectives. To achieve this goal, decision makers not only must identify dysfunctional policies, they also must attain a configuration of political forces that supports a new set of expectations, rules, and practices to supplant the old ones.

New Partnership, New Triumvirate, or New Network?

In the judicial, institutional reform context, these ideas are particularly applicable because, as we will demonstrate, the termination of remedial decrees and the removal of judicial supervision is an elongated process focusing on which set of expectations, rules, and practices should follow the removal of judicial supervision. These expectations are played out in a complex network of political forces, with various groups pursuing sometimes complementary and sometimes competing goals. As with the formation and implementation of the remedial decree, the "new judicial partnership" (Bazelon 1976; Rosenbloom 1987)—and sometimes the "new triumvirate" (O'Leary and Wise 1991)—are critical to how the process ensues.

The "judicial partnership," or the so-called collaborative relationship between judges, public administrators, and legislatures has evolved to a new level. First, the sheer number of public institutions and programs operating under court orders and supervision has expanded, to the point that for many programs, judicial involvement is a recurring presence. "The remedial orders in many institutional suits—involving schools, prisons, mental hospitals, and the like—have placed many state institutions virtually under the control of federal district judges" (Friedman 1992, 748). In many program areas, courts' involvement in program administration has changed from episodic to near long-term involvement. Finally, the extent of court involvement in the administration of public institutions under court order has both broadened and deepened. For some institutions, courts have ordered the construction of new buildings, devised educational programs, hired state officials, and raised taxes to pay for ordered improvements (O'Leary and Wise 1991; Friedman 1992, 754).

Over the years, court involvement in a widening array of policy areas and administrative matters has involved many more actors than just administrators, meaning the term "collaboration" is insufficient to denote the myriad relationships that have developed. For instance, the large budgetary expenditures that federal courts have mandated as part of their formulated remedies inevitably have crossed over into legislative prerogatives and directed legislative action.

"Partnership" denotes a bipolar relationship characterized by equal or balanced power relations with mutual accommodating interactions directed at pursuit of a common goal. However, it is evident that the increasing involvement and power of federal district court judges in public program administration has given rise to their preeminent power position (O'Leary and Wise 1991; Rosenbloom 1987; Driver 1979). The courts have not hesitated to order sweeping changes, even if the costs and administrative burdens stretch the jurisdiction's capacity to the breaking point. In addition, many far-ranging remedies have revealed that parties far beyond the proximate administrators are brought into the courts' directives. The relationships are more than bipolar. Even the term "new triumvirate" (O'Leary and Wise 1991) may not fully capture the nature of the relationships: Often the players easily number more than three, and the relationships among them are not static, but dynamic.

Under a remedial decree, judges engage in the process of policy implementation. "Policy implementation is what develops between the establishment of an apparent intention on the part of government to do something, or to stop doing something and the ultimate impact in the world of action" (O'Toole 1999, 4). Focusing on implementation helps us to analyze the dynamics and effectiveness of judicial supervision of reform of public institutions. In the institutional reform setting, judicial policy implementation develops between the establishment of the initial remedial decree and its ultimate impact on the institution being reformed and on the client groups whose rights are being vindicated. Such implementation involves multiple organizations, and thus it is a task of interorganizational implementation. As such, the judge confronts a world of multiple actors—more than one government, agency, or interest group—whose cooperation, and even coordination, are crucial for implementation success. In addition, the clients or targets of the policy are typically more than passive recipients; they are usually among the parties who must be active in the implementation of the decree (O'Toole 1999, 4). This is certainly true of the implementation of institutional reform remedies such as school desegregation orders. Among the targets of these orders are thousands of school children and their parents, who make decisions about school attendance and other issues that ultimately determine the success of the reform effort.

As the public administration literature discusses, networks of organizations have a profound impact on policy implementation and its effectiveness (O'Toole 1997; Provan and Milward 2001). The nature of networks and network management provides insight into the dilemmas and tasks facing the institution-reforming federal court. "Networks are structures of interdependence involving multiple organizations or parts thereof, where one unit is not merely the formal subordinate of the others in some large hierarchical arrangement. Networks exhibit some structural stability but extend beyond formally established linkages and policy legitimated ties" (O'Toole 1997, 45). This describes the multiple actors involved in the implementation of school desegregation decrees. To illustrate, the actors involved in the Kansas City Metropolitan School District (KCMSD) case include:

- KCMSD superintendent
- KCMSD Board of Education
- Missouri State Department of Elementary and Secondary Education
- Missouri Attorney General's office
- Missouri legislature
- Court-appointed Desegregation Monitoring Committee (three different versions)
- Individual plaintiffs
- KCMSD parents and children
- Interest groups formed by parents and children concerned about specific issues (such as sports, foreign languages, arts, theater)
- Teachers
- Unions
- Contractors, builders, and architects
- Consultants
- Ethnic groups (such as the African American community)
- Parents and children in adjacent school districts
- Federal district court judge
- Federal court of appeals
- U.S. Supreme Court.

Even at first glance, it is apparent that only some of the organizations (for instance, the federal courts) appear to operate in a strong hierarchical setting. Even this is deceiving because the judicial system, in fashioning and implementing public institution remedial decrees, does not work in a top-down hierarchical fashion. Historically, the higher-level courts have not provided much direction about the methods for structuring remedial decrees, but they have expected the lower-level courts to confront situations and shape the remedial program in response. Only much later, if at all, have the appellate courts entered into the decision making, and then only with respect to specific legal issues. In addition, federal district court judge-supervisors facing the array of participants in the network would be well served by the warning of network researchers that in networks, administrators cannot be expected to exercise decisive leverage by virtue of their formal position (O'Toole 1997, 45). Unfortunately, as we will demonstrate, district court judges have not always seen their situation from this perspective.

When district court judges design remedial decrees, they confront highly charged issues in a multiorganizational setting. To be effective, the judges need to mobilize other individuals, institutions, and groups to work through difficult problems and tensions so they can attain concrete changes in program quality. Washington asks a question that is central to that mobilization: "To what extent do decisions of the courts create, clarify, or confuse the actions of policymakers, the superintendent, and the bureaucracy in efforts to achieve quality K–12 public education in a desegregated, multicultural environment?" (Washington 1997, 481).

The Evolution of U.S. Supreme Court Decisions, 1990–2000

To understand how the federal court in Kansas City arrived at its position in addressing whether to continue or terminate judicial supervision of the school system, it is necessary to briefly review the appellate decisions that provide the framework for judicial decision making about termination in the school setting. It must be recognized, assuming there will be appeals, that three courts—district, appellate, and Supreme Court—may be involved in the decree termination decision, and the conditions demanded for termination most likely will evolve from the interplay of the judges on these courts. As Cooper (1988, 28) points out, the trial judge's decisions in formulating the institutional changes required of a public entity are a function of (1) the doctrinal limits ordained in appellate court decisions, and (2) how the trial judge sees the flexibility factors and uses the resulting judicial policy range. However, the doctrines of public institution reform have been very broad and come under the judicial rubric of "equitable remedies." The U.S. Supreme Court has stated, "The scope of the district court's equitable powers to remedy past wrongs is broad, for breadth and flexibility are inherent in equitable remedies" (*Swann v. Charlotte-Mecklenburg Board of Education*, 402 U.S. at 281 [1976]). This stance has resulted in much uncertainty about how the evolution of remedy implementation will occur in any given case because there are no defined and stable legal standards for district courts to employ.

Recently, however, as federal court supervision of public institutions has stretched over decades, the Supreme Court has seen the necessity of nudging the district courts toward ending their supervision of public institutions. As a result, the Court has begun to play a more directive role in indicating which considerations district judges should use when terminating judicial decrees in institution cases. . . .

. . . Cooper points out three sets of problems, however, that the courts face in making their decisions about termination: (1) In instances when implementation of the court's order stretches over a long period of time, the circumstances under which the original case was brought change, and determining the level of compliance with the order as it was issued becomes complex; (2) plaintiffs wish to use the existing remedy process to address new problems; (3) the administrators under court order may not want the court order terminated because, rightly or wrongly, they see the court's continuing involvement as a way to obtain needed funds and support from state legislatures or local communities that would not be forthcoming without such judicial leverage (Cooper 1997, 431–432). All three sets of problems faced the courts in *Missouri v. Jenkins*. . . .

The Evolution of Management and Implementation Challenges, 1990–2000

By 2000, $1.7 billion had been poured into the KCMSD in response to the court directive, yet the Department of Elementary and Secondary Education had just stripped the KCMSD of its accreditation. Despite the new triumvirate formed among the public administrators of the KCMSD, the courts, and the Missouri legislature, only six of 75 schools met all state standards. Even though the court decision had "empowered" and "enabled" (O'Leary and Wise 1991, 322) the KCMSD to implement new programs, build new schools, renovate old schools, and increase salaries, the district's graduation rate was 56.5 percent, compared to 77.4 percent for the state. Notwithstanding the fact that no other school district had ever received such an infusion of court-ordered resources, 90 percent of the district's tenth-graders scored in the bottom two of five levels on the state's math test.

Public administrators throughout the United States were jealously eyeing the superb budgetary situation of the KCMSD. Nevertheless, only 11 percent of seventh graders were considered proficient readers, compared to 31 percent for the state as a whole. Even though the implementation of the desegregation case provided the KCMSD, in Judge Clark's words, with facilities and opportunities "not available anywhere in the country" (*Jenkins v. Missouri*, No. 77–0420-CV-W-4 [W.D. Mo. July 30, 1993], order granting extension of desegregation plan), the school district was more segregated at the end of the implementation period than it was before the court order. In twenty years, the number of students in the KCMSD had dropped from 70,000 to 29,500. By 2000, the KCMSD was, according to the new superintendent, "a train wreck."[3]

While there are historical, socioeconomic, and legal factors contributing to the disaster in Kansas City, Judge Whipple wrote that he believed "the KCMSD's ability to use the court as a shield from responsibility and accountability impact[ed] its motivation to take actions necessary to be an effective school district" (*Jenkins v. School District*, 73 F. Supp. 2d at 1079). Thus, the challenges faced by the KCMSD reflect two things: the difficulties of managing under federal court supervision of this magnitude, and the limits of judicial intervention. Throughout the case, remedies grew, and the defendant KCMSD sought numerous modifications, often enlargements, to the original decree. With the incremental increase in the scope of the remedy came the long reach of the court into nearly every facet of school administration. The court decision posed formidable challenges in public budgeting and finance, personnel, infrastructure management, strategic planning, and intergovernmental relations. . . .

Evaluating the Impact of Court Supervision in Kansas City

In response to the original findings of racial discrimination in the KCMSD, Judge Clark articulated three goals of his desegregation program. First, the plan was devised to attract majority (Caucasian) students to the KCMSD. Second, the court sought to implement a high-quality education program in the KCMSD, whether or not a significantly desegregated school population ever resulted. Third, the court stated that its long-term goal was to "make available to all KCMSD students educational opportunities equal to or greater than those presently available in the average Kansas City, Missouri, metropolitan suburban school district" (*Jenkins v. Missouri*, 639 F. Supp. 19, at 54 [W.D. Mo. 1985]).

How does one assess the success, or lack thereof, of court-ordered changes in the context of these goals? There is no doubt that significant discrimination, which manifested itself partly as segregation, existed in the KCMSD at the beginning of the *Missouri v. Jenkins* case. It is a sad irony that in 2000, while a significant number of Caucasian students were drawn to the KCMSD, in the end the district was more segregated than it was before the court decision.[10] While one can certainly count the number of white, black, Latino, and other students before and after the desegregation plan, it is more difficult to gauge whether the programs implemented were of high quality and equal to or greater than options offered elsewhere. These difficult and complex goals are at the heart of many management challenges faced by the KCMSD. While under judicial supervision, other tough questions include whether desegregation decrees can eliminate differences in student performances caused by poverty, family structure, and other socioeconomic factors. Can good intentions alone move a school district forward?

An earlier district court case had found that racial segregation had caused lower achievement in the KCMSD. After $1.7 billion had been pumped into the school district, buildings had improved but standardized test scores showed little improvement over all, and in fact had declined in several schools. Citing the earlier district court decision, one court of appeals stated that it was not enough to implement special programs in the school, but the KCMSD and the state had to demonstrate their effectiveness in improving student achievement. This, however, was overturned by the Supreme Court, which said that achievement on test scores was not necessarily required. By 2000, the KCMSD had lost state accreditation, partially because of failing test scores. Several competing masters, with only the best intentions, have laid down competing orders. Which policy is the KCMSD to follow?

Recently, many schools have abandoned their magnet theme and have gone back to being neighborhood schools. Further, the number of racially isolated schools in the KCMSD has jumped from 16 to 27 from 1996 to 1999, despite years of desegregation litigation. Were the court's efforts a success? The multiple goals and the confusion surrounding them make this a difficult question to address. No single perspective is likely to be satisfying. To examine a range of perspectives, we asked three key actors in the implementation of the court decision and received three distinctly different answers.

No, the court's efforts were not successful, according to Fifi Weideman, a parent of children in the school district and a KCMSD school board member. Weideman read a court-mandated statement found on an application to a KCMSD magnet school: "The goal of the Kansas City Missouri School District is to desegregate." "Shouldn't it be to educate?" Weideman asked. She continued, "The court decision fractured neighborhoods by bussing children. The extensive transportation provided to the children, sometimes even by taxi, kept the parents out of the schools. The court removed community, care, commitment, and concern. School issues became depersonalized, disenfranchising and disempowering parents. There was desensitization to the human element. They focused on buildings and forgot the cultural issues such as disruptive students. The court never asked the parents what they needed. They made parents and family unimportant. Everyone says, 'There's nothing I can do.' The focus was on the implementation of the court decision, not on the best interests of the children. The children were somehow lost in all of this."[11]

Yes, the court decision was successful in terms of infrastructure development and the creation of new programs, such as specialized magnet schools, says former DMC member Eugene Eubanks. The problem was not with the judge or the court decision, but with poor implementation by imperfect human beings who made unwise choices. "We assumed people were more able than they actually are," lamented Eubanks. He continued, "No one was able to bring the key entities together. The condition of the schools as documented by the courts was deplorable and untenable. The litigation was badly needed. Seven hundred million dollars for buildings for children is a success. The problem is, just because you build the building doesn't mean that the teaching will be good. Unfortunately you can't force a cultural change just because the law is on your side. A learning organization was never developed. The heavy reliance on the court never allowed individuals to grow up and walk."[12]

Yes and no, the courts' efforts were both successful and unsuccessful, according to KCMSD chief of staff Jack Goddard. Yes, in terms of infrastructure development and the jobs that came with it, but, no, in terms of education: "For the twenty-year duration of litigation surrounding the KCMSD, the focus was not on new or innovative education ideas, but on 'black versus white.' (Latino and Asian residents were largely left out of the educational discussions because of the nature of the original lawsuit and because of the way the court framed the issues.) The court decision forced administrators to concentrate on the past history of desegregation, not forward on community and education. The court decision quashed innovation because of all the legal hoops that had to be jumped through. The ultimate irony is that twenty years of litigation and $1.7 billion failed to address the core issue of education."[13]

Despite these failings, at the time this article was written, the district court was supporting the removal of judicial oversight from the KCMSD, maintaining the court had done all it could do. As the district court attempts to pull out of the implementation of *Missouri v. Jenkins,* the elaborate network that has developed because of the court case is making judicial policy termination a challenge. At one juncture in the case, for example, Judge Whipple wrote that "the large number of chefs in KCMSD's kitchen has contributed to administrative instability, leading some of the district's past administrators and superintendents to leave KCMSD rather than be prodded in different directions" (73 F. Supp. 2d 1079).

Hundreds of small bureaucracies have formed around the issues of the case, from the purchasing of textbooks to infrastructure development. These networks of bureaucracies are not about to willingly fade away. In the end, with the KCMSD's dependence on court-driven funding has come a dependence on continued court supervision. The court has become a convenient scapegoat and a shield keeping the KCMSD from accepting responsibility.

The Process for Terminating Court Supervision of Public Institutions

As discussed earlier, termination is a process, not a single, sudden act of closure. To terminate dysfunctional or outmoded practices, decision makers not only must agree on which policies and practices are outmoded, they also must attain the requisite configuration of political forces that support a new set of expectations, rules, and practices. The KCMSD situation is a perfect example. The successful termination of judicial oversight in the *Missouri v. Jenkins* case is a complex and ongoing process focused on which set of expectations, rules, and practices should follow the removal of judicial supervision. The process is so difficult because these expectations have been articulated by competing groups in a complex network of political forces, with some pursuing complementary goals and others pursuing competing goals.

In the end, the federal courts themselves, as the final arbiters, must determine the expectations, rules, and practices that should prevail in the termination decision. At issue in the school desegregation context are questions about judicial capacity to further reduce segregation and increase integration, the responsibility of the courts to determine the quality of education in a school district, and the weight to be placed on state and local control of a school system.

With regard to judicial capacity, there is considerable debate over just how much integration has been brought about by the courts (Heise 1996; Armor 1995; Teitelbaum 1995; West 1994; Brown 1993; Schuck 1993; Orfield and Monfort 1992; Rosenberg 1991). There is not space to reprise the whole debate here, but suffice it to say that considerable argument and evidence has been presented on both sides of the issue. We do not conclude from this that the weight of the evidence suggests federal courts have had an insignificant impact on integration of local schools. To the contrary, a reasonable conclusion is that they have had a considerable impact.[14] Nonetheless, the issue the federal courts now face is to assess the potential for further positive impact of court supervision over the integration of school districts that have been under supervision for decades.

The issue is not whether to discontinue all court involvement in safeguarding or vindicating the rights of minorities in public schools. The Constitution and federal law provide ready avenues of redress for any violations of rights by school authorities. Rather, the issue is, after a long period of close court supervision of a school system, will continued direct court supervision of school operations cause more integration or less? Of course, this determination will have to be made by federal courts examining the local situation, but some national studies suggest the prospects for further large gains may be modest. Two national studies show that most school desegregation took place between 1968 and 1972, with only small improvements after that period (Orfield and Monfort 1992; Armor 1995, 169–174). One reason for declining improvement is that white students constitute a declining proportion of students in large urban school systems. According to a national survey by the U.S. Department of Education, during the twenty-year period since the beginning of affirmative desegregation policies, the percentage of white public school students in larger school systems has fallen from 73 percent to 52 percent of total enrollment, while the percentage of black students has increased from 19 percent to 25 percent, the percentage of Hispanic students has increased from 6 percent to 17 percent, and the percentage of Asian students went from less than 1 percent to 4.5 percent (see Steele et al. 1993).

The opportunities for meaningful desegregation are increasingly affected and limited by changing demographics and the declining proportion of white students. The space within which even the most prescient and competent court can act is shrinking. As one desegregation analyst put it, "Indeed, if white enrollment losses continue, especially in larger systems that enroll most minority students, then black and Hispanic exposure to white students can be expected to drop in future years regardless of the degree of racial balance within these systems, at least in the absence of extensive interdistrict desegregation policies" (Armor 1995, 174). In other words, despite the court's best intentions, changing demographics may yield a student population that is less diverse than desired. Therefore, barring a sudden change in the Supreme Court's stance on ordering interdistrict remedies, federal district courts will have to decide just what the possible zone of conceivable improvement is from continued judicial supervision, even if everything they envision goes as they have planned. Of course, their decision should also be informed by estimates of the likelihood of achieving planned changes. A second aspect of judicial capacity that federal courts will have to decide is just how equipped they are to deepen their involvement in the operational management of large, complex public services such as school systems. Even with unprecedented resources, the federal court in Kansas City has experienced enormous difficulties in achieving a stable school organization, let alone a system that is delivering quality education. The responsibilities of network management involved in an urban school system are difficult even under the most favorable circumstances. Given the challenges of urban education today, combined with the inevitably contentious relationships among numerous network participants, it is not surprising if these challenges become daunting during litigation.

With regard to the courts' responsibility for determining the quality of education in a school district, there is a debate in the federal appellate courts over whether this lends itself to an adjudicatory solution. From one side, proponents see this as a "vestiges-of-segregation" issue. They argue, as the court of appeals did, that until the educational performance of students in formerly segregated school districts rises to the level of other students in the state, then the court must supervise to end the vestiges of segregation (112 S.Ct. 630 [1991], J. Marshall dissenting). However, the Supreme Court majority in *Freeman* perceived that introducing the use of test scores as a measure of educational quality was an insistence on academic goals unrelated to the effects of legal segregation. A challenge for the courts is the disentanglement of all of the factors that affect educational quality and assumption of judicial responsibility for those stemming from the legal violation. That is a most difficult proposition, and the long-time tendency in Kansas City was for the judge to ignore this complexity and treat the whole of educational quality in Kansas City as a judicial responsibility.

Responsibility for educational quality is obviously an issue for public officials. From the beginning, school officials in Kansas City saw the federal court as an instrument for gaining additional resources. The goal of improving educational quality is incredibly difficult, and there is a temptation to allow the court to assume responsibility for both extracting the resources to pursue it and to assume accountability for meeting it. Judge Whipple, in his termination decision, cited a long list of dislocations caused by the litigation and concluded: "These byproducts of court oversight suggest that retention of judicial control may be more disruptive than beneficial to KCMSD. The court is drawn even closer to this conclusion by the fact that the KCMSD and the Kansas City community have repeatedly used the court's presence as a shield from responsibility" (*Jenkins v. School District* 73 F. Supp. 2d at 1079).

The issue is, at what price are public officials avoiding accountability and hiding behind the court?

This leads to the issue of how much weight to place on state and local officials being responsible for managing public services. The Supreme Court has said this is a major factor to be figured into the calculus of withdrawing judicial supervision. As we have seen, however, there is a clash of perspectives over how much weight to place on this. On the one hand, if school officials reverted to segregative practices, the Constitution would not permit the reassertion of local control. However, once the officials have demonstrated good-faith compliance with the court's remedy for a considerable period of time, this factor is supposed to be accorded increasing weight in the calculus. The issue then becomes what constitutes good-faith compliance and how long it must be demonstrated to establish the requisite intent. The expectation of what will happen once judicial supervision is relinquished is a most contentious issue, and one that is at the center of the termination decision.

Conclusion

Weighing these issues and mediating among the competing expectations is clearly a complex task, and one that is subject to strident arguments from many sides. The process is far from straightforward: It is tied up in political processes among a network of many actors. That is why the termination process of judicial supervision of public services is so difficult. The federal courts may have reached a point where they need to consider the answers to several questions in conjunction with the termination decision.

Will continued judicial supervision make the likelihood of achieving policy objectives better or worse? The district court judge, in deciding to terminate his court's supervision of the KCMSD, clearly concluded that continued court supervision was unlikely to increase integration or to advance educational quality. In fact, he cited several factors indicating the school district's officials were hiding behind the court, neither taking responsibility for pursuing the policy goals nor managing effectively to achieve them.

Has the original authoritative rationale for judicial supervision run its course? The incremental process of remedy formation and implementation admits of the possibility of "mission creep," and judges need to step back and ensure their authority for supervision is still solidly grounded in the law, or they risk losing legitimacy. In Kansas City, the rationale for the court's involvement was the violation of the Constitution. Judge Whipple, in deciding for termination of court supervision, found the KCMSD was not engaged in discrimination and had not been doing so for years. Thus, in the court's view, the legal foundation for continued judicial supervision had evaporated.

Are the costs of the remedy under continued court supervision exceeding the benefits achieved or likely to be achieved? While it is difficult to assign costs to constitutional rights, after courts assume executive and legislative functions in governing a public service for a long period of time, they also assume the obligation to examine the costs they are levying on the people and to compare them to the benefits achieved. With over $1.7 billion infused into the KCMSD—but with both integration and educational quality decreasing—the court must face the reality of the limits of judicial intervention in this case at this point in time.

Quality education for all KCMSD students without discrimination and without continued judicial supervision is an achievable goal. Clearly, the courts have been instrumental in ending and remedying discrimination and the other legal wrongs within the KCMSD. It is time for the public management and educational experts in the KCMSD to take back responsibility for quality education of the children. But as we have demonstrated in this analysis, breaking up is hard to do.

Notes

. . .

3. Interview with KCMSD chief of staff Jack Goddard, October 2000.

. . .

10. At least one author has observed that even in integrated schools, the classrooms themselves are segregated (West 1994).

11. Interview with KSMSD school board member Fifi Weideman, October 2000.

12. Interview with former DMC member Dr. Eugene Eubanks, October 2000.

13. Interview with KCMSD chief of staff Jack Goddard, October 2000.

14. "In districts that have formal desegregation plans, racial imbalance has been reduced by nearly half, according to the index of dissimilarity, most of this occurring by 1980. Moreover, desegregation plans have led to a reduction in the percent of black students in predominantly minority schools" (Armor 1995, 208).

References

Armor, David J. 1995. *Forced Justice.* New York: Oxford University Press.

Bazelon, David L. 1976. "The Impact of the Courts on Public Administration." *Indiana Law Journal* 52(1): 101–110.

Behn, Robert D. 1978. "How to Terminate a Policy: A Dozen Hints for the Would-Be Terminator." *Policy Analysis* 4(3): 393–413.

Biller, Robert P. 1976. "On Tolerating Policy and Organizational Termination: Some Design Considerations." *Policy Sciences* 7(1): 133–149.

Brewer, Garry. 1978. "Termination: Hard Choices-Harder Questions." *Public Administration Review* 38(4): 338–344.

Brewer, Garry, and Peter deLeon. 1983. *Foundations of Policy Analysis.* Homewood, IL: Dorsey.

Brown, Wendy R. 1993. "School Desegregation Litigation: Crossroads or Dead End?" *Saint Louis University Law Journal* 37(3): 923–937.

Cameron, James N. 1978. "Ideology and Policy Termination." In Judith May and Aaron Wildavsky, eds., *The Policy Cycle,* 301–328. Beverly Hills, CA: Sage.

Cooper, Phillip J. 1988. *Hard Judicial Choices: Federal District Court Judges and State and Local Officials.* New York: Oxford University Press.

———. 1997. Court Involvement in Operations of State and Local Institutions. In Phillip J. Cooper and Chester A. Newland, eds., *Handbook of Public Law and Administration,* 424–439. San Francisco: Jossey-Bass.

deLeon, Peter. 1978. "A Theory of Policy Termination." In Judith May and Aaron Wildavsky, eds., *The Policy Cycle,* 279–300. Beverly Hills, CA: Sage.

———. 1987. "Policy Termination as a Political Phenomenon." In Dennis Palumbo, ed., *The Politics of Program Evaluation,* 173–199. Beverly Hills, CA: Sage.

Driver, Colin S. 1979. "The Judge as Political Powerbroker: Superintending Structural Change in Public Institutions." *Virginia Law Review* 65(1): 43–106.

Frantz, Janet. 1992. "Reviving and Revising a Termination Model." *Policy Sciences* 25(2): 175–189.

Friedman, Barry. 1992. "When Rights Encounter Reality: Enforcing Federal Remedies." *California Law Review* 65(2): 735–797.

Heise, Michael. 1996. "Assessing the Efficacy of School Desegregation." *Syracuse Law Review* 46(4): 1093–1117.

Jones, Charles O. 1997. *An Introduction to the Study of Public Policy.* 3rd ed. Monterey, CA: Brooks/ Cole.

Nagel, Robert F. 1978. "Separation of Powers and the Scope of Federal Equitable Remedies." *Stanford Law Review* 30(4): 661–724.

O'Leary, Rosemary, and Charles Wise. 1991. "Public Managers, Judges, and Legislators: Redefining the 'New Partnership.'" *Public Administration Review* 51(4): 316–327.

Orfield, Gary, and Franklin Monfort. 1992. *Status of School Desegregation: The Next Generation.* Washington, DC: National School Boards Association.

O'Toole, Laurence J. 1997. "Taking Networks Seriously." *Public Administration Review* 57(1): 45–52.

———. 1999. "Research on Policy Implementation: Assessment and Prospect." Paper presented at the Fifth National Public Management Research Conference, December 2, College Station, TX.

Provan, Keith G., and H. Brinton Milward. 2001. "Do Networks Really Work? A Framework for Evaluating Public-Sector Organizational Networks." *Public Administration Review* 61(4): 414–423.

Retell, Michael A. 1996. "Communities and the Courts: A Dialogic Approach to Educational Reform." *Yale Law and Policy Review* 14(1): 99–139.

Roach, Kent. 1991. "The Limits of Corrective Justice and the Potential of Equity in Constitutional Remedies." *Arizona Law Review* 33(3): 859–903.

Rosenberg, Gerald N. 1991. *The Hollow Hope: Can Courts Bring About Social Change?* Chicago: University of Chicago Press.

Rosenbloom, David. 1987. "Public Administrators and the Judiciary: The 'New Partnership.'" *Public Administration Review* 47(1): 75–83.

Schuck, Peter. 1993. "Public Law Litigation and Social Reform." *Yale Law Journal* 102(5): 1763–1786.

Steele, Lauri, Roger E. Levine, Christine H. Russel, and David J. Armor. 1993. *Magnet Schools and Issues of Desegregation, Quality, and Choice.* Palo Alto, CA: American Institutes for Research.

Teitelbaum, Joel B. 1995. "Issues in School Desegregation: The Dissolution of a Well-Intentioned Mandate." *Marquette Law Review* 79(2): 347–375.

Washington, Charles W. 1997. "Race, Education, and the Legal and Administrative Systems." In Phillip J. Cooper and Chester A. Newland, eds., *Handbook of Public Law and Administration,* 479–502. San Francisco: Jossey-Bass.

West, Kimberly. 1994. "A Desegregation Tool that Backfired: Magnet Schools and Classroom Segregation." *Yale Law Journal* 103(6): 2567–2592.

CHAPTER 20

REDISCOVERING PRINCIPLES OF PUBLIC ADMINISTRATION

The Neglected Foundation of Public Law

RONALD C. MOE AND ROBERT S. GILMOUR

Over the past five decades, the field of public administration has gradually lost its theoretical distinctiveness. Today, public administration has largely abandoned or forgotten its roots in public law—in the Constitution, statutes, and case law—and has accepted, to varying degrees, the generic behavioral principles of management as taught in schools of business. In this intellectual climate, those who study government and those who are practitioners of governmental management were understandably caught off guard by the sheer audacity of the entrepreneurial management advocates, actively led by no less a personage than the Vice President of the United States. The entrepreneurial management model outlined first in Osborne and Gaebler's popular book, *Reinventing Government,*[1] and later in the Vice President's *National Performance Review Report,*[2] seemed to many practitioners and major professional organizations of public administration, not as a challenge to fundamental values, but simply as the next logical step in the grand synthesis of management science.

The difficulty is that this grand synthesis does not comport with the daily experience of managing government agencies and programs. This discontinuity between the contemporary management theory synthesis and reality has been difficult for public administrators to articulate since most have lost touch with the theoretical foundation of their field's intellectual tradition. That foundation is in public law, not in behavioral theories of management.[3] Ironically, the legal constraints and demands in the governmental work environment are evident enough. To a considerable extent they are evident in the business world as well. Nonetheless, the fact is that the private and governmental sectors are based on fundamentally different streams of legal doctrine: one traditionally rooted in judge-made common law, protecting rights and asserting duties in the relations of private individuals; the other founded on the body of the Constitution and the Bill of Rights and articulated by a truly enormous body of statutory, regulatory, and case law to ensure continuance of a republican form of government and to protect the rights and freedoms of citizens at the hands of an all-powerful state.

The intent of the authors is to revisit the protective purposes of the Constitution as designed by the framers and the basic tenets of our administrative state as adapted by their successors (legislators, presidents, jurists, and other government officials) to meet contemporary administrative realities. It is our understanding that the basic theory guiding governmental organization and management—structures, processes, and procedures—is to be found in public law, that it is valid today, and that it will remain so as long as the Republic endures. The principles that make up this theory can in many settings embrace useful precepts such as those of "management by objectives" (MBO) or "total quality management" (TQM) and they can accommodate and be enhanced by an almost infinite variety of technological innovations. But such techniques and advances are not—and cannot be—a substitute or replacement for the traditional, constitution-based method of doing the public's business. To accept such a substitution would be to trade away the constitutionally protected, known means of ensuring accountability for yet to be established measures of government performance.

Protective Purposes of the Constitution

As a matter of cultural preference, intensified by the experiences of colonial dependency, the Revolutionary War, and the operation of fledgling states during the Confederation period thereafter, the framers of the Constitution consciously designed a government better suited to frustrate the concentration of political power than to govern effectively. As James Madison expressed the common assumption that led to this result: "The accumulation of all powers, legislative, executive, and judiciary in the same hands . . . may be justly pronounced the very definition of tyranny."[4] Separated institutions (a bicameral Congress, a president, and "one supreme Court") were delegated different elements of shared powers, which somehow had to be coordinated if government was to function at all.[5]

Not only were the branches of government separated, but each was held accountable differently to voting citizens: Congress directly (though not originally the Senate, which was selected by state legislatures until adoption of the Seventeenth Amendment in 1913); the president indirectly through the Electoral College; and the Supreme Court and federal judiciary even more indirectly through the mechanisms of presidential appointment, Senate confirmation, and potentially, congressional impeachment. At the same time, institutional impediments to direct citizen participation in government protected the government from some surge of momentary popular passion.

The purpose of such an unwieldy design was to prevent an over-concentration of power in any one branch (or in the impassioned mob); and, most critically, through the separation of governing institutions, to protect the people from the tyrannous exercise of governmental power. Such a scheme also identifies the responsible institutions and officials with the powers they may exercise so that citizens seeking change or redress for official wrongdoing can direct their efforts accordingly.

The long-term result of this structure is in some respects closer to the original expectations of the framers than even the most optimistic among them might have expected: continuation of a now ancient struggle for marginal advantage among the three branches. What was not anticipated is the increasing inclination of the branches to accept—even to initiate—delegation of governmental functions and power to novel locations and institutional arrangements both in and outside the structure of government.

The protective purposes of the framers' separated-institutions design has been eroded with respect to all three fundamental functions of government (legislative, executive, and judicial) in virtually every realm of federal policy making. This observation is not meant to revive moribund arguments about whether the primary functions of the three branches of government should be "hermetically sealed" in each; they have not been and cannot be. But when medical doctors in the employ of private insurance carriers are delegated legal authority to adjudicate Medicare claims authoritatively and without review by federal courts or when Congress locates a federal commission in the judicial branch, consisting of both judges and nonjudges who will authoritatively write sentencing and probation law affecting those convicted of federal crimes, questions about the continued protections of the framers' constitutional design are bound to be raised.[6] More to the point of the argument advanced here are powers to agents and the indiscriminate delegations of executive entities wholly or partially outside the executive branch or even the government itself and the current full-scale attack on the principle of hierarchy within the executive branch.

The president, as "chief executive," can hardly be held accountable to the constitutional mandate to "take Care that the Laws be faithfully executed," (Article II, Section 3) if those laws are not his to enforce and the agents created by such laws are beyond his control. For example, when the Department of Energy or the Environmental Protection Agency contracts with private consultants to prepare official speeches and congressional testimony, to write binding regulations (law), to counsel regulated parties on compliance, and then to adjudicate enforcement decisions under agency rules, it is virtually impossible for the president or anyone else to call responsible officials to account.[7] The possibilities for abuse of government power in such situations are manifest.

Fragmentation of the Accountable Executive

Although questions were raised by delegates at the Constitutional Convention regarding how best to organize the executive branch they were creating, the Constitution is nearly silent on organizational matters.[8] This paucity of language in the fundamental document respecting executive structure and management belies the framers' concern for organization, which was far more evident in the first session of Congress when one of the first orders of business was legislation creating the three great departments: Treasury, State, and War.[9] The heads of these departments were directly responsible to the president and were his agents (and thus the agency chiefs were removable by him),[10] but accountable for policy purposes to Congress. All the particular functions of the newly created executive branch, except delivering the mail, were entrusted to these departments.

With respect to fundamental authorities and lines of accountability, however, the executive branch has never been a pristine unity. From the decision in the first Congress to give the comptroller in the Department of the Treasury a substantial degree of legal autonomy within the department,[11] down to the present day "independent prosecutors" functioning in an uneasy relationship with the executive branch[12] not all officers have been directly accountable to the president.[13] These exceptions notwithstanding, the prevailing organizational norm has historically been toward an executive accountable to the president.

Reinforcing the hierarchical concept of the accountable executive has been the view that authority ought to be assigned by delegation from the president or department heads to subordinate officers rather than being assigned directly by Congress to a nondepartment head.[14] The first substantial breaks with the theory of the accountable executive did not occur until the creation of the Civil Service Commission in 1883 and the Interstate Commerce Commission in 1887. Subsequently, more independent regulatory commissions have been added—Federal Trade Commission, Federal Communications Commission, Securities and Exchange Commission, among others. For many years, such organizational departures were most likely to be taken where governmental functions to be performed were largely of a quasi-judicial nature, suggesting an appropriate insulation from the executive chain of command, representation of bipartisan points of view, assurance of procedural fairness, and decisions supported by a full rendering of the facts of a "case."

Today, the executive branch with clear lines of responsibility and accountability to the president is no longer the ideal organizational model sought by either the president or Congress. Disaggregation of governmental agencies and functions is, arguably, the dominant operating philosophy today. While disaggregation may not be the articulated general objective, as a consequence of myriad specific decisions, it has become the general policy in practice.

Disaggregation (not to be confused with decentralization) takes several forms. The most visible form of disaggregation involves organizations. The "break-up" of the old Department of Health, Education, and Welfare into two executive departments (Department of Heath and Human Services and Department of Education) and one large independent agency (Social Security Administration, probably in transit to department status) is an obvious case. But there are other forms of disaggregation as well. Within the Office of Management and Budget (OMB), for instance, a subordinate unit, the Office of Federal Procurement Policy, has been assigned authorities and functions directly by Congress, a practice that tends to fragment the internal management of OMB.

Agencies are intentionally located at the fringes of the executive branch, outside the vertical lines of accountability to the president (Legal Services Corporation, for example) or outside the executive branch altogether (such as the National Endowment for Democracy). And there are the "instrumentalities of government," such as the government-sponsored enterprises (for example, the Federal National Mortgage Association, "Fannie Mae," and Student Loan Marketing Association, "Sallie Mae") that are privately owned but assigned by Congress limited attributes of the government.[15]

Another form of disaggregation concerns the coverage of general management laws. Increasingly, the objective of sponsors of legislation, whether members of Congress, executive agencies, private interest groups, or consulting firms is to obtain exemption from the general management laws (the Budget and Accounting Act; Administrative Procedure Act; Freedom of Information Act; Paperwork Reduction Act; Federal Property and Administrative Services Act; Government Corporation Control Act, among others) for their preferred agencies and activities. Provisions in management laws that are perennial targets for exemption are those covering funding, personnel, procurement, access to agency records, and policy review and audit procedures.

Evidence of OMB resistance to this disaggregating process is scant. Indeed, OMB has prompted and supported considerable disaggregation on its own as illustrated by its 1993 approval for an independent agency called the Corporation for National and Community Service.[16] Furthermore, OMB has recently integrated much of the remainder of its management personnel and capability into the "budget side" of the agency.[17] One consequence of the current absence of a "managerial voice" near the president is that bills are increasingly written and forwarded to Congress by agency legal staffs, or outside consultants, or written by (quite often) congressional committee staffs themselves, absent a review for management consequences once such proposals become law. Monumentally complex administrative arrangements imbedded in health care reform legislation advanced by both branches offer a major recent example of this practice. With the long-term retreat of presidents from their organizational management responsibilities[18] and the downgrading of the central management agencies, the traditional foundation of governmental administration has been further undermined. Most recently a self-conscious effort is underway to replace it with a behavioral-based, entrepreneurial model (referred to by proponents as "public management") of administering government agencies.[19]

Paradoxically, as the executive branch disaggregates organizationally and governmental management functions are assigned increasingly to private parties,[20] the need for effective central management remains; indeed it increases. A president can only "manage" the executive branch if he is supported by sound management laws with general applicability, administered by a central management agency charged with building managerial capacity in the agencies and ensuring political accountability of program managers. Otherwise, the institutional presidency may become tantamount to a separate branch of government, independently developing its own line operations, such as those of Iran-Contra or the National Heath Care Reform Task Force.

Laws intended to provide a foundation of public administration and a framework for managerial accountability, equity, and fairness in dealing with citizens have been eroded substantially. Such laws have suffered over the years from particularistic increments with little interest shown by either the president or Congress in periodic comprehensive reviews and integrative updating. Government management as a field has been permitted to fragment into several hundred separate management laws[21] only some of which have been written with understanding and appreciation for how this part relates to other parts and the whole. All too often, specific political objectives have been permitted to overstep their functional policy boundaries in ways that can only be described as wasteful of scarce resources and confusing to citizens. Numerous hastily funded weapons acquisition programs of the early 1980s and the federal health care and welfare systems are ready cases in point. In each of these policy areas, the operative concern was arguably the use of disaggregation and organizational complexity to obscure rather than to enhance program accountability and as a means of blame avoidance while retaining some elements of program control.

The federal government is not (nor should it be) a loose collection of several hundred semi-autonomous agencies, officials, and quasi-private proxies, all seeking to establish their own missions, designating their own favorite citizens ("customers"), following their own management rules, and defining their own standards of success. Public law is the under-appreciated "cement" that binds the separated powers of the administrative state, ensures political and legal accountability of its officials, and restrains abuses of administrative discretion and conflicts of interest.

The distinguishing characteristic of governmental management, contrasted to private management, is that the actions of governmental officials must have their basis in public law, not in the pecuniary interests of private entrepreneur and owners or in the fiduciary concerns of corporate managers. The hierarchical structure found in the executive branch is designed more to ensure accountability for managerial actions than to promote control over employees. The value of accountability to politically chosen leaders outranks the premium placed on efficient, low-cost service. It is less a question of pursuing one value at the expense of the other, however, than it is a matter of precedence in the event of conflict.

The "red tape" decried in the *NPR Report* (presumably "red tape" is a metaphor for undesired laws and regulations) is in large measure a consequence of the loss of capacity within the executive branch to view management as a single, comprehensive function in which elements of the managerial function (e.g., financial, information, and personnel management systems, and organizational design management) must be coordinated and integrated. The organizational disaggregation and fragmentation of management laws in the executive branch is not a sign that the principles of public law and administration are outdated, but that they have been neglected, avoided for purposes of expedience, and misapplied.

Principles of Public Administration

What follows are ten principles that have been historically fundamental to the administration of the federal government. They are not "laws" (with the possible exception of first three principles discussed) which apply in all situations. Rather, they are principles, which means that they are generalizations that, through experience over the years, have been variously and widely understood to be axiomatic "givens" in American public administration in the interest of the effective and accountable management of government.

1. The purpose of agency management is to implement the laws passed by Congress as elected representatives of the people.

This statement of the purpose of government management is fundamental to order under our Constitution. As a matter of direct delegation under Article I, Congress makes the laws, establishes offices and departments, and appropriates necessary determined funding. The missions and priorities of agencies are determined by law, not by the president or by the department heads, either collectively or separately. While comity and cooperation among Congress, the president, and the agencies are the bases for most relationships between the branches, the authoritative element in the relationship is clear. Management of the executive branch, both in terms of process and behavior, is ultimately dependent upon Congress and the law. Moreover, Congress (individual members, committees, institutional subordinates, and staff) is deeply involved in setting and overseeing both the broad dimensions and detailed particulars of programs, processes, procedures, work rules, and management performance standards. In one policy area after another, what were once broad, unspecified statutory delegations of power to the executive have been laced with nearly countless requirements, limits, directions, prohibitions, personnel restrictions, deadlines, hammers, "no-expenditure" clauses, and other means of asserting direct congressional access to detailed policy development and program administration.[22]

In the private sector, there are compliant boards of directors that occasionally challenge the policies and decisions of management, but they can in no way be compared to the supervision provided agency management by Congress. Repeatedly, outside "CEOs" brought in to "reinvent" or "re-engineer" this program or that agency along private sector lines are shocked to find that they must meticulously obey laws and regulations and are answerable to Congress for their actions.[23] This congressional involvement in the detailed direction of executive management is not aberrational behavior nor is it a political strategy employed by an "imperialistic" Congress. Because of Congress's immense legislative powers to organize and control the orientation, even the very existence of every aspect of executive branch management, Congress has always had the potential—frequently realized in contemporary practice—to be a veritable co-manager of policy and program implementation. Whenever there is a vacuum in executive branch leadership, direct congressional intervention in the details of administrative management is a distinct probability.[24]

2. The president is the chief executive officer of the executive branch and commander-in-chief of the armed forces and as such is responsible for the execution of the laws.

The Constitution provides in Article II that "the executive Power shall be vested in a president . . ." and that "he shall take Care that the Laws be faithfully executed. . . ." It is neither possible nor desirable for the president to be involved in all executive actions taken in his name, but it is possible, through proper delegation, diligent execution of central management laws, and strong central management agencies to ensure that the president's institutional interests in an integrated executive branch are protected.

Presidents must remember, if not discover anew, that the key tool for managing the executive branch, broadly understood, is found in the general management laws and their subordinate regulations and executive orders (for example, the Paperwork Reduction Act establishing the Office of Information and Regulatory Affairs and Executive

Orders 12,291 and 12,498 instituting central review of executive branch regulations in that office on behalf of the president).

Considered collectively, these laws permit a politics of general management with the burden of proof for exceptions resting on the supplicants. The alternative, increasingly the case in practice, is a politics of exceptional management where each agency's management structures and processes are determined in its enabling legislation, as amended. Agency-specific politics tends to place the president at a disadvantage in meeting his executive responsibilities. Furthermore, the growth in the number of agencies and programs not within the executive branch or under the authority of the central management agencies has created a burgeoning "quasi-government" effectively outside accountability to the president or anyone else.[25]

3. Executive branch managers are held legally accountable by reviewing courts for maintaining procedural safeguards in dealing with both citizens and employees and for conforming to legislative deadlines and substantive standards.

Article III's vesting of "the judicial Power of the United States . . . in one Supreme Court, and in such inferior Courts as the Congress may . . . establish" created the framework for judicial review of executive action. Over time reviewing courts gradually developed legal doctrines that expose executive actions to judicial scrutiny and hold the government and its officials legally accountable for their acts. In 1946, this developing body of case law was regularized and codified as the Administrative Procedure Act, subsequently amended (for example, by the Freedom of Information, Privacy, and Federal Tort Claims acts) to extend the scope of these doctrines, as elaborated by reviewing courts, still further. By the early 1970s, federal judges had begun to remark upon "a new era in the history of long and fruitful collaboration of administrative agencies and reviewing courts"[26] a "new partnership"[27] between the executive and judicial branches. In this collaboration, senior partners on the bench regularly, if not altogether consistently, probe the actions of administrators to ascertain their fealty to law and legislative intent, their basis in substantial evidence and procedural fairness, and their openness to the public as well as to reviewing courts. Such standards are wholly different and far more demanding than those imposed on private sector officials.

4. Political accountability for the implementation of policy and law requires a clear line of authority from the president to the heads of the departments and agencies and from them to their subordinates.

Political accountability necessarily assumes legally based hierarchical reporting structures. As the first Hoover Commission Report succinctly stated in 1949: "[The] organization and administration of the Government . . . must establish a clear line of control from the president to these department and agency heads and from them to their subordinates with correlative responsibility from these officials to the president, cutting through the barriers which in many cases made bureaus and agencies partially independent of the Chief Executive."[28]

Despite the obviousness of the proposition as a matter of matching constitutional authority with public responsibility, hierarchical structures are currently out of favor. In the private sector, such organizational arrangements are thought counterproductive to an "information age" environment and, therefore, inappropriate for twenty-first century government as well. The important distinction between the sectors, however, is not to be found in the relative degrees of technological advancement; rather it relates to legal requirements. In the executive branch, the president is required to ensure that certain actions are forthcoming that may or may not be of his choosing. Changes in policy generally have to be approved by Congress and ordinarily involve changes in law. Openness to congressional, judicial, and public scrutiny of department and agency decision-making processes is a hallmark of the governmental sector operating under public law; not so in the private sector.

5. Policy and program objectives specifically agreed to and incorporated into enabling legislation, subject to reasonable and articulate standards of measurement and compliance, facilitate effective implementation.

Basic enabling legislation is central to proper and effective management of policies and programs. Such legislation should, at the outset, be as precise as possible as to the substantive intent and specific objectives of the law and, as well, the lines of authority, responsibility, and oversight—by organization, official office, and legislative committee. Political agreement on precise policy and program objectives and levels of performance has characteristically been difficult. It is far easier to agree upon lofty goals ("a cleaner environment") than upon costly and highly contested specifics and standards of performance. Quite often legislative intent has been left vague or contradictory by design to facilitate congressional agreement. In such instances, however, programmatic specifics will be supplied by administrators and reviewing courts.[29] Thereafter, Congress will almost certainly revisit such issues (virtually forced to do so by events and the fruits of unpalatable choices made by others), though its subsequent involvement will just as surely be encumbered by the stakeholders in less than desirable policies already in place.

6. The congruence of statutory responsibility for policy or program performance and administrative authority and resources makes possible the achievement of statutory objectives.

There is a growing divergence between the agencies and officers responsible for policies and programs and the entities and persons that actually implement them. This incongruence takes three forms. First, programs are increasingly designed to involve a number of agencies, often located in more than one department or outside the government altogether. If clear lines of authority and accountability are to be ensured, laws should provide, to the maximum degree possible, that implementation responsibility is assigned to one department or agency. Where policies and programs involve more than one agency, coordinating authority should be delegated to one agency and a responsible senior official.

Second, central management agencies should be required to approve the contracting-out of management functions (e.g., payroll) by one agency to another. Practices such as off-loading (where one agency contracts with another agency to do its contracting) should be carefully reviewed from several perspectives, including their possible impact upon the capacity of agency management to retain its integrity and skill base.[30]

Third, while it has been federal policy since the earliest days of the Republic to rely on private contractors for many goods and services, recent practices have placed third parties in policy and management roles with control over resources.[31] Although often described as creative public-private partnerships functioning in a competitive environment, in practice these partnerships are increasingly skewed toward the interests of private parties. Substantive program results, once the principal basis for judging managerial performance, are being displaced by managerial process standards. To re-establish, where it has been neglected, the congruence between statutory responsibility and managerial practices, it is necessary to recognize the critical role that legal instruments (contracts) play in the management of proxy agencies. It is also necessary for agencies to have—in-house—the expertise and the resources to superintend such instruments effectively.

7. Authority and responsibility for policy and program performance are located with certainty in single administrators, not in plural executives, interagency committees, or representative boards.

The Federalists, reflecting on their administrative experiences with plural executive bodies while waging a war against a global power and during the subsequent Confederation period, were adamant in their opinion favoring a single-administrator-headed department.[32] President George Washington insisted that single officials bear the responsibility for administration rather than boards.[33] Since government agencies were understood to be unlike private corporations, in which diversity of ownership required a board to represent the several owners, during the nineteenth century little use was made of such boards at the federal level.

Beginning with the Progressive era, however, the plural executive option has been employed more frequently, particularly with respect to regulatory fields and government corporations. In neither of these fields, however, is a plural executive necessary and is only occasionally preferable.[34] From the managerial standpoint, the advantages of a single administrator are fairly obvious, most notably the ability to act promptly and decisively. In terms of legal authority, a single-administrator executive ensures that authority is not dispersed among board members with resultant impairment of accountability to the president and Congress.[35]

Increasingly, boards are being established as the legal source of authority for agencies (illustrated by the U.S. Postal Service) with the administrator (chief executive officer) being selected by the board rather than the president, thus making this individual an "inferior officer," not subject to Senate confirmation. This use of boards is further complicated by the inclusion of officers from other agencies (usually departmental Secretaries), a practice of dubious worth.[36]

8. Public accountability requires that inherently governmental functions and tasks be performed by officers of the United States and their government-employed subordinates.

Notwithstanding an apparent national preference for the delivery of government services by private-sector contractors, common understanding has it (and "official" policy agrees) that the basic functions of government should be carried out by government officials. There is a collective sense, generally, that such functions as the making of law binding on citizens, authoritative adjudication of disputes, control over elections for government office, the unconsented taking of private property, the exercise of coercive force over others, and the denial of private rights on behalf of the state are peculiarly those of the state. While there may be specific exceptions (the consent of private parties to binding, nonreviewable private arbitration, for example), it is understood that such functions involve an exercise of fundamental powers of the "sovereign" which should not be delegated to private parties.

Official policy for the contracting out of activities by federal agencies both reflects and articulates this view, declaring that certain functions are inherently governmental in nature, which "include those activities which require either the exercise of discretion in applying Government authority or the use of value judgment in making decisions for the Government. . . ."[37] Furthermore, official guidelines prohibit the use of private consulting services where "work of a policy, decision-making or managerial nature . . . is the direct responsibility of agency officials."[38] Nevertheless, investigations have repeatedly found that private contractors perform essential government work, including the writing of legally binding regulations, rule enforcement and administrative adjudication, while at the same time consulting for private corporations directly affected by these basic governmental activities.[39] Almost by design, widespread practices of this sort frustrate any serious attempt to hold government officials accountable for the implementation of fundamental government policy.

9. Departures from the principles of government organization are made only when functions to be performed or truly exceptional circumstances require them and when political and legal accountability are otherwise ensured.

Throughout the nineteenth century and well into the twentieth, departures from the accountable executive model of organization were made only when functions undertaken ranged well beyond straight-forward execution of the law. For example, government acceptance of novel administrative roles in the extensive adjudication of competing claims between the government and private parties (e.g., federal trade and communications regulation) or among private parties (e.g., resolution of management-labor disputes) or when the government took on the management of large, revenue-producing enterprises (e.g., hydroelectric power generation), provided ample grounds to argue the case for organizational experimentation. Even so, the burden of persuasion—to demonstrate that the novelty and character of the new function or the exigencies of war or nationwide emergency justified such innovation and that political and legal accountability of the new structures could be ensured—rested with the experimenters.

10. Executive management capacity is increased by regular reviews of general and specific management laws and regulations to incorporate the best available government sector management practices and to eliminate requirements and practices that are no longer relevant or productive.

Over recent decades, the functions performed by the federal government have not only increased in number, but have become more complex technically, more demanding legally, and more expensive. At the same time, the executive branch has suffered from years of disinvestment in organizational structures, personnel, and support services.[40] There has been little investment in recruiting, training, supporting, and retaining executive talent. Increasingly, the executive branch has become "hollow" with agencies and programs being placed at risk through inadequate management resources and greater dependence upon private contractors and consultants to perform basic management functions.[41] We have been living off the capital, both intellectual and managerial, inherited from earlier generations. Now this capital has been depleted and the whole infrastructure of government has been weakened.[42]

The response of the president and Congress to this disparity between demands and resources has been to rely largely upon the budget process to substitute for difficult management decisions. Management should be a capacity-building activity and in the federal government this means that both enabling and general management laws have to be properly written and regularly reviewed and revised. There has to be in place a trained, professional, nonpartisan management corps to implement the politically based policies of successive Congresses and presidents. And capacity building requires a management system that is not dependent upon short-term, often marginally trained, political appointees.[43] Only when these conditions are met will "reforms" of governmental management (e.g., TQM) take on a permanent character and make sense within our constitutional order. There are no legal or structural reasons preventing creative management from becoming a reality.

Principles of the Entrepreneurial Management Paradigm

The ten public law principles discussed above provide a basic theoretical framework through which the administrative state is managed (Table 20.1). The entrepreneurial management advocates, however, have found most of this framework to be obsolete, an impediment to "making government work better and cost less." In a word, they say that the government is "broken,"[44] and it cannot be fixed by the traditional public law approach to management. This "old way," to use the Vice President's phrase, must be displaced by

Table 20.1

The Principles of Public Administration

1. The purpose of agency management is to implement the laws passed by Congress as elected representatives of the people.

2. The president is the chief executive officer of the executive branch and Commander-in-Chief of the armed forces and as such is responsible for the execution of the laws.

3. Executive branch managers are held legally accountable by reviewing courts for maintaining procedural safeguards in dealing with both citizens and employees and for conforming to legislative deadlines and substantive standards.

4. Political accountability for the implementation of policy and law requires a clear line of authority from the president to the heads of the departments and agencies and from them to their subordinates.

5. Policy and program objectives specifically agreed to and incorporated into enabling legislation, subject to reasonable and articulate standards of measurement and compliance, facilitate effective implementation.

6. The congruence of statutory responsibility for policy or program performance and administrative authority and resources makes possible the achievement of statutory objectives.

7. Authority and responsibility for policy and program performance are located with certainty in single administrators, not in plural executives, interagency committees, or representatives boards.

8. Public accountability requires that inherently governmental functions and tasks be performed by officers of the United States and their government-employed subordinates.

9. Departures from the principles of government organization are made only when functions to be performed or truly exceptional circumstances require them and when political and legal accountability are otherwise ensured.

10. Executive management capacity is increased by regular reviews of general and specific management laws and regulations to incorporate the best available government sector management practices and to eliminate requirements and practices that are no longer relevant or productive.

a "new way" of government management and new principles of public administration.[45] The NPR Report argues that "four key principles" must be followed in the future if federal government management is to be a success.

(1) Cast Aside Red Tape

Effective, entrepreneurial governments cast aside red tape, shifting from systems in which people are accountable for following rules to systems in which they are accountable for achieving results. They streamline their budget, personnel, and procurement systems— liberating organizations to pursue their missions. They reorient their control systems to prevent problems rather than simply punish those who make mistakes. They strip away unnecessary layers of regulation that stifle innovation. And they deregulate organizations that depend upon them for funding, such as lower levels of government.

(2) *Customer Satisfaction*

Effective, entrepreneurial governments insist on customer satisfaction. They listen carefully to their customers—using surveys, focus groups, and the like. They restructure their basic operations to meet customers' needs. And they use market dynamics such as competition and customer choice to create incentives that drive their employees to put customers first.

(3) *Decentralize Authority*

Effective, entrepreneurial governments transform their cultures by decentralizing authority. They empower those who work on the front lines to make more of their own decisions and solve more of their own problems. They embrace labor-management cooperation, provide training and other tools employees need to be effective, and humanize the workplace. While stripping away layers and empowering front-line employees, they hold organizations accountable for producing results.

(4) *Work Better and Cost Less*

Effective, entrepreneurial governments constantly find ways to make government work better and cost less—reengineering how they do their work and reexamining programs and processes. They abandon the obsolete, eliminate duplication, and end special interest privileges. They invest in greater productivity, through loan funds and long-term capital investments. And they embrace advanced technologies to cut costs.[46]

These "key principles" are expanded upon and defended in the NPR Report and are offered as not only theoretically defensible but as a practical guideline for federal management success. It is not clear, however, whether these principles constitute any kind of comprehensive theory (propositions subject to disproof) or if they have direct practical utility in organizing the administration of government. Is casting aside "red tape," however that term may be defined, really a useful guide for organizational design and management or is "red tape" simply a symptom of some other and more fundamental theoretical problem? Indeed, a case can be made that the *NPR Report* and the whole reinventing government exercise is largely a story of unexamined assumptions about government (e.g., the government and private sectors are alike in the essentials and respond similarly to management incentives and processes) being elevated to the status of Holy Writ.[47]

The critical point to recognize is that what is taking place is a fundamental clash of cultures, simplified to the extreme as a clash between the legal and business cultures for acceptance of their principles by the government management community. This article has attempted to explain the public law paradigm of federal government management and to indicate that this framework is likely to remain paramount irrespective of the immediate appeal of the entrepreneurial management paradigm. The problem is that the importance of this framework will no longer be considered fully legitimate or subject to comprehensive applicability. The legal symmetry that was carefully nurtured over two centuries is rapidly becoming frayed with exceptions and compromised processes.

As the previously protected line of demarcation between the governmental and private sectors is continually breached, the reasonable certainties of governmental administration are becoming uncertainties with decisions based more upon immediate political expediency and symbolic action rather than upon principles of effective governmental administration. By meshing the sectors, it is uncertain whether we are privatizing the governmental sector or governmentalizing the private sector. What is certain, however, is that political accountability for government programs, whether assigned to federal agencies or to third and fourth parties, is being weakened. There is an increasing disconnect between the legal values and practices embedded in the regime and the management values and practices being imposed upon the federal agencies by the entrepreneurial management paradigm.

The Management Crisis

The federal government now faces a management crisis. On this, and this alone, the partisans of the public law and entrepreneurial management paradigms can agree. The paradigm partisans diagnose the causes of this crisis differently; hence their prescriptions are at odds.

The NPR Report depicts the problem as one of "layer upon layer" of laws, rules, and regulations hamstringing the federal manager. They attack the hierarchical system, per se, and advocate a relatively nonhierarchical system patterned after what they believe is the successful system used in the private sector. They view most (or one-half to be specific) federal middle managers as parasites clogging the system and costing billions of dollars unnecessarily.[48] As this is written, the implementation phase to eliminate "useless" middle managers is well underway as is the plan to substantially weaken the already beleaguered central management agencies. The substantial "downsizing" of the management corps and capacity of the federal government has been written into law (P.L. 103–226) and runs into direct conflict with the new demands being assigned the federal government (although not discussed here, massive new demands upon the states as well).

The *NPR Report* argued that it had captured the imagination of the federal agency manager because it promised freedom from the "mindless constraints" of bureaucracy and implicitly from Congress as well. The definition of success was to be determined internally ("customer satisfaction"), apart from legal requirements.

The entrepreneurial management paradigm largely rejects the notion that the federal administrative state is a product of the law and the legal culture. Indeed, the clear implication is that the "good manager" of the future will be the risk-taker, the one who is willing to ignore the "unnecessary" rules, relations, and control systems to get the job done right—and less expensively. There is little need to change the laws, the answer lies principally in changing attitudes and behavior.[49]

The much maligned public law management paradigm, on the other hand, recognizes first and foremost, that the federal government is organized and tasked by laws passed by Congress. Congress has been, is now, and will continue to be a central player in the politics and management of the administrative state. No promises, rhetoric, or behaviorist posturing will change this reality. The real issue is how to make this legal system, with its hierarchies and rules, work to the advantage of the federal manager, not the disadvantage. It is a legal problem calling for a legal answer.

First, the federal manager is overregulated and needs to be deregulated.[50] Management laws and accompanying regulation are in need of tough, systematic review by both Congress and the president. This review process will require something, however, that no longer exists: a central management agency and a president who is committed to the institutional heath and prerogatives of the executive branch. The reduction in management capacity within OMB, and especially the loss of capacity to evaluate legislation from an organizational management perspective, was evident most recently in the nonplayer role of OMB during the critical, hectic legislative drafting stage for the proposed, but unaccepted, new national medical system. The increasing awareness of the decline in management capacity government-wide[51] reopens the issue of whether a separate Office of Federal Management needs to be established as a prerequisite for a constructive "reform of the executive branch."[52]

To reduce unnecessary regulations and to create more effective informal norms of official behavior will require a concerted and determined effort by line agencies, general management agencies, and congressional oversight committees in an endeavor that is inevitably time consuming, tedious, and difficult. The reason is that each regulation, whether directed internally or externally to government, was enacted or promulgated in response to a problem or crisis. Internally, such rules are put in place to prevent the occurrence or recurrence of an actual or apparent opportunity for fraud, conflict of interest, or other abuse of public funds or power.

Public funds (tax dollars), after all, are not freely given in voluntary market exchanges for goods and services; they are legally confiscated from citizens, by force if necessary. Moreover, the armed might of federal enforcement to collect such funds, maintain order, and control behavior according to federal law will not be stayed by a call to a local law enforcement official or private security guard. At this level—and one senses the presence of this level upon every contact with federal enforcement—the private and governmental sectors are fundamentally different. It is for this reason that the standards for governmental control and enforced adherence to prescribed processes and procedures are—and have to be—so much higher than those of the private sector.

Conclusion

Law-based principles of public administration are not quaint proverbs; nor are they impediments to sound government management practices. They provide the necessary foundation for a growing and evolving administrative system. The principles not only protect the citizenry from an overbearing, arbitrary, and capricious use of government power, they permit substantial public involvement in the processes of developing rules and regulations. The problem is not that the public law paradigm ("the old way") has failed but rather that it has succeeded so well that crucial protections and advantages it provides are taken for granted and neglected. The principles of public administration articulated here work, but the price for having them work well is high. New generations of public administrators must be trained in the fundamentals of their field and not simply be taught glib aphorisms from another and very different field to serve as ersatz theory.[53]

While it may be tempting and easy to forget, ignore, or circumvent principles of public administration founded in American public law, in doing so, we leave ourselves vulnerable. The entrepreneurial management model is not and cannot be a substitute for political and legal accountability. Moreover, unchecked, free-ranging private agents of federal power will not long be tolerated. Such "privatization" of governmental authority and power will almost inevitably be regovernmentalized by Congress and the judiciary—more laws, regulations, procedures, and control systems (red tape) applied to the private sector.

Rather than continue the contemporary drift toward an ever deeper misunderstanding and active confusion of critical differences between public and private sector management, a far better course would be to recognize the particular strengths and responsibilities of each sector. The critical distinction between the sectors has been, and will continue to be, their relationship to the power of the sovereign. Federal government institutions are agents of the sovereign and function under public law. Private institutions are not agents of the sovereign and function under private law. This distinction is critical and provides the theoretical foundation of public administration.

Notes

1. David Osborne and Ted Gaebler, *Reinventing Government: How the Entrepreneurial Spirit is Transforming the Public Sector from Schoolhouse to State House, City Hall to Pentagon* (Reading, MA: Addison-Wesley, 1992).

2. U.S. Executive Office of the President, *National Performance Review, From Red Tape to Results: Creating Government That Works Better and Costs Less* (Washington, DC: U.S. Government Printing Office, 1993). Hereafter this Report is referred to as NPR Report.

The NPR awarded itself high marks for accomplishment in its first year, particularly in eliminating "executive" middle management. U.S. Executive Office of the President, *National Performance Review: Status Report* (Washington, DC: U.S. Government Printing Office, 1994). Only slightly less laudatory is Donald F. Kettl's assessment for Brookings, *Reinventing Government? Appraising the National Performance Review* (Washington, DC: Brookings Institution, 1994). For a more critical status report, see: U.S. General Accounting Office, Management Reform, *Evaluating NPR Results*, GGD94-203R, September 1994.

3. Two studies by the authors predating the "reinventing exercise" have attempted to question the wisdom of ignoring fundamental doctrines of public law as applied to administration and to point out consequences of a departure from this intellectual tradition. Barbara Hinkson Craig and Robert S. Gilmour, "The Constitution and Accountability for Public Functions," *Governance* 5 (January 1992): 46–67; Ronald C. Moe, "Exploring the Limits of Privatization," *Public Administration Review* 47 (November/December 1987): 453–460.

4. *Federalist 47*; Clinton Rossiter, ed., *The Federalist Papers* (New York: Mentor Books, 1961), p. 301.

5. For an explanation of the difficulty of administration in this environment, see David H. Rosenbloom, "Public Administrative Theory and the Separation of Powers," *Public Administration Review* 43 (May/June 1989): 219–226.

6. Indeed such concerns have been raised by litigants before the Supreme Court, but in each instance that court's majority found that the structural innovation in question did not stray beyond permissible bounds of the separation of powers doctrine: *Scweiker v. McClure*, 456 U.S. 188; *Mistretta v. U.S.*, 448 U.S. 361 (1989).

7. U.S. Congress, Senate, Committee on Governmental Affairs, Subcommittee on Federal Services, Post Office, and Civil Service, *Hearing: Use of Consultants and Contractors by the Environmental Protection Agency and the Department of Energy*, 101st Cong., 1st sess. (Washington, DC: U.S. Government Printing Office, 1990); Committee on Governmental Affairs, *Hearings: Department of the Environmental Act of 1990*, 101st Cong., 2d sess. (Washington, DC: U.S. Government Printing Office, 1990).

8. There are only two indirect references to the question of administrative organization to be found in the Constitution, namely that the President " . . . may require the Opinion, in writing, of the principal Officer in each of the executive Departments, upon any subject relating to the Duties of their respective Offices," and that "the Congress may by Law vest the Appointment of such inferior Officers, as they think proper, in the President alone, in the Courts of law, or in the Heads of Departments." (Article II, Sec. 2, paras. 1 and 2)

9. Discussion of the acts creating the three "great departments" may be found in James Hart, *The American Presidency in Action, 1789: A Study in Constitutional History* (New York: Macmillan, 1948), chap. 7.

10. Louis Fisher, *Constitutional Conflicts Between Congress and the President*, 3d ed. (Lawrence: University Press of Kansas, 1991), chap. 3.

11. Representative James Madison described to his colleagues in the first Congress, his views on why the comptroller of the Treasury Department ought not be directly accountable to the President. "I question very much whether [the President] can or ought to have any interference in the setting and adjusting of the legal claims of individuals against the United States. The necessary examination and decision in such cases partake too much of the Judicial capacity to be blended with the Executive. . . ." 1 *Annals of Congress* (1789), p. 614.

12. Kary J. Harriger, "Separation of Powers and the Politics of Independent Counsels," *Political Science Quarterly* 103 (Summer 1994): 261–286.

13. Charles Tiefer, "The Constitutionality of Independent Officers as Checks on Abuses of Executive Power, *Boston University Law Review* 63(1983): 59–103.

14. In the administration of James Monroe (1817–1825), the President objected to a proposal to establish the Patent Office as an agency independent of any executive department. He argued that such a proposal would result in a usurpation of his powers as President. "I have always thought that every institution of whatever nature soever it might be, ought to be comprised within some one of the Departments of the Government, the chief of which only should be responsible to the Chief Executive magistrate of the Nation. The establishment of inferior independent departments, the heads of which are not, and ought not be, members of the administration, appears to me to be liable to many serious objections, which will doubtless occur to you." 2 *American State Papers*, Mis., p. 192.

15. Thomas H. Stanton, "Federal Credit Programs: The Economic Consequences of Institutional Choices," *The Financier* 1 (February 1994): 20–34.

16. The Corporation for National and Community Service, although designated a "corporation" under the Government Corporation Control Act, does not meet the criteria normally associated with corporations (e.g., revenue producer). P.L. 103-82; 107 Stat. 873.

17. The National Performance Review *Report* in 1993 rejected earlier recommendations to rebuild OMB's management capacity (see, e.g, National Academy of Public Administration, *Revitalizing Federal Management: Managers and Their Overburdened Systems*, 1983) and indirectly proposed that OMB not have a separate management component whatever. A subsequent OMB reorganization has largely implemented this NPR suggestion. (U.S. Office of Management and Budget, "Making OMB More Effective in Serving the Presidency: Changes in OMB as a Result of the OMB 2000 Review," *OMB Memorandum* No. 94–16, March 1, 1994.) As a result, the General Management Division was integrated with budget analysis into five Resource Management Offices (RMOs) structured along

budgetary functional lines. Insofar as designed management functions remain in OMB, they are located in much reduced statutory elements of the agency (e.g., Office of Federal Procurement Policy). The integration of management functions and personnel within the larger budgetary side of the Agency is permanent and represents, to the critics of OMB 2000 and its philosophy, the final act of subservience of management values to budgetary priorities. Alan Dean, Dwight Ink, and Harold Seidman, "OMB's 'M' Fading Away," *Government Executive* 26 (June 1994): 62–64.

18. Ronald C. Moe, "Traditional Organizational Principles and the Managerial Presidency: From Phoenix to Ashes," *Public Administration Review* 50 (March/April 1990): 129–140; Peter M. Benda and Charles Levine, "OMB's Management Role: Issues and Strategy in U.S. Congress, Senate, Committee on Governmental Affairs," *Office of Management and Budget: Evolving Roles and Future Issues,* Committee print. 99th Cong., 2d sess. (Washington, DC: U.S. Government Printing Office, 1986): 73–146.

19. Advocates of "public management theory" see themselves as rejecting traditional public administration and instead synthesizing the insights of various behaviorist disciplines with business school approaches (case studies) to change the means of "governance." Thus, government management, in their view, would shift from adherence to red tape (laws and regulations) toward "results," however that term may be defined by the managers. As Don Kettl notes: "Public management researchers sometimes contend that we do not know enough to make predictions or develop models; instead we ought simply to observe what works and what does not, and to draw from those observations some propositions that managers can employ." Barry Bozeman, ed., *Public Management: The State of the Art* (San Francisco: Jossey-Bass, 1993), p. 58. The reinventing government exercise is an attempt, without a theoretical basis, to put the public management paradigm ("if it works, it must be right") into practice, hence the large number of supporters within the government contractor community and academe that have an economic and dispositional stake in the "success" of NPR.

20. U.S. General Accounting Office, *Government Contractors: Are Service Contractors Performing Inherently Governmental Functions?* GGD-32-11, November 1991; Donald F. Kettl, *Government By Proxy: (Mis)Managing Federal Programs* (Washington, DC: CQ Press, 1988); Lester Salamon, "Rethinking Public Management: Third-Party Government and the Changing Forms of Government Action," *Public Policy* 29 (Summer 1981): 255–275.

21. For an overview of general management laws and regulations administered by the Office of Management and Budget, consult U.S. Congress, Senate, Committee on Government Affairs, *Office of Management and Budget: Evolving Roles and Future Issues,* prepared by the Congressional Research Service. S. Print 39–134, 99th Cong., 2d sess. (Washington, DC: U.S. Government Printing Office, 1986), pp. 395–675.

22. Robert S. Gilmour and Alexis A. Halley, ed., *Who Makes Public Policy? The Struggle for Control Between Congress and the Executive* (Chatham, NJ: Chatham House, 1994), chapter 12. Throughout the *NPR Report* and related literature, Congress is either ignored or awarded hostile treatment. The entrepreneurial management philosophy seeks to alter the fundamental political power relationships of the government favorably to the executive branch, although nor necessarily toward the President, and away from Congress. As Donald Kettl, an NPR partisan ("the NPR invasion cannot be allowed to fail," *Reinventing Government,* p. 6) correctly observes:

> First, "reinventing government" seeks the transfer of power from the legislative to the executive branch. In the Vice President's report, Congress is notable principally for its rare appearance. When it does appear, it is usually as an unindicted co-conspirator responsible for undermining effective management. The NPR criticizes Congress for micromanagement and for unpredictable budgetary decisions. Almost all of what the NPR recommends, in fact, requires that Congress give up power. (Beyond the Rhetoric of Reinvention: Driving Themes of the Clinton Administration's Management Reforms," *Governance,* 7 July 1994: p. 309.)

23. A recent news account illustrates the difficulties often encountered by hard-charging private sector executives who suddenly find out they must be accountable for their actions to higher authority,

the Congress. "Representatives Jack Brooks and John Conyers Jr. gave the head of the General Services Administration [Roger W. Johnson] a dressing-down yesterday, contending that possible changes in the works at GSA run counter to policies established by Congress." Stephen Barr, "Hill Leaders Reprove GSA Chief on Yielding Authority," *Washington Post,* March 25, 1994, p. A-21. In retrospect, Johnson realized that he had overlooked one detail in his grand scheme for changing GSA: Congress. "On Capitol Hill, he was a bull in the federal china closet—cocky, rushing in to change an agency he had not taken the time to figure out, and neglecting to inform Congress, where six major committees are authorized to oversee what the GSA does." Faye Fiore, "Idealist: Washington Realities Set In for GSA Chief Johnson," *Los Angeles Times,* July 14, 1994, p. A-1.

24. Gilmour and Halley, *Who Makes Public Policy?* Only occasionally has the federal judiciary intervened to enjoin a congressional role in the execution of statutory programs, and then only when Congress insinuated itself or its agents statutorily into formal positions of executive power. Exceptional cases such as *Buckley v. Valeo,* 424 U.S. 1 (1976), which overruled congressional appointment of officials to perform executive functions; *Immigration and Naturalization Service v. Chadha,* 462 U.S. 919 (1983), overcoming the congressional veto of executive actions; and *Bowsher v. Synar,* 106 S.Ct. 3181 (1986), which ruled improper the formal participation of a congressionally controller officer, the Comptroller General of the United States, in the execution of the Gramm-Rudman-Hollings deficit reduction act best serve to underscore the larger point.

25. Harold Seidman, "The Quasi World of the Federal Government," *The Brookings Review* 6 (Summer 1988): 23–27.

26. *Environmental Defense Fund v. Ruckelshaus,* 439 F.2d 584, 597 (D.C. Cir. 1971).

27. *Greater Boston Television Corp. v. FCC,* 444 F.2d 841, 851 (D.C. Cir. 1971).

28. U.S. Commission on Organization of the Executive Branch of the Government, *The Hoover Commission Report* (New York: McGraw-Hill, 1949), p. 7.

29. A characteristic example is offered by implementation of the Occupational Safety and Health Act of 1970, in which Congress issued a regulatory mandate resting on such broad and vague definitions as "a standard which requires conditions" or adopts means and measures that are "reasonably necessary or appropriate to provide safe or healthful employment and places of employment" [SEC. 3(8)] and "which most adequately assures, to the extent feasible, on the basis of best evidence available, that no employee will suffer material impairment of health or functional capacity" during a working lifetime [SEC. 6(b)(5)]. The Occupational Safety and Heath Administration's efforts to promulgate rules to implement these instructions were subsequently found wanting when the judiciary parsed these words while attempting to divine congressional intent for the exercise of administrative discretion. See *Industrial Union Department, AFL-CIO v. American Petroleum Institute,* 448 U.S. 607 (1980); also *American Trade Manufacturers Institute v. Donovan,* 452 U.S. 490 (1981).

30. U.S. Congress, Senate, Committee on Governmental Affairs, Subcommittee on Oversight of Government Management, *Off-Loading: The Abuse of Inter-Agency Contracting to Avoid Competition and Oversight Requirements,* Staff Report (Washington, DC: Senate Governmental Affairs Committee, 1994).

31. Donald F. Kettl in his book, *Sharing Power: Public Governance and Private Markets,* describes this growing reliance by the federal government on its private partners. "In its eager pursuit of the competition prescription, government has—for a remarkable variety of reasons—too often surrendered its basic policy making powers to contractors." (Washington, DC: Brookings Institution, 1993), p. 13.

32. Characteristic of such opinions at the time, Alexander Hamilton expressed his preference for single administrators as follows: "A single man, in each department of administration would be greatly preferable. It would give us a chance of more knowledge, more activity, more responsibility, and, of course, more zeal and attention. Boards partake of a part of the inconveniences of larger assemblies. Their decisions are slower, their energy less, their responsibility more diffused. They will not have the same abilities and knowledge as an administration by a single man." *The Works of Alexander Hamilton,* J.C. Hamilton, ed., 7 v. (New York: John F. Trow, 1850–51), I, pp. 154–155 (September 3, 1780).

33. Leonard D. White, *The Federalists: A Study in Administrative History* (New York: Macmillan, 1948), p. 513.

34. Regulatory activities are a principal function of virtually all agencies and such agencies can be led by single administrators (e.g., Food and Drug Administration) or by boards (e.g., Consumer Product Safety Commission). Similarly, there is no inherent reason why government corporations need to be managed by boards, and several function without boards (e.g., St. Lawrence Seaway Development Corporation). Harold Seidman, "The Theory of the Autonomous Government Corporation: A Critical Appraisal," *Public Administration Review* 12 (Spring 1952): 31–32.

35. President Franklin D. Roosevelt was opposed in principle to boards as administrative agents. In speaking of the Civil Service Commission to Louis Brownlow, Roosevelt lamented: "[T]he statute requires that I appoint three persons to the board, and no more than two of them can be members of the same political party. Of course, I know it is set up to keep bipartisan control over the civil service, but the way it works, the President is handicapped in trying to find out what the commission wants. If they come into this office and I ask them a question, all three of them have to go out in the corridor or some place, hold a caucus, and come back and answer me. If anything comes up that doesn't admit of a two-to-one vote of 'yes' or 'no,' then they listen, and sometimes weeks later they may give me some sort of answer. I would like to deal with one man alone." Louis Brownlow, *A Passion for Anonymity: The Autobiography of Louis Brownlow, The Second Half* (Chicago: University of Chicago Press, 1949), pp. 420–421.

36. The Pension Benefit Guarantee Corporation (PBGC), an agency within the Department of Labor, provides evidence of the problems associated with boards of directors that include officials of other departments. The board of directors of the PBGC has three members: the Secretary of the Treasury, the Secretary of Commerce, and as Chairman, the Secretary of Labor. "Such arrangements," according to a National Academy of Public Administration Report, "inherently cause confusion as to the corporation's status and the role of the Secretary of Labor. To have cabinet officers serve as directors of a subordinate unit of an executive department, other than their own, places them and the head of that department in an anomalous position. Can the Secretaries of the Treasury and Commerce give orders to the Secretary of Labor? On the other hand, are the Secretaries of the Treasury and Commerce, when acting as PBGC directors, in any way required in formulating policies to conform to the policies and procedures of the Secretary of Labor?" Not surprisingly, although the bylaws call for "regular meetings," the board never met between March 1982 and April 1991. *Study of the Pension Benefit Guarantors Corporation's Corporate Status* (Washington, DC: National Academy of Public Administration, 1991), pp. 5–6.

37. U.S. Office of Management and Budget, *OMB Circular No. A-76,* para. 6e.

38. U.S. Office of Management and Budget, *OMB Circular No. A-124,* para. 7B.

39. U.S. General Accounting Office, *Government Contractors: Are Service Contractors Performing Inherently Governmental Functions?* GGD-92–11, November 1991.

40. Charles A. Bowsher, Comptroller of the United States, "The Emerging Crisis: The Disinventment of Government," Webb Lecture, National Academy of Public Administration (2 December 1988).

41. Mark Goldstein, *America's Hollow Government* (Homewood, IL: Business One Irwin, 1992), U.S. General Accounting Office, *Government National Mortgage Association: Greater Staffing Flexibility Needed to Improve Management,* GAO/RCEDD-93–100 (Washington, DC: General Accounting Office, 1993).

42. U.S. Congress, House, Committee on the Budget, *Management Reform: A Top Priority the Federal Executive Branch,* Comm. print, 102 Cong., 1st sess. (Washington, DC: U.S. Government Printing Office, 1991).

43. Criticism of what is believed to be excessive reliance upon short-term political appointees for agency management is to be found in National Commission on the Public Service, *Rebuilding the Public Service* (Washington, DC: National Commission on the Public Service, 1989). The Commission was chaired by Paul Volcker and is commonly referred to as the Volcker Commission. As reported by the Volcker Commission:

From 1964 to 1984, the proportion of political appointees who stayed in position 1.5 years or less was 41.7 percent for cabinet secretaries, 62 percent for deputy secretaries, and 46.3 percent for under secretaries. From 1979 to 1986, noncareer members (political appointees) of the Senior Executive

Service remained in office an average of twenty months. Fully 40 percent of the political executives throughout the government stayed in their positions less than one year. In contrast, 70 percent
of the career executives have been with their agencies for ten years and fifty percent of them for
fifteen years (p. 168).

See also James P. Pfiffner, "Political Appointees and Career Executives: The Democracy-Bureaucracy
News in the Third Century," *Public Administration Review* 47 (January/February 1987): 57–65.

44. *NPR Report*, p. 6.

45. Vice President Al Gore explains why, in his view, public administration requires a new, entrepreneurial management theory. "Two relatively recent developments have dramatically shifted the premises on which traditional public and private sector management has been based: (1) a new understanding
of how best to employ human capacity; and (2) the new role of information technology in transforming
the manager's job." Al Gore, Jr., "The Job of the Federal Executive," *Public Administration Review* 54
(July/August 1994): 317.

46. *NPR Report*, pp. 6–7.

47. See Ronald C. Moe, "The 'Reinventing Government' Exercise: Misinterpreting the Problem,
Misjudging the Consequences," *Public Administration Review* 54 (March/April 1994): 111–122.

48. The *NPR Report* argues that the mandatory halving of supervisory ranks will be salutary as the
excess supervisors now harm the work of the Federal Government and cost unnecessary monies. "Most
of the personal reductions will be concentrated in the structures of overcontrol and micromanagement
that now bind the federal government: supervisors, headquarters staffs, personnel specialists, budget
analysts, procurements specialists, accountants and auditors. These central control structures not
only stifle the creativity of line managers and workers, but they consume billions per year in salary,
benefit, and administrative costs." *NPR Report*, pp. iii–iv. It is interesting to note that two categories
of supervisors and technical personnel not included in this listing of "parasites" are lawyers and
political appointees.

President Bill Clinton argues that in reducing the civil service, he is reducing the size of the government and therefore is not a "traditional liberal." "[We are] reducing the Federal Government by 272,00—
certainly not a traditional liberal thing to do—to the smallest Federal Government we've had since
Kennedy was President." Monies "saved" by reducing the civil service will go into a Violent Crime
Reduction Trust Fund. "The Trust Fund will ensure that the entire Crime Bill will be paid for, not with
new taxes, but by reducing the federal bureaucracy to its lowest level in 30 years." *Weekly Compilation
of Presidential Documents* 30 (August 30, 1994): 1712, 1701.

49. The example most discussed in the *NPR Report* of how to change management behavior without
having to change laws involves the Inspectors General in the several departments and agencies. The
NPR Report is particularly harsh on Inspectors General, the "reform" of the 1970s. In the reinvented
government, the IGs will not be so zealous in their pursuit of "waste, fraud and abuse." "Today, they
audit for strict compliance with rules and regulations. In the future they should help managers evaluate
their management control systems." The answer to the problem of overzealous IGs is to reculturate
them to think and act less like IGs and more like entrepreneurial managers. "Congress need pass no
legislation to make this happen. Promoting the efficiency and integrity of government programs was
part of the IG's original mandate. But such change will require a cultural revolution within many IGs'
offices. . . ." *NPR Report*, p. 32.

50. "Reduction in the administrative rules and regulations is clearly necessary to ease the problems
confronting the Federal manager. . . . The most fundamental need is for a philosophy of Federal management which is aimed at enhancing the role and accountability of the manager." National Academy of
Public Administration, *Revitalizing Federal Management: Managers and Their Overburdened System*
(Washington, DC: National Academy of Public Administration, 1983), p. viii.

51. Amy Goldstein and Spencer Rich, "Immunization Program Falters Here, Across U.S.," *Washington Post,* October 18, 1994, p. A-1.

52. *Revitalizing Federal Management,* pp. 11–13; Ronald C. Moe, "The HUD Scandal and the Case
for an Office of Federal Management," *Public Administration Review* 51 (July/August 1991): 298–307.

Statement of Rep. Leon Panetta, "Office of Federal Management Act of 1991," *Cong. Rec.*, June 25, 1991, pp. H5038–5041.

53. An interesting side debate underway is whether or not the *NPR Report* is properly cast as being in the tradition of the earlier presidential commissions that recommended fundamental changes in the executive branch (e.g., Hoover Commission in 1949), or if the *NPR Report* and the entrepreneurial management paradigm constitute a major departure from this tradition. Kettl sees the *NPR Report* as being in the tradition of the earlier Reports, especially the Hoover Commission (*Reinventing Government,* p. 4). Peri Arnold, on the other hand, argues persuasively that the *NPR Report* constitutes a break in this tradition and represents a very different management philosophy and political agenda than that of, say, the Hoover Commission. "Reform's Changing Role: The National Performance Review and the Stages of Executive Reorganization," *Public Administration Review* 55 (September/October 1995): 407–417.

INDEX

ABOUT THE EDITORS

Julia Beckett is an associate professor in the Department of Public Administration and Urban Studies at the University of Akron. She received a J.D. from Washington University in Saint Louis and a Ph.D. in Public Administration from the University of Colorado at Denver. Her work has appeared in *Public Administration Review, The American Review of Public Administration,* and *Public Budgeting, Accounting and Financial Management.* From 2002 to 2005, she was the contributing editor of the Public Law Category of the *Encyclopedia of Public Policy and Public Administration.*

Heidi O. Koenig is an associate professor in the Division of Public Administration at Northern Illinois University. She holds a J.D./M.A. from the University of Nebraska–Lincoln and a Ph.D. degree in Public Administration from Syracuse University. Her work has appeared in *Public Administration Review, International Journal of Public Administration* and *Public Administration & Management: An Interactive Journal.* From 1996 to 1999, she was the editor of Oyez, Oyez, a column on law and public administration in *Public Administration Review.*